# THE LEGAL NATURE OF
# THE UNIT TRUST

# The Legal Nature of the Unit Trust

KAM FAN SIN

*sometime Julius Stone Scholar of
the University of New South Wales*

CLARENDON PRESS · OXFORD
1997

Oxford University Press, Great Clarendon Street, Oxford OX2 6DP

Oxford New York
Athens Auckland Bangkok Bogota Bombay
Buenos Aires Calcutta Cape Town Dar es Salaam
Delhi Florence Hong Kong Istanbul Karachi
Kuala Lumpur Madras Madrid Melbourne
Mexico City Nairobi Paris Singapore
Taipei Tokyo Toronto Warsaw
and associated companies in
Berlin Ibadan

Oxford is a trade mark of Oxford University Press

Published in the United States
by Oxford University Press Inc., New York

A catalogue record for this book is available from the British Library

Library of Congress Cataloging in Publication Data
Sim, Kam Fan.
The legal nature of the unit trust/Kam Fan Sin.
p. cm.
Includes bibliographical references and index.
1. Mutual funds—Law and legislation—Great Britain. I. Title.
IN PROCESS
346.41'0922—dc21 97–28129
ISBN 0–19–876468–5

1 3 5 7 9 10 8 6 4 2

Typeset by Cambrian Typesetters, Frimley, Surrey
Printed in Great Britain on acid-free paper by
Bookcraft Ltd., Midsomer Norton, Somerset

TO

HOK CHING, HOK WEN and HOK AO

# Foreword

*The Honourable Sir Anthony Mason, AC, KBE*
*Chief Justice, High Court of Australia, 1987–1995*
*Chancellor, University of New South Wales*
*National Fellow, Research School of Social Sciences,*
*Australian National University*

In a world awash with legal publications, *The Legal Nature of the Unit Trust* is a much needed and comprehensive examination of a topic that has been largely neglected by legal commentators. Like some other legal innovations, the unit trust was an ingenious response to the demands of commerce. The unit trust was a response to the demand for a suitable investment vehicle. It is a hybrid, resting partly in trust and partly in contract and, as the author demonstrates in Chapter 1, the unit trust has close historical links with the law of corporations, notably through the deed of settlement company. Lawyers who do not have an eye to legal history may not appreciate just how extensive was the role of the trust in the emergence of the limited liability company.[1]

The author's in-depth exploration of the relationship between trust and contract as principal elements in the unit trust is not only instructive but also timely and appropriate. As a result of commercial mishaps, mainly afflicting property trusts, Australia has generated a significant body of case law on unit trusts. And the publication of this book comes at a time when the courts, in England, Australia and elsewhere, are giving weight to the policy consideration that the certainty and security of commercial transactions call for caution and circumspection in making equitable remedies, particularly proprietary remedies, available in relation to such transactions. This policy consideration may lead to some modification of the incidents of the law relating to traditional trusts when that law is applied to trusts in a commercial setting. Lord Browne-Wilkinson's speech in *Target Holdings Ltd* v *Redferns*,[2] which was concerned with a bare trust in a commercial setting, no doubt surprising to some traditional equity lawyers, may be a harbinger of future developments.

Be that as it may be, *The Legal Nature of the Unit Trust* is a valuable contribution to our understanding of the law relating to unit trusts. It not

[1] See *Elders Trustee an Executor Co Ltd* v *EG Reeves Pty Ltd* (1987) 78 ALR 193 at 229.  [2] [1995] 1 AC 421.

only draws on the lessons of history and exhibits analytical skills of a high order, but also draws attention to and discusses, where appropriate, the authorities in a number of jurisdictions.

Cambridge, 1 July 1997

# *Preface*

This book travelled many miles. It had its gestation in Hong Kong in my occasional encounters of unit trust problems after the black Monday of 1987. When my family moved to Sydney in 1992, my proposal to write a thesis on unit trusts was received with enthusiasm by Professor Michael Chesterman. After the completion of this thesis in 1995, my publication enquiry with this publisher was also responded to with no less enthusiasm.

Practical issues on unit trusts cannot be solved without answering a basic question of what a unit trust is. This work is an attempt to give a doctrinal answer to it. It does not seek to consider taxation and regulatory issues on unit trusts, unless they implicate on this question, and in respect of which major practitioners' texts may be consulted. In this endeavour, an effort has been made to exhaust unit trust cases in common law jurisdictions having unit trusts modelled on those of the United Kingdom.

I am grateful to all organisations and individuals providing me with scheme particulars, prospectuses, deeds and documentary materials, including Advance Asset Management Ltd, AMP Investment Management Ltd, ANZ Funds Management Ltd, BT Asset Management Ltd, Mr Richard Chamberlin of Freshfields, London, Commonwealth Funds Management Ltd, Cornwall Stodart, Solicitors, Melbourne, Jardine Fleming Australia Management Ltd, Friends Provident Life Assurance Co Ltd, Howard Funds Management Ltd, National Australia Bank Ltd (Investment & Trust Services), Mr N W Reid of Linklaters & Paines, London, National Australia Financial Management Ltd, Rothchild Australia Asset Management Ltd, Schroders Australia Management Ltd, Schroders Australia Property Management Ltd, Mr L E Taylor, Chief Solicitor and General Counsel of Commonwealth Bank Group, and Wardley Investment Services (Australia) Ltd. I have also relied on documentary materials obtained through enquiry desks of many financial institutions. I am also grateful to Professor Paul Redmond for a copy of the rare book *Formoy's Historical Foundations of Modern Company Law*; to the United States Securities and Exchange Commission (Division of Investment Management) for its report 'Protecting Investors: a Half Century of Investment Company Regulation'; to Investment Management Regulatory Organisation Ltd for a copy of the 'Report on Financial Services and Trust Law', prepared by Professor D J Hayton and to the University of London Library for a copy of C H Walker's thesis on 'Unit

Trusts', a thesis submitted in 1938 for the degree of Doctor of Philosophy (in Economic History) of that University.

Various individuals have made comments on this work at different stages. As this work puts forward a particular thesis of what a unit trust is, I may not have adopted every opinion generously given to me. Nevertheless, I am grateful to all. In order to complete this book, I spent my last summer in England. During my stay, the Institute of Advanced Legal Studies and the Oxford University kindly permitted me to use their libraries. I am grateful to Professor David Hayton of King's College, University of London, for his valuable comments as a reader for the publisher. He also took the trouble to introduce me to practitioners who provided me with useful information. My gratitude is also due to Mr Graham Moffat of the University of Warwick for his valuable support to the publication of this book.

I would like to thank the staff members of the Law Library of the University of New South Wales for their assistance of more than half a decade. In particular, Ms Lynette Falconer helped me to update my manuscript through electronic media before it went to the publisher.

I am particularly indebted to Professor Michael Chesterman and Professor Ian Ramsay of the University of Melbourne (formerly a member of the University of New South Wales) for their thorough guidance and willingness to accord priority to my consultation when I was writing my thesis. Indeed, this book cannot reach this stage and be in its present form without the support given by Professor Chesterman. He has been an inspiring teacher, tolerant of new ideas and willing to answer queries whenever I knocked on his door. When I was doing research on this book in England, I was fortunate enough that he happened to be there. Assistance of all kind was given to me and my family.

At a late stage of this book, I also had the benefit of the wisdom of the Honourable Sir Anthony Mason, who kindly undertook to read the manuscript and to make valuable comments within a very short period of time. Sir Anthony's legal contributions, both in his judgments and scholarly writings, are universally acclaimed. I am deeply honoured that the Foreword of this book is written by him.

I would also like to record my deep appreciation for the award of the Julius Stone Scholarship by the Faculty of Law of the University of New South Wales, which has alleviated the financial, if not other, burden occasioned to my family during my full time study as a PhD student. The Faculty also provided me a travel grant to England to complete this book, in respect of which I also gratefully acknowledge.

I am also grateful to the editorial staff of the publisher, particularly Mr Rob Dickinson and Ms Myfanwy Milton, for their assistance in the production of this book.

My final thanks go to my wife, Ha Ping Helen, for her continuing support and for having been a litmus paper of many ideas put forward in this book.

Despite the generous support of so many people, I alone am responsible for all errors and omissions.

I have endeavoured to state the law from materials available to me as on 2 March 1997.

Kam Fan Sin
Faculty of Law,
University of New South Wales,
1 August 1997.

# Contents

# Contents

# Abbreviations

| | |
|---|---|
| *Australian Ency. F & P, Vol. 3* | *Australian Encyclopaedia of Forms and Precedents*, Vol. 3, 2nd edn. (rev.), Butterworths Australia, 1985. |
| Cheshire and Fifoot | Cheshire and Fifoot, *Law of Contract*, 6th Australian edn. by Starke, Seddon and Ellinghaus, Butterworths Australia, 1992. |
| *Chitty* | *Chitty on Contracts*, 27th edn. by Guest, Sweet and Maxwell, 1994. |
| Day and Harris | Day and Harris, *Unit Trusts*, Oyez, 1974. |
| Ford and Lee | Ford and Lee, *Principles of the Law of Trusts*, 3rd (looseleaf) edn., LBC Information Services, 1996. |
| Greig and Davis | Greig and Davis, *The Law of Contract*, Law Book Co., 1987. |
| *Hanbury and Martin* | *Hanbury and Martin's Modern Equity*, 14th edn. by Martin, Sweet and Maxwell, 1993. |
| Holdsworth | Holdsworth, *A History of English Law*, 2nd edn., Methuen and Sweet and Maxwell, 1937. |
| Jacobs | Jacobs, *Law of Trusts in Australia*, 6th edn. by Meagher and Gummow, Butterworths Australia, 1997. |
| Macfarlanes | Macfarlanes, *Collective Investment Schemes: the Law and Practice*, FT Law and Tax, 1996. |
| Megarry and Wade | Megarry and Wade, *The Law of Real Property*, 5th edn., Stevens, 1984. |
| Moffat | Moffat, *Trusts Law: Text and Materials*, 2nd edn., Butterworths, 1994. |
| Pettit | Pettit, *Equity and the Law of Trusts*, 7th edn., Butterworths, 1993. |

Scott

Scott, A. W., *The Law of Trusts*, 4th edn. by Fratcher, Little, Brown & Co, 1987.

*Snell*

*Snell's Equity*, 29th edn. by Baker and Langan, Sweet and Maxwell, 1990.

*Underhill and Hayton*

*Underhill and Hayton's Law Relating to Trusts and Trustees*, 15th edn. by Hayton, Butterworths, 1995.

Waters

Waters, *Law of Trusts in Canada*, 2nd edn., Carswell, Toronto, 1984.

# Table of Statutes

# Table of Statutory Instruments

# Table of Cases

CANADA

UNITED STATES

# Introduction:
# The Conceptual Question

The trust is a charismatic institution. It has won the imagination of generations of lawyers and historians;[1] has laid claim to be the greatest and most distinctive achievement performed by Englishmen in the field of jurisprudence;[2] and has been honoured as an instrument of law reform.[3]

The trust is a property institution. It was and still is an institution that serves the property-owning class. Its reputation is built on its versatility to manipulate the facets of ownership: title, control, and benefit.[4] With this versatility, it has since its early days leaped out of the family circle and has ventured into the commercial arena. It is a ready tool to achieve co-ownership by individuals as well as what in functional terms is ownership by groups as quasi-entities.[5] With this ability, it was instrumental in mobilizing the capital of the wealthy and the humble, shaping the trading monopolies into joint-stock companies, breaking the duopoly of the Crown and the Parliament in making corporations, and ultimately forcing registered companies into existence.[6] Underlying all these is the trust's ability to segregate capital from its management and the capitalists from the traders. From its involvement in direct trading enterprises, the trust has also found its way into indirect investment.

It is in the context of indirect investment that the concept of the unit trust emerged. In the contemporary market-place, a unit trust is initiated by a professional fund management company commonly called the manager. It is constituted by a trust deed executed between a manager and a trustee, which provides that assets of investors, commonly called the unitholders, will be held on trust by the trustee to be invested in such manner as may be directed by the manager in accordance with the terms of

---

[1] Maitland and Scott, for example.

[2] Maitland, 'The Unincorporate Body', in Fisher, *The Collected Papers of F. W. Maitland*, Vol. III, Cambridge UP, 1911 (William S. Hein reprint, Buffalo, 1981) p. 272.

[3] Scott, 'The Trust as an Instrument of Law Reform' (1922) 31 *Yale LJ* 457.

[4] Moffat, pp. 5–11.

[5] For example, gifts to them may be validated as gifts for purposes indirectly benefiting individuals (*Re Denley's Trust Deed* [1969] 1 Ch. 373; *Re Lipinski's Will Trusts* [1976] Ch. 235) or as gifts to such bodies subject to the contractual constitutions (*Re Recher's Will Trusts* [1972] Ch. 526; *Re Goodson* [1971] VR 801; *Re Lipinski's Will Trusts*, ibid.; *Re Bucks. Constabulary Widows' and Orphans' Fund Friendly Society (No. 2)* [1979] 1 All ER 623; *Universe Tankerships Inc. of Monrovia* v. *International Transport Workers Federation Conservative* [1983] 1 AC 366; *News Group Newspapers Ltd.* v. *SOGAT 1982* [1986] ICR 716).                                    [6] See ch. 1, ss. 1–3A, *post*.

the trust deed.[7] Rights, which are calculated in terms of the value of underlying assets, are created by this trust deed in the form of units. They are then subscribed to by investors and are dealt with and disposed of by them as intangible properties. The manager may undertake to repurchase units itself or in some cases to arrange for the units to be redeemed by the trustee out of the trust fund. Alternatively, though rarely, units may be sold or purchased in the stock exchange. This form of investment arrangement is very common in common law countries although the regulatory regimes may differ. It is regarded as an alternative to the company as an investment vehicle. And like the company, it has been used for commercial activities other than investment.[8]

In discussing this form of arrangement, Gower has described the limited company as the product of the marriage of the trust and the corporation and the unit trust as 'the offspring of a later union between the trust and the limited company'.[9] If this metaphorical statement is true, the unit trust is, sadly, an orphan that has been abandoned both by trusts law and company law. It does not receive any significant treatment in any trusts texts.[10] The term is not traceable in the index of *Lewin* and, until recently, that of *Underhill and Hayton*.[11] The same picture is also true of company texts. Except for Gower[12] and Pennington,[13] the unit trust has seldom been discussed in company law textbooks.[14] Even for Gower and Pennington,

---

[7] The terms of an authorized unit trust under the Financial Services Act 1986 are also governed by the provisions of the Financial Services (Regulated Schemes) Regulations 1991 which may take effect both as a matter of law and as implied terms: see ch. 2, s. 2A(2), *post*.

[8] e.g., as a trading vehicle: Hayton, 'Trading Trusts' in Glasson, *International Trust Law* (looseleaf), Chancery Law Publishing, 1992, paras. B5.14–B.5.20; Ford and Hardingham, 'Trading Trusts: Rights and Liabilities of Beneficiaries' in Finn (ed.), *Equity and Commercial Relationships*, Law Book Co., 1987, p. 54.

[9] Gower, *The Principles of Modern Company Law*, Stevens & Sons, 1954, p. 229. In 1923, Magruder, a professor of Harvard Law School, also described the business trust as 'the offspring of a union between the unincorporated joint stock company and the trust' (23 *Columbia LR* 423 at 424.)

[10] The space that leading texts devote to the unit trust speaks for itself: *Underhill and Hayton*, 1 page; Pettit, *Equity and the Law of Trusts*, 7th edn., Butterworths UK, 1993, 1 page; Waters, less than 2 pages and only as part of the discussion of the trust as a substitute for incorporation; Jacobs, 2½ pages; Sheridan and Keeton, *The Law of Trusts*, 11th edn., Barry Rose, 1983, 1 paragraph; Parker & Mellows, *The Modern Law of Trusts*, 3rd edn., Sweet and Maxwell, 1974, only 1 paragraph. Hayton and Marshall, *Cases and Commentary on the Law of Trusts*, 9th edn., Sweet and Maxwell, 1991 and Maudsley & Burn's *Trusts & Trustees: Cases and Materials*, 4th edn. by Burn, 1990 do not have any discussion on the unit trust at all. This is also true of *Lewin on Trusts*. While the second edition of Ford and Lee has a full chapter on public unit trusts, '[t]he justification for special treatment of public unit trusts in this work is that they attract a special gloss of enacted law . . .' (at p. 1062). It is expunged from its third (looseleaf) edition.

[11] The term 'unit trust' only appears in the 15th edn. published in 1995.

[12] *Supra*.        [13] *The Principles of Company Law*, Butterworths, 1959.

[14] As with trusts texts, the pages devoted by company books are minimal: *Palmer's Company Law*, 25th (looseleaf) edn. by Morse, et al., Sweet and Maxwell, 1992, 2 pages; Ford and Austin *Principles of Corporations Law*, 7th edn., 1995, 1 paragraph.

the discussion on unit trusts eventually disappeared when their works were subsequently revised.[15] This position may be a result of the perception that the unit trust is 'merely an extension of the private trust into the commercial field'[16] that involves no new conceptual analysis. The few monographs devoted to unit trusts[17] do not attempt to change this perception as their main focus is on the impact of statutory regulations.[18]

This conceptual abandonment is the point of departure of this work. Notwithstanding the comment from high authority that the unit trust is 'an expression now well known and understood',[19] the question that this work seeks to investigate is a simple one: what is a unit trust? It starts with the assumption that lawyers are a conservative lot that prefer convention to invention[20] and proceeds on the premise that this offspring of the trust and the limited company cannot be described without knowing its parents. A description of what a unit trust is can only be meaningful in terms of its points of resemblance to and difference from the trust and the company. This, inevitably, brings, by way of introduction, a historical excursion into how the trust has acted as a facilitator in the mobilization of capital of groups of people with a common objective, be it trading or investment.[21] In the process, it will be realized that, by nature and unlike the contract, the trust is not a constitutive tool for aggregates of individuals. Our admiration of the flexibility of the trust should not conceal the fact that, to

---

[15] Pennington originally devoted a full chapter to the history and operation of the unit trust as an investment scheme. When the 3rd edn. appeared in 1973, the whole chapter was removed. Gower's treatment of the unit trust was in the context of his comparison of the limited company and other associations. This also disappeared from the 5th edn., published in 1992.

[16] Gower, *The Principles of Modern Company Law*, Stevens & Sons, 1954, p. 229.

[17] Day and Harris, *Unit Trusts*, Oyez, 1974; Macfarlanes, *Collective Investment Schemes: the Law and Practice*, FT Law & Tax, 1996 (which is based on Linklaters & Paines, *Unit Trusts: The Law and Practice*, Longman Professional UK, 1989, which in turn is the successor of Day and Harris); Vaughan, *The Regulation of Unit Trusts*, Lloyd's of London Press, 1990; Hughes, *The Law of Public Unit Trusts*, Longman Professional, 1992.

[18] The aim of Day and Harris is 'to provide a concise summary of the law and practice relating to unit trusts, particularly in regard to authorised unit trust schemes' (preface, p. iii). The nature of the unit trust is not its focus. 'The subject matter of [Hughes] is an examination of the legal principles relating to public unit trusts in Australia' (Hughes, ibid., p. ix) and '[t]he point of this book is to examine the most significant issues relating to public unit trusts' (p. xii). In his preface (p. x), the learned author expresses the view that the unit trust 'is "a hybrid institution" which does not fit comfortably in either [corporations law or trust law]. A public unit trust is a creature of trust law which is intended to operate wholly as a commercial "entity".' No explanation has been given as to its hybrid nature. The learned author's discussion of the nature of a public unit trust in ch. 1 gives the impression that '[t]he distinguishing feature of public unit trusts is that they are regulated [under the Australian Corporations Law]', (p. 7). This is consistent with the treatment of the subject in the rest of the book.

[19] Per Wynn-Parry J in *Re AEG Unit Trust (Managers) Ltd.'s Deed* [1957] 1 Ch. 415 at 419.

[20] They would not draw up unit trust deeds without precedents.

[21] Ch. 1, *post*.

function in this way, the trust had to be grafted onto the contractual constitution of the unincorporated company. As an extension of the express trust in the investment field, the unit trust, like its corporate parent, has contractual ingredients which ultimately set it apart from other express trusts.[22] The contractual ingredients will be demonstrated in chapter 2 in two ways.

First, it will suggest that the trust in a unit trust is a contractual creation. A trust in a unit trust exists because this is an agreed term. The 'three certainties' exist because there is mutual intention that the property will be held on trust and not in any other capacity and because the subject matters and objects have been agreed. This contrasts with the position of a private trust *inter vivos* whereby the certainty rules are concerned with the ascertainment of the donative wishes of a settlor and the implementation of those wishes in default of a trustee.

This study argues that the unit trust deed is a contract by showing that the contract can, but the trust alone cannot, explain the 'relationships', 'obligations', and 'rights' found in a unit trust. 'Relationships', 'obligations', and 'rights' are the three aspects that have been used by jurists in defining the trust.[23] They therefore provide convenient anchors for understanding the nature of a unit trust. The contents of the 'relationships',[24] 'obligations',[25] and 'rights'[26] of the trustee, the manager, and the unitholders will form the subject of discussion of the remainder of this book.

In the process, points of similarity to and differences from the express trust used as a gift-making device will be apparent and the conclusion that the unit trust is a species of its own will be almost self-evident. In particular, the following major conclusions are drawn.

In a unit trust, the trust is being used, contractually, as a holding device to achieve collective ownership of unitholders themselves, rather than as a means of disposition in favour of objects of the unitholders' benefaction. This basic position implies that rights and obligations of all these three parties may be derived from contract, trust or both. This contractual—and non-gift—character means that the unit trust should not be subject to rules relating to perpetuities or the rule in *Saunders* v. *Vautier*, but may be subject to the doctrine of frustration. Its dual trust and contractual

[22] Ch. 2, *post.*
[23] Definition in terms of the relationship of the trustee and the beneficiaries: Keeton and Sheridan, *American Restatement of Trusts*, and Scott (see ch. 2, s. 2B(1) ); in terms of the trustees' obligations: *Lewin, Underhill and Hayton*, and Pettit (see ch. 2, s. 2C(1) ); in terms of the rights of beneficiaries: *Story* (see ch. 2, s. 2D(1) ).
[24] Between its participants, the manager, the trustee, and the unitholders: ch. 3, *post.*
[25] Of those who manage the trust: ch. 4, *post.*
[26] Of unitholders: ch. 5, *post.*

characters will give parties remedies both at law and in equity, depending on the nature of a particular dispute.

It also follows from this contractual and consensual character that the relationships created in a unit trust are not monolithic—i.e. not purely trust relationships. There is the possibility that the relationships may be characterized as some other species of contractual relationships. Viewed as a single entity, and compared with its predecessor the deed of settlement company, there is a possibility for it to be considered as a large partnership or association giving rise to the danger of infringing the prohibition against large unincorporated business associations contained in the Companies Act. However, the conclusion drawn from the analysis is that the parties are not associating for the purpose of carrying on business with a view of profit. In the majority of cases, the trustee is investing as a trustee—though subject to the directions of the manager. Even if it is possible to find any investment business carried on in a unit trust, it is carried on by the trustee. It is also the conclusion that there is no partnership or general agency subsisting between the trustee and the manager, and that the manager is not a general agent of the unitholders. The trustee, the manager, and the unitholders are contracting as independent parties whereby the trustee agrees to act as a trustee and the manager to manage the trust assets for all unitholders.

A trust analysis cannot fully describe the relationships at the individual levels between the trustee and the manager, the manager and the unitholders, and the trustee and the unitholders. The expansion of fiduciary principles will mean that in some factual circumstances fiduciary relationships may be created amongst them. In particular, the manager, as a party dominating the investment decision process, may be characterized as a fiduciary of the unitholders in many facets of the trust operations and therefore may be subject to fiduciary duties of loyalty and, as argued, of skill and care. However, the content of the duties of a manager forms an interesting contrast with that of the trustee, as the approaches of contract, tort, and trust law may be different in relation to a person whose office is derived from contract (the manager) and one whose office is both contractual and equitable (the trustee). The sharing between the trustee and the manager of powers and functions that hitherto have been vested in the single person of a trustee of a private trust is also a characteristic feature of a unit trust. In the discussion, powers in a unit trust have been classified as directory powers, veto powers, advisory powers or delegation powers. It suggests that a distinction must be made between a beneficial power and a fiduciary power. It concludes that in all cases, a party subject to the direction, veto, or advice or to whom responsibility is delegated is not bound to follow an instruction from the power holder if such instruction may result in a breach of statutory or contractual obligation. In the case of a fiduciary power, the power is also subject to the additional requirement that the instruction must not be given in breach of any of the power holder's fiduciary duties.

The contractual use of the trust as a means to combine investors' capital suggests that the rights of investors are predominantly contractual. There is, in this regard, a striking similarity between units and shares. The analysis shows that a unit is a single chose in action, and therefore a kind of personal property, which is transferable and in many cases redeemable. It is a chose comprising a bundle of contractual rights as well as rights conferred by statute. In ordinary cases, the trust fund of a unit trust may be characterized as a sum of capital and a unit only confers on its owner a right in money, being a proportion of the net value of the trust fund calculated and realizable as the trust deed may provide; a unitholder has no right in individual assets.

# 1

## *Evolution of the Unit Trust*

A necessary characteristic of any collective investment vehicle is the passive part played by investors in the conduct of the investment activities of the vehicle. This involves the segregation of those who provide the money from those who manage it. The trust is a natural candidate by reason of its ability to segregate the title and management of properties from their beneficial enjoyment. The company, likewise, separates the capitalists and the traders and therefore offers an alternative form. Historically, the trust owed its origin to the use and the company owed its to trading monopolies in the age of imperialism. In this sense, one would argue that the trust and the company are two competing forms with distinct origins.[1]

However, as the history of the two unfolds, the picture is not so clear-cut. In fact, the two concepts did and do closely interweave. As Maitland has observed, 'some day when English history is adequately written one of the most interesting and curious tales that it will have to tell will be that which brings trust and corporation into intimate connection with each other'.[2] Despite the passage of time, it seems, this intimacy has not dissipated. In fact, investment companies in England and Scotland are still called 'investment trusts'. The purpose of the short historical account that follows is to demonstrate the intimacy of the trust and the company and how history can give a better perception of what the unit trust is. There are four themes:

(1) It is true that at many points in time the company and the trust competed for popularity amongst investors. This owed much to the perception or misconception of risks associated with the form. However, there were many instances where they complemented and aided the development of each other. At the early stage of the company, the trust was the device to enable the company to hold properties. The highest watermark was reached when the deed of settlement company was used to overcome the objection by the state to the corporate form. Of course, the

---

[1] Cf. Moffat, pp. 15–17. Generally, see Cooke, *Corporation, Trust and Company: an Essay in Legal History*, Manchester UP, 1950.

[2] 'The Unincorporate Body' in Fisher, *The Collected Papers of F. W. Maitland*, Vol. III, Cambridge UP, 1911 (William S. Hein reprint, Buffalo, 1981) p. 272.

deed of settlement company was also the parent of the earliest unit trusts.
(2) There was a cross-cultivation of principles. This was a necessary
consequence of (1). During the early history of the company, equity had
already established a coherent body of law in relation to the trust. The fact
that companies were within equity's jurisdiction meant that trust concepts
had become a ready source of principles of corporate relationships, such as
the duty of the directors towards the company. Recently, there are signs of
a reverse cultivation: in unit trust problems that have been encountered in
the company context, courts have been prepared to apply company law
principles—apparently based on the justification of their common
parentage of the deed of settlement company.[3]
(3) They share a common legal characteristic, namely, that their constitutions are contractual in nature. The early joint stock company and the deed
of settlement companies were conceived as large partnerships where the
contractual nature would not have been doubted. The account in this
chapter traces the link between the unit trust and the deed of settlement
company. This account reinforces the argument in chapter 2 that the trust
by nature is not a constitutive tool as it is basically an obligation
institution—involving the imposition of trustees' duties upon legal owners.
Any arrangement involving enforceable promises rests with the contract.
Both the deed of settlement and the unit trust can only be understood in
terms of the contract.
(4) Liquidity of investment is another theme in the history of the two. The
joint stock concept was an investment concept; it involved a segregation of
the investors from the traders. This was achievable only with the invention
of shares as a species of properties and with the commercial and
subsequent judicial recognition of their transferability. Transferability was
achieved long before the introduction of registered companies. Units in
unit trusts of course 'inherit' this feature. In addition, managers of unlisted
trusts offer redemption of units at a price reflecting the underlying asset
value. Redeemability is further development of the liquidity feature of
investment.

### 1. THE TRUST AND THE EARLY JOINT STOCK COMPANIES: 1600–1720[4]

The development of the company form owed much to Britain's imperialistic
expansion of overseas trade in the sixteenth century. The earliest type of

---

[3] See s. 5F, *post*.
[4] See Scott, *The Constitution and Finance of English, Scottish and Irish Joint-Stock Companies to 1720*, Cambridge, 1912 (Peter Smith reprint, 1951); Holdsworth, Vol. VIII, pp. 206–19.

company was the regulated company. This was an extension of the guild principle in the foreign sphere. Each member of a regulated company traded on his own account and the liability of each was separate from the company. A charter was usually obtained in order to monopolize the trade for members. The company was an instrument of the government to ensure that 'the trade with which it was concerned was conducted in accordance with the commercial policy of the state'.[5]

At a later stage, the partnership idea[6] invaded the regulated company and the company became a joint enterprise of all members rather than a trade protection society. This evolution probably was a result of voyages that had become more expensive and risky. The joint stock concept was clearly one of sharing of trading risk and return. The history of the famous East India Company (which received its charter to trade in the Indies in 1600) was revealing of this evolution.[7]

From our perspective, it was the application of this joint stock concept to investment that is interesting. One important episode was the formation of the Bank of England in 1694[8] for the purpose of lending to the government the capital subscribed by members. The members were in effect making investments, the return of which was the interest promised by the state.[9] In modern parlance, the Bank of England was a vehicle of the government for securitizing the loan to it.

According to Holdsworth, it was this idea behind the Bank of England that became the foundation of the grandiose scheme of the South Sea Company.[10] Thus, the idea of shares as a form of investment property had taken its roots in this period, in spite of the fact that the nature of shares had not been determined. This was reflected in the number of companies formed and the frenetic level of share activities of the day, especially in the

---

[5] Holdsworth, Vol. VIII, p. 206.

[6] Which was in essence the ancient *societas* idea.

[7] All members were, in addition to their private trade, given the option to subscribe to joint stocks of varying amounts. During the first 50 years of its operation the company traded on a series of temporary (and sometimes coexisting) separate joint stocks. In 1613, the joint stock had to be subscribed for a succession of voyages for a fixed period of 4 years. In 1657 permanent stocks were introduced. Finally, in 1693, private trading by members was forbidden and a joint stock to run for 21 years was raised: Scott, *supra*, Vol. II, pp. 89 *et seq.*; Cooke, *Corporation, Trust and Company*, Manchester UP, 1950, pp. 58–9. Note that the years given here are based on Scott, Cooke and Holdsworth. These differ from those given in Gower, *The Principles of Modern Company Law*, 5th edn., Sweet and Maxwell, 1992, p. 21.

[8] Holdsworth, Vol. VIII, pp. 211–12; Scott, *supra*, Vol. I, p. 397.

[9] Scott, id., describes the phenomenon thus: 'Not only was all the capital subscribed by the members of the Bank of England lent to the State, but, in addition, a further sum was taken from the deposits of customers. Thus none of the share capital was available for the business of banking, and the loan made by the Bank to the State became in fact a fund of credit, to support the operations of the institution.' For details of the capital structure of the Bank of England, see Vol. III of Scott, *supra*, pp. 206–7.

[10] Holdsworth, Vol. VIII, at pp. 212–13.

last decade of the seventeenth century. In 1692, there was established a paper[11] on prices of stocks and shares. Also developed were mechanisms of stock exchange dealings, put and call options, specialized businesses of stock brokers and jobbers, and tariff charges by them. The degree of market sophistication can perhaps be seen from the market malpractices of market-rigging by share dealers and misleading prospectuses which were detailed in the Report of the Commissioners of Trade in 1696.[12]

In relation to this phase of the history of the joint stock company as an investment vehicle—and the shares as investment properties—it is submitted that two seemingly unconnected strands can be identified.

The first is that the adventurous mentality of the mercantile community had clearly impacted on the experiments in corporate forms in a similar fashion as it had on foreign trade. This driving force was stimulating development so rapidly that there was a very real gap between commercial practice and legal doctrines. In general, apart from ideas of personal liabilities for trading associations[13] and of mutual agency amongst partners,[14] the nature of the company and its shares was not appreciated. The line between corporate and unincorporated societies was generally disregarded by the commercial community.[15] Even societies considered themselves free to undertake activities outside the businesses for which they were incorporated.[16] Nor was any distinction drawn between the status of a joint stock company and a partnership.[17] More specifically, shares were readily transferable without regard to the nature of underlying assets of the company and also without regard to whether the company was incorporated or not. The modern method of transferring shares on the registers of companies emerged as early as the 1600s. This was apparent from a law report of a case[18] involving the East India Company.[19] According to Scott,[20] the shares of the East India Company were widely traded in the company's early years and in many cases by way of auction, in

---

[11] The word 'paper' was used by Holdsworth, ibid.; presumably, this was a newspaper.

[12] Holdsworth, Vol. VIII, p. 214.

[13] *Edmunds* v. *Brown and Tillard* (1668) 1 Lev. 237; *Salmon* v. *The Hamborough Company* (1671) 1 Ch. Cas. 204; Holdsworth, Vol. VIII, p. 203.

[14] *Lane* v. *Williams* (1693) 2 Vern. 277; *Pinkney* v. *Hall* (1697) 1 Ld. Raym. 175.

[15] Holdsworth, Vol. VIII, p. 215. [16] Id.

[17] Holdsworth, Vol. VIII, pp. 219–21.

[18] *Johnson* v. *East India Company* (1679) Rep. Temp. Finch 430, where the transferee with notice of fraud was ordered to transfer back the shares to the rightful owner. This was done by joining the company as a defendant.

[19] Which received its first charter in 1600 granting it monopoly of trade with the Indies.

[20] *The Constitution and Finance of English, Scottish and Irish Joint-Stock Companies to 1720*, Cambridge, 1912 (Peter Smith reprint, 1951) Vol. 1, p. 161.

the same way as the East India commodities. The transfer method was also used by other statutory companies in this period.[21] To sum up, there was an 'extreme poverty of the ascertained rules of law applicable to commercial societies, whether corporate or unincorporate'.[22] In the words of Formoy, '[t]he period from 1600 to 1720 is a history rather of particular companies than a history of any broad development of the law'.[23]

The history of this phase—and the gap between commercial practice and legal theory—are best summed up in the words of an American author, Smith:[24]

The English courts from Coke's day until long after the American Revolution are busy with boroughs, colleges, hospitals and ecclesiastical establishments; rarely do they have to deal with commercial corporations. Kyd's work on corporations (1793), the first comprehensive treatise, could as well have been written in 1600 for all the light it throws upon such questions as the rights of stockholders, limitations upon liability, or the internal set-up of business corporations. Here, if ever, have we an instance of a great social institution evolving unaided by contemporary judicial intervention. The courts, like Lot's wife, were looking backward; the merchants and capitalists were looking ahead.

The second strand of development in this period was Chancery's acquisition of jurisdiction over corporations and partnerships.[25] Both corporations and partnerships had been matters within the jurisdiction of the common law courts.[26] Had Chancery not intervened, the tales of the trust and the company would never have been told and there would be no interaction of their principles.

It appeared that Chancery's jurisdiction was founded on two principles. The first was that equity intervened where the forms of action at common law prevented any remedy. '[T]hough a corporation had a good cause of action against one of its members, by the rules of law no action could be

[21] e.g., Greenland Company, 1692, Bank of England, 1694, and National Land Bank, 1695 (Cooke, *Corporation, Trust and Company*, Manchester UP, 1950, p. 73).

[22] Holdsworth, Vol. VIII, p. 215.

[23] Formoy, *The Historical Foundation of Modern Company Law*, Sweet and Maxwell, 1923, p. 3.

[24] *Cases and Materials on Development of Legal Institutions*, West Publishing, 1965 (which, as noted in its preface, is based on Goebel, *Cases and Materials on the Development of Legal Institutions* (1946) ) p. 664.

[25] At this stage, the jurisdiction overlapped with that of the common law courts. It was not until the time of Lord Mansfield that their respective jurisdictions over commercial law were demarcated: Holdsworth, Vol. VI, p. 636.

[26] It must be borne in mind that the seventeenth century was a period during which the common law courts had won overriding jurisdiction in all matters of mercantile and maritime law over the Admiralty; they had just expanded into matters of bills of exchange, promissory notes, banking, insurance, bankruptcy, and bailment: Holdsworth, Vol. VI, pp. 634–5.

brought upon it; for any such action must have been brought in the name of the corporation, so that the person sued would have been one of the persons suing.'[27] Secondly, jurisdiction was also acquired on the basis that rights acknowledged at law were not effectively enforced by courts of law, so as to produce a mockery of justice. The court of equity was able to give remedies that were necessary to do justice but were not available in common law courts. These included taking the accounts of partnerships, compelling contribution between partners, discovery, and injunctions preventing breaches of good faith. There were also partnership rights not recognized at law such as conversion of partnership properties into money.[28]

These two currents eventually met in the century that followed. Following the logic of economics, the share market inevitably moved into its falling cycle. Litigation ensued. The fact that companies were within equity's jurisdiction played an important part in the application of trust principles to company law and the subsequent development of the unit trust. Trust law was a well established body of principles at the beginning of the eighteenth century when the court was asked to determine rights of members of the company. It was natural that the court would look to the established rules of the trust. Given its nature as a means of dealing with properties, the trust was particularly well placed to resolve issues involving property rights. The company, even though unincorporated, was held to be the trustee of the members of the company properties.[29] The status of directors was also held to be that of trustees.[30]

[27] Spence, *The Equitable Jurisdiction of the Court of Chancery*, Lea and Blanchard, 1846 (William S. Hein reprint, 1981) Vol. I, p. 641. The same was true of partnerships: 'An action between a partner and the firm, or between two firms having a common member, was impossible at common law.' (Pollock, *Law of Partnership*, 6th edn., Stevens & Sons, 1895.)

[28] Spence, ibid., p. 665.

[29] *Child* v. *Hudson's Bay Co.* (1723) 2 P Wms. 207 at 208–9 where Lord Macclesfield said that 'the legal interest of all the stock is in the company, who are trustees for the several members'. It was also admitted by the parties in *Bligh* v. *Brent* (1837) 2 Y & C Ex. 268, the leading case on the nature of shares in a deed of settlement company (discussed in ch. 5, s. 2C(2)&(3), *post*). Cooke, *Corporation, Trust and Company*, Manchester UP, 1950, p. 69. This proposition that a company holds its property on trust for its members *qua* members is no longer arguable: *Macaura* v. *Northern Assurance Co. Ltd.* [1925] AC 619 at 626; *Hood Barrs* v. *IRC* [1946] 2 All ER 768 at 775; *Short* v. *Treasury Commissioners* [1948] 1 KB 16 at 122; *Bank voor Handel en Scheepvaart* v. *Slatford* [1953] 1 QB 248 at 269.

[30] *Charitable Corporation* v. *Sutton* (1742) 2 Atk. 400 at 405–6, per Lord Hardwicke. The same principle applies to an unincorporated company: *Benson* v. *Heathorn* (1842) 1 Y & CCC 326. Cooke, *supra*, pp. 74–6; Keeton, 'The Director as Trustee' (1952) 5 *Current Legal Problems* 11. Contra, Sealy, 'The Director as Trustee' [1967] *CLJ* 83; the learned author attributes the trustee appellation to the 'limited vocabulary of the day' when the 'trustee' in a strict sense was not separately distinguished from the expression 'fiduciary', which happened only in the nineteenth century: ibid., at 86.

## 2. DEED OF SETTLEMENT COMPANIES AFTER THE BUBBLE ACT: 1720–1800[31]

The twenty years preceding the passage of the Act of 6 Geo. I, c. 18 (1720), popularly know as the Bubble Act, was a period of company boom and share speculation. This boom is often referred to as the South Sea Bubble, a name clearly associated with the South Sea Company, which introduced a grandiose share scheme in 1719. It was for the protection of this scheme against competition that the Bubble Act was enacted and 'the passage of the Act was shortly followed by a financial crash of Homeric proportions, and public hysteria no longer saw the company as a goose which laid eggs of gold but as a monster from the book of Revelation'.[32]

The immediate consequence of the crash was litigation on rights of the parties. As discussed in the preceding section, trust principles were utilized by the court as a means of settling joint stock issues. However, it was the use of the trust by businessmen to achieve the corporate objective that achieved far-reaching success.

The Bubble Act was an Act to make it illegal to act or presume to act as a corporation and have transferable shares without a charter. In simple terms, it was intended to impose a general prohibition on unincorporated companies.

Understandably, in the years immediately following the passing of the Act, applications for charters were numerous. If charters could have been obtained easily, the story of the trust in group organization for investment or trading would have had to end with this Act. The British Government's response to these applications was chilling, probably regarding companies as 'disturbers of financial peace'.[33] The result was the emergence of the deed of settlement company as a new business vehicle.

In the words of Maitland, the deed of settlement company was a use of the trust to make corporations without troubling King or Parliament.[34] Whilst this colourful description might have highlighted the versatility of the trust and the ingenious use of it by commercial lawyers of the day, one

---

[31] DuBois, *The English Business Company after the Bubble Act 1720–1800*, 1938 (Octagon Books reprint, 1971).

[32] Goebel, Editor's Introduction to DuBois, *supra*, p. viii.

[33] The words of Goebel, ibid., p. x. As pointed out by DuBois, the law officers of the Crown regarded the Act as an embodiment of the Government's policy against formation of companies with transferable shares (p. 12).

[34] Fisher, *The Collected Papers of F. W. Maitland*, Vol. III, Cambridge UP, 1911 (William S. Hein reprint, Buffalo, 1981) p. 283. Maitland probably has in mind the case of *Sutton's Hospital* (1615) 10 Coke Rep. 1a, [1558–1774] All ER Rep. 11 where Lord Coke declared that a corporation must be created by one of the four means: by the common law (as the King himself); by authority of Parliament; by the King's charter; or by prescription.

wonders whether at the same time it buried the true nature of the deed of settlement company of this period. A closer examination of its features is required.

(1) There was no doubt that the deed of settlement company was largely an avoidance measure. By nature, it was a revival of the joint stock company that existed before the passing of the Bubble Act. The only difference was that its constitution was tailored not to infringe the provisions of the Bubble Act, which, according to prevailing legal opinion,[35] was aiming at the creation of companies with transferable shares.[36] The deed of settlement was a constitution of a business company making provisions 'for the management of the business affairs of the company as a going concern, rather than the disposition of properties amongst the objects of the wishes of a settlor. A reading of precedents of such deeds from old books[37] makes this clear. A deed of settlement usually appointed directors and managers of the company's affairs, auditors of accounts, and other officers as might be required. It defined the number of shares, the method and restrictions of transfer, the mode of calling of general meetings of proprietors, their rights at such meetings, procedures for arbitration, and a variety of rules on regulating the internal affairs of the company. As a later development, there were provisions that each shareholder could only be liable to the extent of his shares.[38] The provision

---

[35] The status of legal opinions in that century must not be underestimated. 'On advice of counsel' was the keynote of the developments in the realm of business organization after the passing of the Bubble Act. (DuBois, *supra*, pp. 3 *et seq.*) As Goebel, *supra*, p. xiii, points out, '. . . it is obvious that the lawyers' opinions must be ranged with the law reports as a source of law. This is not merely because lawyers formulated the rules upon which great enterprises were conducted with a minimum resort to the tribunals, but because they carried the authority of a respected profession. If ever the civic advantage of a select and competent bar needs demonstration it can be found in the unexampled confidence which underlay this habit of consultation.'

[36] DuBois has pointed out that the opinions of Sergeant Thomas Pengellery, which were typical of the opinions given, stressed again and again that it was the creation of transferable shares that was the dominant issue in the prohibitions of the Bubble and that no attempt was made to define what 'presuming to act as a corporation' might be (DuBois, *supra*, pp. 3–5).

[37] Collyer, *A Practical Treatise on the Law of Partnership*, Sweet, Stevens and Maxwell, 1832, App. No. IX, pp. 734–59 is probably the most detailed. Unfortunately, its American edition (with American notes, by Phillips and Pickering) published by Merriam in 1839 omits the precedents, See also Wordsworth, *The Law of Joint Stock Companies*, 3rd edn., John Littell, 1843; Wordsworth, *The Law of Railway, Banking, Mining and Other Joint Stock Companies*, 5th edn., William Benning & Co, 1845. Descriptions of the deed of settlement in other texts also support the view that it functioned as a constitution of a business company: Smith, *A Compendium of Mercantile Law*, 6th edn. by Dowdeswell, Stevens, Norton and Sweet, 1859, pp. 59–110; Formoy, *The Historical Foundation of Modern Company Law*, Sweet and Maxwell, 1923, pp. 40–3.

[38] Such provisions were recognized as valid between shareholders and third parties dealing with the company with knowledge of such provisions: see Cooke, *supra*, p. 87, citing *Hallett* v.

for the holding of properties on trust typically only occupied one or two clauses.

(2) In a company for carrying on businesses, those who actively made the business decisions would naturally become the focus of its constitution. As Sealy has pointed out,[39] the directors were a distinct working body, though the persons of the trustees and the directors might overlap in some instances. This body was contemplated by the deed to be the focal point, as elaborate provisions were made regarding their powers, responsibilities, and the conduct of their meetings. It was through this body that day-to-day business was carried out. Thus, a joint stock company has been described as:

a company having certain amount of capital, divided into a greater or smaller number of transferable shares, managed for the common advantage of the shareholders *by a body of directors* chosen by and responsible to them.[40]

An active role by the directors was clearly recognized.

(3) Lest the importance of the trust may be downplayed, it should be said that a body of trustees to hold the properties for the company was an imperative in the deed of settlement. The common law had laid down already that an unincorporated group could not own property as a group. Without properties, a company did not have much scope for action. But '[t]he use of the equitable trust to serve the common purpose of a group was no new thing in the eighteenth century'.[41] If the role of the trustees was compared with that of the directors, its passive nature was most apparent. This was reflected in a common provision that the trustee shall stand possessed of the properties 'in trust for the company, and shall apply and dispose of the same in such manner, for the benefit of the company, as the board of directors shall, conformably to the duties imposed on them by these presents, from time to time order or direct'.[42] There was usually no provision for decision making by the trustees. It is fair to say that the trust was merely a holding device to enable the real and personal properties of the company to be held and also to facilitate the bringing and defending of suits in respect of the company's properties.[43] The decision-making role regarding such properties was vested in the directors.

*Dowdall* (1852) 21 LJQB 98; *Re Waterloo Life Assurance Co.* (1864) 33 Beav. 542; *Re Medical, Invalid and General Life Assurance Society* (1871) (*Griffiths' Case*) 6 Ch. App. 374; (*Spencer's Case*) 6 Ch. App. 362; *Re Family Endowment Society* (1869) 5 Ch. App. 118; *Re European Assurance Society* (1875) (*Hort's Case*) 1 Ch. D 307; (*Grain's Case*) 1 Ch. D 315.

[39] Sealy, 'The Director as Trustee' [1967] *CLJ* 83 at 84.
[40] Wordsworth, *The Law of Joint Stock Companies*, 3rd edn., John Littell, 1843, p. 2, citing an American author, McCulloock (emphasis added).
[41] Cooke, *Corporation, Trust and Company*, Manchester UP, 1950, p. 86.
[42] Collyer, *supra*, cl. 98.
[43] *Metcalf* v. *Bruin* (1810) 12 East 400. But, as DuBois has noted, there were instances where legal proceedings might be difficult: DuBois, *supra*, pp. 220–1.

Three observations may be made in respect of the three features just identified. First, from a commercial perspective, the trust was merely part of the larger constitutional framework established by the deed of settlement. The legal character of the deed of settlement was a contract between the shareholders who had put up the capital to be 'managed for the common advantage of the shareholders *by a body of directors* chosen by and responsible to them'.[44] The shareholders were of course a new class of investors who would not actively manage their own money.[45] In this sense, therefore, the trust was created by a contract and was part of that contract's terms. The contractual nature of the deed of settlement was recognized in a case on the method of transfer of shares[46] and also by all textbooks. Formoy, for instance, says, '[t]he deed of settlement was in effect a deed of partnership. It consisted *in a mutual covenant* between a few of the shareholders acting as trustees for the purpose, and the other shareholders whose names appeared in the schedule, to carry out the provisions contained in the deed.'[47] An examination of the precedents in such texts also confirms that the deed of settlement took the form of a deed of mutual covenants. As a deed of covenants, it was simply a contract under seal. This contractual nature was certainly active in the mind of the draftsmen of the day. There were provisions requiring transferees of shares to execute a deed of covenant to abide by the deed of settlement,[48] provisions which obviously were dictated by the privity doctrine.

The second point is that the trust, as a part of the deed of settlement, played an important part in avoiding the Bubble Act. It sustained the continued growth of the company form which would otherwise have been suppressed. In terms of developing a body of company law principles, company disputes during this period were largely resolved by Chancery judges by resort to trust concepts.

Thirdly, what the trust ultimately supported was a furtherance of the joint stock concept developed by companies formed before the Bubble Act. The shadow of the Bubble Act meant that some sort of restrictions were necessary in regard to free transfer of shares, but this did not halt the emergence of shares as a species of properties in their own right.

Here, the interpenetration of the company and the trust concept is more

---

[44] See text accompanying fn. 40, *supra*.

[45] Under a typical deed of settlement the proprietors were to assemble only once or twice a year.

[46] *Ashby* v. *Blackwell and Million Bank* (1765) Amb. 503: see the discussion below on validity of 'transfer' as a method of disposing shares.

[47] Formoy, *The Historical Foundation of Modern Company Law*, Sweet and Maxwell, 1923, p. 40 (emphasis supplied); Wordsworth, *The Law of Joint Stock Companies*, 3rd edn., John Littell, 1843, pp. 11–12; Smith, *A Compendium of Mercantile Law*, 6th edn. by Dowdeswell, Stevens, Norton and Sweet, 1859, p. 59.

[48] Collyer, *supra*, cl. 117; Cooke, *supra*, pp. 86–7.

subtle. Apparently, transferability of shares and transfer on books as a method of disposition of shares were 'company practices' developed in the previous century.[49] During the Bubble period, there were many modes of transfer of shares, including transfer by deeds and endorsement on share certificates, but transfer on books remained the most common.[50] Logically, in a deed of settlement company, if there was a trust of properties, the transfer of shares should take the same form as the assignment of beneficiaries' interests under a trust. But validity of the transfer method was never doubted, and in 1765 this received judicial recognition in *Ashby* v. *Blackwell and Million Bank*.[51] Lord Northington justified the transfer method on the basis that it was part of the contractual agreement as to holding of shares and their disposal to be found in the deed of settlement.[52] The Chancery judges were pragmatic enough to give effect to company practice in the transfer of 'equitable interests (in the trust)' of company shareholders. This was at a time when equity had not yet reached the stage of recognizing shares as properties distinct from companies' underlying assets.

The next development in the same vein was the recognition of shares as a species of property. Initially, judges in a series of cases concerning the New River Company took the view that shareholders were the equitable owners of underlying assets.[53] In the middle of nineteenth century, in another series of cases,[54] the court was asked to determine whether shares were personalty or realty for the purpose of the Mortmain Acts and section 4 of the Statute of Frauds. The conclusion reached was that shares were personalty unconnected with the underlying assets. This was held to be the nature of shares of both deed of settlement companies and companies

---

[49] It is clear from DuBois, *The English Business Company after the Bubble Act 1720–1800*, 1938 (Octagon Books reprint, 1971), that transfer on books was the method used by deed of settlement companies such as Sun Fire Office, the Temple Brass Mills, and the West New Jersey Society (pp. 360 and 405 n. 106). These companies were established in 1707, 1695, and 1692 respectively (pp. 218, 493, and 494). The history of methods of transfer of shares in deed of settlement companies will be examined in greater detail in the context of transferability of units in unit trusts: ch. 5, s. 4B, *post*.    [50] DuBois, ibid., pp. 358–62.

[51] (1765) Amb. 503.    [52] Ibid. at 506.

[53] *Drybutter* v. *Bartholomew* (1723) 2 P Wms. 127, *Townsend* v. *Ash* (1745) 3 Atk. 336, *Stafford* v. *Buckley* (1750) 2 Ves. Sen. 171, *Swayne* v. *Fawkener* (1696) Show. PC 207, *Sandys* v. *Sibthorpe* (1778) Dick. 545. Other early cases on the same point were referred to in the judgment and counsel's arguments in *Bligh* v. *Brent* (1837) 2Y & C Ex. 268. For further discussion, see ch. 5, s. 2C(3), *post*.

[54] *Bligh* v. *Brent* (1837) 2Y & C Ex. 268; *Humble* v. *Mitchell* (1839) 11 AD & E 205; *Duncuft* v. *Albrecht* (1841) 12 Sim. 189; *Sparling* v. *Parker* (1846) 9 Beav. 450, *Walker* v. *Milne* (1849) 11 Beav. 507; *Ashton* v. *Lord Langdale* (1851) 4 De G & Sm. 402; *Myers* v. *Perigal* (1852) 2 De GM & G 599; *Watson* v. *Spratley* (1854) 10 Ex. 222. A discussion of these cases appears in ch. 5, s. 2C(2), (3), and (5), *post*.

incorporated by Acts of Parliament. This was achieved by treating the issue
as one of construction of the deed of settlement or the incorporating Act.
In 1839, in *Humble* v. *Mitchell*,[55] shares of a deed of settlement company
were recognized as choses in action. This conclusion was confirmed by the
House of Lords in 1886 in *The Colonial Bank* v. *Whinney*.[56] This
development of the conception of shares as a species of properties in their
own right was of utmost importance in the subsequent distinction made by
the court between unincorporated companies and partnerships.[57]

   To sum up, the trust saved the joint stock company from statutory
suppression and the pragmatism of Chancery judges had permitted
company practices to cultivate trust principles. The deed of settlement
company of this period was therefore an offspring of the joint stock
company and the trust. Perhaps, it was the most important development in
the history of both company law and trust principles for it was also the
parent of both modern registered companies and the unincorporated

---

[55] (1839) 11 AD & E 205.                    [56] (1886) LR 11 AC 426.

[57] This was most explicit in the judgment of James LJ in *Re Agriculturist Cattle Insurance Co.* (1870) LR 5 Ch. 725 at 733: 'Ordinary partnerships are essentially in kind and not merely in the magnitude of the partnership or the number of partners different from joint stock companies. Ordinary partnerships are by the law assumed and presumed to be based on the mutual trust and confidence of each partner in the skill, knowledge and integrity of every other partner. As between the partners and the outside world (what ever may be their private arrangements between themselves), each partner is the unlimited agent of every other in every matter connected with the partnership, that being the relation between partners; of course, when the Court had to consider whether a partner could substitute or let in some other person for or with him or whether a partner's executor could claim to succeed him, there could be no difficulty in saying that this could not be done without the consent of all the partners. The death of a partner, therefore, necessarily put an end to the partnership so far as he was concerned; and as in the absence of express stipulation the right of the representative was to have all the assets realised and divided, it necessarily put an end to the whole subject-matter of the partnership. . . . But it is because these were the ordinary partnership—it was to escape from these, that joint-stock companies were invented. That was the very cause and reason of their existence. At first they existed under the favour of the Crown, which gave them charters of incorporation, and nobody ever supposed that the holders of stock in the Bank of England, or the East India Company had anything to do with the law of partnership or were partners. But there were large societies on which the sun of royal or legislative favour did not shine, and as to whom the whole desire of the associates, and the whole aim of the ablest legal assistants they could obtain, was to make them as nearly a corporation as possible, with continuous existence with transmissible and transferable stock, but without any individual right in any associate to bind the other associates, or deal with the assets of the association. A joint-stock company is not an agreement between a great many persons that they will be co-partners, but is an agreement between the owners of shares, or the owners of stock, that they or their duly recognised assigns, the owner of the shares for the time being, whoever they may be, shall be and continue an association together, sharing profits and bearing losses . . . if he is liable under any contracts or obligation, or in respect of any act of the body, it is not because they are the contracts, obligations, or acts of his partners or partner, but because they are the contracts, obligations and acts of the quasi-corporate body (under present legislation the actual body corporate) by its properly constituted agents.'

investment trusts of the late nineteenth century. The deed of settlement was the progenitor of articles of association, since the early pieces of companies legislation in England required all companies to have deeds of settlement as their constitution.[58] It was also the model of trust deeds of unit trusts in the late 1860s, the most famous of which appeared in the litigation of *Smith* v. *Anderson*.[59]

3. THE EMERGENCE OF THE UNIT TRUST IN THE
NINETEENTH CENTURY

## A. The New Investors and the Struggle for Limited Liability

The Bubble Act was repealed in 1825. The Joint Stock Companies Registration and Regulation Act of 1844[60] made incorporation by registration generally available and limited liability was given to such registered companies by the Limited Liability Act of 1855. With these advancements in the features and incidents of the limited company, one would have thought that the limited company had become 'the means by which huge aggregations of capital required to give effect to their discoveries were collected, organised and efficiently administered'[61] and that the deed of settlement or the trust would have been displaced as a vehicle for investment or trading. Yet the trust re-emerged in 1868[62] as a form of collective investment. This re-emergence of the trust has never been accounted for.[63] The clue, it is submitted, lies in the widening of the class of market players and in the events leading to the enactment of the Limited Liability Act of 1855.

---

[58] The Chartered Companies Act 1837 and the Joint Stock Companies Act 1844: see Formoy, *The Historical Foundation of Modern Company Law*, Sweet and Maxwell, 1923, p. 41.

[59] (1880) 15 Ch. D 247, discussed in ch. 3, s. 1, *post*.

[60] Hunt, *The Development of the Business Corporation in England 1800–1867*, Harvard UP, 1936 (Russell & Russell edition, 1969), describes this Act as one that 'marks an epoch in the history of English company law' (p. 94).

[61] *The Economist*, 18 Dec. 1926, quoted by Hunt, *The Development of the Business Corporation in England 1800–1867*, Harvard UP, 1936 (Russell & Russell edition, 1969), p. 116.

[62] The Foreign and Colonial Government Trust. This form of investment trust was based on the deed of settlement: see the discussion below.

[63] The only detailed account of the trust as an investment vehicle in this period is ch. 2 of Walker's unpublished thesis 'Unit Trust' submitted for the degree of Ph.D. in Economics in the University of London in 1938, which is substantially published as 'Unincorporated Investment Trusts in the Nineteenth Century' (1940) 15 *Economic History* 341. Walker's thesis forms the part of Gower's account of the history of the unit trust in his *The Principles of Modern Company Law* (4th edn., 1979, pp. 266–72; this account was omitted in the 5th edn.). Walker's thesis, however, does not attempt to explain why all of a sudden the trust was used in 1868 even though limited liability was available.

The history of the limited company in the nineteenth century has been traced by Hunt in his book, *The Development of the Business Corporation in England 1800–1867.*[64] From his vivid account, it is clear that up to the year 1855, England had experienced three booms[65] in the trading of shares, which were all followed by liquidation of companies. Each of these booms appeared to have dwarfed its predecessor in size. They can be traced back to the end of the Napoleonic war, the immediate consequence of which was an abundant supply of capital that was no longer absorbed by war expenditure.

There was a significant difference in the composition of investors in this period from those of the previous era. They included a significant number of trustees who emerged as a group that played a role in the Government's decision to give limited liability to registered companies. The South Sea Bubble had inhibited the range of permitted trustee investment in line with the expectation of the new wealth-owning class, who were predominantly directors and shareholders of business companies. Until the first statutory widening of trustee investment, Chancery judges were still labouring under the shock of the South Sea Bubble of the last century. Trustees were only permitted to lay out trust properties 'either in well-secured estate (i.e. on mortgage) or upon Government Stock'.[66] Shares were not permitted investments until 1859.[67] The response of the new wealth-owning class was to insert broad investment powers for their trustees.[68] As a result, trustees became a group of active investors in shares. This led the Royal Commission of 1854 to come to the view that as there was a lack of control by trustees in the management of companies in which they invested it was 'only fair to secure them from any further loss than the sum already

---

[64] *Supra.*

[65] The first boom was in the years 1824 and 1825 which was described by Hunt, *supra*, as 'a veritable avalanche of extravagent promotions and general speculation' (p. 30) and which seemed to have had its inception in foreign loans, especially to new governments of South America. The second was the joint stock bank 'mania' (p. 61) of 1834–6 which was followed by the violent liquidations of 1836–7. The third was the railway boom, which emerged shortly after the passing of the Act of 1844 (pp. 90–115). During this boom, with the vast expansion of the railway network, there was immense interest in railway companies. Investment was facilitated through the concurrent rise of stock exchanges. The total capital raised for railroads rose from £65 m. to £200 m. between 1844 and 1848 (p. 105).

[66] *Pocock* v. *Reddington* (1801) 5 Ves. 794 at 800, per Lord Alvanley. There were cases to the effect that investment in mortgages was not suitable: *Raby* v. *Ridehalgh* (1855) 7 De GM & G 104. This was only confirmed by the Law of Property Act 1859, s. 32.

[67] The Trustees' Relief Act of 1859 permitted trustees to invest in stocks of the Banks of England and Ireland and in East India Stock.

[68] Despite the absence of statistics, it was probable that they were inserted widely in trust instruments. This was reflected from the continuous demands to widen the range of investment. Acts extending the range of trustee investment were passed in 1867, 1871, 1875, and 1882: Keeton, 'The Evolution of Trustee Investments' in *Modern Developments in the Law of Trusts*, North Ireland Legal Quarterly, 1971, p. 48.

invested'.[69] The Royal Commission therefore supported the introduction of limited liability. In this way, developments of the company and the trust have impacted on each other.

The more significant group of investors were working people with no business expertise and with no desire to participate in the management of business. Naturally enough, they did not wish to have responsibility or liability for trading activities of the businesses in which they invested. Shares in small denominations emerged in the mid-1830s,[70] apparently to attract this new class of investors to put their savings in shares. Indeed, the Government in England responsible for the passing of the Limited Liability Act of 1855 was in many respects motivated by concerns about the working class raised in reports such as the Report of Select Committee on Investments for the Savings of the Middle and Working Classes 1850, the Report of Select Committee on the Law of Partnership 1851, and the First Report, Royal Mercantile Law Commission 1854.[71] The frauds of the 1840s amongst the savings banks were regarded as a threat to the 'provident habits of the labouring classes' and it was said that there should be an outlet of savings of the 'frugal and industrious of the humble classes'.[72] In political terms, the strive for limited liability can be seen as a struggle for equality for the masses. '[T]he working classes should have the fullest opportunity of trying experiments for themselves.'[73] The joint stock principle would prove 'an instrument of immense latent capacity for elevating the whole labouring class'[74] but the law, as it stood, prevented 'the marriage of skill and capital by means of limited liability'.[75]

The passage of the Limited Liability Act 1855, which extended limited liability to all joint stock companies, therefore inevitably meant not only 'the emancipation of joint-stock enterprise'[76] but also the germination of a new class of investors in shares. The Act of 1855 was repealed but re-enacted the following year. A consolidation Act was enacted in 1862.[77]

---

[69] The Royal Commission's Report of 1854, App. p. 76, quoted by Hunt, *supra*, p. 131.

[70] Hunt, *supra*, p. 72.

[71] Hunt, *supra*, p. 116, fn. 5.

[72] The annual amount of savings by 'the poorer part of the community' was about £3 m.: *Economist* VIII (1850) p. 537, quoted in Hunt, *supra*, p. 119, fn. 23.

[73] Hansard, CXIX, 679; quoted in Hunt, *supra*, p. 125.

[74] *Money and Morals: a Book for the Times* (1852) pp. 203–4, quoted by Hunt, *supra*, p. 121, fn. 33.

[75] Hansard, CXIX, 682; quoted in Hunt, ibid.

[76] *The Times*, 16 Jan. 1865, quoted in Hunt, *supra*, p. 145. The emancipation took the form of conversion of private firms into companies and also the establishment of new enterprises, such as joint stock banks, finance companies etc.: see Hunt, *supra*, ch. VII.

[77] This Act was described by Palmer, *Company Law*, 7th edn., 1909, p. 1, as 'the Magna Carta' of English company law.

## B. The Unit Trust as a Revival of the Deed of Settlement Company

With the issue of limited liability resolved, the registered company became particularly attractive as a collective investment vehicle. The first invest- ment companies appeared in Scotland in 1860[78] and in England in 1863.[79] The practical reason for the formation of such companies was believed to be the diversification of risks for this new class of investors.[80] In their legal nature, they did not differ from the registered company that engaged in trading activities.

In the meantime, England entered the 'stormy decade'[81] of the 1860s. The first half of this decade witnessed a spectacular surge of joint stock banks and finance and discount companies, which in turn acted as a stimulus to promoters of companies in fields such as manufacturing, trading, hotel, building, insurance, and mining. There was also conversion of established private firms into limited companies. The width of company formation inevitably exacerbated the panic that was to come. Hunt described the panic of 1866:

The failure of Overend, Gurney, Ltd on May 10, 1866 precipitated the panic of Black Friday. No single bankruptcy had ever caused 'so great a shock to credit'. There ensued the greatest agitation ever known in the City. Several banks failed within the week and a number of the new credit companies, 'framed on the French model', were summarily crushed. 'We have called this panic "financial" ', the editors of *The Times* explained on one of the fateful days, 'because the new Finance Companies feel the effects most severely.' In their wake, of course, followed many of the new promotions in other fields—over 200 of them were snuffed out in less than three months.

Limited liability suddenly became extremely unpopular; it had 'palpably and plainly intensified a panic;' indeed many were disposed to father on it all the disasters that had occurred. A universal outcry against all joint stock companies broke forth. The country was discouraged and suspicious, the House of Commons almost hostile.[82]

---

[78] The first investment trust company was the Scottish American Investment Company incorporated in 1860 under the Joint Stock Companies Act 1856: Pennington, *The Investor and the Law*, Macgibbon & Kee, 1968, p. 217 (but the name of the company given in Hanson, *Dictionary of Banking and Finance*, Pitman, 1985, is South American Investment Company).

[79] The London Financial Association and the International Financial Society formed in 1863 were believed to be the first two investment trust companies in England: Grayson, *Investment Trusts: Their Origin, Development, and Operation*, John Wiley & Sons, 1928 (Arno Press reprint, 1975), p. 14.

[80] This was a class that 'became exceedingly chary of the new avenues of investment constantly opened abroad, but nevertheless became more and more eager for larger returns upon invested capital' (Grayson, *supra*, p. 16).

[81] The words of Lord Goschen, *Essays and Addresses on Economic Questions* (1905) 'Introductory Note' p. 1, quoted in Hunt, *supra*, p. 145.

It was against this background that the first unit trust emerged two years later. The Foreign and Colonial Trust was formed in 1868.[83] At this time, of the 7,056 of the companies formed since 1844[84] only 2,967 remained.[85] The distaste for the company was apparent from the underlying investments of the Trust. It consisted solely of fixed interest investment and promised fixed interest returns.[86] In terms of investors' sentiment at the time, '[f]ixed interest suggested something removed from the dangers of "limited liability," "joint stock," and "profit on the stock" '.[87] Thus, it is fair to suggest that it was a misconceived evil in the concept of limited liability[88] that lay behind the first appearance of the unit trust. There was no indication that at this stage people were enticed by the ability of the unit trust to return their capital to them, an advantage perceived by modern investors to be important.[89] In fact, one characteristic shared by all trusts in this period was that a trust would return the capital to investors when there was surplus income, by way of a tender and a draw.[90] The Foreign and Colonial Trust did not expect all certificates to be redeemed and capital returned until the end of twenty-four years.

Several observations can be made in respect of the unit trust of this period.

---

[82] Hunt, *supra*, pp. 153–4; all footnotes omitted.

[83] The trust deed was dated 1 June 1868: Walker's unpublished thesis 'Unit Trust' *supra*, p. 14; Walker, 'Unincorporated Investment Trusts in the Nineteenth Century' [1940] *Economic History* 341.

[84] The year in which the registered company was introduced.

[85] See 'the Table of Companies Formed and Remaining, 1844–1868' in Hunt, *supra*, p. 157.

[86] The underlying investments were listed in Table I of Walker's unpublished thesis 'Unit Trust' *supra*, p. 19; Walker, 'Unincorporated Investment Trusts in the Nineteenth Century' [1940] *Economic History* 341 at 343. All trusts during this period provided a fixed rate of interest return.

[87] Walker, 'Unincorporated Investment Trusts in the Nineteenth Century' [1940] *Economic History* 341 at 354.

[88] Considering that limited liability was the evil, the House of Commons in fact appointed a committee on the Limited Liability Acts. However, the committee countenanced all objections to limited liability and in fact 'extended and completed' the concept by recommending that reduction of capital be permitted with the consent of creditors: Hunt, *supra*, p. 155–6. In fact, the true evil was the margin of uncalled capital in most issues, which tempted investors to subscribe for liability beyond their means (Hunt, ibid.).

[89] Day and Harris, p. 1, give reduction of capital as a reason for the growth of the unit trust. If the learned authors are referring to early unit trusts, this proposition is very doubtful. The rule that a company cannot reduce its own capital appeared to have been decided in 1882 in *Guinness* v. *Land Corporation of Ireland* (1882) 22 Ch. D 349 (Knight, 'Capital Maintenance' in Patfield (ed.), *Perspectives on Company Law: I*, Kluwer Law International, 1995, p. 52). It was settled only in 1887 in *Trevor* v. *Whitworth* (1887) 12 App. Cas. 409, much later than the first appearance of the unit trust.

[90] A trust deed usually provided that the trustees shall apply the surplus income to redeem certificates from certificate holders through a tender and that if there was any further surplus remaining, a draw would be held in front of a notary public to decide which certificates would be redeemed: e.g., clauses 6–12 of the deed creating the Submarine Cables' Trust (*Smith* v. *Anderson* (1879) 15 Ch. D 247 at 250).

(1) It is clear that before the first unit trust was introduced, the company had already been adopted as a vehicle for collective investment. But as the story of the company unfolded, it suffered a public perception as being of high risk. Yet risk was something which both the investment company and the unit trust were supposed to avoid. Diversification of risks was a theme of the first investment company. It was also the purpose advertised by the Foreign and Colonial Government Trust.[91] Thus, as suggested above, there was perceived to be a real need to find an alternative form of vehicle for collective investment. The trust was the natural candidate. Indeed, *The Economist* described the Foreign and Colonial Government Trust as 'an evident attempt to avoid the now unpopular name of Company'.[92]

(2) If the trust was to be used as the company's alternative, there was no reason why the deed of settlement should not become the model. An examination of the precedents in the law reports[93] reveals the unit trust's resemblance to the deed of settlement company. This view of the nature of the unit trust deed appears to be shared by counsel for the plaintiff in *Sykes* v. *Beadon*,[94] the first case on the nature of the unit trust in this period.

(3) The unit trust deed took the form of a deed of mutual covenant. A reading of the trust deed recited in the report of *Smith* v. *Anderson* illustrates this. The trust deed was intended to be made between the trustees and all the certificate holders, with one acting as an agent for all:

The trust was constituted by a deed dated the 6th of September 1871, between Sir James Anderson and five other persons (thereinafter called the said trustees) of the one part, and Philip Rose (thereinafter called the covenantee), 'for and on behalf of all the holders for the time being of the certificates hereinafter mentioned,' of the other part: whereby after reciting . . . [the recitals] the trustees jointly and severally covenanted with the covenantee, his executors, administrators, and assigns, for and on behalf of all the holders for the time being of the said certificates, as follows . . . [the full terms of the trust deed followed][95]

---

[91] The Trust was advertised in its prospectus as a plan 'for enabling the public to make investments in foreign and colonial securities without encountering the special risk incidental to any single purchase'. Particulars of the Trust were reported in the 'Money-Market & City Intelligence' of *The Times*, 20 Mar. 1868, which was reproduced in full in Merriman, *Unit Trusts and How They Work*, 2nd edn., Pitman, 1959, pp. 1–2.

[92] 28 Mar. 1868, quoted in Walker's unpublished thesis 'Unit Trust' *supra*, p. 14; Walker, 'Unincorporated Investment Trusts in the Nineteenth Century' [1940] *Economic History* 341; Merriman, *Unit Trusts and How They Work*, 2nd edn., Pitman, 1959, pp. 1–2.

[93] *Sykes* v. *Beadon* (1879) 11 Ch. D 170; *Smith* v. *Anderson* (1879) 15 Ch. D 247.

[94] (1879) 11 Ch. D 170 at 185 where counsel for the plaintiff are reported to have submitted that '[the trust] is not an "association for the acquisition of gain" within the meaning of the 4th section [of the Companies Act 1862]. It is in terms a trust, not an association for carrying on business for gain. Its nature is shewn by the trust deed, which is, in substance, a deed of settlement . . .' Leading counsel was Chitty QC.

[95] (1880) 15 Ch. D 247 at 248–9.

As it is a deed of mutual covenants, the trustees and the certificate holders are in a contractual relationship. This was recognized by the two first instance judgments of Jessel MR in *Sykes* v. *Beadon*[96] and *Smith* v. *Anderson*.[97] Jessel MR treated the trust deed as a contract in his decision that the unit trust constituted an unregistered association for the acquisition of gain. Although the Court of Appeal subsequently overturned both decisions in *Sykes* v. *Beadon*[98] and in *Smith* v. *Anderson*,[99] it appeared that this contractual point was not raised.

(4) Management of the trust was in the hands of the trustees, who were given the power to sell the portfolio assets in certain specified circumstances. Given the 'fixity' of underlying investments intended by these trusts, it would appear that no 'organ' similar to the directors was required. Yet, a committee of certificate holders to be chosen annually at the general meeting was provided for. This was a close following of the deed of settlement. Arguably, this structure was unnecessary and it was criticized as 'a kind of double government in the trustees and certificate holders'.[100]

(5) Units were treated in all respects as shares.[101] They were issued to the public in the same manner as shares. According to Walker, 'they were applied for on the basis of a prospectus in the same way as shares, though there is some indication that lists generally did not close very quickly. It was customary, therefore, to state in the prospectus the minimum total subscription necessary for the trust to operate . . .'[102] They were also traded on the stock exchange.[103] This similarity should not obscure the fact it was contemplated in the unit trust deed that units would eventually be redeemed. The redemption procedure at this infant stage of the unit trust was very complicated, but it significantly distinguished the joint stock company, which was supposed to continue indefinitely.

The most striking feature of these trusts was not so much their legal characteristics as the high rate of return they promised.[104] At the very

---

[96] (1879) 11 Ch. D 170.      [97] (1880) 15 Ch. D 247.      [98] *Supra.*

[99] *Supra.*

[100] *Economist*, 28 Mar. 1868, quoted in Walker's unpublished thesis 'Unit Trust' *supra*, p. 13; Walker, 'Unincorporated Investment Trusts in the Nineteenth Century' [1940] *Economic History* 341.

[101] The word 'shares' was actually used in the prospectus of the Submarine Cables' Trust (*Smith* v. *Anderson* (1879) 15 Ch. D 247 at 256).

[102] Walker's unpublished thesis 'Unit Trust' *supra*, pp. 17–18; Walker, 'Unincorporated Investment Trusts in the Nineteenth Century' [1940] *Economic History* 341 at 343.

[103] e.g., *Sykes* v. *Beadon* (1879) 11 Ch. D 170 at 181.

[104] Walker in his thesis has analysed the yields required to fulfil the promises made by the trusts. (Table III 'Income Yield Required on Underlying Securities'—Walker's unpublished thesis 'Unit Trust' *supra*, p. 38; Walker, 'Unincorporated Investment Trusts in the Nineteenth Century' [1940] *Economic History* 341 at 349.) They ranged from 6.2% to 8.9%. In reading these figures, the restricted range of underlying investments as well as the period over which this level had been maintained must be borne in mind.

moment when the first of these trusts, the Foreign and Colonial Government Trust, appeared, *The Economist* attacked its promised yield as extravagant.[105] After some initial success, some of the trusts defaulted in paying the interest promised. The first instance involved the Share Investment Trust, which went into partial default in 1876. With defaults, litigation followed. In 1877, the certificate holders of the Government and Guaranteed Securities Permanent Trust brought an action against their trustees to have (*inter alia*) the trust administered by the court. This was the case of *Sykes* v. *Beadon*.[106] It was heard by Jessel MR in 1879 on a demurrer by a retired trustee, claiming that the trust was an association consisting of more than twenty persons for the acquisition of gain[107] not having been registered under the Companies Act 1862 and accordingly was an illegal association. The Master of the Rolls allowed the demurrer on the ground that the association was illegal and that the trust deed therefore constituted an illegal contract.

Within one month[108] after the judgment in *Sykes* v. *Beadon*[109] was given, an action was commenced by Smith, a certificate holder of the Submarine Cables' Trust on behalf of all certificate holders, against the trustees of the Trust. This was the leading case of *Smith* v. *Anderson*, which was heard before the Master of the Rolls in December 1879 and in January 1880. As Chitty QC, leading counsel for the defendant trustees, admitted, the action was defended entirely with a view to test the correctness of *Sykes* v. *Beadon*[110] at the Court of Appeal.[111] Chitty QC was the leading counsel who argued the legality of such trusts in *Sykes* v. *Beadon*.[112] The case reached the Court of Appeal in July 1880 and *Sykes* v. *Beadon* was reversed.

Despite the swiftness with which the case of *Smith* v. *Anderson* was brought and heard, all unit trusts were in the process of being reorganized as companies or being wound up when the Court of Appeal gave its judgment. Thus, before the legal battle was fought, the trust had already lost all its commercial ground to the company as an investment vehicle. By this time, more than a decade had elapsed since the panic of 1866. The concept of limited liability was better understood; and the company must

---

[105] 28 Mar. 1868, quoted in Walker p. 13; p. 241.

[106] (1879) 11 Ch. D 170.

[107] Since the Companies Act 1844, there was a prohibition on the formation of unincorporated companies, associations, and partnerships for gain where the members exceeded 25. (This was reduced to 20 by the Companies Act 1856.)

[108] Judgment was given by the Master of Rolls on 11 Feb. 1879 (see 11 Ch. D 170). Action was commenced by Smith in Mar. 1879 (*Smith* v. *Anderson* (1880) 15 Ch. D 247 at 257).

[109] (1879) 11 Ch. D 170.          [110] (1879) 11 Ch. D 170.

[111] As noted in the first instance judgment of Jessel MR: (1880) 15 Ch. D 247 at 258. Jessel MR also agreed that '[t]here really are no substantial difference between that case and the present'.          [112] *Supra*.

have consolidated itself as an attractive trading vehicle. The conversion of trusts into companies seemed to be a natural outcome when investment trusts could not fulfil their expectation as collective investment vehicles. After 1880, the Submarine Cables' Trust was the only trust in existence. It came to its natural end in November 1926 when the last 333 certificates were redeemed. As noted by Walker,[113] the Submarine Cables' Trust had 'a very fine record':

An investment of £90 in 1871 brought to the purchaser of a certificate an almost unbroken income at the rate of 6 2/3 per cent. for a period of from one to fifty-five years, plus repayment at a premium of 33 1/3 per cent., plus a cash payment at the end of 55 years of more than one and two-thirds times the original investment.

### 4. THE REBIRTH OF THE UNIT TRUST IN THE 1930S

#### A. American Origins

The company had triumphed over the trust as a collective investment vehicle—though it was under the misnomer of the 'investment trust', a term which is probably to be attributed to the fact that the majority of the investment companies in this period were converted from trusts. Investment companies grew in number and, with the exception of the Baring crisis of 1890, there was relative stability until the end of the First World War. The years after the war were difficult and investment companies had to shift their investments from fixed-interest debentures or preference shares to shares in American companies. With increasing financing and business activities in America, American influence became important. Interestingly, the modern form of unit trusts in Britain has its origin in the United States.[114]

The trust and the company in America interacted in a similar fashion to their English counterparts. The first notable use of the trust was its use as an alternative to incorporation. It was called the 'business trust', 'Massachusetts trust', or 'common law trust'.[115] It took the form of a

---

[113] Walker's unpublished thesis 'Unit Trust' *supra*, p. 60; Walker, 'Unincorporated Investment Trusts in the Nineteenth Century' [1940] *Economic History* 341 at 354.

[114] *Fixed Trusts: Report of the Departmental Committee Appointed by the Board of Trade*, 1936 (Cmd. 5259), para. 7.

[115] American literature on business trusts is voluminous; for recent accounts, see Jones, 'The Massachusetts Business Trust and Registered Investment Companies' in Youdan (ed.), *Equity, Fiduciaries and Trusts*, Carswell, 1989, pp. 161–79, which is a similar account of Jones, Moret and Storey, 'The Massachusetts Business Trust and Registered Investment Companies' (1988) 13 *Delaware Journal of Corporate Law* 421; Rosenbalm, 'The Massachusetts Trust' (1964) 31 *Tennessee LR* 471. For historical interest and a brief comparison with the English development see Cook, 'The Mysterious Massachusetts Trusts' (1923) 9 *American Bar Association Journal* 763.

declaration of trust by the trustee, who would carry on business. The beneficial interest under the trust was divided into transferable shares. The business trust was used in the majority of states where state corporation statutes were unduly burdensome and restrictive. It flourished in the state of Massachusetts to circumvent the statutory prohibition against a corporation dealing in real estate—a prohibition which had its roots in the Mortmain Statutes.[116] As a logical extension, the Massachusetts trust was and still is used as a vehicle for collective investment in real estate in many states under the name of 'real estate investment trust'. This use of the trust for collective investment has not taken root in England or in any other common law countries that modelled on the English statutory regulation of unit trusts.

The form of the trust that influenced subsequent developments in England was the unit investment trust that emerged in 1924 as a result of an American businessman's desire to increase the public ownership in his company. His company's share was selling at $400 a share, which presumably was then a very high price. He 'deposited' a share to his bank in exchange for ten bankers' receipts which represented pro rata interests.[117]

This form did not, however, gain immediate popularity. In fact, between 1925 and 1929, the company, under the name 'investment company', was the predominant form of collective investment in America. These investment companies were highly geared and speculative. In many instances, they were created by promoters as a means to dispose of their unwanted stocks. When the fateful crash of October 1929 and the Great Depression came, the value of shares in such investment companies was shattered.[118]

It was not long before the investing public linked the proportion of their losses to abuses and malpractices in the management of such companies. The investors turned to the unit investment trust because it eliminated the management. The unit investment trust was then commonly referred to as the contractual trust because it was governed by an agreement between a management company, called the 'depositor', and a trustee, under which certificates were issued against the deposit of specified securities in fixed proportion. The idea, and hence the attraction after the Crash of 1929, was

[116] Jones, ibid., at 163.

[117] Harman, 'Emerging Alternatives to Mutual Funds: Unit Investment Trusts and Other Fixed Portfolio Investment Vehicles' [1987] *Duke Law Journal* 1045 at 1050–1. Harman also gives an account of unit investment trusts' history and its recent resurgence as a collective investment scheme in the US.

[118] On average, $1 invested in 1929 in such shares was worth 5 cents by the end of 1937: Arnaud, *Investment Trusts Explained*, Woodhead Faulkner Ltd., 1977, p. 6.

that the underlying investments were more or less fixed with very little discretion to the depositor to change them.[119]

The peak of these unit trusts was reached in the summer of 1931 when it was realized that the United States was in more than a minor recession. The fall in the value of underlying securities was reflected in the prices of these fixed trusts. The pendulum had therefore to swing back to investment vehicles which would give professional management. The 'flexible' unit trust, with power given to the management company to change the underlying portfolio, emerged in America.

## B. Importing the Unit Trust from America

In the meantime, the Wall Street Crash of 1929 did not have such a severe effect on British investment companies as on their American counterparts. This was mainly due to their longer experience in investment and the fact that the majority had made timely sales of their American investments. The slow recovery and the unexpected length of the bear market caught many investment companies which returned to the American market too soon. Nevertheless, investment companies were generally in a healthy state, with not a single company being liquidated.[120] Naturally, therefore, when the American fixed unit trust was first marketed in Britain in 1930, comments from the *Financial News* and *The Economist* were negative.[121]

In August 1930, International Investment Deposit Certificates were marketed in Britain. The certificates were units from a Switzerland fixed unit trust which had Société Internationale de Placements as its manager and the Union Bank of Switzerland as its trustee. At the same time, discussion also took place between a London broker and the manager of a company, Municipal and General Securities Company Limited. Municipal and General Securities Company Limited was controlled by an American company JG White & Co. Inc.,[122] which was the marketing agent of the American fixed trust, All-America Investors Corporation Trust. After negotiation and discussion, the First British Fixed Trust was formed under a trust deed dated 22 April 1931 with Municipal and General Securities Company Limited as the manager and the Lloyds Bank as the trustee. The trust deed was based on 'the All-America Investors' with some modifications,[123] notably the provision that the manager undertook to reacquire

---

[119] Harman, ibid., at 1050–1.  [120] Arnaud, ibid.

[121] Walker's unpublished thesis 'Unit Trust' *supra*, p. 95.˙

[122] Through its British subsidiary J. G. White & Co. Ltd.

[123] The differences in the provisions of the two are discussed in Walker's unpublished thesis 'Unit Trust' *supra*, pp. 99–102. According to Walker, despite the variations, the counsel who settled the trust deed was of the opinion that the trust had 'obvious signs of its American origin'.

units issued at a price based on the value of the underlying investments. As in the American counterpart, a holder could surrender a whole unit in exchange for the underlying securities.

In terms of legal analysis, this was a departure from the investment trusts of the last century. It was the first time that the trust was established through a contract between a professional manager and a trustee. This differed in form from the deed of settlement, which was a deed of mutual covenant between the trustee and a certificate holder on behalf of all certificate holders. Further, this new form of unit trust contemplated the possibility that the holder of one unit could exchange it for its underlying assets. By contrast, the cases on deed of settlement companies had by this time moved towards holding that (as a matter of construction) a member did not have any interest in underlying assets and that the shares in such companies were personalty.[124]

This 'American import' was received by the financial press with scepticism, if not hostility.[125] Economic conditions were not very encouraging. No other unit trust was formed until June 1932, when the National Fixed Trust was formed. The growth of fixed trusts was slow. Soon it came to be realized that such trusts prevented the manager from responding to market conditions by changing the composition of the portfolio. On the other hand, managers had built up the goodwill of unit trusts and the investing public became accustomed to the principles of the unit trust.

In April 1934, flexibility was introduced into the Foreign Government Bond Trust managed by Municipal and General Securities Co. Ltd.[126] The principle of depositing securities with the trustee was retained, but instead of there being a number of identical units, each divided into a specified number of sub-units, there was simply one pool of securities divided into a number of 'bond-units', with each unit representing a proportion of a changeable collection of securities. This is the flexible trust. As a legal form, this was a major step forward towards the modern form of the unit trust.

Broadly speaking, since the Foreign Government Bond Trust, there emerged two types of flexible trusts, the cash fund type and the appropriation type.[127] In a cash fund trust, the issue price of further units was calculated by dividing the value of assets (plus all charges and

---

[124] See s. 2 of this ch., *ante.*

[125] All major financial newspapers, including *The Economist*, were critical of the scheme: Walker's unpublished thesis 'Unit Trust' *supra*, pp. 105–8.

[126] Walker's unpublished thesis 'Unit Trust' *supra*, p. 149.

[127] According to Walker's unpublished thesis 'Unit Trust' *supra*, p. 137, the two terms were given by a Mr Piercy. For mechanics of these two and arithmetical examples, see Merriman, *Unit Trusts and How They Work*, 2nd edn., Pitman, 1959, pp. 18–29; Pennington, *Company Law*, 2nd edn., Butterworths, 1967, pp. 760–2.

expenses) by the number of issued units. In an appropriation trust, the basic principle was that the assets (or cash) must be appropriated by the manager before new units were issued. The manager had first to decide the number of new units to be issued. It then purchased permitted assets whose prices bore the same proportion to the total value of the trust fund as the number of new units bore to the number of existing units. New units were then issued to the manager who might then sell to new investors. The resale price might however vary from day to day as those of existing units and this created a risk to the manager. For this reason, the appropriation type no longer exists today.

In December 1935, the Municipal and General Securities Co. Ltd. invited subscriptions to the Limited Investment Fund without the initial step of making a cash deposit with the trustee. This method was followed by two of its funds issued in early 1936.[128] This became the standard method of operation used by all modern unit trusts. With the emergence of the flexible trust, the fixed trust gradually fell into disuse.[129]

Accordingly, within just a short span of five years, the unit trust matured into its modern form. This rapid development could, to some extent, be attributed to extensive advertising[130] but there were structural features that contributed to its success.

First of all, the unit trust did not emerge as an alternative to the company. In fact, when the unit trust was first introduced in 1931, the company was a well-understood concept and the investment company had weathered the storm of the Depression. As the Anderson Committee has observed in 1936 in its report on unit trusts,[131] '[m]ost investment trust companies have the advantage of managements who combine long experience with expert knowledge of securities; and on a long view, British investment trust companies as a whole can claim to have served well the interests of those who have entrusted their savings to them'.

The success of the unit trust owed much to the fact that it had fulfilled a gap that the company did not provide adequately—liquidity. It is true that, by this time, shares had achieved the status as choses in action readily transferable in the share market. Investors could liquidate their investment easily. However, this could only be done at a price that reflected the forces

---

[128] Midland and Southern Investment Fund and Scottish & North Country Investment Fund, Mar. 1936: Walker's unpublished thesis 'Unit Trust' *supra*, p. 150.
[129] Interestingly, in the 1980s the fixed trust re-emerged in the United Kingdom in the form of the single property ownership trust, a vehicle that achieved subdivision of a property ownership in a readily transferable form: see s. 5D, *post*; Sinclair, 'Property Income Certificates (PINCs) Explained' (1987) 6 (Issue 4) *IFLR* 6 at 7; Macfarlanes, paras. A3.0740–0870.
[130] This was recognized as one of the factors: *Fixed Trusts: Report of the Departmental Committee Appointed by the Board of Trade*, 1936 (Cmd. 5259) (hereinafter cited as *Fixed Trusts Report*), para. 31.  [131] *Fixed Trusts Report, supra.*

of demand and supply rather than the value of underlying assets. For small investors, the determination of prices of shares in investment trust companies was no easy thing. This was summed up by the Anderson committee:

> The capital of an investment trust company . . . is subscribed once and for all at the time of issue; an investor who subsequently wishes to buy its shares can only do so through the Stock Exchange; and there may be no stock or shares available when he wishes to buy. Moreover, expert knowledge is required to form even an approximate idea of the relation between the price that must be paid for the shares and the value of the securities in which an interest is thereby acquired.[132]

At this time, investment had become more proximate to savings as more people of comparatively small means looked for alternatives to savings banks.[133] In the first unit trust, the First British Fixed Trust, the manager undertook to reacquire units at a price that reflected the underlying asset value. Thus, '[t]he investor can buy units at any time at a price which he knows will correspond to the prices of the underlying securities, subject only to the charges and profits made by the management company'.[134] The unit trust therefore offered the advantage of redeemability that the company could not offer, since by this time the doctrine of maintenance of capital had fully developed.[135]

To sum up, the unit trust offered both transferability and redeemability, whilst company shares could be transferred but not redeemed.

In view of the speed with which the fixed trust had developed into the flexible trust, it is fair to suggest that the public did not perceive owning the beneficial interest in underlying assets as an advantage over the investment trust company.[136]

### C. The Impact of the Prevention of Fraud (Investments) Acts

In December 1935, the Stock Exchange in London published a Report on

---

[132] *Fixed Trusts Report, supra*, para. 19. Other disadvantages of the investment trust companies outlined in the report: 'The capital of an investment trust company is usually divided between debentures, preference shares and ordinary shares, with the result that a fluctuation in its income means a more than proportionate variation in the earnings available for the ordinary shareholder. Again, the proportion of the earnings of an investment trust company that will be distributed in dividends is determined at the discretion of the directors. The securities held by most investment trust companies include many which are not widely known, the merits of which the average investor is incapable of assessing . . .'

[133] *Fixed Trusts Report, supra*, paras. 17–18.

[134] *Fixed Trusts Report, supra*, para. 19.

[135] *Trevor* v. *Whitworth* (1887) 12 App. Cas. 409.

[136] This point was conceded by the Anderson committee in its *Fixed Trusts Report, supra*, para. 20.

Fixed Trusts recommending legislation to protect the investing public.[137] This was followed by the appointment in March 1936 of a Departmental Committee of the Board of Trade 'to enquire into Fixed Trusts in all their aspects and to report what action, if any, is desirable in the public interest'.[138] The committee considered it necessary to enquire into flexible trusts as well and accordingly adopted the term 'unit trust' as comprehending both types of trusts.[139] It reported in July 1936. This report was most important as its recommendations became the cornerstone of subsequent legislation in the United Kingdom and in jurisdictions that adopted the English legislative model.

Three years later, the Prevention of Fraud (Investments) Act was passed. This Act was the outcome of both the Fixed Trust report and the report on 'operations known as share pushing and share hawking'.[140] This 1939 Act was replaced by the Prevention of Fraud (Investments) Act 1958.[141] The 1958 Act was important because under section 17 the Board of Trade 'may'[142] authorize unit trust schemes which complied with certain criteria. Authorization was necessary if the units were to be sold to the public as the general prohibition on the possession or distribution of circulars did not apply to those containing an invitation or information 'made or given by or on behalf of the manager under an authorised unit trust scheme with respect to any securities created in pursuance of that scheme'.[143] As a condition of authorization, the Department was to be satisfied as to certain matters with regard to the manager and the trustee of the unit trust.[144] In addition, the trust deed was required to provide for certain matters specified in the Schedule of the Prevention of Fraud (Investments) Act 1958.

From a doctrinal viewpoint, the Act was important in two respects. In

---

[137] The subcommittee of the Stock Exchange had drawn up draft regulations, but, as it recognized, such regulations could only give protection to investors of fixed trusts that sought listing on the Stock Exchange. The subcommittee concluded that it was inadvisable to put the regulations into force as the full measure of protection could only be achieved by legislation: *Fixed Trusts Report, supra*, para. 4. A summary of the Stock Exchange subcommittee's report appears in App. of Merriman, *Unit Trusts and How They Work*, 2nd edn., Pitman & Sons, 1959. [138] *Fixed Trusts Report, supra*, p. 5.
[139] Ibid., para. 6.
[140] The 1939 Act was enacted also to deal with fraudulent share pushing raised in the Bodkin Committee's report (Cmd. 5539 of 1837): Gower, *Review of Investor Protection: a Discussion Document*, HMSO, 1982, para. 3.01.
[141] This was an Act consolidating the 1939 Act with the amendments made by the Companies Act 1947: Gower, ibid.
[142] This word gives the Department uncontrolled discretion in authorizing unit trust schemes: *Allied Investors' Trust Ltd* v. *Board of Trade* [1956] Ch. 232.
[143] S. 14(3)(a)(iv). For other effects of authorization, see Gower, *Review of Investor Protection* (Cmnd. 9125), HMSO, 1984, para. 8.04.
[144] Ibid., s. 17(1).

the first place, it stipulated as a condition of authorization by the Department of Trade that there must be a dual management structure of the manager and the trustee. As the Department's authorization was necessary for the trust to be marketed to the public, in practical terms, the Act has 'concretized' the unit trust structure imported by Municipal and General in the early 1930s. Other forms of collective investment, such as the Massachusetts trust, or other contractual schemes, such as limited partnerships, were not known to have been marketed to the public. This is attributed to the conditions under which authorization was given.

The second aspect is important in terms of the liquidity of the unit trust. This arose from the Department of Trade's interpretation of its power of authorization. The Department took the view that the First Schedule prohibited it from authorizing a unit trust scheme that invested in property other than 'securities' as defined by the Act. The term 'securities' did not cover cash, money market instruments, and freehold or leasehold property. As a result, property trusts could not be authorized. An authorized unit trust would invariably invest in securities which could be liquidated easily in secondary markets. Thus, if a manager faced a large number of redemption requests, it could easily fulfil its obligation to buy back units by selling the requisite quantity of portfolio assets.

In summary, the modern form of the unit trust emerged in England in the 1930s. It flourished by filling in a gap left by the company as a vehicle of collective investment. It enabled investors not only to buy units from the manager at a price that reflected the value of underlying assets but also to redeem them in a similar manner. Thus, the concept of redemption added another feature of liquidity to the unit trust. This flexibility was enhanced under regulating statutes which, in effect, confined investments of such unit trusts to securities that were readily marketable.

### 5. THE UNIT TRUST AND THE FINANCIAL SERVICES REVOLUTION

Proposals for more sophisticated regulation of the management of unit trusts had been made in the context of company law reform in the United Kingdom[145] but were never implemented. After the collapse of some investment firms in the late 1970s and of Norton Warburg in 1981, Professor L. C. B. Gower was invited to make a study on investor protection in the United Kingdom. He reported in 1984, recommending a new regulatory system for investment business, including unit trusts and other collective investment schemes. The Government followed this up

---

[145] *The Report of the Company Law Committee* (the Jenkin's Committee) (Cmnd. 1749), HMSO, 1962.

with the publication of a white paper 'Financial Services in the United Kingdom: A New Framework for Investor Protection'.[146] In 1986, the Financial Services Act was enacted.

The Act was enacted against a background of competition, deregulation, technological advancement, and globalization of financial markets. There were an increasing number of overseas collective investment schemes operating in the United Kingdom. The adoption by the Council of the European Community of a Directive on the coordination of laws, regulations, and administrative provisions relating to undertakings for collective investment in transferable securities (the UCITS)[147] also signified opportunities for expanding into the European markets by British fund management firms.

## A. Authorized Unit Trusts

Section 76(1) provides:

. . . [A]n authorised person shall not—
(a) issue or cause to be issued in the United Kingdom any advertisement inviting persons to become or offer to become participants in a collective investment scheme or containing information calculated to lead directly or indirectly to persons becoming or offering to become participants in such a scheme; or
(b) advise or procure any person in the United Kingdom to become or offer to become a participant in such a scheme,
unless the scheme is an authorised unit trust scheme or a recognised scheme under the . . . provisions of this Chapter.

Under this section, advertisement[148] inviting persons to become participants of a collective investment scheme can only be issued by an authorized person[149] if the scheme is either an authorized unit trust scheme or a

---

[146] Cmnd. 9432, HMSO, 1985.
[147] Dir. 85/611/EEC as amended by Dir. 88/220/EEC. This Directive is given effect to by ss. 75–95 of the Financial Services Act 1986.
[148] The term 'advertisement' is defined in s. 207(2) to include 'every form of advertising, whether in a publication, by display of notices, signs, labels or showcards, by means of circulars, catalogues, price lists or other documents, by an exhibition of pictures or photographic or cinematographic films, by way of sound broadcasting or television or by inclusion in any programme service (within the meaning of the Broadcasting Act 1990) other than a sound or television broadcasting service, by the distribution of recordings, or in any other manner'. Further, 'an advertisement or other information issued outside the United Kingdom shall be treated as issued in the United Kingdom if it is directed to persons in the United Kingdom or is made available to them otherwise than in a newspaper, journal, magazine or other periodical publication published and circulating principally outside the United Kingdom or in a sound or television broadcast transmitted principally for reception outside the United Kingdom' (s. 207(3) ).
[149] An authorized person is a person authorized under Ch. III of the Financial Services Act 1986 (s. 207(1) ). In general, a manager or a trustee is an authorized person by virtue of its

recognized scheme under the Act. If a collective investment scheme is established in the United Kingdom, it can only be authorized under the Act if it is a unit trust scheme.[150] Unit trusts, open-ended investment companies, and other forms of schemes established outside the United Kingdom need only be recognized by the Securities and Investments Board under the Act.[151] From 6 January 1997, open-ended investment companies that fall within the UCITS Directive may also be formed in the United Kingdom.[152]

A unit trust may be authorized under the Act if the scheme complies with the regulations made under section 81.[153] In addition, the manager and the trustee must be independent of each other, must be corporate bodies incorporated in the United Kingdom or a member state of the European Community, having a place of business in the United Kingdom, and must be 'authorized persons' authorized to carry on investment business and neither must be prohibited from acting as a manager or a trustee. The name of the scheme must not be undesirable or misleading; and the purpose of the scheme must be reasonably capable of being successfully carried into effect. The participants must be entitled to have their units redeemed at a price related to the net value of the property to which the units relate and determined in accordance with the scheme, or alternatively, the scheme must require the manager to ensure that participants are able to sell their units on an investment exchange at a price not significantly different from the price at which the manager would otherwise be obliged to redeem.[154]

The system of authorization of unit trusts, in broad terms, can be regarded as inherited from the repealed Prevention of Fraud (Investments)

---

membership of a recognized self-regulating organization (s. 7), although it is possible to obtain direct authorization by the Securities and Investments Board (s. 25). In respect of the operation of an authorized unit trust scheme, a manager and a trustee has to be a member of the Investment Management Regulatory Organisation Limited (IMRO). The Securities and Futures Authority Limited (SFA) regulates the management activities of a non-authorized unit trust, a single property scheme, and authorized unit trusts dedicated to options, futures or contracts for differences, land or other property-related assets, and warrants to subscribe or purchase securities and membership of SFA will also confer the authorized person status. In respect of the marketing activities of a unit trust scheme, a manager has to be a member of the Personal Investment Authority Limited (PIA) unless the marketing activities are not carried out on a substantial scale, in which case IMRO will regulate the marketing activities of the manager concerned. For further details, see Macfarlanes, para. A3.0060 *et seq.*

[150] Ss. 76(1), 77, and 78.

[151] Ss. 76(1), 86(1), 87(1), and 88(1).

[152] The Open-Ended Investment Companies (Investment Companies with Variable Capital) Regulations 1996, made under s. 2(2) of the European Communities Act 1972.

[153] S. 78(1): the Secretary of State (now the Treasury: the Transfer of Functions (Financial Services) Order 1992) must be furnished with a copy of the trust deed and a certificate by a solicitor that all statutory requirements have been complied with.

[154] S. 78 (2)–(6).

Act 1958. However, there is one significant difference. Under the Prevention of Fraud (Investments) Act 1958, the regulatory requirements as to the terms of the unit trust deeds by the Department of Trade and Industry are imposed as matters of its discretion. All terms are by nature the terms of the trust deeds. Now, under the Financial Services Act 1986, if a unit trust is to be authorized, it must comply with the regulations made under section 81. These regulations may cover

the constitution and management of authorised unit trust schemes, the powers and duties of the manager and trustee of any such scheme and the rights and obligations of the participants in any such scheme[155]

and

may make provision as to the contents of the trust deed[156]

Section 81(3) provides that

regulations under this section [81] shall be binding on the manager, trustee and participants independently of the contents of the deed and, in the case of the participants, shall have effect as if contained in it.

Thus, the terms of the regulations, despite the fact that they are requirements similar to those imposed by the Department of Trade and Industry, are different in legal character. They operate both as a matter of law and as implied terms. If there is a breach by the manager or the trustee, it may be liable to unitholders for breach of statutory duty and may be subject to disciplinary actions of the relevant self-regulating organization to which it belongs.[157]

A second important feature of the new regime is the hybrid nature of the scheme particulars. Scheme particulars are required by regulation 3 of the Financial Services (Regulated Schemes) Regulation 1991. Scheme particulars function very similarly to a prospectus as a disclosure document, containing 'the information necessary for investors to be able to make an informed judgment of the investment proposed in them'.[158] In the case of UCITS schemes, they are necessary to fulfil the prospectus obligation under the UCITS Directives. Under the regulations, they differ from prospectuses in three aspects. First, scheme particulars have a continuing function after units have been subscribed. There is an obligation on the part of the manager to keep the scheme particulars up to date from time to time.[159] Secondly, the manager is under an obligation to ensure the correctness of the whole document.[160] This may be contrasted with the

---

[155] S. 81(1); s. 81(2) provides for specific matters that may be covered by the regulations.
[156] S. 81(3).  [157] See ch. 2, s. 2A(2) and ch. 5, s. 3C, *post*.
[158] UCITS Dir., Art. 28 para. 1.
[159] The Financial Services (Regulated Schemes) Regulations 1991, reg. 3.07.
[160] The Financial Services (Regulated Schemes) Regulations 1991, reg. 3.06.

position of a director of a company which issues new shares: the director may not be responsible for the whole of the listing particulars.[161] Thirdly, the scheme particulars may contain some of the terms of the unit trust. This position may not be expected by investors but is the result of the operation of some of the provisions of the regulations and section 81(3).[162]

There is no question that the very elaborate provisions of the Financial Services (Regulated Schemes) Regulations 1991 play an important role in the shaping and evolution of the unit trust. However, it must be stressed that authorization under the Financial Services Act 1986 serves only to legitimize the issue of advertisements by managers inviting subscription for units. Authorization under the Act has no effect whatsoever on the validity of the constitution of a particular unit trust. Validity is a matter of equitable principles.

## B. Non-Authorized Unit Trusts[163]

The promoter of a unit trust may not necessarily wish to obtain authorization under the Financial Services Act 1986. This may be because it is targeting a specialized group of investors. Under section 76(2), advertisement of a non-authorized unit trust may be issued to an authorized person or a person whose ordinary business involves the acquisition and disposal of property of the same kind as the property, or a substantial part of the property, to which the scheme relates. Section 76(3) also permits regulations to be made exempting schemes from the prohibition against advertisement[164] so long as it does not involve promotion to the general public. The relevant regulations are the Financial Services (Promotion of Unregulated Schemes) Regulations 1991 made by the Securities and Investments Board.

Under regulation 1.04[165] of these Regulations an authorized person may promote an unregulated scheme to a person who is already a participant in an unregulated scheme or who has been, in the last thirty months, a participant in such a scheme. This is permissible so long as the scheme promoted is either the same scheme, or any other scheme whose underlying property and risk profile are both substantially similar, or another scheme which is intended to absorb or take over the assets of that

---

[161] Under s. 152 of the Financial Services Act 1986, a director may accept responsibility for or authorize only part of the contents of any listing particulars.

[162] See the discussion in ch. 2, s. 2A(2), *post*.

[163] The term 'non-authorized unit trust', instead of 'unauthorized unit trust', is used to describe a unit trust that has not been authorized under s. 78 of the Financial Services Act 1986 as the latter has a connotation of illegitimacy. This follows the usage in Pennington, *The Law of the Investment Market*, Blackwell Law, 1990.

[164] S. 76(1) of the Financial Services Act 1986.

[165] This regulation contains a table of promotion which is permitted.

scheme, or a scheme units in which are being offered by its operator as an alternative to cash on the liquidation of that scheme. In addition, an unregulated scheme may also be promoted to an established customer or newly accepted customer of the promoter if reasonable steps have been taken to assess the suitability of the scheme for that customer. It may also be promoted to certain permitted and exempted persons, non-private customers, persons eligible to participate in schemes constituted under the Church Funds Investment Measure 1958, Charities Act 1960 or Charities Act (Northern Ireland) 1964, eligible employees, and persons exempted from capital gains tax or corporate tax on capital gain. Promotion can also be made to a potential investor who requests an unauthorized person to include him on a list of persons willing to receive information on unregulated collective investment schemes investing in a particular type of property.

The terms of a non-authorized unit trust are not subject to the regulations made under section 81 of the Financial Services Act 1986. The provisions of Financial Services (Regulated Schemes) Regulations 1991 relating to scheme particulars also do not apply, though they apply to offshore schemes recognized under section 87 or section 88 of the Act. The constitution of the unit trust will be entirely a matter of those promoting the scheme. Usually, it is constituted by a trust deed made between the manager and the trustee. The terms may also be similar to those contained in the Financial Services (Regulated Schemes) Regulations 1991. It is also possible for such a scheme to be constituted by a deed poll executed by a trustee.

The most common example of a non-authorized unit trust is a property unit trust that invests in real property[166] and not in shares of companies that invest in real property. The reason for this is historical. Under the Prevention of Fraud (Investments) Act 1958, the Department of Trade and Industry took the view that it had no power to authorize unit trusts that did not invest in securities. As a result, property trusts could not be authorized. With the introduction of the property fund as one type of authorized unit trust under the Financial Services (Regulated Schemes) Regulations 1991 and also with the making of the Financial Services Act 1986 (Single Property Schemes) (Exemption) Regulations 1989 by the Secretary of State, it is not certain whether non-authorized property trusts will become less common. A non-authorized unit trust may also be formed as an exempt unit trust which will be invested exclusively by unitholders wholly exempt from capital gains tax or corporation tax on capital gains.[167]

---

[166] The close-ended property trusts in *Galmerrow Securities Ltd.* v. *National Westminster Bank plc*, unreported, Harman J, 20 Dec. 1993 are examples.

[167] Item 9 of the Table in the Financial Services (Promotion of Unregulated Schemes) Regulations 1991.

## C. Offshore Unit Trusts Recognized under the Financial Services Act 1986

The trust has been utilized for collective investment purposes in a number of common law jurisdictions, including the Isle of Man, Jersey, Guernsey, Bermuda, Hong Kong, Australia, and New Zealand. Such unit trusts may be promoted to persons falling within section 76(2) or the Financial Services (Promotion of Unregulated Schemes) Regulations 1991. If a scheme is to be promoted to the public without infringing section 76(1), it has to be recognized under section 86, 87 or 88 of the Financial Services Act 1986. Under these three sections, a scheme may be recognized whether it is a corporate, trust or contractual scheme. Section 86 applies to schemes constituted in member states of the European Community and Gibraltar.[168] As the trust is not a common vehicle in those jurisdictions, it is unlikely for an offshore unit trust to be formed in any state in the Community. An offshore unit trust may be recognized under the Act if it is constituted in a country or territory designated by the Secretary of State for the purpose of section 87. If a particular scheme is not eligible under either of these two sections, it can apply for individual recognition by an order of the Securities and Investments Board under section 88.

Like a non-authorized unit trust, the constitution of an offshore unit trust is not subject to the regulations made under section 81 of the Financial Services Act 1986. Consequently, with the exception of Part 3 and Part 14, which are not made under section 81, the whole of the Financial Services (Regulated Schemes) Regulations 1991 does not apply to recognized schemes. Schemes recognized under section 87 and 88 are subject to the scheme particulars provisions in Part 3[169] and Part 14 contains specific regulations on information and documents to be submitted to the Securities and Investments Board and facilities to be maintained in the United Kingdom. The end result is that the relationships of the manager, the trustee, and unitholders are determined by the terms of the trust deed. In practice, offshore trusts are more flexible and innovative in terms of provisions and features.

## D. Single Property Unit Trusts

Although the Financial Services (Regulated Schemes) Regulations 1991 permit a property fund to be authorized under the Financial Services Act

---

[168] The Financial Services Act 1986 s. 208.
[169] Scheme particulars requirements do not apply to s. 86 schemes because the UCITS Directive requires such schemes to provide prospectuses.

1986, it is not possible for a scheme with a single property to fulfil the requirements laid down by the Regulations.[170] At the same time, with the escalating value of real properties in the commercial sector, the number of investors ready and willing to purchase such properties is limited. This is likely to result in an illiquid property market. Conceptually, a company or a trust that pools investors' money to purchase a single property will provide the solution. Such a vehicle enables those with inadequate means to achieve collective ownership. It is a form of collective investment.

Because such a single property vehicle cannot be an authorized unit trust, it will be subject to section 76(1) of the Financial Services Act 1986 when it is marketed to the public. Consequently, exemption has to be provided if liquidity purpose is to be achieved. This is provided by section 76(4)–(6) and the regulations made thereunder.

The relevant regulations are the Financial Services Act 1986 (Single Property Schemes) (Exemption) Regulations 1989 made by the Secretary of State and the Financial Services (Single Property Schemes) (Supplementary) Regulations 1989 made by the Securities and Investments Board.[171] The former specify the terms of conferring exemption and the latter regulate the marketing and ongoing operation of such schemes.

It is possible for both corporate-based and trust-based schemes to obtain exemption under the Financial Services Act 1986 (Single Property Schemes) (Exemption) Regulations 1989.[172] Under section 76(5) and (6) of the Act, a single property scheme can obtain exemption only if the property of the scheme consists of '(a) a single building (or a single building with ancillary buildings) managed by or on behalf of the operator of the scheme' or '(b) a group of adjacent or contiguous buildings managed by him or on his behalf as a single enterprise'. In both cases it can be 'with or without ancillary land and with or without furniture, fittings or other contents of the building or buildings in question'. A building is a structure of considerable size and intended to be permanent or at least to endure for a considerable time.[173] It seems that it must form part of the land and change the physical character of the land.[174] However, for the building to

---

[170] A property fund can invest up to 80% of the trust money in immovables but only 15% in value of the property may consist of any one immovable, but there is no breach if the property appreciates subsequently unless the value exceeds 25%: the Financial Services (Regulated Schemes) Regulations 1991, reg. 5.32 and 5.38.

[171] The power to make regulations under s. 76(4) has not been delegated to the Securities and Investments Board. Such power is now vested in the Treasury (SI 1992 No. 1315). However, the power to make supplemental regulations for the marketing and operation of single property schemes has been delegated: the Financial Services Act 1986 (Delegation) (No. 2) Order 1988.

[172] Reg. 6(1).

[173] *Stevens* v. *Gourley* (1859) 7 CB NS 99 at 112; *Moir* v. *Williams* [1892] 1 QB 264 at 270.

[174] *Cheshire CC* v. *Woodward* [1962] 2 QB 126.

qualify the scheme as a single property scheme under the Act, it is not necessary that it is one single structure. A single building with ancillary buildings is covered. So are 'contiguous'[175] buildings as well as buildings 'adjacent'[176] to each other—though not physically connected. The extent of proximity is not provided. This seems to be a question of fact but adjacent and contiguous buildings must be managed as one single enterprise.

In regulating single property schemes, the Financial Services Act 1986 (Single Property Schemes) (Exemption) Regulations 1989 take the approach of dictating the terms of the trust deed. If the terms are not complied with, there is no exemption. The rights and obligations of the manager, the trustee, and unitholders are determined by the terms of the trust deed. The parties' relationships are not governed by a hierarchy of regulations, terms of trust deed, and scheme particulars as in the case of an authorized unit trust.

There are two other distinct features. First, units of a single property scheme must be listed in a recognized investment exchange.[177] This provides for the liquidity of investments to investors. In practice, the unit trust will also be subject to the Stock Exchange listing requirements. Secondly, the Regulations require the trust deed to provide 'for the trustee to hold the land and the building or group of adjacent or contiguous buildings forming part of the property subject to the scheme on trust for sale . . . for participants in proportion to their respective entitlements as determined by the number of units in respect of which they are registered'.[178] Thus there is a trust for sale of the real property in favour of unitholders as tenants in common in the proportion as may be determined by the number of units. This creates in favour of each unitholder an interest in the underlying assets. This forms an interesting contrast to the rights of unitholders in an authorized unit trust and indeed the majority of unit trusts.[179]

### E. Open-Ended Investment Companies: The Battle of Form Continues

The trust appears to be the form of collective investment scheme favoured by the Financial Services Act 1986. This is because, as mentioned before, if a

---

[175] In order for buildings to be regarded as contiguous, they must physically touch each other: *Haynes* v. *King* [1893] 3 Ch. 439 at 448; *James A Jobling & Co. Ltd.* v. *Sunderland County Borough Assessment Committee* [1944] 1 All ER 207.

[176] This word means 'near': *Re Ecclesiastical Commissioners for England's Conveyance* [1936] Ch. 430.

[177] The Financial Services Act 1986 s. 76(6)(b).

[178] Reg. 6(b)(vi).

[179] See the discussion of the right of a unitholder in underlying assets in ch. 5, s. 2, *post*.

collective investment scheme is established in the United Kingdom, it can only be authorized under the Act if it is a unit trust scheme.[180] If a scheme operator intends to use the company form as a scheme vehicle, this can be formed under the Companies Act 1985 as any other companies and it will not be regulated under the Financial Services Act 1986 as a collective investment scheme.[181] This means that an investment company—which is often called an investment trust—can only provide liquidity to investors by being listed in the Stock Exchange as it cannot redeem shares on a regular basis under the Companies Act 1985.[182]

By contrast, companies which redeem their capital from investors from time to time have been operating in other countries for many years. Under the Act, they can be promoted in the United Kingdom as recognized schemes.[183] They are specifically mentioned in the Act as 'open-ended investment companies'.

The trust is not a concept well understood in Europe. In commercial terms, unit trusts formed in the United Kingdom have additional obstacles to overcome when they are promoted in Europe. In the Government's white paper 'Financial Services in the United Kingdom: A New Framework for Investor Protection'[184] it was proposed that the law should be amended to allow open-ended investment companies to be formed in the United Kingdom. After over one decade of industry lobbying, the Government has decided to introduce open-ended investment companies as collective investment vehicles into the United Kingdom.[185] In May 1995, the Treasury published for consultation the Open Ended Investment Companies (Investment Companies with Variable Capital) Regulations. It was intended that these regulations would be made under section 2(2) of the European Communities Act 1972. In October of the same year, the Securities and Investments Board also published for consultation the Financial Services (Open Ended Investment Company) Regulations. The Treasury regulations, commonly referred to as the ECA regulations, were enacted in November 1996 and came into force on 6 January 1997. The Securities and Investments Board made its relevant regulations in 1997 and these came into force on 24 January 1997.

---

[180] Ss. 76(1), 77, and 78.

[181] S. 75(7) provides that 'no . . . body corporate other than an open-ended investment company shall be regarded as constituting a collective investment scheme'.

[182] A company may repurchase its own shares in limited circumstances provided by ss. 162–77.                                                                    [183] Ss. 86–8.

[184] Cmnd. 9432, HMSO, 1985, para. 9.8.

[185] Generally, see Securities and Investments Board, *Regulated Collective Investment Schemes: Key Policy Issues* (Discussion Paper) 1993, paras. 1.12, 2.18–2.25; Securities and Investments Board, *Open Ended Investment Companies* (Consultative Paper 93) 1995; Cornick, 'UK Introduces Open-Ended Investment Company' (1997) 16 (Pt. 2) *IFLR* 29.

In a sense, this is a triumph for the company in collective investments. But it is not accomplished without limitation and concession.

The limitation is that the regulations are in the form of regulations made under the European Communities Act rather than a separate piece of legislation. The implication is that the ECA regulations, as a piece of subsidiary legislation, can only provide a legal framework for open-ended investment companies within the UCITS Directive. In practical terms, this means that open-ended investment companies formed under the ECA regulations can only have as their sole object 'collective investment in transferable securities of capital raised from the public'.[186] They cannot invest in futures and options, deposits, money market instruments or real properties.

Secondly, despite the corporate form which an open-ended investment company may take, its constitutional structure will mirror that of a unit trust. Under the ECA regulations, there must be one designated corporate director which will have the same functions as a manager in a unit trust.[187] There must also be a depository to whom all of the scheme property[188] must be entrusted for safe keeping. Apparently, it is contemplated that the depository will hold the scheme assets on trust for the company (not the investors, as in the case of a unit trust). Both the ECA regulations and the SIB regulations provide for active monitoring roles on the part of the depository.[189] This introduction into the corporate governance of the trust concept is a significant conceptual concession. It recognizes trust principles as a body of law that can be readily adopted to aid the development of the company as a collective investment vehicle.

For commercial reason, therefore, the company has been recognized as an important competitor to the trust in collective investments.

## F. Company Principles in Unit Trusts

A study of the evolution of the unit trust in this new age of financial services will not be complete without a survey of case-law development.

The most significant doctrinal development came from several cases in

---

[186] EC Council Dir. 85/611/EEC as amended by 88/220/EEC, Art. 1.

[187] Reg. 10(6) and reg. 28(4).

[188] Other than tangible movable property: reg. 5 and Sch. 3, para. 2(d) of the Open Ended Investment Companies (Investment Companies with Variable Capital) Regulations 1996 and reg. 6.06 of the Financial Services (Open Ended Investment Company) Regulations 1997.

[189] Sch. 2 of the Open Ended Investment Companies (Investment Companies with Variable Capital) Regulations 1996 and reg. 6.05–6.09 of the Financial Services (Open Ended Investment Company) Regulations 1997. Cf. Art. 14 of the UCITS Dir. It is clear that the roles contemplated by the new regime go beyond those provided by this Act.

Australia. In Australia,[190] unit trusts have the same dual manager-trustee structure as their British counterparts. However, there was one significant aspect which made the Australian development different: unit trusts have never been subject to restrictions on underlying investments. Two forms of unit trusts, mortgage trusts and unlisted property trusts, invested heavily in real estates.[191] With the downturn of the commercial property market, many mortgage trusts and property trusts experienced liquidity problems.[192] Eventually, such problems reached crisis level in July 1991[193] and the Australian Federal Government had to impose a freeze on redemption.[194]

One of the results of this crisis was the unprecedented volume of litigation on unit trusts. Courts were faced with issues that had not been met in the context of private trusts used as a means of disposition. There were issues such as the fiduciary obligation of a promoter of a unit trust,[195] majority unitholders' power to bind minority unitholders,[196] and the right of the trustee to disregard a requisition by unitholders for a unitholders' meeting.[197] These issues had been encountered by registered companies. In coming to a resolution of the incidents of the parties, courts utilized principles developed in company cases. Their direct application to the unit trust context was justified on the ground that both the unit trust and the registered company are siblings with a common parent, the deed of settlement company.[198] Thus, instead of trust principles providing solutions

---

[190] For a more detailed account of the development of unit trusts in Australia, see Sin, 'The Legal Nature of the Unit Trust', a Ph.D. thesis submitted to the University of New South Wales in 1995.

[191] Both did not invest in securities which had ready secondary markets. The mortgage trusts invested in mortgages, which in effect meant that they were lenders on security of real properties. The unlisted property trusts invested in real properties which generated rental income. Like other unit trusts in the UK, the purchase and sale of units in these trusts were conducted by the managers. It was the practice that the manager agreed to redeem units within very short periods of notice, ranging from seven days to one month.

[192] There were other problems in these two crises, including fraud, dishonesty, misleading advertisement, inaccuracy, and inept timing of valuation of trust assets, lack of independence of investment advisers, and the mismatch between long-term investments and short-term redemption.

[193] When fund managers associated with leading banks and insurance companies were unable to fulfil their redemption commitments.

[194] This freeze did not stop the collapse of the unlisted property trusts. It merely delayed the realization of the losses by investors. After the first nine months of the freeze, the assets of unlisted property trusts were valued at $4.5 billion, making a total loss of $4.4 billion from the 1990 value of $8.9 billion. (Australian Law Reform Commission and Companies and Securities Advisory Committee, *Collective Investment Schemes* (Discussion Paper 53), 1992, para. 1.3.)

[195] *Elders Trustee and Executor Co. Ltd.* v. *EG Reeves Pty. Ltd.* (1987) 78 ALR 193.

[196] *Gra-ham Australia Pty. Ltd.* v. *Perpetual Trustees WA Ltd.* (1989) 1 WAR 65.

[197] *Smith* v. *Permanent Trustee Australia Ltd.* (1992) 10 ACLC 906.

[198] In *Elders Trustee and Executor Co. Ltd.* v. *EG Reeves Pty. Ltd.*, *supra*, it was held that a promoter of a unit trust owed the same fiduciary duties of a company promoter. Gummow J

to company problems, company law now provides answers to the trust when it is used as means of collective investment. There has been a reverse cultivation of principles.

justified this analogy by reference to the 'extensive role' the trust played 'in the evolution of the limited liability corporation as an instrument of business endeavour' (*supra*, at 229). In *Gra-ham Australia Pty. Ltd.* v. *Perpetual Trustees WA Ltd.*, *supra*, a unitholder requested the manager to redeem his units immediately after the collapse of the stock market in October 1987. Under the then trust deed, the redemption price was based on the value of the assets seven days before the redemption request. The manager made no payment until after a meeting of unitholders which resolved to amend the trust deed provision so that the redemption price would be based on the current value of the asset. It was held that the power of a majority to amend the trust deed was part of the contract between members and between the manager and the unitholders and was wide enough to make amendments that would defeat vested or accrued rights of a unitholder. The principles in company cases of *Allen* v. *Gold Reefs of West Africa Ltd.* [1900] 1 Ch. 656 and *Peters' American Delicacy Co. Ltd.* v. *Heath* (1939) 61 CLR 457 were held to 'apply equally to a trust deed for a unit trust as they did to a deed of settlement of the kind under which limited companies were once established' (*supra*, at 81). In *Smith* v. *Permanent Trustee Australia Ltd.*, *supra*, the unit trust deed provided that the trustee shall on the requisition of a certain number of unitholders convene a meeting of unitholders. A number of unitholders (the exact number being in dispute) requisitioned the trustee to hold a meeting to pass certain resolutions as ordinary resolutions to require the trustee to take steps to seek listing on the Australian Stock Exchange, to request the Manager to retire, and to appoint a new manager. The defendant argued that the requirements of the requisitions were absurd in that the proposed resolutions either could not be passed as ordinary resolutions or would not be effective. On this issue, Young J held that 'if shareholders requisition a meeting . . . the directors may disregard the requisition completely if the whole of the requisition requires them to do something illegal or completely fatuous [citing the company case *NRMA* v. *Parker* (1986) 6 NSWLR 517] and that the same rule must apply to requisitions under the contractual provisions in a trust deed' (*supra*, at 916).

# 2

# *The Trust and the Constitution of a Unit Trust*

The re-emergence of the fixed trust in 1931 in England[1] marked an important, though subtle, development in the unit trust concept. It was the first time that a unit trust was formed at the initiative of an investment management company.

The *Smith* v. *Anderson*[2] type of trust was set up by a trust deed made between trustees and an investor as an agent for all investors, with the latter subsequently forming a committee amongst themselves. This bore resemblance with the deed of settlement company used for trading purposes in the Bubble period. The unit trust that appeared in the 1930s[3] witnessed the emergence of the manager as a party to the trust deed. This form of arrangement has become the basic structure of unit trusts in England as well as a number of common law jurisdictions.

A trust constituted by a deed executed by the manager and the trustee is conceptually phenomenal. An *inter vivos* private trust used for the disposition of family properties is effected through the execution of a trust deed by the settlor and a complete transfer of properties to the trustee.[4] The terms of the trust deed are the mandate from the settlor. A unit trust deed, by contrast, is constituted without the participation of a settlor. It represents the terms that have been agreed by the manager and the trustee for the provision of their respective services to the unitholders and for the issue of units. It is thus not illegitimate to ask whether the unit trust is a trust at all or whether the unit trust is some other kind of relationship that merely bears the logo of the trust.

This chapter examines the process of creation of the unit trust and how the trust concept has been utilized. It will suggest, in the first two sections, two fundamental tenets:

---

[1] The First British Fixed Trust, established in Apr. 1931 by Municipal and General Securities. See ch. 1, s. 4B, *ante*.

[2] (1880) 15 Ch. D 247.

[3] Which was based on the American unit trusts: see ch. 1, s. 4B, *ante*.

[4] Or by the settlor declaring himself or herself a trustee. Historically, it was also common to dispose of family properties by a marriage settlement which by nature was a contract to settle properties in consideration of the marriage. This is a contract to create a trust and to transfer future property to the trust, not a contract incorporating a trust: see s. 1A(3)(b), *post*.

(1) that the trust in the unit trust is a creation of the contract between the parties; and

(2) that the trust is a device forming part of the contractual terms agreed for investment purposes.

The final section will examine the implications that will follow from these two propositions.

1. THE THREE CERTAINTIES AND CONTRACTUAL CREATION

In order for an express trust to be valid, it has been said that three certainties[5] are essential to a valid trust: certainty of the settlor's intention, certainty of subject, and certainty of object. These three aspects provide a convenient anchor for examining the creation of the unit trust and the contractual ingredients involved.

## A. Intentions

### (1) The Trust as a Gift-Making Device—Intention of the Settlor

Although the trust has a long history of being used for a variety of purposes, the vast body of principles is developed from the trust being used as a means of disposition of property. A person intending to make a gift of property *inter vivos* by means of a trust may do so by declaring himself a trustee of that property which he intends to dispose of or by his transfer of the property to a trustee. In all instances, it is said that there must be an intention to create a trust on the part of the settlor.[6] The intention in this context is far more complicated than is first visualized. It is a unity of two intentions, the intention to make a gift and the intention to make that gift by way of trust. These two intentions need not always overlap, but in this situation, they do.

### (a) The Donative Intent

Conceptually, the intention to make a gift must be distinct from the intention to create a trust. A person may make a gift by simply transferring

---

[5] *Wright* v. *Atkyns* (1823) Turn. & R 143 at 157 per Lord Eldon; *Knight* v. *Knight* (1840) 3 Beav. 148 at 173, per Lord Langdale. See generally, Williams, 'The Three Certainties' (1940) 4 *MLR* 20; Davies, 'The Variety of Express Trusts' (1986) 8 *U Tas. LR* 209.

[6] A testator can likewise establish a trust by appointing a trustee in a will. Since *inter vivos* trusts are the natural comparisons of unit trusts, reference will be made to settlors rather than to settlors and testators.

the assets to the donee without any trust intention whatsoever. He may make a gift to a trust without creating the trust.[7] In these two types of cases, there is no intention to create a trust.

It is well established that the mere existence of a donative wish, without more, will have no legal consequence, for equity will not perfect an imperfect gift. The donor must have done everything which, according to the nature of the property, is necessary to be done in order to dispose of the property in favour of the donee. The court will not, in the absence of any manifestation of an intention to create a trust, find a trust in order to make good the gift despite the disponer's donative intent.[8]

### (b) The Trust Intention

If the distinction between a donative intent and a trust intent is drawn, the majority of cases on certainty of intention, or, to be precise, cases where the donor gives property with precatory words of wish, hope, desire or confidence that the donee will dispose of the property in a particular way,[9] should be understood as cases on the first question of the existence of a donative intent. The court is ascertaining whether there is an intention to make a gift to the person who is the object of the precatory words.

In cases where a private trust is established, the court has satisfied itself that the donor wants to effectuate his donative wish through the method of a trust. In more concrete terms, if the settlor chooses to transfer the property to a transferee to be held on trust, the intention is that the transferee shall acquire the rights of ownership subject to the duties to hold or to manage the property for the enjoyment of the beneficiaries. It is intended that he shall have the status of a trustee, not an absolute owner. If a declaration of trust is the mode intended, there must be an intention on the part of the donor to become a trustee—an intention not only to make a gift but to assume the onerous duties of a trustee. The cases clearly go as

---

[7] For instance, he may make donations to charities, which are trusts set up by others. See also the discussion in s. 1A(2), *post*.

[8] *Milroy* v. *Lord* (1862) 4 DF & J 264; *Richards* v. *Delbridge* (1874) LR 18 Eq. 11 at 15, per Jessel MR; *Jones* v. *Lock* (1865) 1 Ch. App. 25; *Paul* v. *Constance* [1977] 1 All ER 195; *Re Armstrong* [1960] VR 202. Similarly, a contract that benefits a third party does not automatically make the promisee a trustee: *Re Schebsman* [1944] 1 Ch. 83; *West* v. *Houghton* (1879) LR 4 CPD 197; see also ch. 5, s. 3B, *post*.

[9] *Lambe* v. *Eames* (1871) LR 6 Ch. 597; *Re Hutchinson and Tenant* (1878) 8 Ch. D 540; *Re Williams* [1897] 2 Ch. 12; *Re Adams and Kensington Vestry* (1884) 27 Ch. D 394; *Mussoorie Bank Ltd.* v. *Raynor* (1882) 7 App. Cas. 327; *Re Hamilton* [1895] 2 Ch. 370; *Comiskey* v. *Bowring-Hanbury* [1905] AC 84; *Re Steele's Will Trusts* [1948] Ch. 603; *Re Diggles* (1888) 39 Ch. D 253; *Re Altson* [1955] VLR 281; *Re Schar* [1951] Ch. 280; *Re Stirling* [1954] 2 All ER 113; *Re Pugh's Will Trusts* [1967] 3 All ER 337. See *Underhill and Hayton*, pp. 111–16; Ford and Lee, para. 2190–200.

far as saying that if the settlement is intended to be effectuated by one of the above two modes, the court will not give effect to it by applying the other of these modes.[10]

The donative character of private trusts inevitably means that the court's preoccupation is the ascertainment of the subjective intention of the settlor. In this sense, the trust's existence depends on the unilateral intention of the settlor. The trustee's intention is not relevant to trust creation, for the court of equity will execute the trust even if the trustee does not wish to act.[11] This unilateral nature also implies that the court has to adopt a subjective interpretation in construing an instrument purportedly creating the trust, be it a trust deed *inter vivos* or a will, when determining whether a genuine intention to create a trust is present.

### (2)  Unit Trust—Trust Intention without a Settlor

In a private trust *inter vivos*, the settlor is the creator of the trust[12] and it is his unilateral intention that determines the existence of the trust. But in a unit trust, there is no settlor. It is a creation of the trustee and the manager, a transferee of properties and a delegate to whom certain powers have been vested. There are two stages which require consideration. The first is the execution of the unit trust deed by the trustee and the manager. The second is when an investor subscribes units of the unit trust.

The parties to a unit trust deed are the manager and the trustee. In an authorized unit trust, this deed is subject to the Financial Services (Regulated Schemes) Regulations 1991, which in its Part 7 provides for the different roles of the manager and the trustee. In a non-authorized unit trust, matters covered by Part 7 will be catered for by the express provisions of the trust deed. The very fact that the parties are named 'the manager' and 'the trustee' respectively gives rise to the inference that the intentions of the parties to the deed are that the manager is to act as the manager of the unit trust and the trustee the trustee in accordance with the roles contemplated by Part 7 of the Regulations or the trust deed. None of them intends to act as a settlor. This appears to be plainly obvious.

---

[10] *Milroy* v. *Lord*, ibid., at 274, per Turner LJ. Maitland also made a distinction between the intention of a donor making an absolute gift and that of a donor declaring himself a trustee: 'The two intentions are very different—the giver means to get rid of his rights, the man who is intending to make himself a trustee intends to retain his rights but to come under an onerous obligation.' (*Equity: a Course of Lectures* (2nd edn. by Brunyate), 1936, p. 21.)

[11] Trusts do not fail for want of a trustee. The courts of equity have inherent jurisdiction to appoint trustees: see *Underhill and Hayton*, p. 60; Ford and Lee, paras. 8280 *et seq*.

[12] In a testamentary trust, the testator is the creator of the trust. It appears that the draftsman of the Hague Convention on the Law Applicable to Trusts and on Their Recognition uses the term 'settlor' to cover both the creator of an *inter vivos* trust and a testator.

A little more ought to be said about the manager. In *Famel Pty. Ltd.* v. *Burswood Management Ltd.*,[13] French J, in describing the trust deed before him, labelled a manager as the settlor without giving any explanation.[14] The meaning of the word 'settlor' does not appear to have received any judicial consideration. If his Honour used the word 'settlor' to mean a creator, it is a correct description. If the word was used to mean a person settling property by way of gift, it can hardly be a correct description of the manager. Under a unit trust deed, the manager takes active control of investment of money or properties of others. Like a trustee, it has a fiduciary role to play. It is in marked contrast to a settlor of an ordinary trust who divests himself of all beneficial interests. The donative intention is not present. In simpler terms, a manager, *qua* manager in the trust deed, does not have any property to settle.

In most cases[15] the trust deed has a clause whereby the trustee declares itself a trustee of all trust funds paid by unitholders upon trust for the benefit of all unitholders subject to the terms and conditions of the deed and, in the case of an authorized unit trust, the regulations made under section 81 of the Financial Services Act 1986. But there is no trust without property. A trust does not exist at the time of the execution of the trust deed. It only comes into existence at the moment when the first unitholder subscribes his units and pays his subscription money. In some non-authorized unit trusts or offshore unit trusts, the manager agrees in the trust deed to lodge with the trustee, upon demand being made by the trustee, a specified sum of money to constitute the initial trust fund.[16] If any demand is actually made, the manager is made the first unitholder like any investor subscribing units. Indeed, most trust deeds contemplate the holding of units by a manager and provide expressly that in respect of its units the manager can exercise all rights as a unitholder. This provision enables the manager to wear two hats without any problem of conflict of interests. Whilst holding units, it is holding them *qua* unitholder. The provision cannot affect the argument that when it executes the unit trust deed *qua* manager it does not have the intention to become a settlor but only the intention to act as a manager.

The next point of consideration is the time when an investor becomes a

---

[13] (1989) 15 ACLR 572.
[14] Ibid. at 574 where the learned judge said: 'On the same day as the agreement was made, a trust known as the Burswood Property Trust was constituted by a deed between BML as settlor (designated as manager under the deed) and WATL as trustee.'
[15] For an authorized unit trust, this is mandatory: the Financial Services (Regulated Schemes) Regulations 1991, Sch. 1.
[16] Some deeds may provide for an actual amount to be paid by the manager either before or simultaneously with the execution of the deeds.

unitholder. This happens when an investor acquires the units from an existing unitholder or when he subscribes from the manager.

In a transfer situation, the intentions of the transferor and the transferee respectively are to dispose of and to acquire existing interests of a trust. There is no intention to create any trust.

When an investor subscribes for units, can he be regarded as a settlor creating a trust? In *Baldwin* v. *CIR*,[17] the New Zealand Land and Income Tax Act provided that a certain exemption would not be allowed if 'a trust . . . has been created by the taxpayer or by a person who is or has been the wife or husband of the taxpayer or by both the taxpayer and that person'. A taxpayer's father-in-law settled a sum of money in favour of the taxpayer's children with the taxpayer and his wife as the trustees. Subsequently, the taxpayer and his wife transferred properties from another trust into the trust. Macarthur J held that a trust was created by the assignment of properties to the trust settled by the father-in-law. His reason was that '. . . the phrase "a trust has been created" simply means "a trust has been brought into legal existence." No particular method of creation of a trust is indicated by the section . . . [I]f it is shown that trust obligations have been imposed or constituted in respect of certain property by one or more of the specified persons then a trust has been created by that person or those persons within the meaning of the section.'[18]

*Baldwin* was applied to similar facts by Woodhouse J in another New Zealand case, *Tucker* v. *CIR*.[19] His Honour sought to strengthen *Baldwin* on the basis of the intention requirement. He said:

. . . Macarthur J has not excluded the need for intention as a necessary element in the creation of the trust. Indeed his use of the words 'imposed or constituted' themselves imply that there must be a deliberate act of will on the part of the person so dealing with the property to which the words refer. On the other hand the passage explicitly recognises that no particular method need to be adopted in achieving this intention. It is enough if it can be demonstrated that the trust obligations have attached to the property as a result of it. In my view there is no conflict between this judgment and the decision of the Board. . . . [T]he Board considered it to be necessary in the circumstances of the case to put some emphasis upon the element of intention, while Macarthur J in the *Baldwin* case has pointed to the way in which such an intention can be made effective. The important matter is that both elements must be found to co-exist, as in my view they do in the present case. The appellant has never disputed that a trust has actually arisen in respect of the property transferred by him to the trustees; but the original settlor certainly had no part in these transactions. Nor can it be disputed that when the trustees took the property upon trust they did so not in terms of any power of investment, nor as an inadvertent consequence of the transfers made by the appellant, but by a deliberate act of will on his part. In my opinion his intention and purpose was effected and a

---

[17] [1965] NZLR 1.          [18] Ibid., at 6.          [19] [1965] NZLR 1027.

trust created in respect of the property when he made use of the existing trust deed in order that its terms should become applicable to his own dispositions.[20]

Similar facts and issues were considered by the High Court of Australia in *Truesdale* v. *FCT*.[21] In this case, a grandfather settled a nominal sum of money in favour of his grandchild at the request of the father. The father later transferred funds to the trust. The question was whether for tax purposes he created a trust by his transfer. Menzies J, delivering the judgment of the court, rejected the New Zealand cases in the following terms:

> The words 'created a trust' in s. 102 are not, I think, apt to describe the payment of money to a trustee to hold under a trust already constituted. There is an obvious difference between creating a trust in respect of property, on the one hand, and, on the other, transferring property to a trustee to hold upon the terms of an established trust. To read the section as if it applied to such a transfer would be, in the absence of a context, to expand it. Such a reading would be tantamount to saying that the transfer to the trustee of property to be held as part of the assets of an already constituted trust would be to create a second trust, whereas, from the point of view of both the trustee and of the beneficiary,[22] there would be but one trust and the property transferred would be nothing more than an addition to the property subject to the trust . . .[23]

When a unitholder subscribes for units in a unit trust, his position is indistinguishable from the position of the father in *Truesdale*, except that the unitholder is also a beneficiary of the trust fund and no question of making a gift arises. Following the logic of *Truesdale*, a unitholder is not a settlor but only a person transferring property, his subscription money, to the trust. The correctness of *Truesdale*, however, has been questioned[24] and it is worthwhile to consider whether *Baldwin* and *Tucker* offer a better analysis.

On ordinary principles, a person can create as many trusts of same terms for as many beneficiaries as he likes. Likewise, he can create one trust for such beneficiaries. The distinction between the two rests on intention, as equity looks to the intent rather than to the form. The determinative character of the element of intention is clearly recognized by Woodhouse J.[25] However, it is legitimate to enquire into the specific nature of the intention, as an intention to make a gift (to a trust) is not the same thing as the intention to create a trust. The facts of *Baldwin* and *Tucker* can best support a finding of an intention to make use of the existing trust in order

---

[20] [1965] NZLR 1027 at 1030.      [21] (1969) 120 CLR 353.
[22] This reference to the trustee and the beneficiary is puzzling as the issue clearly is the intention of the settlor.      [23] Ibid., at 362.
[24] Jacobs, *Law of Trusts in Australia*, 5th edn., Butterworths Australia, 1986, para. 2913. (The chapter containing this para. is omitted from the 6th edn.)
[25] The part of judgment accompanying fn. 20, *supra*.

that its terms should become applicable to the taxpayer's own disposi-tions.[26] The donative intent is present, but the intention to make use of someone else's trust terms cannot be equated with an intention to create a fresh trust. In short, a transferor of properties to a trust does not intend to create a trust but to give properties to a trust which has been created by someone else.[27] On the basis of this reasoning, it is submitted that *Truesdale* is to be preferred.

The basic intention of each investor in unit trusts is the same: to pool his resources with those of other investors under common professional management on the same terms. If each investor is regarded as a settlor and a new trust is created each time a subscription is accepted, this intention is not given effect to. Nor is it consistent with the accounting provisions[28] and the provisions for meeting of unitholders, found in the section 81 regulations[29] or trust deeds. In truth, unitholders are multiple beneficiaries under a single trust.[30]

This interpretation is supported by *Re AEG Unit Trust (Managers) Ltd.'s Deed*,[31] where Wynn-Parry J held that a unitholder subscribing units in a unit trust is not 'settling' his property for the purpose of the Law of Property Act provision restricting accumulation of income.[32]

The irresistible conclusion is that an investor subscribing units does not have any intention to create a trust in favour of himself but only an intention to add property to an existing trust and to acquire rights as a

---

[26] This is a finding of Woodhouse J, *Tucker* v. *CIR*: [1965] NZLR 1027 at 1030–1.

[27] As argued by Dawson, junior counsel for the appellant in *Truesdale* v. *FCT*, *supra*, in reply: 'The creation of a trust depends upon intention. The parent did not intend to create a trust but to give or appoint money to a trust which was to be created by the settlor.' (1970) 120 CLR 353 at 358. Although this was not adopted expressly by the High Court, Menzies J's judgment, quoted in the text above, implicitly approved this view. Arguments in the same direction were made by Austin in support of *Truesdale*: 'The Income Tax Assessment Act, Section 102(1)(B): Trusts for Unmarried Infant Children' (1974) 4 Tas. LR 137 at 141.

[28] Which invariably treat a unit trust as a single accounting unit.

[29] The Financial Services (Regulated Schemes) Regulations 1991, Parts 9 and 11.

[30] If there are multiple trusts, the trustee owes several duties towards beneficiaries and cannot mix funds of different trusts. If there is one trust, in the event where interests of different unitholders conflict, the question is one of duty of fairness amongst beneficiaries. In *Re Liberal Petroleums Trust* (1985) 64 Alberta LR 243, a unit trustee was liable to pay income taxes in respect of income from Canadian resource properties to non-residents. Some unitholders were non-resident whilst others were resident. The trust deed provided for rateable distribution of net income after payment of certain deductions, including taxes. No distinction was made in the deed between resident and non-resident unitholders. In an application for direction by the trustee, the court held that the payment of tax should be treated as reducing the amounts paid to all unitholders and not only the amounts payable to non-resident unitholders. The court analysed in terms of equitable principles of apportion-ment amongst beneficiaries in one trust. If there were multiple trusts, the non-resident unitholders would have had to bear the tax burden.

[31] [1957] 1 Ch. 415 at 420. Two other grounds given by his Lordship are discussed in s. 3B(2), *post*.          [32] Law of Property Act 1925, s. 164(1).

beneficiary in it in addition to other contractual rights provided by the unit trust scheme.

## (3) Consideration, Contractual Intentions, and Consensus *Ad Idem*

### (a) *Absence of the Settlor*

The absence of the settlor from the creation process of the unit trust can be contrasted with a typical private trust where the terms of the trust are the mandate of the settlor. Conceptually, the absence of a settlor is not novel. Unincorporated joint stock companies, partnerships, clubs, and associations have all lived behind the trust and it does not appear to have been necessary to characterize any person as the settlor. Indeed, in none of the definitions of the trust propounded by jurists and scholars[33] is the settlor regarded as a requisite of the trust institution. The reason is that the trust is equity's institutionalization of the confidence reposed in the trustee for the protection of the beneficiaries, not the settlor. The settlor disappears from the picture after that gift has been effected.

Once the interlocking elements of donative intent and trust intent are disentangled, it is not difficult to accept the proposition that the trust in the unit trust does not have a settlor. If no gift is involved, it would be artificial to characterize a party as a settlor. Thus understood, the absence of the settlor is a feature that negatives the donative element of the trust within the specific context of the unit trust. Where there is a settlor, the trust intention is necessarily that of the settlor alone. His absence therefore also negates the unilateral nature of the trust intention.

The absence of any gift element is simply a corollary of the presence of a bargain that involves exchanges of values, mutual consensus, and intentions to be bound (contractually). All these are ingredients of a contract.

### (b) *Consideration and Promises*

When the trust is used as a method of effecting a gift, it is said that the trust must be completely constituted with the trust property transferred to the trustee. This is because equity will not assist a volunteer or perfect an imperfect gift.[34]

---

[33] See ss. 2B(1), 2C(1), and 2D(1) of this ch., *post*. Art. 2 of the Hague Convention on the Law Applicable to Trusts and on Their Recognition defines, for the purpose of the Convention, a trust as 'the legal relationships created—*inter vivos* or on death—by a person, the settlor, when assets have been placed under the control of a trustee for the benefit of a beneficiary or for a specified purpose'.

[34] Thus, where the transfer to a trustee is intended, the court will not construe that the settlor is making a declaration of trust: see s. 1A(1), *ante*.

There are cases in the law reports that deal with the creation of trusts by contracts. This usually takes the form of enforcing the promise or covenant by the settlor to make a trust.[35] Often, the consideration in exchange for the promise to make a trust is an executed consideration. In other words, the contract to make a trust is a unilateral contract where the consideration is the performance of an act specified by the settlor-promisor, such as the promisee getting married with a certain person.[36] Once the consideration is executed and the settlor-promisor performs his part of the contract, the trust is created and simultaneously the contract is discharged by performance. The trust and the contract remain distinct. Both features reflect the family character of the circumstances in which the trust has arisen.

With the unit trust, the element of consideration operates differently. From a commercial perspective, both the trustee and the manager offer professional investment services,[37] in exchange for fees. In the trust deed, they agree with each other their respective capacities in the unit trust operation and how they are to be remunerated. The regulations made under section 81 of the Financial Services Act may have standardized some of the terms of engagement of the manager and the trustee of an authorized unit trust but they do not alter the nature of the deed: it is their contract, with the considerations being their respective promises.

When an investor subscribes to units from the manager, the manager may sell its own units[38] or may ask the trustee to create new units.[39] Whichever method it adopts, the transaction involved is a bilateral contract. Putting aside the sale charges to which the manager may be

---

[35] Two types of situation feature in texts. The first is where the beneficiary is a party to the contract and therefore can enforce the covenant to make a trust: *Re Ellenborough* [1902] 1 Ch. 697; *Pullan* v. *Koe* [1913] 1 Ch. 9; *Cannon* v. *Hartley* [1949] Ch. 213. The second is where the trustee is the promisee and the beneficiary is not a party and does not provide consideration. A prominent issue has been whether the covenant is enforceable not only by the potential beneficiary but by the trustee at all: *Re Pryce* [1917] 1 Ch. 234; *Re Kay's Settlement* [1939] Ch. 329; *Re Cook's Settlement Trusts* [1965] Ch. 902.

[36] e.g., *Pullan* v *Koe* [1913] 1 Ch. 9.

[37] In *Burns Philp Trustee Co. Ltd.* v. *Estate Mortgage Managers Ltd.*, unreported, Vic. SC, No. 2253 of 1990, 8 June 1990, Smith J, it was contended by the manager that the unit trust deed is a contract of service and hence the court should not make it subject to an interlocutory mandatory injunction to perform the covenant relating making books available for inspection by the trustee or the auditor appointed by it. Such proposition was not rejected by his Honour except that his Honour held that the unit trust deed was 'no ordinary contract of service' and mandatory injunction was granted.

[38] Though the Financial Services (Regulated Schemes) Regulations 1991 contemplate the possibility of the manager acting as the agent of the trustee in dealing with units, a manager usually holds units for its own account (in the 'box'). An incoming unitholder may be buying units held by the manager after they have been redeemed by the manager from a previous unitholder.

[39] The Financial Services (Regulated Schemes) Regulations 1991, reg. 4.06–4.09.

entitled, a unitholder is putting in a sum of money and acquires a unit through which he agrees to be bound by the terms of the trust deed.[40] The consideration is executory: promises are exchanged for counter-promises. The manager promises to act as the manager of the unit trust, to redeem units, and to manage the trust fund in accordance with the trust deed (and the regulations and the scheme particulars, in the case of an authorized unit trust). The trustee promises to act as the trustee, to hold the properties separate from those of the trustee, the manager, or other unit trusts, and to oversee that the manager manages the unit trust in accordance with its terms. The counter-promises of the unitholder are the observance of the unit trust deed and, in the case of an authorized unit trust, the regulations which include provisions for valuation for redemption purposes, meetings, voting and binding effect of majority decisions, and granting of power to the manager and the trustee. It is observable that the unitholder's counter-promise is not exchanged for the promise to create a trust but for promises to undertake certain functions. They are analogous to promises found in contracts for services. The trust arises because of the promises to keep the property apart as a trust fund and of the trustee to act as such. It is the integral part of the promises forming the executory consideration of the parties.

### (c) Mutuality of Intentions and Consensus of Unit Trust Terms

(i) Mutuality in Unit Trust Creation. In the private trust context, the creation of the trust must necessarily be determined by the unilateral intention of the settlor. Likewise, the terms of trusteeship and the conditions of the gifts are his wishes. The trustee can either act or refuse to take up the trusteeship. It is also clear that the beneficiary's agreement to the terms of the trust is unnecessary.

By contrast, the element of consideration and the way it operates in the unit trust relationship are indicative that the transaction is a commercial one. Of course, consideration is only one of the indicia of the existence of contract. For a contract to exist, the court has again resorted to intention as the tool of analysis. Amongst other things, it is used to demarcate those

---

[40] Until recently, it has been the practice that the application form will state that the applicant agrees to be bound by the terms of the trust deed: see the precedents in Day and Harris (p. 173). The binding nature of the trust deed is now impliedly recognized by s. 81(3). It is still the practice of many overseas jurisdictions to incorporate in an application form an express agreement to be bound by the trust deed: e.g., *Australian Ency. F & P*, Vol. 3 (p. 1109). In any event, it can be implied that an applicant agrees to be bound by the terms of the trust deed under which the units are issued: *Gra-ham Australia Pty. Ltd.* v. *Corporate West Management Pty. Ltd.* (1990) 1 ACSR 682 at 687.

promises which the court finds it undesirable to enforce notwithstanding that the promisee may have given consideration.[41]

This approach has found its manifestation in the presumptions of no intention to create legal (contractual) relationship in domestic promises and of such an intention in commercial dealings.[42] Thus, while enforcing a promise to create a trust for the disposition of family properties will have to get over the intention hurdle, it is inconceivable for the intention issue to arise in unit trust dealings, which are commercial by nature. Instead, a contractual intention is presumed when the trust deed is executed and when an investor subscribes for units.

It goes without saying that contractual intentions are mutual in nature, since the very basis of the contract is the consensus of the parties. At all stages of the unit trust transactions, the parties are dealing at arm's length in respect of the provision of investment services. This is true of the dealings between the manager and the trustee. Investors, unlike objects of gifts, have to signify their consent before they become beneficiaries of the trust fund. It follows that the intentions to create or participate in a trust are at all times mutual. This forms a contrast to most private trusts and fits in with a contractual analysis of the intentions of the parties.

(ii) Consensus *Ad Idem* as to Unit Trust Terms. A stronger argument in support of the observation that the unit trust phenomenon is a contractual one and not purely a trust one is that the consensus goes beyond the trust of properties. There are agreements as to a variety of matters that do not relate to it.

At the moment when the trustee and the manager execute the trust deed, there is also an intention to constitute an investment scheme. A unit trust deed may provide in the recital or the operative part that:

It is intended by this deed to establish a trust to be called The . . . Trust which trust shall be administered by the parties to this deed for the benefit of the registered holders of units as herein provided.[43]

---

[41] The 'tool' nature of the intention requirement is well illustrated by the juxtaposition of *Shadwell* v. *Shadwell* (1860) 9 CBNS 159 and *Jones* v. *Padavatton* [1969] 1 WLR 328 by Atiyah in his discussion of the artificial nature of the consideration requirement in *Essays on Contract*, Clarendon Press, 1986, pp. 184–5: in the former case, where an uncle promised to pay his nephew an allowance on his marriage, the whole discussion was in terms of consideration. In *Jones*, where a mother promised her daughter an allowance while she studied for the Bar, the whole discussion was in terms of the intent to create legal relations.

[42] *Chitty*, paras. 2-105–2-120; Greig and Davis, pp. 191 *et seq*; Cheshire and Fifoot, pp. 171 *et seq*.

[43] *Australian Ency. F & P*, Vol. 3, p. 1005, recital B. Recitals are common in many jurisdictions, though not contemplated by the Financial Services (Regulated Schemes) Regulations 1991, Sch. 1.

The intention is clear. Both parties intend that the unit trust deed shall contain the basic provisions that set up the structure of the scheme that will attract investors to join in. In the case of an authorized unit trust, it is an instrument through which the section 81 regulations of the Financial Services Act 1986 will apply, and which in turn bring in some of the provisions contained in the scheme particulars as terms of the unit trust.[44] These documents constitute the scheme by providing the investment philosophy of the scheme, the services to be performed by the trustee and the manager, their remuneration, the pricing of units in it, valuation of underlying investments, treatment of capital and income, redemption procedure, rights of unitholders, and meetings of unitholders. Holding the moneys in trust is only one of the features. When a manager initiates a unit trust and proposes to engage a trustee for it, it reflects the manager's own perception of the investment opportunity and the needs of investors. The scheme adopted therefore gives such rights and makes arrangements that the manager and the trustee consider will satisfy such needs. For example, in some offshore schemes, there may be a guarantee of return of capital or certain level of income, or a life insurance for the unitholders. Facilities may be made for switching between trusts managed by the manager, rapid redemption of units, and access through banks. The possibility of these arrangements in unit trusts demonstrates that unit trusts are not merely trust arrangements of properties but are simply contractual promises between the manager and the trustee that involve trusts. They may also involve contracts with third parties.

Similarly, at the time when an investor becomes a unitholder, he is acquiring more than an interest in the trust fund. He signifies his acceptance of the terms of the trust deed and may also become a party to other contracts arranged as part of the scheme.[45]

### (d) Trust Intention and Contractual Intention

The intention in the unit trust is an integration of a trust intention and a contractual intention. It is a contractual intention to create or participate in a trust. The contract and the trust should not be regarded as two parallel relationships that exist within the unit trust deed. It is part of that contractual arrangement that a party shall act as a trustee and that the properties will be segregated and be held in trust, though their management is vested in the manager. If contracting parties have mutually chosen to adopt the trust institution and its consequential obligations and rights,

---

[44] See s. 2A(2) of this ch., *post.*
[45] e.g., a savings plan. Cheque book facilities provided by a bank are also common in some unit trusts offshore.

there is no reason why the court will not give effect to such an arrangement. But, if the investors had deposited their money with the persons constituting the trustee and the manager as their agents investing on their behalf, the relationship created would be one of creditor and debtor. The line to be drawn between an agency and a trust depends on the mutual intention of the parties.[46] The unit trust deed must contain provisions that enable the court to conclude that the properties are held on trust and are not available to the general creditors of the trustee. Therefore, the intention in the unit trust must necessarily be a mutual intention. That mutuality is derived from the contract between the parties. The trust intention is simply the contractual intention to create or participate in a trust in respect of the money which has changed hands under the terms of the contract. The trust intention therefore is integrated into the contractual intention.

This theoretical position will have dramatic implications for the application of the rules relating to perpetuities, the rule in *Saunders* v. *Vautier*,[47] and the doctrine of frustration.[48]

## B. The *Res* Requirement

### (1) Certainty of Subject Matter

This certainty has two limbs. First, the trust property must be specifically identified or capable of identification. If this is not done by the settlor, no trust is established.[49] Secondly, if the trust property is identified but the beneficial interests of beneficiaries are not certain, those beneficial interests will fail and the trustee will hold the property on a resulting trust for the settlor.[50]

These requirements are gift-making rules. They are the logical consequence of the donative element of the intention to create a trust. If a gift is

---

[46] Such an intention may be inferred from the agreement to segregate the property: cf. *Burdick* v. *Garrick* (1870) LR 5 Ch. App. 233 at 243; *Lyell* v. *Kennedy* (1889) 14 App. Cas. 437 at 463; *Foley* v. *Hill* (1848) 2 HL Cas. 28; *Henry* v. *Hammond* [1913] 2 KB 515 at 521; *Re Nanwa Gold Mines Ltd.* [1955] 1 WLR 1080; *Aluminium Industrie Vaassen BV* v. *Romalpa Aluminium Ltd.* [1976] 2 All ER 552; *Clough Mill Ltd.* v. *Martin* [1984] 3 All ER 982; *Stephens Travel Service International Pty. Ltd.* v. *Qantas Airways Ltd.* (1988) 13 NSWLR 331.

[47] (1841) 4 Beav. 115.

[48] These are examined in 3 of this ch., *post*.

[49] *Palmer* v. *Simmonds* (1854) 2 Drew. 221; *Sprange* v. *Barnard* (1789) 2 Bro. CC 585; *Re London Wine Co. (Shippers) Ltd.* [1986] PCC 121; *Re Goldcorp Exchanges Ltd.* [1995] 1 AC 74; *Hunter* v. *Moss* [1994] 3 All ER 215.

[50] *Boyce* v. *Boyce* (1849) 16 Sim. 476.

intended, it is logical that that gift must be made known. The first limb identifies the subject matter of the gift and the second each donee's quantum or interest in the property constituting the gift. Thus, if the intending donor does not use words clear enough to identify the gift subject or the share in it, it is appropriate to enquire whether he really intends to make that gift.[51] The *res* is simply the subject matter of the gift effected by the trust as a method of disposition.

The gift nature of the trust property of a private trust may be contrasted with the unit trust fund.

(2) Contractual Character and the Certainty Rule

Three points may be made.

First, unlike a private trust corpus, the trust fund of a unit trust is simply not an aggregate of property provided by the settlor by way of gift. The trust corpus has a capital character. No donative intent is present in the unit trust. It does not have any distributive function in the sense that it is a mechanism to distribute one or more gifts amongst a group of beneficiaries. The common characteristic that the trust fund shares with the subject of a private trust is its nature as a fund, namely, that the fund preserves its identity although its contents change.[52] But the fund character is also shared by the capital of an incorporated company.[53]

In the unit trust, the trust corpus consists of moneys belonging to the beneficiaries themselves. They are contributed by unitholders for the purpose of investment, and investment by nature is the use of capital for the purpose of gain, whether such gain is in the form of capital appreciation or income. In substance, unitholders are contributors of capital and the trust corpus has a function no different from share capital of a company.[54]

---

[51] As Sir Arthur Hobhouse has observed in *Mussoorie Bank Ltd.* v. *Raynor*: '[i]f there is uncertainty as to the amount or nature of the property that is given over, two difficulties at once arise. There is not only difficulty in the execution of the trust because the court does not know upon what property to lay its hands, but the uncertainty in the subject of the gift has a reflex action upon the previous words, and throws doubt upon the intention of the testator, and seems to shew that he could not possibly have intended his words of confidence, hope or whatever they may be—his appeal to the conscience of the first taker—to be imperative words.' (1882) 7 App. Cas. 321 at 331.

[52] Maitland, 'Trust and Corporation' in Fisher, *The Collected Papers of F. W. Maitland*, Vol. III, Cambridge UP, 1911 (William S. Hein reprint, Buffalo, 1981) p. 351. 'We conceive that the "trust fund" can change its dress, but maintain its identity.' See also Lawson, *Introduction to the Law of Property*, Clarendon Press, 1958, pp. 30–1.

[53] Lawson, ibid.

[54] Cf. Wrightington defines a Massachusetts business trust as a 'combination of *capital* vested in trustees who issue transferable certificates for shares and execute a declaration of trust designed to provide for the shareholders all the immunities of corporate shareholding'. ('Voluntary Associations in Massachusetts' (1911–1912) 21 *Yale LJ* 311, emphasis supplied.) For the distinction between a Massachusetts trust and a unit trust, see ch. 1, s. 4A, *ante*.

The difference is in form. In the case of company, it is owned by an abstract person, the company. In the case of the unit trust, it is owned by the trustee for the benefit of the unitholders. In theoretical terms, there is no duty on the part of a private trust beneficiary to contribute but it is possible for the unit trust deed to provide for units being subject to calls.[55] This functional distinction may affect the way the court construes the rights of unitholders in underlying assets and whether units constitute choses in action.[56]

Secondly, there is no theoretical problem in the application of the certainty rule in the unit trust context. The rule on certainty of the trust property has been stated as requiring that 'the property to be held by the trustee must be definite at the time at which the creator of the trust purports to create it or else be definitely ascertainable from facts then existing'.[57] From time to time, in a trust deed of a private trust *inter vivos*, the trust property may be defined as including such assets as may from time to time be transferred to the trustee. A marriage settlement is an example. Provisions in unit trust deeds are the same. The trust funds in both private trusts and unit trusts may change as a result of the exercise of investment powers by the trustees. The real difference lies in the fact that this certainty is contractually defined. The capital nature of the unit trust corpus arises from the fact that unit trust transactions are contractual in nature. The unit trust is a means of providing investment services. The unit trust deed embodies the agreement of the manager and the trustee the trust is to be open-ended so that the size of the trust fund can vary.[58] They may also agree to issue units in exchange for investments of investors, i.e., accept contributions *in specie* from investors.[59] In this case, the regulations or the

---

[55] e.g., Schroders Property Fund (formerly known as Darling Property Fund) established in Australia on 23 Feb. 1972.

[56] In a number of deed of settlement company cases, the court regarded interests of members of such companies as represented by mere money. This conclusion was arrived at by characterizing the issue as one of construction and the 'trust fund' was regarded a fund of capital. See the discussion in ch. 5, s. 2C, *post*.

[57] Ford and Lee, para. 4130, citing *Palmer* v. *Simmonds* (1854) 2 Drew 221.

[58] As explained in ch. 1, one of the main reasons for the growth of the unit trust in the UK is such vehicle's ability to redeem its units from investors. Consequently, a close-ended unit trust is not common except in the case of a single property trust. Often, if a close-ended vehicle is intended, it will take the form of an investment trust (company): see ch. 1, ss. 5D and 5E, *ante*.

[59] Reg. 4.05 of the Financial Services (Regulated Schemes) Regulations 1991 makes special provision for a unitization, a process which involves the winding up of a body corporate or collective investment scheme, the transfer of assets of the wound up vehicle to the authorized unit trust, and the issue of units to the investors of the predecessor vehicle. In other circumstances, it appears that reg. 4.08 has to be complied with. This regulation requires the trustee to be satisfied that there is no material prejudice to the interests of participants or potential participants. Many unit trusts overseas have provision for *in specie* contribution though the extent of its being used is uncertain.

trust deed will provide for the discretion of the manager or the trustee to accept or refuse particular investments and provide the valuation method for the exchange of units with the investment properties of the investor. In making any decision as to the contribution to the trust fund, the manager or the trustee is exercising a contractual power. Also, each addition of new trust fund is a result of the contract between the manager and a new unitholder, whereby the latter agrees to buy units from the manager.

In relation to certainty of beneficial interests, an objectively ascertainable benefit must be defined by the trust to enable them to be ascertained.[60] There is no difficulty in applying this rule to a unitholder's interest. When an investor subscribes for units, the units, by nature, define the quantum which that investor, as a unitholder, is entitled to in the trust fund of the unit trust.[61] However, a unitholder's entitlement is contractually defined.[62] While the unit trust is a going concern, the price of the units is calculated by the manager according to the buy-sell formulas laid down in the section 81 regulations or the unit trust deed and which also embody valuation methods for different assets. These provisions exclude other means of calculation. The trust deed provisions also mean that the right to require the trustee to dispose of the underlying assets for the purpose of distribution is altered to the extent that may be provided by those provisions. When the unit trust is terminated, the trust deed often provides for a trust for sale and a unitholder's entitlement will take the form of a proportionate share of the net proceeds of sale.[63] This duality of interests in the trust fund reflects the consensual nature of the transaction.

Thirdly, the management of the trust fund is contractually determined. The centrality of the manager in the management of investments of a unit trust is judicially recognized.[64] The trustee in a unit trust does not have the extensive management power which an ordinary trustee of a private trust may have. This arrangement is achieved by the agreement contained in the unit trust deed.

---

[60] Ford and Lee, para. 5320.

[61] Reg. 2.05 of the Financial Services (Regulated Schemes) Regulations 1991 provides that '[t]he interests of the holders in an authorised unit trust scheme shall consist of units (including fractions of a unit) each unit representing one undivided share in the property of the scheme . . .'

[62] Although a unitholder's interest is not defined in reg. 2.05 of the Financial Services (Regulated Schemes) Regulations 1991 as being subject to the terms of the trust deed or the rest of the regulations, it is implicit in the whole of the Regulations that such right to an undivided share must be subject to the provisions of the trust deed requiring each unitholder to redeem his units through the manager in accordance with the buy-sell formula provided.

[63] See s. 2A(1) of this ch., *post.*

[64] *Parkes Management Ltd.* v. *Perpetual Trustee Co. Ltd.* (1977–1978) ACLC 29,545.

(3) Roles of the *Res* Requirement in the Unit Trust

In a private trust, the trust is a means of disposing of property and the trust assets have a substantive function as being the actual subject of the gift. Often, the certainty or uncertainty of the trust property reflects the gift intention of the settlor.[65] In the unit trust context, it is inconceivable that uncertainties, in terms of the identification of the trust fund and the quantification of the beneficiaries' interests, can arise. This, however, does not downplay the closeness between the *res* requirement and the trust intention. On the contrary, the trust property occupies a significant role in determining the intention to create a trust. It is a determinant of trust intention.

If it is acknowledged that the unit trust is contractual in nature, it is necessary to distinguish other investment services of a contractual nature. Stockbrokers, futures brokers, and investment advisers often provide investment accounts for their clients and customers under which customers deposit their moneys into their clients' accounts. Such accounts may be discretionary accounts whereby brokers will make investment decisions on behalf of customers.[66] Margin facilities can be given to the customer to enable the customer to trade at greater value than his original deposit. Such investment accounts perform a similar function as unit trusts. However, the relationship constituted between a broker and an investor is one of agency. In respect of the money deposited, a debtor-creditor relationship is created.

The distinction between an investment agency, or other debt relationship, and a trust relationship is found in the existence of a trust *res*. It is perfectly clear from a number of cases[67] in the commercial context that segregation of assets was held to be the determining test for establishing that the relationship is one of trustee-beneficiary. The approach is best summed up by Channel J in *Henry* v. *Hammond*:[68]

---

[65] *Mussoorie Bank Ltd.* v. *Raynor* (1882) 7 App. Cas. 321 at 331: fn. 51, *supra*.

[66] They may be 'execution only' accounts such that the broker can only execute buy-sell orders on instructions of the account-holder.

[67] *Re Nanwa Gold Mines Ltd.* [1955] 3 All ER 211; *Barclays Bank Ltd.* v. *Quistclose Investments Ltd.* [1970] AC 567; *Re Kayford Ltd.* [1975] 1 All ER 604; *Carreras Rothmans Ltd.* v. *Freeman Mathews Treasure Ltd.* [1985] Ch. 207; *Stephens Travel Service International Pty. Ltd. (Receivers and Managers Appointed)* v. *Qantas Airways Ltd.* (1988) 13 NSWLR 331; *Thiess Watkins White Ltd.* v. *Equiticorp Australia Ltd.* [1991] 1 Qd. R 82; *Re English & American Insurance Co. Ltd.* [1994] 1 BCLC 649; *Re Fleet Disposal Services Ltd.* [1995] 1 BCLC 345; *Guardian Ocean Cargoes Ltd.* v. *Banco da Brasil* [1994] 2 Ll Rep. 152; *Re Goldcorp Exchange Ltd.* [1995] 1 AC 74; *R* v. *Clowes (No. 2)* [1994] 2 All ER 316.

[68] [1913] 2 KB 515 at 521; *Cohen* v. *Cohen* (1929) 42 CLR 91 at 101; *R* v. *Clowes (No. 2)* [1994] 2 All ER 316 at 325.

. . . It is clear that if the terms upon which the person receives the money are that he is bound to keep it separate, either in a bank or elsewhere, and to hand that money so kept as a separate fund to the person entitled to it, then he is a trustee of that money and must hand it over to the person who is his cestui que trust. If on the other hand he is not bound to keep the money separate, but is entitled to mix it with his own money and deal with it as he pleases, and when called upon to hand over an equivalent sum of money, then, in my opinion, he is not a trustee of the money, but merely a debtor.

The segregation of a separate trust fund, therefore, is crucial to the establishment of the unit trust. In the unit trust, the trust *res* serves a formal function[69] in distinguishing the relationship from any other contractual relationships. The same sum of money could be given to the manager and the trustee as investment agents. In the unit trust, this sum is trust money because it is designated as such by their contract. As a corollary, it can be said that segregation of property is the practical step to effectuate the trust intention.[70]

Apart from the evidential function, the segregation has an important substantive function to play in the unit trust as a medium of collective investment. Unitholders would consider themselves beneficial owners of underlying assets.[71] The very fact that the unit trust fund is trust property means that it does not form part of the property available to the general creditors of the trustee or the manager in their other businesses.[72] As trust property, it brings with it the notion of a higher degree of accountability commonly perceived to be associated with trusts.[73]

The trust fund is also a medium of spreading risk. The trust has

---

[69] i.e., a function similar to writing, witnessing, etc.

[70] Segregation of assets is only an evidence which has to be seen in the context of other evidence before the court. Ultimately, the court has to find an intention to create a trust. Mere segregation without trust intention cannot establish a trust: *Re Fada (Australia) Ltd.* [1927] SASR 590 (cf. *Re Nanwa Gold Mines Ltd.* [1955] 3 All ER 211); *Tit* v. *Waddell (No. 2)* [1977] 3 All ER 129; *Swain* v. *Law Society* [1983] AC 599; *Re Multi Guarantee Co. Ltd.* [1987] BCLC 257; *Walker* v. *Corboy* (1990) 19 NSWLR 382.

[71] Despite the fact that whilst the unit trust is a going concern they are bound by the provisions as to redemption laid down in the unit trust deed.

[72] This can be contrasted with the evidential function of the *res* requirement which is indicative in the dictum of Lord Eldon LC in *Morice* v. *Bishop of Durham* (1805) 10 Ves. 522 at 536–7: 'Wherever the subject, to be administered as trust property, and the objects, for whose benefit it is to be administered, are to be found in a will, not expressly creating trust, the indefinite nature and quantum of the subject, and the indefinite nature of the objects, are always used by the court as evidence, that the mind of the testator was not to create a trust; and the difficulty, that would be imposed upon the court to say, what should be so applied, or to what objects, has been the foundation of the argument, that no trust was intended.'

[73] That accountability flows from the duty nature of the trust institution which courts of equity are jealous to supervise: 'There can be no trust, over the exercise of which [the] court will not assume a control; for an uncontrollable power of disposition would be ownership, and not trust.' (*Morice* v. *Bishop of Durham* (1804) 9 Ves. 399 at 404–5, per Grant MR.)

developed to a stage where it can focus on the preservation of value rather than specific assets. Thus, the unit trust is taking advantage of the changing nature of the *res* to enable investors to spread their risk through a portfolio of assets of different risk characteristics. An investor is putting money in and is getting money out as if the trust is a savings institution but he is not subject to the risk of depreciation of the value of money faced by an ordinary depositor.

The *res* also serves as the yardstick of investment return. The characteristic of a fund is that its content may change though its identity will not. Thus, any change in value over a period of time together with its income accrual will measure the return that portfolio generates. In this sense, it functions no differently from share capital of a company.

Different risk characteristics and return projections of a particular portfolio of assets would suit a particular sector of the investment community. By combining different types of assets in a trust, the manager is able to design a variety of unit trusts. The *res* therefore forms a focal point for uniting like-minded investors to join together to have their moneys commonly managed.[74] It also distinguishes a particular unit trust from other unit trusts managed by the same manager.

## C. Certainty of Objects

Where there are certainties as to intention and subject matter, the trust will be valid only when the objects of the settlor's benefaction are identified with sufficient certainty.[75] In determining whether this certainty is satisfied, it depends on whether the trust is a fixed trust or is a discretionary trust. In the case of a fixed trust,[76] the test is whether a complete list of beneficiaries or potential beneficiaries can be drawn up.[77] In the case of a

---

[74] Hence, the issue whether they 'associate' together: see ch. 3, s. 1B, *post*.

[75] Of course, under the beneficiary principle, the trust must be intended to be directly or indirectly for the benefit of persons unless the trust is for charitable purposes or for a limited anomalous number of non-charitable purposes relating to animals and tombs, etc. A discretionary trust must also be administratively workable. Generally, see *Underhill and Hayton*, art. 8, p. 73 *et seq*.

[76] To be precise, the 'complete list' rule applies to every trust where every object must benefit: see Emery, 'The Most Hallowed Principle—Certainty of Beneficiaries of Trusts and Powers of Appointment' (1982) 98 *LQR* 551, at 553 and 570–2. An example will be a discretionary trust in which the discretion relates only to the quantum of beneficial interests but not the selection of objects. *Borough* v. *Philcox* (1840) 5 My. & C 72 was cited by Emery to support his position: here, the trust was for a testator's 'nephews and nieces, or their children either all to one of them or to as many of them as [the appointor] shall think proper'. The trustee did not discharge his duty of selection and the court held that the trust properties would be distributed equally. To do this, the court must draw up a complete list.

[77] *Re Gulbenkian's Settlement Trusts* [1970] AC 508 at 524.

discretionary trust, since the decision of the House of Lords in *McPhail* v. *Doulton*,[78] the test for validity is the same[79] as that for powers,[80] namely that the trust is valid if it can be said with certainty that any given individual is or is not a member of the class.

Theoretically, therefore, a prerequisite of applying the certainty test to a unit trust is to characterize the unit trust as a fixed trust or a discretionary trust.

A characteristic of a unit trust is that its beneficiaries are of a fluctuating class since unitholders may subscribe for or redeem their units at any time. However, the trust is not a discretionary trust. This is because the beneficiaries are not objects of the dispositive power of the trustee.

A trust is commonly said to be fixed where the answer to the question 'who is entitled to what—and when?' is to be found solely in the trust instrument itself. In this sense the settlor has fixed the beneficial interests.[81] In a unit trust, a unitholder is entitled to a proportionate interest in the capital and income in the trust fund from the moment when he acquires his units. His interest is vested in possession at all times. It follows that a unit trust is a fixed trust and the test to be applied is the comprehensive list test.

Before the problem of applying this test to the unit trust is discussed, it may be useful to briefly examine the underlying rationale of the rule. In *Re Gulbenkian's Settlement Trusts*,[82] when explaining the need for a 'complete list' certainty if the donor directs that a fund should be divided, Lord Upjoin said:

The principle is, in my opinion, that the donor must make his intention sufficiently plain as to the object of his trust and the court cannot give effect to it by misinterpreting his intentions by dividing the fund merely among those present. Secondly, and perhaps it is the more[83] hallowed principle, the Court of Chancery,

---

[78] [1971] AC 424.

[79] The actual word used by Lord Wilberforce in *McPhail* v. *Doulton*, ibid., at 456, was 'similar'. The Court of Appeal in *Re Baden's Deed Trusts (No. 2)* [1972] Ch. 607 confirmed that the two tests for discretionary trusts and powers were identical.

[80] Established in *Re Gulbenkian's Settlement Trusts* [1970] AC 508.

[81] Emery, *supra*, at p. 559. Contrast the definition in *Underhill and Hayton*: 'A fixed trust is a trust in which a beneficiary has a current fixed entitlement to an ascertainable part of the net income, if any, of the trust fund after deduction of sums paid by the trustees in the exercise of their administrative powers of management: the beneficiary has an interest in possession under the trust.' (art. 5, p. 47.) *Quaere*, whether the reference to income is unduly restrictive.                                   [82] [1970] AC 508 at 524.

[83] As pointed out by Emery, *supra*, at p. 551, fn. 4, Lord Upjohn is reported in the All England Reports to have used the word 'most' ([1968] 3 All ER 785 at 792). *McPhail* v. *Doulton* [1971] AC 424 can be seen as an application of this most hallowed principle. Lord Wilberforce accepted *IRC* v. *Broadway Cottages Trust* [1955] Ch. 20 to the extent that 'the test of validity is whether the trust can be executed by the court' but did not agree that 'execution is impossible unless there can be equal division' (at 451).

which acts in default of trustees, must know with sufficient certainty the objects of the beneficence of the donor so as to execute the trust.

These two principles are closely linked in that the first is concerned with the ascertainment of intention whilst the latter is about the carrying out of that intention by the court. Both exemplify that the case-law on certainty requirements is evolving around the trust being used as a method of disposition. Ultimately, the certainty rule is concerned with the dispositive power of the trustee and the distribution function of the trust.

In applying the 'comprehensive list' test, the proper time to consider is the moment when the unit trust is created and not the moment when investors subscribe for units.[84] This is because the certainty rule basically is a rule determining whether a trust is validly created.

Theoretically, there is no problem in drawing up the list of beneficiaries at the moment of the creation of the unit trust. At this point, the manager is most likely to be the only beneficiary if the terms of the trust deed require it to pay a nominal sum as initial trust property. This list of beneficiaries drawn up will be very different from that drawn up subsequently when new unitholders have come and existing unitholders have left. The artificiality of the test is evident.

The true picture perhaps is that the emergence of a new beneficiary is always as a result of this beneficiary contributing to the trust through his contracting with the manager to be bound by the terms of the unit trust deed.[85] At the time of the creation of the trust, the trust is part of the contract made between the manager and the trustee, i.e. the trust deed. This contract provides for the addition of beneficiaries as well as for the withdrawal of beneficiaries. Thus, at this point in time, certainty of objects is by reference to the contracts to be made between investors applying for units and the manager. This analysis is consistent with Lord Upjohn's explanation of the rule. His first reasoning on misinterpreting the donative wish of the settlor does not apply as there is no gift. His second reasoning about the court's acting in default of trustees is basically concerned with ascertainability of beneficiaries if the court is asked to execute the trust. In a unit trust, which is a fixed trust, beneficiaries are ascertainable by reference to the contracts made from time to time in respect of subscription

---

[84] It was established in *Re Hain's Settlement* [1961] 1 All ER 848 that the relevant date for deciding whether the membership of the class of beneficiaries under a fixed trust was ascertainable or not was the date when the trust came into existence.

[85] In most cases of open-ended trusts, by subscription. Where the unitholder is a transferee, the transferee will agree to be bound by the terms of the trust deed in the transfer form: see s. 2B of this ch., *post*. The agreement to be bound may be implied in both situations of subscription and transfer: *Gra-ham Australia Pty. Ltd.* v. *Corporate West Management Pty. Ltd.* (1990) 1 ACSR 682 at 687 and *Elkington* v. *Moore Business Systems Australia Ltd.* (1994) 15 ACSR 292 at 296.

and allotment of units. Thus, in order to take into account the trust in the unit trust, the proper way of expressing the rule is not to suggest drawing of a comprehensive list at the time of creation of the trust. Of course, this list can be drawn up but it is not meaningful at all. A better way of stating the rule, it is submitted, is that there is 'list certainty' at the time of creation of the unit trust because a comprehensive list is 'capable of being drawn up whenever the trust has to be executed by the court'.

This observation reinforces the proposition that a beneficiary, a unitholder, of a unit trust is not an object of a dispositive power; nor an object of benevolence. He is a contracting party who has agreed to a certain trust arrangement in respect of his money.

### D. Summary

It is apparent from the foregoing that the focal point of the three certainties is the intention of the settlor and of that intention the donative element of the settlor is the driving force of the various refinements of the rules relating to intention, subject matter, and objects. This simply shows that the trust has its origin as a gift-device of the landowning class in England.

If we take intention again as a focal point in a unit trust, it can be realized soon that the intention in the unit trust is basically a contractual (and, therefore, a mutual) intention. Once this is acknowledged, the concern is ascertainment of the contractual terms agreed upon by the parties, the manager, the trustee, and the unitholders. A particular term that has been agreed is that moneys belonging to unitholders will be held by the trustee to be invested in accordance with the contractual terms contained in the unit trust deed, which, in the case of an authorized unit trust, may be subject to the regulations made under section 81 of the Financial Services Act 1986.[86] The trust is a holding device of a contractual investment arrangement. It is not a disposition to objects of unitholders. There is certainty of subject matter because it has contractually been agreed that the subscription moneys (both initial and subsequent) are to be the subject matter to be held on trust. There is certainty of objects because the objects are the same persons who have transferred the subject matter to the trustee (or the transferees of such persons). To sum up, the three certainties in the unit trust are contractually defined. But is it not true that all contractual terms are always certain? Otherwise, there is no contract at all. In a sense, therefore, an analysis of the unit trust in terms of the three

---

[86] They are binding on the manager, the trustee, and unitholders independently of the deed and on unitholders as terms of the deed: s. 81(3). Often, they may also be incorporated into the trust deed by reference. The effect of s. 81 on the terms of the unit trust is discussed in s. 2A(2), *post*.

certainties is like squeezing a square into a circle. But this 'squeezing in' has served to unveil the inadequacies of a monolithic analysis—in terms of trusts law alone—of a commercial phenomenon.

## 2. THE UNIT TRUST AS A CONTRACT INCORPORATING A TRUST

A trust may be created by contract but it does not follow necessarily that the trust terms are contract terms. A may agree with B to settle certain properties of A in favour of B upon B's marriage. The terms of the subsequent settlement in pursuance of this agreement will be terms of trust and not contractual terms. In a unit trust, as explained, the elements of consensus of the parties go to the terms of the trust deed as well.[87]

The second proposition, that the trust forms part of the contractual terms of the parties to the unit trust, involves three interwoven themes:

(1) the trust does not, or is not adequate to, explain all elements of the unit trust phenomenon;
(2) the contract offers a better analysis of the terms of the parties' relationships; and
(3) the trust and the contract are two legal institutions that can coexist.

All these themes, especially the first, inevitably bring into focus questions of what a trust is and why does it fail to explain the unit trust. Opinions differ as to how the trust should be defined. It has been defined in terms of 'relationships', 'obligations', and 'rights'. In this section, it will be suggested that the relationships, obligations, and rights that exist in a unit trust cannot be explained adequately in terms of trust principles and that they are contractual in nature as well. The characterization of the relationships amongst the manager, the trustee, and the unitholders will be the subject of discussion in chapter 3. The content of 'obligations' of the manager and the trustee will be examined in chapter 4. The nature and content of 'rights' comprised in a unit will be discussed in chapter 5.

But, first of all, the structure of the unit trust has to be scrutinized.

## A. The Constitution of the Unit Trust

### (1) The Trust in the Unit Trust

A unit trust deed of an authorized unit trust typically contains a declaration by the trustee in the following terms:

---

[87] S. 1A(3)(c) of this ch., *ante.*

Subject to the provisions of this Deed and all regulations made under section 81 of the Financial Services Act 1986 and for the time being in force . . . the property of the scheme (other than sums standing to the credit of the distribution account) is held by the trustee on trust for the holders of the units *pari passu* according to the number of units held by each holder or, in the case where income units and accumulation units are both in issue, according to the number of undivided shares in the property of the scheme represented by the units held by each holder . . .[88]

Regulation 13.03 of the Financial Services (Regulated Schemes) Regulations 1991 provides that 'the trustee shall proceed to wind up the scheme in accordance with regulation 13.04' upon the revocation of the order authorizing the unit trust, the expiration of the duration stipulated in the trust deed, or the amalgamation or reconstruction of the scheme. Regulation 13.04.2 provides that:

the trustee shall, as soon as practicable after the scheme falls to be wound up, realise the property of the scheme, and, after paying thereout or retaining adequate provision for all liabilities properly so payable and retaining provision for the costs of the winding up, distribute the proceeds of that realisation to the holders and the manager (upon production by them of such evidence, if any, as the trustee may reasonably require as to their entitlement thereto) proportionately to their respective interests in the scheme as at the date of the relevant event [triggering the winding up]

In effect, there is a dual trust, or a trust with two limbs,[89] under the combined operation of the trust deed and the Regulations. The primary one is a trust whilst the unit trust scheme is a going concern; it is a trust of the trust fund 'subject to the provisions of the deed and all regulations made under section 81'. It is a trust that contemplates the active management by the manager; it is a trust that does not contemplate realization of beneficiaries' interest other than by way of an agreed method—redemption at a price calculated by an agreed formula. It is a use of the trust for a collective purpose; it is not a use of it as a means of disposition. The secondary one arises from the moment of an event triggering off the winding up of the unit trust. It is a trust for sale or conversion into money for distribution to unitholders on a proportionate basis. The Regulations exclude any role on the part of the manager in the management of the secondary trust. All decisions as to disposal of assets will be made by the trustee. This feature does not seem to be absolutely essential but is implicit in regulation 13.03.1. This structure is one trust

---

[88] The Financial Services (Regulated Schemes) Regulations 1991, Sch. 1.
[89] To borrow Gummow J's description of the *Quistclose* trust (*Re Australian Elizabethan Theatre Trust* (1991) 102 ALR 681 at 691).

because the trust assets and the beneficiaries remain the same. It has two limbs that are of different nature in operation.[90]

In practice, this dual trust structure is also typical in deeds of non-authorized unit trusts and other offshore unit trusts, though the list of winding up events may be more elaborative.[91]

From a functional perspective, the existence of a dual trust structure is easy to understand. The trust fund is like the capital in a company[92] which will be utilized for the objects of the company whilst the company is a going concern and will be distributed to shareholders upon its winding up. The dual trust structure mirrors this corporate arrangement.

### (a) The Primary Trust

The primary trust can be characterized as a purpose trust for the benefit of individuals, a type recognized in *Re Denley's Trust Deed*[93] by Goff J. It is a trust for investment purposes which will benefit individual unitholders. This purpose trust will not create any analytical problem under the conventional beneficiary principle.[94] This is because under the contract constituted by the unit trust deed, the beneficiaries are always ascertained or ascertainable. Why then do we need a purpose trust analysis? There are a few answers. First, as explained above, in applying the 'list certainty' rule to unitholders, the list drawn up at the time of the creation of the trust is very different from that drawn up at any other time. A purpose as an object avoids this problem. This is because a purpose of investing in accordance with the objects stated in the unit trust deed remains constant despite the changes of unitholders. This is analogous to the *Re Denley*

---

[90] A dual trust structure has been recognized in the *Quistclose* line of cases (although the nature of the dual trust in the unit trust is different): *Barclays Bank Ltd.* v. *Quistclose Investments Ltd.* [1970] AC 567; *Re Groom* (1977) 16 ALR 278; *Rose* v. *Rose* (1986) 7 NSWLR 67; Millet, 'The Quistclose Trust: Who Can Enforce It?' (1985) 101 *LQR* 269; Rickett, 'Different Views on the Scope of the Quistclose Analysis: English and Antipodean Insights' (1991) 107 *LQR* 608; and the comment by Gummow J in *Re Australian Elizabethan Theatre Trust* (1991) 102 ALR 681. From an analytical viewpoint, a unit trust will not encounter the difficulty of 'floating' beneficiaries in a *Quistclose* trust because all the beneficiaries remain the same both under the primary trust and the secondary trust.

[91] e.g., *Australian Ency. F & P*, Vol. 3, p. 1009, cl. 2(2); pp. 1017–18, cl. 9(5). Instead of a declaration of a trust, sometimes, the trust deed may provide for the manager to deposit a nominal sum with the trustee to set up the trust. It is commonly provided for the manager to terminate the trust if the trust fund falls below a certain value or where the investment objective ceases to be possible. Some deeds may provide for the winding up of the scheme by a special resolution of a meeting of unitholders.

[92] Or indeed a deed of settlement company or a partnership.

[93] [1969] 1 Ch. 373; applied in *Re Lipinski's Will Trusts* [1976] Ch. 235.

[94] The main issue to be resolved with a purpose trust is the existence of persons with *locus standi* to enforce the trust positively: *Re Astor's Settlement Trusts* [1952] 1 Ch. 540 at 541–2, per Roxburgh J; *Bowman* v. *Secular Society Ltd.* [1917] AC 406 at 441, per Lord Parker.

situation where the purpose of providing a recreation ground for employees of a company remained constant, despite the fact that the employees might change from time to time. Secondly, the reality is that the trust fund is a trust to be invested by the manager according to the investment objective of the unit trust scheme. What a unitholder contracts with the manager is the purchase of units. Units are items of properties in their own right. Whilst the unit trust scheme is a going concern, the interest of a unitholder in the trust fund is in the form of a contractual right to a sum of money; he is only entitled to an amount of money calculated in accordance with the regulations made under the Financial Services Act 1986 or the trust deed[95] and must redeem in the manner prescribed and by paying the manager the relevant charges. He is not entitled to a division of assets. He does not have any proprietary interest in the underlying assets.[96] Since his interest under the primary trust is primarily contractual, it is preferable to characterize the trust as a trust for the investment purpose stated in the unit trust deed. Thirdly, this also ties in with the contractual objective of the unit trust. If the object of the trust subsequently becomes an impossibility, the contract is frustrated and the primary trust will terminate contemporaneously. This reflects the similarity of unit trusts to registered companies and their common origin in the deed of settlement companies.

The disadvantage of the purpose trust analysis is its unorthodoxy; its acceptance by courts is uncertain. An alternative analysis is that the primary trust is an express trust subject to a contract which (*inter alia*) alters the rights and obligations of the trust. This accords with the wordings of the express trust clause of the unit trust deed discussed above.[97] This clause contemplates individuals, rather than purposes, as objects of the trust. In effect, the trust assets are under the collective ownership of all unitholders except that whilst the unit trust scheme is a going concern the trust is subject to the terms of the trust deed. This position is the same as those of deed of settlement companies and unincorporated associations. In these two types of cases, it was recognized that the trustee of a deed of settlement company and the treasurer or officer holding an association's assets will be holding on a bare trust for all present members subject to the

---

[95] Which is by reference to the value of underlying assets.

[96] See ch. 5, s. 2C, *post*.

[97] In Australia, this also accords with another common provision used there: 'The beneficial interest in the trust fund shall be divided into units . . . [E]very unit shall confer an equal interest in the trust fund but shall not confer any interest in any particular part of the trust fund or any investment but only such interest in the trust fund as a whole as is conferred on a unit under the provisions contained in this deed.' *Australian Ency. F & P*, Vol. 3, p. 1009, cl. 3.

contract, which theoretically may specify their immediate division but which invariably provides for their continuing use by future members.[98]

This analysis has an advantage. The winding up provisions[99] are not necessarily exhaustive or they simply may not exist in a particular deed of a non-authorized unit trust or an offshore unit trust. If the unit trust scheme is terminated by breaches or by frustration, the court may be called upon to determine the division of trust property. In such cases, the properties are always held on express trust for the unitholders in proportion to the units each holds. That is consistent with the general expectations of investors.

One thing is clear. Whichever construction is preferred, unitholders will be subject to provisions such as those giving the manager the right to direct the investment and requiring realization of unitholders' interest to be by way of redemption. There is no doubt that whilst the unit trust scheme is a going concern, conventional trust rights and obligations are substantially replaced by rights and obligations expressed in the trust deed, which are contractual in nature, and which may incorporate statutory regulations.[100]

### (b) The Secondary Trust

The trust specified in the winding up provisions is of a secondary nature. Under regulation 13.03 of the Financial Services (Regulated Schemes)

---

[98] In his praise for the trust as providing continuity without incorporation in such ancient unincorporated bodies as the Inns of Court (1422), Lloyds (1720), the London Stock Exchange (1802), and the Jockey Club, Maitland suggests that the original members are owners in equity of the properties of such unincorporated bodies—because a trust for future members would infringe the rule against perpetuities—but they have contracted to observe certain rules that make their ownership in equity a very strange kind: one that is inalienable and not subject to creditors' execution, that ceases on bankruptcy, non-payment of fees, or expulsion, that diminishes in value when a new member is elected, and that does not entitle him to partition. According to Maitland, after a fresh election, there is a fresh contract between the new member and the old member. ('Trust and Corporation' in Fisher, *The Collected Papers of F. W. Maitland*, Vol. III, Cambridge UP, 1911 (William S. Hein reprint, Buffalo, 1981) pp. 321–404 at pp. 377–8.) This conclusion can now be supported in recent cases on the construction of gifts to unincorporated bodies: *Re Recher's Will Trusts* [1972] Ch. 526; *Re Goodson* [1971] VR 801; *Re Lipinski's Will Trusts* [1976] Ch. 235; *Re Bucks. Constabulary Widows' and Orphans' Fund Friendly Society (No. 2)* [1979] 1 All ER 623; *Universe Tankships Inc. of Monrovia* v. *International Transport Workers Federation Conservative* [1983] 1 AC 366; *News Group Newspapers Ltd.* v. *SOGAT 1982* [1986] ICR 716. In these cases, the court held that members of unincorporated groups were in contractual relationships and that gifts to such groups were valid as gifts to their present members as accretions to the groups' funds held by their treasurers subject to such contracts. It was recognized that the treasurer or officer holding the association's assets will be holding on a bare trust for all members subject to the contract, which theoretically may specify their immediate division: see Cross J in *Neville Estates Ltd.* v. *Madden* [1962] Ch. 832 at 849.

[99] Reg. 13.03 of the Financial Services (Regulated Schemes) Regulations 1991.

[100] In practice, the s. 81 regulations may be incorporated into the trust deed by an express clause to this effect. In any event, the Regulations will be 'binding on the manager, trustee and participants independently of the contents of the deed and, in the case of the participants, *shall have effect as if contained in it*' (s. 81(3), emphasis supplied): see s. 2A(2), *post*.

Regulations 1991, the trustee is obliged to proceed to wind up the scheme only when the events mentioned in that regulation happens. Thus, the trustee's obligation to wind up the scheme, and hence the trust for sale, are subject to conditions precedent. If the unit trust deed is a contract, the conditions precedent are of a contractual nature. The parties have agreed upon the manner to deal with their properties if the unit trust scheme is terminated. Thus, upon the happening of all conditions precedent specified, all contractual rights, such as the right to require the manager to redeem within the time stipulated in the Regulations, cease to operate and the secondary trust comes into existence to deal with the distribution of assets. It is like partners agreeing on the manner of disposal of assets upon the dissolution of their partnership. As noted above, if the unit trust scheme is terminated by a manner different from the provisions of this clause, the clause will not operate and the court has to provide a solution.

## (2) Terms of the Constitution of a Unit Trust

The terms of a unit trust are stated in a unit trust deed executed between the manager and the trustee. This is the position of a non-authorized unit trust and of an offshore unit trust unless the law of the relevant jurisdiction provides otherwise.

In the case of an authorized unit trust, the position is more complicated. It appears that the rights and obligations of the parties are governed by a hierarchy of instruments—the regulations made under section 81 of the Financial Services Act 1986, the trust deed, and parts of the scheme particulars.

### (a) The Section 81 Regulations

This complexity arises from the change in regulatory approach under the Financial Services Act 1986.[101] Under this Act, the parties to an authorized unit trust are directly regulated by the section 81 regulations. These regulations may cover the constitution and management of authorized unit trust schemes, the powers and duties of the manager and trustee of any such scheme, and the rights and obligations of the participants in any such scheme.[102] Specifically, they may make provision as to the issue and redemption of units, expenses of the schemes and the means of meeting them, the appointment, removal, powers, and duties of an auditor, investment and borrowing powers, records of the scheme and their

---

[101] Ch. 1, s. 5, *ante*.
[102] S. 81(1); s. 81(2) provides for specific matters that may be covered by the regulations.

inspection, periodical reports, and amendments to the scheme.[103] They may make provision as to the contents of the trust deed.[104] Currently, the section 81 regulations are contained in Part 2, Parts 4 to 13, and Parts 15 and 16 of the Financial Services (Regulated Schemes) Regulations 1991.[105]

Section 81(3) provides that:

regulations under this section [81] shall be binding on the manager, trustee and participants independently of the contents of the deed and, in the case of the participants, shall have effect as if contained in it.

These regulations are binding on the manager, the trustee, and the unitholders independently of the trust deed as a matter of law. Accordingly, it is not possible for the regulations to be modified by the terms of the trust deed and if there is any inconsistency the regulations will override the terms of the trust deed. The Act does not give any power to the Securities and Investments Board to waive or modify the requirements of the regulations. As against the manager and the trustee, breaches of the regulations may give rise to civil actions under section 62 of the Act. Under this section, a contravention of the regulations is actionable as a breach of statutory duty. In addition, the manager or the trustee is deemed to have breached the rules of the relevant self-regulating organization. It may be subject to disciplinary action, including expulsion from such organization and the consequential loss of the status as an authorized person.[106] There is no criminal sanction for their breaches.

As for unitholders, section 81 regulations will also function as implied terms of the trust deed and will be enforceable as if they are contained in it. This subsection (3) assumes that the terms of the trust deed are binding on unitholders, despite the fact that unitholders are not parties executing the trust deed. This is reinforced by the regulation 2.02 and Schedule 1 Part I of the Financial Services (Regulated Schemes) Regulations 1991 which require every trust deed of an authorized unit trust to state that 'the deed is binding on each holder as if he had been a party to it and is bound by its provisions'. If a unitholder is in breach of the terms of the regulations, such a breach will be treated as a breach of contract and be actionable accordingly.

This provision for the enforcement of the section 81 regulations is

---

[103] S. 81(2). But the regulations may not impose limits on the remuneration payable to the manager of the scheme: s. 81(4). This is because this would amount to price control and be incompatible with the Government's competition policy. (*Financial Services in the United Kingdom: A New Framework for Investor Protection*, Cmnd. 9432, HMSO, 1985, para. 10.1.)

[104] S. 81(3).

[105] Part 3 is made under ss. 85, 87(5), and 88(10) of the Financial Services Act 1986 and Part 14 under ss. 86(3), 87(4), 90, and 52 of the Act.

[106] Ss. 62 and 95, which are analysed in ch. 5, s. 3C, *post*.

strange. Terms are implied only in the case of some parties—in this case, the unitholders who are not executing the trust deed. In practice, the section 81 regulations are also binding on the manager and the trustee as implied terms because of a typical provision inserted in the trust deed which provides that:

The regulations made under section 81 of the Financial Services Act 1986 and for the time being in force shall apply to the scheme to the extent that the same are relevant thereto as if the same were reproduced herein save in so far as they are specifically excluded or amended (to the extent permitted in such regulations) by the terms of this deed.[107]

Thus, the section 81 regulations provide a set of implied terms that may change from time to time according to the intention of the regulator rather than the intentions of the parties.

### (b) The Terms of the Deed

Section 81(3) of the Financial Services Act 1986 provides regulations of that section may 'make provision as to the contents of the trust deed'. Regulation 2.02 provides:

1. A unit trust scheme does not qualify to be authorised by an order made under section 78 of the Act unless the scheme is constituted by a deed made between the manager and the trustee which—
(a) conforms with Schedule 1 below, and
(b) (subject to (a) above) makes no provision for matters which are dealt with elsewhere in these regulations.
2. Any power conferred on the manager or on the trustee, or on them together, in these regulations is subject to any express prohibition contained in the trust deed.
3. Part 5 (Investment and borrowing powers) is subject to any restriction imposed by the trust deed under paragraph 13 of Schedule 1.

A trust deed of an authorized unit trust therefore must be executed between the manager and the trustee. It must conform with Schedule 1 of the Regulations. Schedule 1 is divided into two parts. Part I stipulates matters which 'must' be contained in the trust deed and Part II matters which 'may' be contained in the trust deed. The obligatory matters required by Part I are the name of the scheme, the relevant category of funds[108] to which the scheme belongs, the governing law, a provision that

---

[107] This clause may be inserted as an optional provision under para. 22 of Sch. 1: 'Any provision which in all material respects has the same effect as a provision contained, at the time when the provision is made, in the Act or in regulations made under section 81 of the Act.'
[108] Under reg. 2.07, an authorized unit trust must be one of the following categories: (a) a securities fund, (b) a money market fund, (c) a futures and options fund, (d) a geared futures and options fund, (e) a property fund, (f) a warrant fund, (g) a feeder fund, (h) a fund of funds, and (i) an umbrella fund.

the deed is binding on each unitholder, the base currency, the investment powers, declaration of trust of the scheme property by the trustee, and a provision that unitholders' liability is limited to the price of units paid. Optional matters permitted by Part II are the duration of the scheme, the manager's preliminary charge, the periodic charge, the charge on an exchange of units in an umbrella fund, and the charge on redemption, the trustee's remuneration, constituents of property, permitted transactions and borrowing powers, economic or geographic objectives of the scheme, the types of units issued,[109] a provision that unitholders are confined to persons who are exempt from capital gains tax and corporation tax on capital gains otherwise than by reason of residency, provisions regarding issue of unit certificates, a provision authorizing grouping for equalization under regulation 9.08, provisions relevant to pension schemes or charitable schemes, restatement of statutory provisions, and enabling and restricting provisions.

It can be seen that the scope for manipulation of the terms of the unit trust is very limited. The trust deed can impose further restrictions on the powers of the trustee and the manager.[110] Apart from this, the trust deed does not make provision for matters which are dealt with elsewhere in the regulations unless such provision is permitted under the Schedule.[111] Under the optional 'enabling and restricting provisions'[112] of Part II of this Schedule, the trust deed may deal with 'a matter not referred to earlier in [the] schedule the inclusion of which serves to enable the scheme, the manager or the trustee to obtain any privilege or power conferred by [the] regulations' and may contain a provision 'which is expressly contemplated in [the] regulations'. If a particular clause in the trust deed cannot fall within any of these enabling provisions, there is a breach of regulation 2.02 and authorization cannot be obtained. The legal consequence is not entirely clear if authorization was actually obtained. Presumably, the authorization can be revoked under section 79 of the Act.[113] Until revocation, it seems that the effect of section 81(3) of the Act is that regulation 2.02 overrides the clause which should not be inserted in the deed.

### (c) Scheme Particulars

As pointed out in chapter 1, scheme particulars are hybrid in nature. They may contain some of the terms of the trust. In other words, the trust deed is

[109] Units of an authorized unit trust may be issued as accumulation units, income units or both. Other types of units are not permitted.
[110] Reg. 2.02.2 and reg. 2.02.3 cited above.          [111] Reg. 2.01.1 cited above.
[112] Sch. 1, Part II, para. 21.
[113] S. 79(1)(a) empowers the Secretary of State to revoke authorization if it appears to him that any of the requirements for the making of the order are no longer satisfied.

not an exclusive document. This is clearly contemplated by regulation 3.02.2 of the Financial Services (Regulated Schemes) Regulations 1991:

Scheme particulars . . . may contain any other matter—
(a) the inclusion of which is necessary to enable the scheme, the manager or the trustee to obtain any privilege or power granted subject to there being such a provision by these regulations, or
(b) which is expressly contemplated in these regulations.

Although regulations under Part 3, the scheme particulars provisions, also apply to offshore schemes recognized under section 87 and section 88 of the Act, it appears that this particular provision has no effect on them as the other regulations of the Financial Services (Regulated Schemes) Regulations 1991 only apply to authorized unit trusts.[114] Only a provision of scheme particulars of an authorized unit trust can take advantage of regulation 3.02 so as 'to obtain any privilege or power granted' by other provisions of the Regulations. For example, regulation 5.02.4 provides that 'restrictions from time to time included in scheme particulars . . . shall be observed as if they were included in this Part [5]'. Regulation 8.05 enables the manager and its associates to be exempted from an obligation to account for profits made on the issue or cancellation of units 'where the manager has disclosed prominently in the scheme particulars a statement that he or another specified affected person is under no obligation to account to the trustee or to the holder for any profits'.[115]

Thus, in respect of a particular authorized unit trust, some provisions of the Financial Services (Regulated Schemes) Regulations 1991 have to be read in conjunction with the provisions of the scheme particulars. The relevant scheme particulars provision may have been incorporated into the Regulations for that particular scheme, as in the case of regulation 5.02.4. They therefore have a constitutive function. This position may not be expected by investors but must be the result of the combined operation of section 81(3) and regulation 3.02.2 and the enabling regulations incorporating the relevant scheme particulars provisions.

The rationale behind this regulatory arrangement is not entirely clear. It seems that if the section 81 regulations are given the constitutive function of individual unit trust schemes, they must be flexible to cater for special circumstances of individual schemes. The regulations have to incorporate the terms that promoters may decide. Logically, such terms should be contained in the trust deed. However, amendments to the unit trust deed may involve complicated procedures involving calling of unitholders'

---

[114] Apart from Part 14 which contains specific provisions for recognized schemes.
[115] For other examples, see reg. 4.01, reg. 4.03, reg. 8.03, reg. 9.02, and reg. 9.07.

meetings. The scheme particulars appear to an be alternative of conveni-
ence.


## B. A Relationship Analysis

This section discusses whether each of the relevant relationships is
contractual. Characterization of those contractual relationships will be the
subject of chapter 3.[116]

### (1) Keeton and Sheridan's Definition

Keeton and Sheridan[117] define a trust as:

the relationship which arises wherever a person (called the trustee) is compelled in
equity to hold property, whether real or personal, and whether by legal or
equitable title, for the benefit of some persons (of whom he may be one and who
are termed beneficiaries) or for some object permitted by law, in such a way that
the real benefit of the property accrues, not to the trustee, but to the beneficiaries
or other objects of the trust.

Similarly, the express trust is also defined by the American Restatement of
Trusts as:

a fiduciary relationship with respect to property subjecting the person by whom the
property is held to equitable duties to deal with the property for the benefit of
another person which arises as a result of a manifestation of an intention to create
it.[118]

### (2) The Trustee-Manager Relationship

As explained before, the private express trust is primarily founded upon
the donative intention of the settlor whilst the intention in the unit trust is a
mutual intention to utilize the trust for the parties' transaction. If the trust
is looked at as a kind of relationship, as the definitions suggest, it is the
relationship between the trustee and the beneficiary with respect to

---

[116] Ch. 3, ss. 1–4, *post.*

[117] Keeton and Sheridan, *Law of Trusts*, 12th edn. (by Sheridan), Barry Rose, 1993, p. 3.

[118] American Law Institute, *Restatement of the Law: Trusts 2d*, American Law Institute
Publishers, 1959, s. 2. This definition is cited here as well because Keeton and Sheridan's
definition attempts to embrace constructive trusts and resulting trusts and consequently lacks
the element of an express intention featured in the American *Restatement's* definition. Scott,
as the *Restatement's* reporter, logically, approves of this definition: Scott, s. 2.3. The
*Restatement's* definition was approved in a number of cases in the US: see App. to the
*Restatement of Trusts 2d* (1987), s. 2.

property. The settlor is not relevant to the definition of the trust. This is because the trust is a donative device and once the trust is completely constituted he is considered as having parted with his interest and his wishes are being taken care of by the court of equity. The trust is a relational institution that operates at a bipartite level between the persons of the trustee and the beneficiary. The unit trust is a tripartite relationship, involving, by a series of transactions, the trustee, the manager, and the unitholder, with the additional presence of consideration and contractual intentions. The difficulties of an analysis purely in terms of trust are apparent.

The word 'relationship' signifies rights and reciprocal duties. A contractual relationship involves rights and obligations voluntarily and consensually undertaken by the parties. The trust relationship is a relationship having certain characteristics stated in the definitions, namely those with respect to the property which is its subject matter. The rights and duties between the trustee and the manager under the unit trust deed cannot fit into this trust definition. The fact that they are parties to the same deed with the presence of consideration and contractual intention supports a contractual relationship. The contractual nature is also underscored by the possibility that the parent companies of the trustee and the manager may be required to join in the trust deed to guarantee the observance and performance of the obligations contained in the trust deed, a common practice in some offshore jurisdictions.

## (3) The Manager-Unitholders Relationship

The contractual intentions during the subscription of units or the transfer of units have already been adverted to.[119] Whether the manager can be characterized as a trustee or a fiduciary is the subject of the next chapter. At this juncture, it suffices to point out that the application for units may constitute an offer by the investor to be bound by the terms of the trust deed and the regulations and any issue of units by the manager constitutes an acceptance. This argument is by way of analogy to the issue and allotment of company shares and has been accepted by the court.[120] On a similar basis, when units are acquired through transfer, the application made by the transferee, personally or through some agent, to the manager for registration of the transfer of the units in his favour and the issue of a certificate of title in his name bring into existence a contract between the transferee and the manager on the terms of the trust deed.[121] There

[119] S. 1A(3), *ante*.
[120] *Gra-ham Australia Pty. Ltd.* v. *Corporate West Management Pty. Ltd.* (1990) 1 ACSR 682 at 687.
[121] *Elkington* v. *Moore Business Systems Australia Ltd.* (1994) 15 ACSR 292 at 296.

appears to be no difficulty to find a contractual relationship between the manager and unitholders.

## (4) The Trustee-Unitholders Relationship

The unit trustee's relationship with the unitholders typifies the relationship contemplated by the trust definition. Thus, the acquisition of legal title to properties comprised in the trust fund is sufficient to impose a trustee's obligation on the part of the unit trustee. However, in the dual trust structure of the unit trust, the primary trust is expressed to be subject to the terms and conditions of the trust deed and the regulations under the Financial Services Act 1986. The trust deed and the regulations provide for the details that will constitute an investment scheme. Of particular relevance to the trust relationship is the fact that in this scheme the powers usually possessed by a trustee of a private trust are now vested in the manager. The presence of the manager in the management of the trust cannot fit in the bipartite nature of the conventional trust definition.[122] As between the trustee and the unitholders, how this can be achieved also cannot be explained in terms of trust concepts alone.

In addition, promises may be made by the trustee which are independent of the trust of assets. If a unitholder is to enforce such promises, it must be established either that the unitholder is a promisee or that the manager is a promisee holding the promise in trust for the benefit of the unitholders.[123] Either construction is sufficient to support the argument that the unit trust deed embodies more than the ordinary trust relationship between the trustee and the unitholders.

At the same time, there is no impediment to construing a direct contractual relationship between the trustee and unitholders which is in addition to the trust relationship. When an investor subscribes for units or submits a transfer, he is making an offer. His offer is accepted upon issuance of his units or upon his name being entered on the register of units.[124] The application form is often addressed to the manager. Invariably, the cheque is requested to be drawn in favour of the trustee. In

---

[122] More will be said of this changing nature of trusteeship in the ensuing discussion: s. 2C of this ch., *post*.

[123] Cf. *West Merchant Bank Ltd.* v. *Rural Agricultural Management Ltd.*, unreported, 4 Apr. 1996, NSWCA No. 40750/95, where it was held that each unitholder applying for units agreed with the manager to comply with the trust deed and that the manager was holding the benefit of this promise for all unitholders. For a criticism of this decision, see Sin, 'Enforcing the Unit Trust Deed Amongst Unitholders' (1997) 15 *C&SLJ* 108.

[124] *Elkington* v. *Moore Business Systems Australia Ltd.* (1994) 15 ACSR 292. Under reg. 6.03 of the Financial Services (Regulated Schemes) Regulations 1991, the entry of the unitholder's name on the register is conclusive evidence of ownership.

such circumstances it is not difficult to come to the conclusion that the manager is acting as an agent for all parties.[125]

## (5) The Relationship of Unitholders *Inter Se*

The trust concept does not seem fully to explain the relationship amongst the unitholders *inter se*. In an ordinary trust situation, beneficiaries are objects of the donative intent of the settlor; it is not necessary to establish any consensus amongst them. In the case of the unit trust, the trust fund is the capital of the unitholders. The unit trust is their vehicle to achieve their investment purposes. Inevitably and as a minimum, there will be a mechanism for decision making in the unit trust deed in the form of provisions for the conduct of meetings and for voting. Under the Financial Services (Regulated Schemes) Regulations 1991, unitholders associating with the manager are not entitled to vote.[126] Other common provisions for valuation of assets, redemption, and switching between sub-funds of an umbrella trust also affect the rights of unitholders *inter se*.

In *Smith* v. *Anderson*,[127] James LJ held that there were no mutual rights and obligations amongst unitholders, in spite of the provisions for conduct of meetings and for voting in the trust deed before him.[128] The other two judges, Brett and Cotton LJJ, expressed no view on this point but this view is shared by contemporary writers.[129] It was applied by Heerey J in the Federal Court of Australia in *AF & ME Pty. Ltd.* v. *Aveling*.[130]

In *AF & ME Pty. Ltd.* v. *Aveling*, the trust deed of a unit trust listed on the Stock Exchange provided (*inter alia*) that 'a person shall not . . . acquire or be eligible to acquire units in the Trust if any person who is not entitled to any units in the Trust or is entitled to less than 20% of the units

---

[125] i.e., the trustee, the manager itself, and existing unitholders. The manager's authority can either be expressed in the trust deed or be implied. When a person joins a club or an unincorporated association, he contracts with all members through the secretary: *Hybart* v. *Parker* (1858) 4 CB (NS) 209; *Gray* v. *Pearson* (1870) LR 5 CP 568; *Evans* v. *Hooper* (1875) 1 QBD 45. See also *Clarke* v. *Dunraven* [1897] AC 59, discussed in s. 2B(5), *post*.

[126] Reg. 11.07.4.

[127] (1880) 15 Ch. D 247, where, under a trust deed between the trustees and a unitholder representing all other unitholders to constitute a fixed trust, it was held that the unitholders did not form an association for the purpose of carrying on business that has for its object the acquisition of gain by the association or by its individual members.

[128] *Supra*, at 274.

[129] Ford and Hardingham, 'Trading Trusts: Rights and Liabilities of Beneficiaries' in Finn (ed.), *Equity and Commercial Relationships*, Law Book Co., 1987 p. 53 fn. 14. Walsh, 'Unit Trusts' [1978] *Taxation in Australia* 446 at 448; Walsh, 'Unit Trusts' in Grbich, Munn and Reicher, *Modern Trusts and Taxation*, Butterworths Australia, 1978, p. 41; Stewart, 'Unit Trusts—Legal Relationships of Trustee, Manager and Unitholders' (1988) 5 *C & SLJ* 269 at 280; Spavold, 'The Unit Trust: A Comparison with the Corporation' (1991) 3 *Bond LR* 249 at 257. [130] (1994) 14 ACSR 499.

in the trust would, immediately after the acquisition, be entitled to more than 20% of the units in the Trust . . .' and also that the 'Manager may, in its absolute discretion, decline to allot or to register any transfer or transmission of a unit if in the Manager's opinion, the allotment or registration thereof would or might result in or have the effect of causing an infringement or contravention of [the above provision]'.

A unitholder acquired 51 per cent of the units. The manager and the minority unitholders brought an action against this unitholder for breach of the terms of the trust deed. Heerey J held that the unitholders were not in a contractual relationship and could not be liable to each other for breach of the terms of the trust deed. James LJ's view in *Smith* v. *Anderson*[131] was applied without analysis of the modern unit trust situation. His Honour further held that, on construction, the relevant clause 'is not a command but a "restriction" or a statement of disqualifying criteria'.[132] It 'provides a mechanism for preventing would-be infringers or contraveners . . . from becoming registered as unitholders and removing them from the register when they do. But that mechanism is not constructed by the imposition of contractual obligations. Power is given to the manager (and nobody else) to achieve those objects. But that power does not involve contractual obligation on the manager . . . still less on anybody else.'[133]

The view of James LJ and the decision of Heerey J are hard to support on analysis.

First of all, what is a right and what is an obligation? In *Smith* v. *Anderson*, the trust deed provided, amongst other things, for the holding of a meeting annually, voting in such meeting according to units held, not by a show of hands, and the conduct of the meeting according to Table A of the then Companies Act. It included provisions for the appointment and remuneration of auditors to be decided by a resolution of such meeting. It also catered for the unitholders' approval of reinvestment by the trustees. In effect, the unitholders had agreed amongst themselves on a mechanism for action, if necessary, and also that the majority could bind the minority in their decisions within the parameters of the trust deed. If these provisions were regarded as binding amongst unitholders,[134] it is not hard to consider them as creating both 'rights' of the majority in a meeting to make decisions and 'obligations' of the minority to be bound by those decisions. Indeed, it is not difficult to translate these provisions into jural correlatives of right-duty or power-liability in the Hohfeldian sense.

---

[131] (1880) 15 Ch. D 247.          [132] *Supra*, at 523.          [133] Id.

[134] Cotton LJ must have assumed these provisions as effective when his Lordship considered this to be the mechanism to enable certificate holders 'to give such assent as cestuis que trust usually give for a change of securities when they are not incapacitated by infancy or otherwise'. (*Smith* v. *Anderson* (1880) 15 Ch. D 247 at 284.)

But to find a contract, one need not go into such a philosophical analysis. What is necessary is a set of mutual promises, namely, that each agrees with the other to follow the statutory regulations and the provisions of the deed and to pay the redeeming unitholder in accordance with the agreed formula rather than the distribution method of an ordinary private trust. Indeed, if the court wishes, it can come to such a conclusion without resorting to any analysis of this sort. For example, there are many instances where courts have held that the members of an unincorporated group were in contractual relationships and that gifts to such a group were valid as out-and-out gifts to their present members subject to such contracts.[135] No offer and acceptance analysis was ever undertaken in any of these cases. Of course, the concern of judges in such cases was to find or develop a theory whereby such gifts would not be held void. But the finding of the existence of a contractual relationship was a requisite of this theory of validity of gifts to unincorporated groups. It was therefore part of the *ratio decidendi* of each of these cases.

There are two analytical issues that are germane to the conclusion of a contractual relationship amongst unitholders but have not been considered in these cases on gifts to unincorporated groups.

First, intention. The traditional view is that members of voluntary associations are in a consensual, but not contractual, relationship. It was said[136] that '[s]uch associations are established upon a consensual basis, but, unless there were some clear positive indications that the members contemplated the creation of legal relations *inter se*, the rules adopted for their governance would not be treated as amounting to an enforceable contract'. In *Cameron* v. *Hogan*,[137] a member of the Victorian branch of the Australian Labour Party was expelled despite the fact that the effect of expulsion was the loss of the Premiership of Victoria. The court held that it had no jurisdiction to intervene. On the other hand, this case has often been distinguished and there is a vast body of cases in which the court has found that there are contractual intentions amongst members of unincorporated groups.[138]

---

[135] *Re Lipinski's Will Trusts* [1976] Ch. 235; *Re Recher's Will Trusts* [1972] Ch. 526; *Re Bucks. Constabulary Widows' and Orphans' Fund Friendly Society (No. 2)* [1979] 1 All ER 623; *Universe Tankships Inc. of Monrovia* v. *International Transport Workers Federation Conservative* [1983] 1 AC 366; and *Central Office* v. *Burrell (Inspector of Taxes)* [1982] 2 All ER 1; *Re Goodson* [1971] VR 801; *Public Trustee (NSW)* v. *Attorney-General (NSW)* [1985] ACLD 215; *Underhill and Hayton*, pp. 102–8; Lee, 'Trust and Trust-like Obligations with Respect to Unincorporated Associations' in Finn (ed.), *Essays in Equity*, Law Book Co., 1985.  [136] *Cameron* v. *Hogan* (1934) 51 CLR 358 at 370–1.
[137] Ibid.
[138] *Woodford* v. *Smith* [1970] 1 WLR 806; *Grogan* v. *McKinnon* [1973] 2 NSWLR 290; [1974] 1 NSWLR 295; *Burton* v. *Murphy* [1983] 2 Qd. R 32. For a lucid discussion and other cases, see Greig and Davis, pp. 199–213.

These two approaches are not necessarily irreconcilable. It has, for instance, long been accepted that there is a general presumption against an intention to create legal relations in domestic and social settings whilst there is an opposite presumption for promises made in a commercial context.[139] The social-commercial dichotomy provides the philosophical basis for drawing the line between these two groups of association cases. Where property rights are involved, it should be readily inferred that a contractual intention is present.[140] It follows that there is no obstacle to find intentions of unitholders contracting amongst themselves.

The second issue is whether unitholders, a fluctuating body of investors, can contract without knowledge of each other. In *Smith* v. *Anderson*,[141] this was one of the reasons why James LJ came to the conclusion that the unitholders were not in a contractual relationship. However, in *Clarke* v. *Dunraven*,[142] competitors in a regatta of a yacht club signed undertakings that they would obey the rules of the race. These undertakings were addressed to the secretary of the club individually. The House of Lords was not troubled by the absence of knowledge[143] and arrangement amongst the competitors. Nor did their Lordships find it necessary to consider any offer and acceptance.[144] The competitors entering into the race and their undertaking to be bound by the rules to the knowledge of each other were sufficient to create a contract amongst them.[145]

---

[139] S. 1A(3)(c)(i), *ante*.

[140] In *Finlayson* v. *Carr* [1978] 1 NSWLR 657, on a challenge to a decision of the committee of the Australian Jockey Club concerning membership, Waddell J held that 'the assumption underlying the rules [was] that the club would have property, and the members would have special rights and privileges of enjoyment' and that 'the rules must be regarded as creating legal relations between the members, and should be treated as amounting to an enforceable contract' (at 666). See also *Lee* v. *Showmen's Guild of Great Britain* [1952] 2 QB 329 at 341–2; *Nagle* v. *Feilden* [1966] 2 QB 633; *R* v. *Jockey Club, ex p. RAM Racecourses Ltd.* [1993] 2 All ER 225.

[141] (1880) 15 Ch. D 247, where, under a trust deed between the trustees and a unitholder representing all other unitholders to constitute a fixed trust, it was held that the unitholders did not form an association for the purpose of carrying on business that has for its object the acquisition of gain by the association or by its individual members.

[142] [1897] AC 59.

[143] Besides *Clarke* v. *Dunraven*, ibid., when a person joins a club or unincorporated association, he may contract with all other members although he only communicates with the secretary: *Hybart* v. *Parker* (1858) 4 CB (NS) 209; *Gray* v. *Pearson* (1870) LR 5 CP 568; *Evans* v. *Hooper* (1875) 1 QBD 45.

[144] An offer and acceptance analysis of *Clarke* v. *Dunraven* [1897] AC 59 has been provided by Salmond and Williams, *Principles of the Law of Contract*, 2nd edn., Sweet and Maxwell, 1945, p. 71: the first competitor is offering to all subsequent participants an undertaking to be bound by the rules if they all give similar undertaking. The second participant accepts this offer by participating and makes a similar offer for subsequent participants.

[145] Per Lord Herschell, *Clarke* v. *Dunraven* [1897] AC 59 at 63. In Canada, in *McCannell* v. *Mabee-McLaren Motors* [1926] 1 DLR 283, where motor dealers agreed with a

Cases on articles of association of companies are also instructive as to whether unitholders are in contractual relationships. It is true that '[t]he extent to which the articles can bind one member contractually to another is a matter of long-standing debate, but the weight of authority seems clearly to establish that they do have that effect'.[146] This was impliedly recognized in *Borland Trustee* v. *Steel Brothers & Co. Ltd.*.[147]

In *Rayfield* v. *Hands*[148] Vaisey J allowed a shareholder to enforce a pre-emption clause directly against another shareholder without joining the company in the proceedings. Therefore, on the face of it, *Rayfield* v. *Hands* is a strong persuasive authority for arguing that the unit trust deed is a contract between all unitholders. However, Vaisey J said that the principle 'may not be of so general an application as to extend to the articles of association of every company, for it is . . . material to remember that this private company is one of that class of companies which bears a close analogy to a partnership'.[149] This is intriguing because his Lordship was dealing with section 20 of the Companies Act 1948, which could not give rise to any distinction on this basis. A further question is whether the contract established in *Rayfield* v. *Hands* was the effect of the statutory provision or was a contract based on general contractual principle. *Rayfield*

manufacturer to certain restrictions it was held that they had entered into a contract amongst themselves. In *Spike and Rocca Group Ltd.* (1979) 107 DLR (3d) 62, covenants restricting nature of business of tenants were held to be enforceable amongst tenants of a shopping centre although such covenants were contained in leases with the landlord to which other tenants were not parties. *Quaere* if English courts will go as far as *Spike and Rocca Group Ltd.* which is an apparent attempt to avoid the whole body of law on enforcement of covenants.

[146] Per Burt J, *Re Caratti Holding Co. Pty. Ltd.* (1975) 1 ACLR 87 at 99, citing *Borland's Trustee* v. *Steel Brothers & Co. Ltd.* [1901] 1 Ch. 279 and *Rayfield* v. *Hands* [1960] Ch. 1. The issue is whether there is a contract between members in addition to the contract constituted between the members and the company (*Hickman* v. *Kent or Romney Marsh Sheep-Breeders' Association* [1915] 1 Ch. 881). Dicta against include *Welton* v. *Saffery* [1897] AC 299 at 315 per Lord Herschell; *London Sack & Bag Co. Ltd.* v. *Dixon & Lugton Ltd.* [1943] 2 All ER 763 at 765 per Scott LJ; *Re Greene* [1949] Ch. 333 at 340 per Harman J. Dicta supporting include: *Re Tavarone Mining Co., Prichard's Case* (1873) 8 Ch. 956 at 960 per Mellish LJ; *Eley* v. *Positive Government Security Life Assurance Co. Ltd.* (1875) 1 Ex. D 20 at 26 per Amphlett B, (1876) 1 Ex. D 88 at 89–90 per Lord Cairns L; *Browne* v. *La Trinidad* (1888) 37 Ch. D 1 at 12 and 15 per Cotton and Lindley JJ; *Wood* v. *Odessa Waterworks Co.* (1889) 42 Ch. D 636 at 642 per Stirling J; *Salmon* v. *Quinn and Axtens Ltd.* [1909] 1 Ch. 311 at 318 per Farwell LJ (but he qualified this by saying that the court would rarely enforce such a contract). See Wedderburn, 'Company Law—Effect of Articles as Contract—Remedy against Directors' (1958) *CLJ* 148; Gower, 'The Contractual Effect of Articles of Association' (1958) 21 *MLR* 401; Gower, 'Rayfield v. Hands—A Postscript and a Drop of Scotch' (1958) 21 *MLR* 657; Trotman, 'Articles of Association and Contracts' in Farrar, *Contemporary Issues in Company Law*, CCH (NZ), 1987, pp. 33–68 and the New Zealand cases cited therein, and 'The Enforcement of Partnership Agreements, Articles of Association and Shareholder Agreements' in Finn, *Equity and Commercial Relationships*, Law Book Co., 1987, pp. 92–107.

[147] [1901] 1 Ch. 279 and also the Australian decision *Peters' American Delicacy Ltd.* v. *Heath* (1938–1939) 61 CLR 457 at 480.     [148] [1960] Ch. 1.     [149] Ibid., at 9.

v. *Hands* appears to support the latter as his Lordship relied on *Clarke* v. *Dunraven* for his conclusion. Indeed, as Sealy[150] has observed:

[The] contractual basis is, of course, explicitly spelt out by the terms of s 78(1) of the Companies Act (Companies Act 1985 (UK), s 14(1) ), the 'statutory contract'. To my mind, however, it is easy to overstress the importance of this provision. I do not believe that the fundamentally associative nature of the English company *depends* upon the presence of this section in the Act. I would say that the section merely complements and reinforces the view that the Victorian judges would in any case have taken of the matter at common law. They might, to be sure, have disagreed over who had contracted with whom and in what terms but, statute or not, I have no doubt that they would all have agreed that there was a contract there—indeed, not just one, but a network of them; and this not merely because the contract, express or implied, was a favourite 19th-century analytical tool, but because from earliest memory there had been no other way of forming or joining any 'company' (in the broad sense that Lord Lindley and his contemporaries would have understood this term) than by making a contract.

A strong authority on this issue is the decision of the Full Court of the Supreme Court of Western Australia in *Gra-ham Australia Pty. Ltd.* v. *Perpetual Trustees WA Ltd.*.[151] In this case, a unitholder requested the manager to redeem his units immediately after the collapse of the stock market in October 1987. Under the then trust deed, the redemption price was based on the value of the assets seven days before the redemption request. The manager made no payment until after a meeting of unitholders which resolved to amend the trust deed provision so that the redemption price would be based on the current value of the asset. It was held that the power of a majority to amend the trust deed was part of the contract between members and between the manager and the unitholders and was wide enough to make amendments that would defeat vested or accrued rights of a unitholder. The company cases of *Allen* v. *Gold Reefs of West Africa Ltd.*[152] and *Peters' American Delicacy Co. Ltd.* v. *Heath*[153] were applied on the basis that both the unit trust deed and the articles have the same origin in the deed of settlement. Malcolm CJ said:

In my opinion all of the propositions [on amendment of articles stated in *Peters' American Delicacy Co. Ltd.* v. *Heath*] apart from the first which relates to the statutory power, apply equally to a trust deed for a unit trust as they did to a deed of settlement of the kind under which limited companies were once established. In the present case *the contract between the unitholders themselves and between the manager and the unitholders* contained provision for alteration of existing or

---

[150] 'The Enforcement of Partnership Agreements, Articles of Association and Shareholder Agreements' in Finn, *Equity and Commercial Relationships*, Law Book Co., 1987, pp. 92–107 at pp. 92–3.               [151] (1989) 1 WAR 65.               [152] [1900] 1 Ch. 656.
[153] (1939) 61 CLR 457.

accrued rights. Even if the alteration constituted a breach of an existing contract between the manager and any individual unitholder, such a breach would not invalidate the amendment. The fact that the alteration diminished, prejudiced or altered the rights of unitholders was not sufficient to prevent the alteration from being validly made.[154]

Thus, *Gra-ham Australia Pty. Ltd.* v. *Perpetual Trustees WA Ltd.*. recognized that the unit trust deed constituted a binding contract for otherwise the provision relating to the majority's power to amend the trust deed would not be binding on the redeeming unitholder.

The reasoning of Malcolm CJ,[155] however, may be questioned. His Honour relied on *Allen* but *Allen* was a case dealing with the contract between the company and the shareholder, not the contract between shareholders. It was held that an amendment of the articles to create a lien on the shares of a shareholder was effective. *British Equitable Assurance Co. Ltd.* v. *Baily*[156] was the deed of settlement company case cited to justify his Honour's reliance on company cases. There, the deed of settlement contained provisions for the making and alteration of by-laws by members, including by-laws relating to the allocation of profits in favour of participating policy holders. Under the policies that were issued the policy holders agreed to 'conform to and abide by the deed of settlement and by-laws . . . of the company in all respects'. It was held that amendments to the by-laws were binding on policy holders. Apparently, it was a case of the contractual effect of the deed of settlement on the unincorporated company and an outsider under a contract that incorporated the deed. Thus, these two cases do not directly support *Gra-ham Australia Pty. Ltd.* v. *Perpetual Trustees WA Ltd.* Much of the doubt might have been cleared up if his Honour had dealt with the question of the existence of a contract between all unitholders and examined the effect of *Clarke* v. *Dunraven*[157] and *Rayfield* v. *Hands*.[158]

*Clarke* v. *Dunraven*[159] was relied upon by Handley JA in *Elkington* v. *Moore Business Systems Australia Ltd.*[160] to support his opinion that there was a contractual relationship amongst unitholders. In this case, a clause in a unit trust deed incorporated the Companies (Acquisition of Shares) (NSW) Code and Regulations and 'any corresponding legislation or regulations which may from time to time replace or operate in substitution therefor'. The specific provisions of the Code in force when the trust deed

---

[154] At 81; emphasis supplied. The principles in *Allen* and *Peters' American Delicacy* have to be read in the light of *Gambotto* v. *WCP Ltd.* (1995) 182 CLR 432.
[155] With whom Nicholson J agreed (at 92). Pidgeon J gave judgment in terms similar to Malcolm CJ and agreed that 'one would look to the company cases and the building society cases to determine what restrictions there may be [on the power to modify the unit trust deed]' (at 91).          [156] [1906] AC 35.          [157] [1897] AC 59.
[158] [1958] 2 All ER 194.          [159] [1897] AC 59.          [160] (1994) 15 ACSR 292.

was executed required an offeror who acquired 90 per cent or more of the
shares subject to offers under a takeover scheme to acquire the shares of
any dissenting shareholders. An offeror who had acquired 98.59 per cent of
units sought to compulsorily acquire the remaining units according to this
clause. A minority unitholder sought injunctive and other relief to prevent
the compulsory acquisition of their units. The trustee and the manager
were not parties to the proceedings. The court held that such a clause was
valid and binding upon the appellant, a unitholder who had obtained his
units by transfer from an original unitholder. In respect of the appellant's
submission that there was no privity of contract between the offeror and
the minority unitholder, his Honour said:

[The appellant] relied upon the decision of Heerey J in *AF & ME Pty. Ltd.* v.
*Aveling*[161] for the proposition that the terms of the trust deed did not constitute or
evidence a contract binding on the unitholders between themselves. With respect
there may well be an implied consensual compact on the terms of the deed which
bound the unitholders for the time being.[162]

*Clarke* v. *Dunraven*[163] was cited to support his Honour.[164]

   *Aveling* also received criticism in another recent case, *West Merchant
Bank Ltd.* v. *Rural Agricultural Management Ltd.*[165] The facts of this case
were hardly distinguishable from *Aveling* except that this was an action
between a unitholder and the manager. Sheller JA[166] disagreed with
Heerey J in *Aveling* that the relevant restriction on acquisition of units by a
unitholder was not a promise. His Honour held that when the unitholder
applied for the issue of units it agreed with the manager to comply with all
provisions of the deed and that the manager was holding the benefit of this
promise for all unit holders.

   The position now is this. James LJ's view in *Smith* v. *Anderson*[167] was
that there was no contract amongst unitholders in the unit trust before his
Lordship. This was applied in *AF & ME Pty. Ltd.* v. *Aveling*.[168] On the

[161] (1994) 14 ACSR 499.                                     [162] Ibid., at 296.
[163] [1897] AC 59. *Macqueen* v. *Frackelton* (1909) 8 CLR 673 was also quoted.
[164] Arguably, Handley JA's comments on the contractual relationship between unitholders
and his rejection of *AF & ME Pty. Ltd.* v. *Aveling, supra,* can be regarded as obiter because
his Honour upheld the opinion of the court below that 'the appellant's units at all times were
subject to the power of compulsory acquisition conferred by [the deed] which formed an
integral and inseverable element in his property in those units' (ibid., at 296). This reasoning
is explained in clearer terms by Bryson J in the court below: 'The units are a species of
property created by the deed; by the whole of the deed and not by any particular part of it,
and their nature as property is created by and can be understood only from the whole of the
deed. They are trust interests, derive their existence from the trust and are conditioned by
whatever conditions the trust imposes on them.' (1994) 13 ACSR 342 at 350.
[165] Unreported, 4 Apr. 1996, NSWCA No. 40750/95. For a criticism of this decision see
Sin, 'Enforcing the Unit Trust Deed Amongst Unitholders' (1997) 15 C&SLJ 108.
[166] With whom Mahoney and Powell JAA agreed.              [167] *Supra.*
[168] *Supra.*

2. The Constitution of a Unit Trust

other hand, the interpretation of the particular clause in *Aveling* was rejected by a higher court and a contractual relationship was recognized in *Gra-ham Australia Pty. Ltd.* v. *Perpetual Trustees WA Ltd.*[169] and *Elkington* v. *Moore Business Systems Australia Ltd.*[170] Further, James LJ's view is very hard to reconcile with the reasoning in *Clarke* v. *Dunraven*[171] and in a number of cases on gifts to unincorporated groups, on the contractual nature of constitutions of unincorporated associations, on the contractual nature of articles of association.

## (6) A Single Multipartite Relationship

So far, the relationship analysis is at different levels of the unit trust relationships. If the starting-point is the angle of contract law, the unit trust deed is a single contract with three different parties or groups of parties.[172] In fact, trust deeds invariably provide that each unitholder is to be bound as if each has been a party. A typical provision will state:

This deed is binding on each unitholder *as if he had been a party to it and so had covenanted to be bound* by its provisions and had authorised and required the trustee and the manager to do all such acts and things as this deed may authorise require or permit them to do.[173]

Even without such a provision, the House of Lords decision of *Clarke* v. *Dunraven* is wide enough to support such a conclusion. Indeed, Malcolm CJ regarded the unit trust deed as 'the contract between the unitholders themselves and between the manager and the unitholders'.[174]

This multipartite contract is constitutive in nature. It defines the roles of the parties: the manager as the investment specialist, the trustee as the custodian of properties, and the unitholders as investors taking the risk. It defines the trust's objective. It also makes provisions for the creation, issue, redemption, and cancellation of units, investment of trust funds, register of unitholders, transfer and transmission of units, accounts, and audits, meetings and voting, and winding up of the scheme. It cannot be denied the trust deed[175] has the same function as the deed of a deed of

---

[169] *Supra.*      [170] *Supra.*      [171] *Supra.*

[172] There may be more than three parties if the parent companies of the trustee and the manager join in.

[173] Provision to this effect is mandatory for an authorized unit trust (the Financial Services (Regulated Schemes) Regulations 1991, Sch. 1, Part I). It is very common in other jurisdictions (e.g., *Australian Ency. F & P*, Vol. 3, p. 1060, cl. 47).

[174] See the quotation accompanying fn. 154, *supra. Quaere*, whether he would regard the trustee as a party if the issue arose.

[175] Together with the regulations made under the Financial Services Act 1986, in the case of authorized unit trusts.

settlement company, the articles of association of an incorporated company or the constitution of a club or an association. In each case, there are constituent elements of an organization involving the parties.[176]

## C. An Obligation Analysis

This section discusses the contractual nature of the unit trust obligations. The split of these obligations between the trustee and the manager is examined in chapter 4.[177]

### (1) Lewin's Definition

Keeton and Sheridan's 'relationship' definition has the advantage of highlighting that a trustee's duties are matched by corresponding rights[178] in the trust objects.[179] This echoes the philosophy behind the beneficiary principle that there must be someone to enforce the trustee's duties. Within this relationship, it cannot be denied that the centre point of our trust jurisprudence is founded upon the decision of the Chancellors to compel a trustee to do what conscience required him to do with respect to the property which was transferred to him. As Lewin[180] observes:

[t]he word 'trust' refers to the duty or aggregate accumulation of obligations that rest upon a person described as a trustee. The responsibilities are in relation to property held by him, or under his control. That property he will be compelled by a court in its equitable jurisdiction to administer in the manner lawfully prescribed by the trust instrument, or where there be no specific provision written or oral, or to the extent that such provision is invalid or lacking, in accordance with equitable principles.[181]

---

[176] The organizational character is examined in ch. 3.

[177] The 'split of trusteeship' between the trustee and the manager is analysed in terms of directory powers, veto powers, delegation powers, and advisory powers. Ch. 4 will analyse the fiduciary duties of both parties in relation to these powers.

[178] As Roxburgh J has observed in *Re Astor's Settlement Trusts* [1952] 1 Ch. 540 at 541–2: 'The typical case of a trust is one in which the legal owner of property is constrained by a court of equity so to deal with it as to give effect to the equitable rights of another . . . Prima facie, therefore, a trustee would not be expected to be subject to an equitable obligation unless there was somebody who could enforce a correlative equitable right.'

[179] With the anomalous exceptions of trusts for maintenance of animals, monuments, and graves and for the saying of masses and of the fact that charitable trusts are enforced by the Attorney General.

[180] *Lewin on Trusts*, 16th edn. by Mowbray, Sweet and Maxwell, 1964, p. 3.

[181] Similarly, *Underhill and Hayton* define a trust as 'an equitable obligation, binding a person (who is called a trustee) to deal with property over which he has control (which is called the trust property), for the benefit of persons (who are called the beneficiaries or cestuis que trust), of whom he may himself be one, and any one of whom may enforce the

Thus, the trustee is vested with not only the legal title to the trust property but also the responsibility of managing it in the interest of the beneficiaries. That responsibility gives a beneficiary an equitable right *in personam* against him for due administration.

## (2) Unit Trust Obligations: Centrality of the Manager

In a unit trust, management is vested in the manager, not the trustee.[182] In crude terms, there is a split of trusteeship between the trustee and the manager. But, subtly, the difference is more than that. The donative character of a private trust implies that the management power originates from a settlor in the trust instrument. In a unit trust, the power of management is derived from the contract to which the trustee and the manager are parties—the unit trust deed. From a commercial perspective, the unit trust is a financial product of the manager. It is part of its strategy of offering financial services. It has financial stakes in the venture, both in terms of revenue generated from its office as the manager and from its goodwill in general.

In *Parkes Management Ltd.* v. *Perpetual Trustee Co. Ltd.*,[183] this central position of the manager was recognized by the New South Wales Court of Appeal. Hope JA said:[184]

The manager was the source and origin of the trust, and subject to what might be regarded as supervision by the trustee, substantially carried out the trust. In effect, the manager was the entrepreneur of an investment scheme, which contemplated that both it, and those who contributed money to the scheme, should derive financial benefit. The appointment of a trustee is understandably required by statute in this case as a safeguard to ensure that the interests of the unit holders are maintained, but the manager also had this obligation, and in a sense also supervised the activities of the trustee. To the unit holders, the identity of the manager must have been a matter of considerable significance. To the manager, its office was the source of valuable rights.

---

obligation. Any act or neglect on the part of a trustee which is not authorised or excused by the terms of the trust instrument, or by law, is called a breach of trust.' (*Underhill and Hayton*, art. 1.) This definition was approved in *Green* v. *Russell* by Romer LJ [1959] 2 QB 226 at 241 and in *Re Marshall's Will Trusts* [1945] Ch. 217 at 219 by Cohen J. *Underhill and Hayton's* definition is also adopted by Pettit with the following added '. . . or for a charitable purpose, which may be enforced at the instance of the Attorney-General, or for some other purpose permitted by law though unenforceable' (Pettit, p. 23).

[182] The Financial Services (Regulated Schemes) Regulations 1991, reg. 7.02 *et seq.*

[183] (1977) CLC 29,545.

[184] *Supra*, at 29,551. His judgment was agreed to by Moffitt P and Mahoney JA. In *Elders Trustee and Executor Co. Ltd.* v. *EG Reeves Pty. Ltd.* (1987) 78 ALR 193 at 228, Gummow J also described the manager as 'the entrepreneur of the enterprise'.

Later in the judgment he also said:[185]

[The manager's] position in the whole scheme was central to that scheme and its removal in a very real sense changed in an important way the character of the scheme.

For as long as the unit trust is a going concern, the manager has assumed the trust's management function; it logically follows that the nature of trusteeship has changed. The trustee's role is one of ownership without the management responsibility which is vested in the trustee in a private trust.[186] How is this achieved? There is no question that the respective powers and responsibilities have been negotiated by the trustee and the manager prior to the execution of the trust deed. Of course, in the case of an authorized unit trust, such negotiation is within the regulatory framework of the Financial Services Act 1986 and its regulations. In this sense, the trust deed allocates the functional roles of the parties that provide investment services to the unitholders: the trustee as a custodian of the properties and the manager as investment decision maker. It is only when the unit trust is terminated that the trustee will assume all functions as a private trustee.[187]

The manager is not the title holder of the trust fund and its responsibilities to the unitholders, as beneficiaries of such fund, cannot fall within the definition of the trust. Whether they are fiduciary in nature is another issue. The point is: they must be primarily contractual in nature. Any breach on the part of the manager cannot be regarded as a breach of trust.[188]

In short, the unit trust deed alters the functional character of trusteeship by vesting in the manager the management functions which would otherwise be in the hand of a trustee. The trust is by nature an obligation respecting property derived from the donative wishes contained in the trust instrument. That obligation may be supplemented by rules of equity. But once we move out of the property-holding domain and into the provision of (investment) services on a consensual basis (which is what has happened in the process of hiving off the management function), the trust simply offers no satisfactory doctrinal explanation.

From a contractual perspective, the unit trust deed is a contract for

---

[185] *Supra*, at 29,554.

[186] From the perspective of a manager, it is appointing a trustee to carry out a custodian function. Conceptually, however, the emergence of the manager would also mean that the trustee has an oversight function over the manager. See the discussion in this section below.

[187] S. 2A(1), *ante*.

[188] Cf. the reference to breach of trust in *Underhill and Hayton's* definition of the trust: fn. 181, *supra*. Of course, the manager may be in breach of fiduciary duty—if it is a fiduciary in the circumstances.

(investment) services. Under this contract, the manager is providing the services of investing on behalf of others and the trustee is another party providing part of those services contemplated. This element of services cannot easily be squeezed into the concept of trusteeship, although in a sense a trustee in a private trust is also providing services to the settlor.[189] This is because the trust is in essence a property transfer; it is not a contractual agreement. Trust duties and beneficial rights are always defined with respect to the subject matter of the trust.

This is in fact an element of rigidity of the trust when it is compared in this context to the contract. A contract is a form of private law making where parties establish their own obligations.[190] It is a foundation for exchange of promises without any reference to any property. It is flexible enough to bring in parties who are not in a property relationship.[191] It is also flexible enough to let the parties select only some of the trustee's obligations that equity implies while at the same time to define new roles for the trustee resulting from the emergence of the manager.

Regulation 7.09 of the Financial Services (Regulated Schemes) Regulations 1991 provides that the trustee is under a duty to take reasonable care to ensure that the manager manages the scheme in accordance with the regulations and does not exceed its investment powers. Insofar as this regulation has been incorporated into the trust deed to which all unitholders have been deemed parties, it can be said that in the case of an authorized unit trust there is a contractual obligation owed to unitholders to supervise the manager. However, even in the absence of this specific statutory provision, case-law seems to recognize such a watchdog or oversight obligation.[192]

## D. A Rights Analysis

This section seeks to argue that rights of unitholders are contractual in nature. Chapter 5 will discuss the content of such rights and also the nature of units.[193]

---

[189] Which equity presumes to be gratuitous.

[190] Greig and Davis, p. 68.

[191] Such as the manager, banks (if units are linked to savings accounts or automatic teller machines), and insurance companies (if units are linked to insurance policies).

[192] This function is recognized by Young J in *The Application of Permanent Trustee Nominees (Canberra) Ltd.*, unreported, NSWSC (Eq. Div.) No. 4216 of 1985, 24 June 1985, citing *Parkes Management Ltd.* v. *Perpetual Trustee Co. Ltd.* (1977–1978) ACLC 29,545.

[193] Ch. 5 will suggest that a unit is a chose in action comprising a bundle of contractual and statutory rights and that, usually, a unit will not confer on its owner any interest in underlying assets while the trust is a going concern.

## (1) Story's Definition

When a court of equity enforces a trustee's obligation with respect to the property that has been transferred to him, the court does so in order to protect the beneficiary. Therefore, if the emphasis is on the converse of the obligations involved, as in *Story's Commentaries on Equity Jurisprudence*, it can be said that:

[a] trust, in the most enlarged sense in which that term is used in English Jurisprudence, may be defined to be an equitable right, title, or interest in property, real or personal, distinct from the legal ownership thereof.[194]

Because the trust makes possible the separation of legal ownership from its beneficial enjoyment, it is a device that can achieve collective ownership by a group. It is to this kind of use that the trust has been put in the unit trust. One of the advantages of the unit trust is diversification of assets and risks. It enables unitholders to pool their resources together to acquire assets of substantial size that would normally only be available to the rich. Risk is diversified as the trust can acquire a far greater number of different assets than an individual can. In a sense, therefore, a division of properties is possible through the unity of legal ownership in the person of the trustee.

The trust, as emphasized by Story, is an institution that fastens upon the trust assets. Beyond this, the trust cannot explain unit trust rights that arise otherwise.

## (2) Unitholders' Rights

At a collective level, the unit trust is a vehicle for collective investment which is an alternative to the company. Whilst beneficiaries are generally passive, there is ultimately a mechanism for collective decisions not dissimilar to its corporate counterparts.[195] The decisions reached are binding upon the trustee and the manager. Invariably, annual meetings and reporting requirements are provided in unit trust deeds.[196] The trust

---

[194] *Story's Commentaries on Equity Jurisprudence*, 13th edn. by Bigelow, Little, Brown & Co., 1886 (1988 reprint by Rothman & Co.), s. 964, approved by Brett LJ (with whom Bramwell LJ agreed) in *Wilson* v. *Lord Bury* (1880) 5 QBD 518 at 530.

[195] S. 2B(5) of this ch., *ante*.

[196] As in *Smith* v. *Anderson* (1880) 15 Ch. 247. Unitholders' meetings of an authorized unit trust may be convened under reg. 11.07 of the Financial Services (Regulated Schemes) Regulations 1991, but the powers of such meetings are limited to matters that are 'required or expressly contemplated by [the] regulations' to be resolved by members (reg. 11.08). Such matters are the removal of the manager (reg. 7.17), modification of trust deed (reg. 11.02), change of scheme particulars (reg. 11.04), amalgamation (reg. 11.05), and reconstruction (reg. 11.06).

deed or the regulations confer rights upon all unitholders collectively while the unit trust is a going concern. In a private trust, beneficiaries collectively hardly have any right beyond terminating the trust and calling for the transfer of all trust assets. If the trustee is carrying on business as the settlor has provided in the trust deed and if that business is carrying on profitably, beneficiaries do not have any right[197] over the management of the business if the business is to continue.[198] The reason is simply that the trustee is carrying out the wish of the settlor. In a unit trust, the contractual relationships provide the difference. Obviously, the rights which a unitholder may have against the manager are beyond any trust analysis.

At the level of each individual unitholder, the difference between units and a beneficiary's interest in a private trust is even greater. Units are a form of property in themselves. They are choses in action except that the manager invariably provides a ready market for their disposal. Each unit is, generally speaking, transferable on the register of unitholders.[199] For some close-end trusts overseas, units are also traded on the Stock Exchange. Units bear close resemblance to shares of companies. By contrast, beneficiaries of private trusts have interests in trust properties which are not readily marketable. The status of units as choses in action is achieved by contractual arrangements, primarily by the redemption provisions[200] and secondarily by the provision of a unit trust register as a means of transfers.[201]

## (3) The Manager's Rights

In the relationship analysis above, the trust cannot explain the relationships between the manager and other parties. Similarly, it cannot explain adequately the manager's rights either.

The rights of the manager in a unit trust scheme were examined in *Parkes Management Ltd.* v. *Perpetual Trustee Co. Ltd.*[202] in the context of the manager's standing to challenge the trustee's decision to require the

---

[197] As distinct from remedies.

[198] Save in the exceptional case where the settlor confers on the beneficiaries rights to interfere.

[199] In an authorized unit trust, a trustee has no discretion to refuse a transfer other than the very limited exceptions specified in reg. 6.12. The major exception is a transfer resulting in the transferor or the transferee holding below the minimum holding specified in the scheme particulars.

[200] For an authorized unit trust, this is provided by Part 4 (Pricing and dealing) of the Financial Services (Regulated Schemes) Regulations 1991.

[201] For an authorised unit trust, this is provided by Part 6 (Title and transfer) of the Financial Services (Regulated Schemes) Regulations 1991. A transfer on register takes effect by way of novation: ch. 5, s. 4, *post*.

[202] (1977–1978) ACLC 29,545.

manager to retire. In this case, the manager covenanted in the unit trust deed to retire 'if the trustee certifies in writing to the manager that it would be in the interest of the unitholders for the manager to retire'. This is the same provision required by the Department of Trade and Industry under the Prevention of Fraud (Investments) Act 1958[203] and is analogous to regulation 7.17.1(d) of the Financial Services (Regulated Schemes) Regulations 1991.[204] The New South Wales Court of Appeal held that the manager has standing to challenge the validity of the certificate issued by the trustee. As pointed out earlier, the office of the manager was recognized by Hope JA as 'the source of valuable rights'.[205] His Honour said:

It is submitted for the Trustee that it is only a beneficiary who can challenge the exercise by a trustee of a power upon any of the equitable grounds which have been described and that the Manager is not a beneficiary. There would appear to be three answers to this submission. Firstly, that the Manager was a beneficiary; secondly, that the provisions of cl. 20(1) of the Deed entitled the Manager to ensure that the Trustee exercised any power under the Deed bona fide without indirect motive, and with a fair consideration of the issues; and thirdly, that being a party to the Deed the Manager was entitled to challenge the certificate if the requirements of the relevant provision, on its proper construction, were not satisfied.[206]

His Honour's three answers to the submission by counsel were crucial to the case.[207] In support of the first answer, his Honour gave two reasons: the manager was entitled to remuneration out of the trust income and it held issued units which were not subscribed. If the manager held unissued units, it was holding those units *qua* a unitholder. The trust deed did nothing more than permitting the manager to be a unitholder. But it was never suggested by Parkes Management that it was suing in a capacity other than that of the manager. This reason therefore was a weak one.

The suggestion that remuneration constitutes an interest in the trust fund is an interesting one, but no authority was given by his Honour. Perhaps,

---

[203] Extracted in Day and Harris, pp. 159–66 at 166.

[204] Which provides that the manager shall be subject to removal by notice in writing given by the trustee if 'for good and sufficient reason the trustee is of the opinion and so states in writing that a change of manager is desirable in the interest of the holders'. However, under s. 82 (3) of the Financial Services Act 1986, the approval of the Secretary of State (now the Treasury) is required. It seems that, on the authority of *Parkes*, the decision of the trustee under reg. 7.17.1(d) may be challenged even though the approval of the Secretary of State has been obtained. Indeed, if reg. 7.17 is incorporated into the trust deed expressly (which is often the case) contractual remedies will be available. This point has not been tested in court.

[205] Text accompanying fn. 184, *ante*.

[206] Ibid., at 29,553. Both Moffitt P and Mahoney JA concurred.

[207] Arguably, these are very artificial: see ch. 3, s. 2C, *post*.

*Re Pooley*,[208] *Re Thorley*,[209] and *Re Duke of Norfolk's Settlement Trusts*[210] may support the proposition. In *Re Pooley*,[211] an attesting trustee under the will was held not entitled to any remuneration under an express provision of the will. The remuneration was treated as a legacy for the purpose of the Wills Act provision that precluded attesting witnesses from claiming under the will. In *Re Thorley*,[212] it was held that the trustees' emoluments for carrying on the testator's business were legacies subject to legacy duty. In *Re Duke of Norfolk's Settlement Trusts*, the question was whether the court has an inherent jurisdiction to increase the trustee's remuneration beyond that provided in an express provision of the trust. The Court of Appeal accepted that on the authorities of *Re Pooley* and *Re Thorley* remuneration constitutes a beneficial interest. However, it was held that such an interest was of a special kind that would not be subject to the principles of *Chapman* v. *Chapman*[213] and that the court has power under its inherent jurisdiction to increase or vary the amount of remuneration.

All these cases are cases on trustees. If they apply to the manager, the manager can be regarded as having an interest in the trust assets. However, the manager's remuneration will qualify as a beneficial interest in the unit trust assets only if the trust deed provides that such remuneration is to be paid out of the unit trust capital or income. If, on construction of the unit trust deed, the unitholders collectively are under a contractual obligation to pay the manager and payment out of the trust assets is only a means of payment, then it cannot be regarded as having trust interest in the assets.

Further, another important right of the manager is the front-loads added to the purchase and sale prices of units. This arises from provisions dealing with issue and redemption of units and also from those dealing with the pricing of units. These provisions impose contractual obligations on unitholders to follow the buy-sell arrangements and create reciprocal rights on the manager.

The second and third grounds given by Hope JA also support the view that the manager's interests are contractual. Clause 20(1) of the deed in *Parkes Management* provides that:

---

[208] (1888) 40 Ch. D 1.     [209] [1891] 2 Ch. 613.     [210] [1982] 1 Ch. 61.

[211] *Supra*; the same conclusion was reached in *Re Dunstan* [1931] VLR 222.

[212] *Supra*; the same conclusion was reached in *Re Knox* (1911) 30 NZLR 522.

[213] [1954] AC 429 which held that the court did not have an inherent jurisdiction to alter the terms of the trust in the interest of beneficiaries except in the limited cases of salvage, emergency, maintenance, and compromise. But a wider view of the court's inherent jurisdiction was taken by the New South Wales case of *Tickle* v. *Tickle* (1987) 10 NSWLR 581. The court, however, has statutory powers to approve variations on behalf of persons under incapacity: see *Underhill and Hayton*, art. 49, pp. 473–4.

20. The Trustee hereby covenants with the Manager and with the intent that the benefit of the said covenant shall enure not only to the Manager, but to the unit holders jointly and to each of them severally, that:—
(1) The Trustee will act continuously as such Trustee under the trusts herein set forth until such trusts are determined as herein provided or it has retired or been removed from the trusts in the manner herein provided and will exercise all due diligence and vigilance in carrying out its functions and duties and in watching the rights and interests of the holders of the interests to which the Deed relates.[214]

To his Honour, this clause 'points strongly to the special position and interest of the Manager in the whole venture and in the activities of the Trustee'.[215] It appears that the manager was a promisee holding the benefit of this covenant for itself as well as for the unitholders. The contractual covenants therefore were the source of the manager's rights. The third ground needs no further elaboration: parties to a contract can enforce the terms of the contract.

### (4) The Trustee's Rights

Now the rights of the trustee. The office of trusteeship is gratuitous[216] but express charging clauses in private trusts are valid, and very common in modern times. The unit trustee's remuneration therefore has a counterpart in the private trust. However, they are of different origins.

In *Re Duke of Norfolk's Settlement Trusts*,[217] Walton J, at first instance, held that the court has no power to vary an express charging clause because that was a contract between a settlor of a private trust and the trustee.[218] On appeal, however, Fox LJ regarded any contractual analysis as unreal because the trustee might have no knowledge of the trust at the time of execution by the settlor and might decline to act. The conclusion of his Lordship was:

. . . it seems to me to be quite unreal to regard [powers to charge remuneration] as contractual. So far as they derive from any order of the court they simply arise from the court's jurisdiction and so far as they derive from the trust instrument itself they derive from the settlor's power to direct how his property should be dealt with'.[219]

His Lordship therefore held that the court has power to vary express charging clauses.

---

[214] *Underhill and Hayton*, at 29,550.
[215] Ibid., at 29,553, when elaborating on the second ground.
[216] *Robinson* v. *Pett* (1734) 3 P Wms. 249; *Underhill and Hayton*, art. 60, pp. 639 *et seq.*
[217] [1982] 1 Ch. 61.
[218] The other reason was that *Chapman*, *supra*, precluded the court from varying such a clause. This, as discussed above, was also rejected by the Court of Appeal.
[219] [1982] 1 Ch. 61 at 77. Brightman LJ delivered a concurring judgment and Cumming-Bruce LJ agreed.

It has already been said that the trust in the unit trust is a contractual creation and that there is no settlor. The amount of the remuneration is a result of contractual negotiation between the manager and the trustee and is accepted by unitholders as part of the unit trust deed[220] by which they agreed to be bound. Therefore, the proper analogy is to the case where remuneration is payable by virtue of a contract made between the trustee and the beneficiaries.[221] Such contracts for remuneration have always been enforceable as ordinary contracts so long as the beneficiaries are *sui juris*,[222] fully informed, and not subject to any undue influence.[223]

If the agreement as to remuneration is analogous to a contract between a trustee of a private trust and beneficiaries, the reasoning of the Court of Appeal in *Re Duke of Norfolk's Settlement Trusts*[224] does not apply to unit trusts. Indeed, the reasoning of Walton J, at first instance, that courts have no jurisdiction to vary contracts applies.

In *Application of Trust Company of Australia re Barclays Commercial Property Trust*,[225] a trustee of a unit trust made an *ex parte* application for an order that the trustee be authorized to pay $90,000 out of the trust fund to the trustee in addition to the remuneration specified in the unit trust deed on the basis of additional work done. Waddell CJ in Equity applied *Re Duke of Norfolk's Settlement Trusts* without any analysis. This is particularly surprising since it was admitted by the trustee that the same result could be achieved by amending the unit trust deed which, under its terms, required a special resolution in a meeting of unitholders. Based on the contractual analysis above, it is submitted that this case was wrongly decided.[226]

### E. Conclusion: A Trust Embedded on a Contract

To sum up, a unit trust deed is a contract that establishes an investment scheme. It makes provision for rights and obligations on a consensual

---

[220] For an authorized unit trust, the amount is actually stated in the scheme particulars but the trust deed usually makes provision to this effect: see reg. 8.02 and reg. 8.03 of the Financial Services (Regulated Schemes) Regulations 1991.

[221] *Re Sherwood* (1840) 3 Beav. 338; *Douglas* v. *Archbutt* (1858) 2 De G & J 148; *Underhill and Hayton*, art. 60(b), p. 639.

[222] *Re McLean* [1937] NZLR 100; *Re Gambling* [1966] SASR 134.

[223] *Ayliffe* v. *Murray* (1740) 2 Atk. 58; *Re Darling* [1925] SASR 262.

[224] [1982] 1 Ch. 61.

[225] Unreported, NSWSC (Eq. Div.) No. 1033 of 1993, 19 Mar. 1993.

[226] The judgment of his Honour was mainly concerned with the appropriateness of an *ex parte* application. The only reason for not calling a meeting of unitholders and for not making an *inter parte* application joining a defendant to represent unitholders was costs, as estimated by the applicant. Although his Honour emphasized that the circumstances of the case were unusual, it is submitted that this decision was wrongly decided also in this respect. In effect, the unitholders had paid more than they had contractually agreed and without their knowledge. If their rights were affected, they ought to have been joined as parties.

basis. As part of that contract, it employs the trust as a holding device. With the trust, its trust incidents follow. Inevitably, some of those incidents may not be compatible with the mutual intentions of the parties. In this respect, therefore, the trust deed makes provisions for alteration of those trust incidents, in addition to its scheme provisions.

Despite some occasional observations against the trust being introduced into commercial transactions,[227] it appears that there is no doctrinal impediment for the trust to be embedded on the contract. As Maitland has pointed out in his 'Trust and Corporation',[228] the Inns of Court, with its constitution taking shape before 1422,[229] Lloyds, doing business in 1720,[230] the London Stock Exchange, with its deed of settlement drawn up in 1802,[231] and the Jockey Club, the 'most important and august tribunal' in England,[232] have all 'lived behind the trustee wall'.[233] To him, the original

---

[227] Bramwell LJ in *New Zealand and Australian Land Co.* v. *Watson* (1881) 7 QBD 374 at 382 said: '. . . I do not desire to find fault with the various intricacies and doctrines connected with trusts, but I should be very sorry to see them introduced into commercial transactions . . .' This dictum was adopted by Channel J in *Henry* v. *Hammond* [1913] 2 KB 515. In *Neste Oy* v. *Lloyds plc* [1983] 2 Lloyd's Rep. 658 at 665, Bingham J also shared this 'general disinclination . . . to see the intricacies and doctrines connected with trusts introduced into everyday commercial transactions'. Their views were also shared by Meagher JA in *Walker* v. *Corboy* (1990) 19 NSWLR 382 at 439. There is also no lacking of academics of same sentiment. Goodhart and Jones refer to the *Quistclose* trusts and *Romalpa* clauses as 'the infiltration of equitable doctrine' ('The Infiltration of Equitable Doctrine into English Commercial Law' (1980) 43 *MLR* 489). Heydon, Gummow and Austin, *Cases and Materials on Equity and Trusts*, 4th edn., Butterworths Australia, 1993, para. 2316 also said the combination of trust and contract is conceptually undesirable. Similarly, the court was against the imposition of a fiduciary relationship on the contract in such a way as to alter the operation which the contract was intended to have according to its true construction (*Hospital Products Ltd.* v. *US Surgical Corporation* (1984) 156 CLR 41 at 97 per Mason J and *Kelly* v. *Cooper* [1993] AC 205 at 215 per Lord Browne-Wilkinson) or to achieve priority over other creditors (*Re Goldcorp Exchange Ltd.* [1994] 2 All ER 806) or to obtain proprietary remedy (*Westdeutsche Landesbank Girozentrale* v. *Islington LBC* [1996] 2 WLR 802). Perhaps, the true approach is that stated by Priestley JA in *Walker* v. *Corboy* (1990)19 NSWLR 382 at 386: 'It seems to me to be prudent not to approach the question whether equitable doctrines are applicable in a commercial situation with the thought in mind that one should be disinclined to give a positive answer to the question. The question simply is, do the particular circumstances attract equitable rules. There is no reason to regret one answer rather than the other. If there are express agreements between parties to a commercial transaction, or a series of commercial transactions, requiring the application of equitable rules for their working out, then it is difficult to see that commercial life will be any the worse for those rules, which in one very real sense are as much legal rules as are common law rules, being applied. In situations where there is no express agreement, then ultimately whether a court will apply equitable rules will depend upon the court's understanding of the expectations of the parties implicit in their dealings with one another in the commercial milieu in which the particular dispute has arisen. It is to these areas that the court's factual and evacuative attention should be directed and upon which decision should be based.'

[228] Fisher, *The Collected Papers of F. W. Maitland*, Vol. III, Cambridge UP, 1911 (William S. Hein reprint, Buffalo, 1981) pp. 321–404.                    [229] Ibid., p. 370.

[230] Ibid., p. 372.                    [231] Ibid., p. 373.                    [232] Ibid., p. 376.

[233] Ibid., p. 369, meaning all properties are owned by trustees.

members are owners in equity of the properties of such unincorporated bodies—because a trust for future members would infringe the rule against perpetuities—but they have contracted to observe certain rules that make their ownership in equity a very strange kind: one that is inalienable and not subject to creditors' execution, that ceases on bankruptcy, non-payment of fees or expulsion, that diminishes in value when a new member is elected, and that does not entitle him to partition.[234]

Interestingly, conclusions similar to Maitland's analysis were reached in recent cases on the construction of gifts to unincorporated bodies.[235] In these cases, the court held that members of unincorporated groups were in contractual relationships and that gifts to such groups were valid as out-and-out gifts to their present members subject to such contracts. It was recognized that the treasurer or officer holding the association's assets will be holding on a bare trust for all members subject to the contract, which theoretically may specify their immediate division.[236]

A trust of assets may also be found in provisions of partnership agreements. It was also used in deeds of settlement of unincorporated companies.[237]

Besides unincorporated bodies, trusts are also used in many types of contracts and have been held valid. For example, a supplier's contract may provide for the title to goods unsold by its buyer to remain in the supplier and for the proceeds of sale of goods sold by its buyer to be held separately on trust for itself until it has received payment in full for the goods

---

[234] Ibid., 377–8. According to Maitland, after a fresh election, there is a fresh contract between the new member and the old member.

[235] *Re Recher's Will Trusts* [1972] Ch. 526; *Re Goodson* [1971] VR 801; *Re Lipinski's Will Trusts* [1976] Ch. 235; *Re Bucks. Constabulary Widows' and Orphans' Fund Friendly Society (No. 2)* [1979] 1 All ER 623; *Universe Tankships Inc. of Monrovia* v. *International Transport Workers Federation Conservative* [1983] 1 AC 366; *News Group Newspapers Ltd.* v *SOGAT 1982* [1986] ICR 716.

[236] The position was explained by Cross J in *Neville Estates Ltd.* v. *Madden* [1962] Ch. 832 at 849: '[A gift to an unincorporated association] may be a gift to the existing members not as joint tenants, but subject to their respective contractual rights and liabilities towards one another as members of the association. In such a case a member cannot sever his share. It will accrue to the other members on his death or resignation, even though such members include persons who became members after the gift took effect. If this is the effect of the gift, it will not be open to objection on the score of perpetuity or uncertainty unless there is something in its terms or circumstances or in the rules of the association which precludes the members at any given time from dividing the subject of the gift between them on the footing that they are solely entitled to it in equity.'

[237] In fact, some early cases had held that the company was a trustee for shareholders. The leading case was *Bligh* v. *Brent* (1837) 2 Y & C Ex. 268, which also held that shares did not confer interest in assets of the company.

supplied.[238] It may also exist in an agency contract,[239] a loan agreement[240] or a contract for subscription of shares.[241] Indeed, there is no limit to arrangements involving the combination of contract and trust. And there is also no doctrinal objection. In rejecting counsel's submission that a loan contract cannot coexist with a trust, Lord Wilberforce said in *Barclays Bank* v. *Quistclose Investments Ltd.*:[242]

> There is surely no difficulty in recognising the co-existence in one transaction of legal and equitable rights and remedies . . . I can appreciate no reason why the flexible interplay of law and equity cannot let in these practical arrangements, and other variations if desired: it would be to the discredit of both systems if they could not.

Given the generality of the language used by Lord Wilberforce, there is no reason why his comments are not of general application and are limited to the specific loan situation under consideration in that case.[243]

### 3. IMPLICATIONS AND OBSERVATIONS

### A. Introduction: Trust Rules and Property Law

Some brief conclusions can be drawn from the analysis in the last two parts.

We have examined the trust rules relating to the existence of the trust and have seen how difficult some of them are to fit in the unit trust milieu. The difficulty arises principally from the donative quality of the trust intention and the fact that many trust rules presuppose this quality.

We have also used trust definitions by various jurists as tools for analysing the terms of the unit trust deeds from the angles of relationship, obligations, and rights. These three facets will receive further elaborations in ensuing chapters.[244] It is debatable which definition best describes the trust concept. But, whatever that may be, ultimately it is a matter of emphasis and personal predilection and is beyond the purpose of this work.

---

[238] *Aluminium Industrie Vaassen BV* v. *Romalpa Aluminium Ltd.* [1976] 2 All ER 552. But this type of contractual provision has limitations: *Clough Mill Ltd.* v. *Martin* [1984] 3 All ER 982; *Re Bond Worth Ltd.* [1980] Ch. 228.

[239] *Stephens Travel Service International Pty. Ltd. (Receivers and Managers Appointed)* v. *Qantas Airways Ltd.* (1988) 13 NSWLR 331.

[240] *Barclays Bank Ltd.* v. *Quistclose Investments Ltd.* [1970] AC 567.

[241] *Re Nanwa Gold Mines Ltd.* [1955] 1 WLR 1080; *Foreman* v. *Hazard* [1984] 1 NZLR 586.

[242] [1970] AC 567 at 580–1.

[243] *Stephens Travel Service International Pty. Ltd. (Receivers and Managers Appointed)* v. *Qantas Airways Ltd.* (1988) 13 NSWLR 331 at 341, per Hope JA.

[244] Being chs. 3, 4, and 5 respectively.

However, the linking point of all these definitions and the 'vein' of the trust concept is the equitable conception of property. It is not disputable that the trust relationship is a relationship respecting property, that the trustee's obligation is with respect to property, and that the rights of beneficiaries relate to the trust property. The trust, having originated from feudal uses of land, followed closely and adapted itself to changes in forms of property brought about by economic and social changes, such as the development of stocks, shares, bonds, and other intangible personal property. This is reflected in the changes in the composition of the trust fund and in the perception of the trust as a means to preserve value rather than specific assets.[245] The essence of the trust is simply that it is a means to achieve fragmentation of ownership (both between different generations and amongst the same generation) as well as collective ownership.

Fragmentation of ownership is achieved in a private trust by a settlor transferring his property to the trustee who holds for the benefit of a number of beneficial 'transferees'. The trust channels fragments of proprietary interests to beneficiaries. Between the settlor and the beneficiaries, the trust is a property transfer. It is logical that the trust is used as a gift device.

If one diverts the focus to the trustee and the confidence reposed in him, it is not inappropriate to suggest that the trust is a holding device. Obviously, it is the office of trusteeship that enables property to be held for different individuals. This holding function is an essential ingredient to the trust's achievement of being able to channel proprietary interests to succeeding generations. This temporal ability to hold property for generations raises the possibility of property being withheld from circulation in society and, as a consequence, brings property law rules on alienation to the trust arena.

It is the holding function of the trust, rather than its transfer function, which is seized upon by the unit trust. Of course, the trust has a long history of being used as a holding device for a variety of commercial and social purposes.[246] In the unit trust, as explained before, there is no element of gift and the transfer function is absent. Instead, it is a consensual transaction that uses the trust to achieve collective ownership. In the private trust, it is a 'downward' transfer to beneficiaries in order to achieve fragmentation of ownership. In the unit trust, it is an 'upward' transfer from beneficiaries themselves to the trustee in order to achieve collective ownership. From a functional perspective, therefore, the absence of the settlor is easy to understand: if there is no transfer function,

---

[245] For the evolution of this change, see Chesterman, 'Family Settlements on Trust: Landowners and the Rising Bourgeoisie' in Rubin and Sugarman (eds.), *Law, Economy and Society, 1750–1914: Essays in the History of English Law*, Professional Books, 1984, pp. 124–67. [246] See s. 2E of this ch., *ante.*

there is no transferor—the settlor. It is not correct to say that in the unit trust the settlors and the beneficiaries are the same persons; the true picture is that there is no settlor and the trustee contracts to hold the property under the contract amongst the manager, the beneficiaries, and the trustee.

A contract is a consensual transaction and does not as such involve any transfer. The contractual character and lack of transfer function in the unit trust bring into question the applicability to it of many property rules that have been applied to the trust. These include rules relating to perpetuities, the rule in *Saunders* v. *Vautier*, and resulting trusts.

## B. Rules Relating to Perpetuities and Alienation

A consistent policy of property law over the centuries has been to prevent property from being unnecessarily tied up and so removed from commerce. There are two ways in which a settlor of a private trust may offend this policy. The first is by creating a succession of future interests and so postponing to a remote period the time when the property will vest in a person for an absolute interest. The other is by imposing a restraint upon the beneficiary's ability to alienate his interest.

### (1) Remoteness of Vesting[247]

The classic case-law position is stated by Gray: '[n]o interest is good unless it must vest, if at all, not later than twenty-one years after some life in being at the creation of the interest'.[248] The rule has been modified by the Perpetuities and Accumulations Act 1964.[249] It is generally perceived that

---

[247] See generally, Ford, 'Unit Trusts' (1960) 23 *MLR* 129 at 137–8 (criticized by Jacobs, p. 68, fn. 18; *Underhill and Hayton*, art. 11, pp. 165 *et seq.*; Megarry and Wade, pp. 240 *et seq.*; Morris and Leach, *The Rule Against Perpetuities*, 2nd edn., Stevens, 1962; Maudsley, *The Modern Law of Perpetuities*, Butterworths, 1979; Sappideen and Butt, *The Perpetuities Act 1984*, Law Book Co., 1986.

[248] J. C. Gray, *The Rule against Perpetuities*, 4th edn., by R. Gray, Little, Brown & Co., 1942, s. 2.

[249] 'Under the Perpetuities and Accumulations Act 1964, effective as of 16 July 1964 for instruments taking effect on or after that date (not being the exercise of a special power contained in a pre-16 July 1964 trust), it is possible to wait and see what actually happens until it becomes absolutely clear that a future interest is certain to vest outside the perpetuity period and only then is the interest void and unless it can be saved by application of the statutory class-closing rules in section 4 of the Act or by section 5 dealing with the unborn widow problem. The Act also replaces casually relevant lives by a list of statutory lives in being and allows a specific number of years not exceeding eighty to be chosen as the perpetuity period so long as expressly specified in that behalf. . . . Only when a future interest is void under the common law rule against remoteness is there to be applied the "wait and see" provisions and the statutory lives provisions of the 1964 Act.' *Underhill and Hayton*, p. 168.

the rule limits the duration of the unit trust scheme and leads to adoption of the royal lives perpetuity clause by unit trust deed:

The trust shall be deemed to have commenced on the date of this deed and unless determined pursuant to any other provision of this deed shall determine on the date being one day before the twenty-first anniversary of the death of the last survivor of the lineal descendants of His Late Majesty, King George VI living at the date of this deed.[250]

It is submitted that there is in fact no legal restriction on the duration of a unit trust scheme. This is for two reasons. In the first place, within the operation of the rule itself, an operating unit trust scheme does not infringe the rule because there will be no vesting outside the perpetuity period.[251] Secondly and more fundamentally, it is submitted that the rule does not apply to unit trusts at all, by reason of the contractual nature of the unit trust scheme.

First, assuming the rule does apply to unit trust schemes, there is no infringement. The rule is not a rule against a duration longer than the perpetuity period; it is satisfied if all interests vest within the perpetuity period. It is concerned with the commencement of interests. A unit trust scheme can be longer than the perpetuity period if all interests are vested in possession within the period. A new unitholder who subscribes for units will have his interests vested in possession the moment when his units are issued. Once his interests are vested in possession, the rule is satisfied. Through successive transfers, a transferee may acquire his status as such outside the perpetuity period; but this is irrelevant because that transferee is acquiring a vested interest. In relation to close-end trusts,[252] this position is supported by the classic statement of Barker J in the Massachusetts business trust case of *Howe* v. *Morse*:[253]

The [business] trust involves no future limitations, no restraint upon alienation, and no accumulation either of income or of principal. The provisions by which the trust fund may be at some time held for the benefit of persons not shareholders at its inception, and who may become such at a period more remote than that allowed by the rule, are not future limitations made by the trust deed, in the sense in which the word 'limitation' is used in speaking of the operation of the rule. If there shall ever

---

[250] Another common practice is to use the statutory 80-year perpetuity period: 'The trust shall be deemed to have commenced on the date of this Deed and subject to the provisions of this Deed shall determine eighty years after the date of this Deed.' A provision as to the duration of an authorized unit trust is optional: the Financial Services (Regulated Schemes) Regulations 1991, Sch. 1, Part II.

[251] Even in the absence of a perpetuity clause.

[252] It is not possible for close-end unit trusts to be authorized under the Financial Services (Regulated Schemes) Regulations 1991 but a single property trust may take the form of a close-end trust.

[253] 55 NE 213 at 213–14 (1899).

be a shareholder other than those in which the whole equitable estate was absolutely vested at the inception of the trust, that shareholder will not take his interest by virtue of a limitation in the trust deed, but because of his succession, by virtue of the general principles of law, to the property of the original shareholder. The new shareholder, with reference to the rule, is in the same situation as a person who, after the expiration of all lives which were in being when a fee or an estate tail was created, and of a further period of 21 years, takes the fee by the operation of the law which makes property vendible by, or descendible from the owner, and not by virtue of a limitation in the instrument which created the fee. The entire ownership is never for a moment uncertain nor unvested, and at every moment each owner can freely dispose of his property, and at each moment it can be transferred to his creditor by the ordinary processes of the law, and at each moment the trust can be terminated at the will of the owners of the equitable interest.

Thus, for close-end funds with all units issued at the commencement of the unit trust scheme, the rule is not infringed.

Perhaps the real challenge comes with the open-ended trusts where authorized unit trusts are most typical.[254] Here, from time to time, units are created, issued, redeemed, and cancelled as may be necessary. Ford[255] suggests that in such circumstance 'there is a possibility of a nomination outside a relevant perpetuity period so that vesting is postponed'. However, this remains arguable. This is because at all times of the life of the unit trust, all interests are vested in possession; no interest in the existing unit trust fund can be said to have any possibility of being vested in future. At the moment when a new unitholder subscribes for units, the manager is not directing the trustee to exercise a power of appointment of existing interests in the trust. There is no future interest in the existing trust fund to which the rule applies. The new unitholder subscribing for units is transferring his own assets, the subscription money, into the trust. Before any new unit is being subscribed for, there is no property in the unit trust being tied up; all interests are vested. So far as the subscribing unitholder is concerned, the question of tying up his property cannot arise until he subscribes for units, but when he subscribes for units his interests are vested in possession immediately. The rule thus is not infringed.

The second submission is that the rule of remoteness of vesting does not apply to contract. The reality is that the unit trust deed is a contract and the holding of assets by a trustee is only part of that scheme. A unit, like a share, comprises a bundle of contractual rights.

In Gray, it is stated that '[t]he Rule against Perpetuities concerns rights

---

[254] If units are bought back by the manager, no perpetuity problem arises for the reasons given by Barker J in *Howe* v. *Morse, supra.*

[255] Ford, 'The Unit Trust as a Production Joint Venturer' [1985] *AMPLA Yearbook* 1 at 2; A similar view is shared by the Companies and Securities Law Review Committee, *Prescribed Interests*, Discussion Paper No. 6, 1987, p. 107.

of property only and does not affect the making of contracts which do not create rights of property'.[256] Morris and Leach also say: 'The Rule against Perpetuities is a doctrine of the law of property, not of the law of contract. Thus, generally speaking, neither the Rule against Perpetuities nor any related rule invalidates a contract calling for payment, even contingent payment, beyond the perpetuity period.'[257] Both texts contain numerous cases to support the non-application of the rule to contract. But of course the line between contract and property is more easily said than drawn. A contract to buy land creates an interest in land; so do restrictive covenants touching and concerning land. So, the position regarding the contractual exception to the perpetuity rule needs a deeper analysis.

Contracts primarily create personal obligations and are therefore not subject to the rule against perpetuities. A new unitholder, whether he subscribes for units or is a transferee,[258] is a contracting party with the manager, the trustee, and other unitholders. As a contracting party, he cannot be heard to say that he is not bound by the contract on the ground of perpetuity. Insofar as the unit trust is a going concern, the primary rights in the units are in terms of enforcing the agreements of the manager and the trustee to pay the redemption price and to perform their respective duties of investment and of supervision.[259] Those covenants are personal obligations.

In *Walsh* v. *Secretary of State for India*,[260] the House of Lords held that a personal obligation to pay is not subject to the rule. In this case, a person transferred funds to the directors of the East India Company to set up a trust with the directors as trustees providing pensions for disabled soldiers of the company and the company covenanted to repay to him such monies if the company should discontinue its military force. That happened eighty-eight years later. It was held that the covenant was enforceable. Lord Westbury explained:

The obligation of the East India Company is not an obligation in the nature of a duty of retransfer . . . but it is a common personal contract entered into by the East India Company, not to pay out of any specific fund—not to render back any definite trust security—but, out of its general revenues, if a certain event should happen, to repay the representatives of the [donor].[261]

---

[256] Gray, *supra*, s. 329.

[257] Morris and Leach, *supra*, p. 219; see also Megarry and Wade, pp. 287–92.

[258] Transfer of units takes the form of novation: see ch. 5, s. 4B, *post*.

[259] This is because the primary trust is subject to the terms of the contract and contractual rights override trust rights: see s. 2A of this ch., *ante*.

[260] (1863) 10 HL Cas. 367. See also *Witham* v. *Vane* (1883), reported in Challis, *The Law of Real Property*, 3rd edn., 1911, p. 440; *Keppell* v. *Bailey* (1843) 2 My. & K 517 at 527; *South Eastern Ry. Co.* v. *Associated Portland Cement Manufacturers (1900) Ltd.* [1910] 1 Ch. 12; *Sharpe* v. *Durrant* (1911) 55 SJ 423; *Hutton* v. *Watling* [1948] Ch. 26.

[261] Ibid., at 379.

A stronger case is the decision of Farwell J in *Borland's Trustee* v. *Steel Brothers & Co. Ltd.*[262] A company's articles of association provided that a shareholder should, upon demand, transfer his shares upon certain terms and to certain persons. Farwell J held that a share was not a sum of money settled by the shareholder but was an interest measured by a sum of money and made up of various rights contained in the contract, including the right to a sum of money of a more or less amount. As will be seen later, this statement is an extension of a long series of cases holding that shareholders in unincorporated deed of settlement companies did not have an interest in the underlying assets. This is a characteristic shared by units. Farwell J further held that the perpetuity rule has no application to the relevant article because incidents making up shares are contractual in nature. If a unit trust deed is also contractual in nature, Farwell J's reasoning below equally applies. He said:

. . . [I]n my opinion the rule against perpetuity has no application whatever to personal contracts. If authority is necessary for that, the case of *Witham* v. *Vane*[263] is a direct authority of the House of Lords; and to my mind an even stronger case is that of *Walsh* v. *Secretary of State for India.* . . . I have said that these articles are nothing more or less than a personal contract between Mr Borland and the other shareholders in the company. . . . Mr Borland was one of the original shareholders, and he and his trustee in bankruptcy are bound by his own contract. I do not know that I am concerned to consider the case of other shareholders who come in afterwards; but if I am, *the answer so far as they are concerned is that each of them on coming in executes a deed of transfer which, in the terms in which it is executed, makes him liable to all the provisions of the original articles. Mr Borland cannot be heard to say there is any repugnancy or perpetuity in the covenant he has entered into*[264]
. . .

Following the reasoning of Farwell J, an investor subscribing for units is bound by the terms of the trust deed as an original contracting party. A transferee is also a contracting party by reason of the execution of a transfer form.[265] As contracting parties they 'cannot be heard to say there is any repugnancy or perpetuity in the covenant he has entered into'.[266]

When a unit trust scheme is terminated, a bare trust or a trust for sale may come into existence (under the termination clause).[267] The condition precedent to the existence of this trust is the termination of the unit trust scheme. Hence, it does not exist at all when the unit trust scheme is an operating one. This trust is no different from an ordinary private trust as the contractual provisions have already been terminated. It will be subject

---

[262] [1901] 1 Ch. 279.                                   [263] *Supra.*
[264] *Supra*, at 289–90; emphasis supplied.
[265] This takes the form of a novation: ch. 5, s. 4B, *post.*
[266] Per Farwell J, *supra.*          [267] See s. 2A of this ch. *ante.*

to the perpetuity rule but, at this point in time, all interests are vested in the unitholders who together may terminate the trust at any time.

## (2) Accumulations[268]

An accumulation of income can be contrary to the common law, as offending against the rule against remoteness. It may also offend the statutory limitations on the time for which an accumulation may continue as laid down in sections 164–6 of the Law of Property Act 1925.[269] The issue here concerns the power of the manager to direct the trustee in unit trusts to accumulate income from investments.[270]

Section 164(1) of the Law of Property Act 1925 provides that:

No person may by any instrument or otherwise settle or dispose of any property in such manner that the income thereof shall . . . be wholly or partially accumulated for any longer period than one of [the relevant accumulation periods]. In every case where any accumulation is directed otherwise than as aforesaid, the direction shall (save as hereinafter mentioned) be void; and the income of the property directed to be accumulated shall, so long as the same is directed to be accumulated contrary to this section, go to and be received by the person or persons who would have been entitled thereto if such accumulation had not been directed.

In *Bassil* v. *Lister*,[271] a testator directed to pay out of the rents and income of his property the premium upon a policy of insurance effected by him on the life of another. It was held that such direction was valid for the whole life of the insured and was not an accumulation subject to the Thellusson Act, the predecessor of section 164. Turner VC considered the origin of the statute to be against the direction of Thellusson in his will that his property to be invested in land and the rents and profits of the land was to be accumulated.[272] In his view, the law was against dispositions of property for accumulation of rents, profits, and income, *qua* rents, profits, and income, beyond the prescribed period and not dispositions having reference to bargains or contracts entered into for other purposes than the mere purpose of accumulation.[273] A payment of insurance premiums,

---

[268] See generally, Ford, 'Unit Trusts' (1960) 23 *MLR* 129 at 138–40; Megarry and Wade, pp. 300 *et seq.*; Morris and Leach, *supra*, ch. 11; Maudsley, *supra*, ch. 7; *Underhill and Hayton*, art. 11(1)(b), pp. 179 *et seq.*; *Theobald on Wills*, 15th edn., by Clark, Sweet and Maxwell, 1993, pp. 631–8.

[269] Which are derived from the Thellusson Act, 39 & 40 Geo. 3, c. 98. This Act was enacted in response to the case of *Thellusson* v. *Woodford* (1805) 11 Ves. 112 which was seen as permitting unreasonably wide powers for settlors and testators.

[270] The accumulation clause in *Re AEG Unit Trust (Managers) Ltd.'s Deed* [1957] 1 Ch. 415 being an example. For authorized unit trusts, see reg. 9.05 of the Financial Services (Regulated Schemes) Regulations 1991.   [271] (1851) 9 Hare 177.

[272] Obviously, a very narrow construction was placed by his Lordship.

[273] Ibid., at 181 and 183.

which would become part of the general fund of the insurance company, was not an accumulation.

*Bassil* v. *Lister* was applied to the provisions for accumulation of income in the unit trust deed in *Re AEG Unit Trust (Managers) Ltd.'s Deed.*[274] In this case, a unit trust deed provided that as soon as the amount of net income became available for distribution to unitholders in respect of any accounting period, the balance after distribution, if any, should be added to the capital and should thereupon cease to be available for distribution. Wynn-Parry J held that the unitholders did not 'settle' or 'dispose of' property within the meaning of section 164 of the Law of Property Act 1925.[275] Nor did the transaction fall within the mischief of that provision. His Lordship did not analyse the contractual nature explicitly but many passages of Turner VC in *Bassil* v. *Lister*[276] were cited to support the exclusion of the unit trust from the statutory accumulation provisions. Therefore, it can be inferred that his Lordship has taken the view that the contractual nature excluded the statutory provisions.[277]

### (3) Restraints on Alienation

Trusts which impose restrictions on the alienation of property that has once been given absolutely to the beneficiary are void.[278] This is because such restrictions are inconsistent with the ownership of the property given.

In general, unit trusts do not often restrict the right of unitholders to transfer to any person. This is reflected in regulation 6.12 of the Financial Services (Regulated Schemes) Regulations 1991 which applies to authorized unit trusts. That regulation contemplates minimum holding requirements, pension schemes and charitable schemes to be the main reasons for imposing restrictions, although it is possible for the trust deed of an authorized unit trust to specify categories of persons that may become unitholders. Unit trusts in tax havens often impose residency restrictions. This may be due to local tax exemption of foreign unitholders or because of the extraterritorial reach of the tax and securities law of some countries

---

[274] [1957] 1 Ch. 415.
[275] Which provides that no person may by any instrument or otherwise settle or dispose of any property in such manner that the income thereof shall . . . be wholly or partially accumulated for any longer period than one of the relevant perpetuity periods.
[276] (1851) 9 Hare 177.
[277] Counsel for the manager, Elphinstone, has stressed that *Bassil* v. *Lister* should apply on account of the commercial and contractual nature of a unit trust: [1957] 1 Ch. 414 at 418 and 419. His Lordship must have accepted counsel's argument given his heavy reliance on *Bassil* v. *Lister*.
[278] *Brandon* v. *Robinson* (1811) 18 Ves. Jun. 429 where the condition that a life interest 'should not be grantable, transferable or otherwise assignable' was held to be void.

such as the United States. It is of interest to examine the validity of such restrictions.

Within the repugnancy doctrine itself, partial restraints are valid if they do not substantially deprive the owner of his power of alienation. It has been held for instance that a condition is valid if it restrains disposition to an excepted class.[279] It seems that the real distinction is whether a purported alienation in breach of the covenant will confer a right of re-entry or result in cesser of the absolute interest or whether a breach will give rise to a right of damages or will enable the relevant party to seek injunctive relief.[280] Thus, resident restrictions commonly found in unit trusts are valid because only transfers to a limited class are excepted and breach of these restrictions only gives the manager or the trustee a right to obtain contractual remedies.

If restrictions on assignment are found in a contract, no one will doubt their validity. Parties to a contract are bound to observe all contract terms, whether negative or positive in nature, unless the contract itself is void or unenforceable on grounds of public policy or illegality. In *Borland's Trustee* v. *Steel Brothers & Co. Ltd.*[281] the repugnancy argument was also raised. This was rejected by Farwell J on the reasoning that the articles of association constitute a contract by which the shareholders are bound. Accordingly, the provision was valid.

## (4) Policy Considerations

Policy considerations behind the perpetuity rules occupy the pages of many texts.[282] Briefly, the rules are against the dead hand's attempt to bind property against the desires of the living generation thereby withdrawing capital from circulation for commercial purposes. Not only is this element absent from the unit trust but, ironically, the unit trust is a medium that encourages the circulation of capital. It is a vehicle through which capital for investment can be assembled from many individuals. It is a medium for investment services that gives an opportunity to those without professional

---

[279] Coke upon Littleton, 19th edn., with notes by Hargrave and Butler, 1832; *Doe d. Gill* v. *Pearson* (1805) 6 East 173; *Re Macleay* (1875) LR 20 Eq. 186. But these cases have been doubted in *Re Rosher* (1884) 26 Ch. D 801, and not followed in *Re Brown* [1954] Ch. 39. See *Theobald on Wills*, 14th edn., by Clark, Sweet and Maxwell, 1982, pp. 646–9.

[280] *Caldy Manor Estate Ltd.* v. *Farrell* [1974] 3 All ER 753, where a covenant not to sell land separately from adjoining land was held not to be an unlawful restraint since the breach would only give rise to nominal damages or enable the covenantee to obtain an injunction.

[281] [1901] 1 Ch. 279.

[282] Maudsley, *supra*, ch. 9; Morris and Leach, *supra*, pp. 26–9, 303–6. See also Emery, 'Do We Need a Rule Against Perpetuities?' (1994) 57 *MLR* 602.

knowledge to put their capital into use. Any mischief of the sort targeted by perpetuity rules simply does not exist in the unit trust context.

Thus, whether on technical analysis or on policy justifications, the rules against perpetuities should have no application to unit trusts.

## C. The Rule in *Saunders* v. *Vautier*

Texts and commentaries on unit trusts frequently state that 'all the unit holders, if of full age and capacity, could, under the principle of *Saunders* v. *Vautier*,[283] join in requesting the trustee to terminate the trust'.[284] This principle is generally believed to have a status above the express provisions of the trust deed.[285] It is of considerable significance to draftsmen of unit trust deeds to know whether this rule applies to unit trusts and whether a clause expressly excluding it is effective. Before this question is answered, it is necessary to ascertain what this rule is.

This rule is an interesting one because it differs from the actual decision of the case and also because of the difference in treatment given by wills texts and trusts texts respectively.[286] There are three statements of principle for which the case is cited. The narrowest two appear mostly in wills texts.

The narrowest interpretation sees the rule as an application of the general principle that conditions repugnant to the estate previously given are void. The most lucid treatment can be found in *Theobald*.[287] *Saunders* v. *Vautier* is cited for the statement that:

> ... when vested interests have once been given, restrictions postponing the enjoyment of the property beyond the age of majority are void, unless the property is otherwise disposed of in the meantime.[288]

Similar statements can be found in *Jarman on Wills*[289] and *Williams on*

---

[283] (1841) 4 Beav 115.

[284] Day and Harris, p. 16; Walsh, 'Unit Trust' in Grbich, Munn and Reicher, *Modern Trusts and Taxation*, Butterworths Australia, 1978, p. 36 at p. 71; Ford, 'Public Unit Trusts' in Austin and Vann (eds.), *The Law of Public Company Finance*, Law Book Co., 1986, pp. 400 and 413; Ford and Lee, *Principles of the Law of Trusts*, 2nd edn., Law Book Co., 1990, para. 2304.5 (this ch. no longer appears in the 3rd edn., of this work).

[285] *Underhill and Hayton*, p. 712, citing *Re AEG Unit Trust (Managers) Ltd.'s Deed* [1957] Ch. 415, discussed below.

[286] In Manitoba Law Reform Commission, *Report on the Rule in Saunders v. Vautier*, Report No. 18, Winnipeg, 1975, and Waters, p. 963, the two interpretations as a rule against accumulation and as a rule of termination are noted by reference to *Theobald* and *Underhill and Hayton*.

[287] *Theobald on Wills*, 15th edn., by Clark, Sweet and Maxwell, London, 1993, pp. 646–9.

[288] Ibid., p. 648.

[289] *Jarman on Wills*, 8th edn., by Jennings, Sweet and Maxwell, London, 1951, p. 572.

*Wills*[290] and are supported by Lindley LJ in the Court of Appeal in *Harbin* v. *Masterman*:[291]

. . . [N]otwithstanding the general principle that a donee or legatee can only take what is given him on the terms on which it is given, yet by our law there is a remarkable exception to the general principle. Conditions which are repugnant to the estate to which they are annexed are absolutely void, and may consequently be disregarded. This doctrine, I apprehend, underlies the rule laid down in *Saunders* v. *Vautier*, and was enunciated with great clarity by Vice-Chancellor Wood in *Gosling* v. *Gosling*.[292]

The second interpretation is that *Saunders* v. *Vautier* is a rule against accumulations. In Theobald, it is stated that:

Where there is an absolute vested gift made payable at a future event, with a direction to accumulate the income in the meantime and pay it with the principal, the court will not enforce the trust for accumulation, in which no person has any interest but the legatee.[293]

This is an adoption of Lord Davey's statement in *Wharton* v. *Masterman*:[294]

That principle [of *Saunders* v. *Vautier*] is this: that where there is an absolute vested gift made payable at a future event, with direction to accumulate the income in the meantime, and pay it with the principal, the Court will not enforce the trust for accumulation in which no person has any interest but the legatee, or (in other words) the Court holds that a legatee may put an end to an accumulation that is exclusively for his benefit.

The widest version of the rule appears in article 72 of *Underhill and Hayton*:[295]

If there is only one beneficiary, or if there are several (whether entitled concurrently or successively) and they are of one mind, and he or they are not

---

[290] *Williams's Law Relating to Wills*, 6th edn., by Sherrin, Barlow and Wallington, Butterworths, London, 1987, Vol. 1, p. 326.
[291] [1894] 2 Ch. 184, approved on appeal to the House of Lords: *Wharton* v. *Masterman* [1895] AC 186. [292] (1859) John. 265.
[293] *Supra*, p. 636; *Jarman on Wills, supra*, p. 383; *Williams' Law Relating to Wills, supra*, p. 721. [294] [1895] AC 186 at 198.
[295] *Underhill and Hayton*, p. 700. See *Gosling* v. *Gosling* (1859) Johns. 265 at 272 per Page Wood VC; *Re Cotton's Trustees* (1882) 19 Ch. D 624 at 629 per Fry J; *Stephenson* v. *Barclays Bank* [1975] 1 All ER 625 at 637, quoted below as text accompanying fn. 303, *infra*; *Wilson* v. *Wilson* (1950) 51 SR (NSW) 91 at 94 per Street J; *Perpetual Trustees WA Ltd.* v. *Walker* [1982] WAR 22. This rule also applies to discretionary trusts: *Re Smith* [1928] Ch. 915; *Re Beckett's Settlement* [1940] Ch. 279; *Sir Moses Montefiore Jewish Home* v. *Howell & Co. (no. 7) Pty. Ltd.* [1984] 2 NSWLR 406 at 411 per Kearney J. This principle does not represent the position of states in the US: Scott, s. 337, the leading case being *Claflin* v. *Claflin* 20 NE 454 (1889).

under any disability, the specific performance of the trust may be arrested, and the trust modified or extinguished by him or them without reference to the wishes of the settlor or the trustees.

Apart from the words 'modified or',[296] the view outlined in this article is shared by texts such as *Snell*,[297] Moffat,[298] Parker and Mellows,[299] Jacobs,[300] Ford and Lee,[301] and Waters.[302] Indeed, it is also stated as an elementary principle by Walton J in *Stephenson* v. *Barclays Bank*:[303]

(1) In a case where the persons who between them hold the entirety of the beneficial interests in any particular trust fund are all *sui juris* and acting together ('the beneficial interest holders'), they are entitled to direct the trustees how the trust fund may be dealt with. (2) This does not mean however, that they can at one and the same time override the pre-existing trusts and keep them in existence. Thus, in *Re Brockbank*[304] itself the beneficial interest holders were entitled to override the pre-existing trust by, for example, directing the trustees to transfer the trust fund to X and Y, whether X and Y were the trustees of some other trust or not, but they were not entitled to direct the existing trustees to appoint their own nominee as a new trustee of the existing trust. . . . (3) Nor, I think, are the beneficial interest holders entitled to direct the trustees as to the particular investment they should make of the trust fund. I think this follows for the same reasons as the above. Moreover, it appears to me that once the beneficial interest holders have determined to end the trust they are not entitled, unless by agreement, to the further services of the trustees. . . . (4) Of course, the rights of the beneficial interest holders are always subject to the right of the trustee to be fully protected against such matters as duty, taxes costs or other outgoings . . .

The second interpretation best accords with the facts of *Saunders* v. *Vautier* and the statement of Lord Langdale MR in the case itself.[305] The repugnancy interpretation is a step backward but closer to the origin of the

---

[296] Which appear to be inconsistent with *Re Brockbank* [1948] Ch. 206.
[297] *Snell*, pp. 233–4.                                             [298] Moffat, p. 235.
[299] Parker and Mellows, *The Modern Law of Trusts*, 6th edn. (by Oakley), Sweet and Maxwell, 1994, pp. 524–5.                              [300] Jacobs, para. 2308.
[301] Ford and Lee, paras. 16090–16100.
[302] Waters, pp. 962 *et seq.*, noting the narrow construction as well.
[303] [1975] 1 All ER 625 at 637.                              [304] [1948] Ch. 206.
[305] In *Saunders* v. *Vautier* (1841) 4 Beav. 115, a testator bequeathed certain stocks on trust to accumulate the dividends until the beneficiary should attain the age of 25 and then to transfer the capital together with the accumulated dividends to him. It was held that on construction the interest was vested although the testator intended to postpone the enjoyment; consequently the beneficiary was entitled to claim the whole fund on attaining majority. Lord Langdale MR said: 'I think that principle has been repeatedly acted upon; and where a legacy is directed to accumulate for a certain period, or where the payment is postponed, the legatee, if he has an absolute indefeasible interest in the legacy, is not bound to wait until the expiration of that period, but may require payment the moment he is competent to give a valid discharge.'

rule.[306] The wider interpretation positively confers a right of premature termination on all beneficiaries acting collectively. These three interpretations therefore reflect the historical progression of the recognition of the rights of beneficiaries as equitable owners.[307] It is of interest to note that this is also reflected in a new sentence found in the new edition of *Underhill and Hayton*.[308] During this progression, one common theme has not changed: it is a rule of gift—which is about the wish of a donor and the right[309] of the donee. The question now is: should this gift rule be further extended into the contractual relations of the unit trust?

In its narrowest form, the rule makes void any limitation on a gift which is repugnant to the right of enjoyment of that gift. Obviously, 'where there is what amounts to an absolute gift, that absolute gift cannot be fettered by prescribing a mode of enjoyment'.[310] Nothing of this sort happens in the unit trust because there is only a contract. If the relationships of the trustee, the manager, and the unitholders are contractual, it follows that the contract must be terminated in the manner agreed between the parties or by mutual consent. It also goes against common sense to say that the unitholders can together terminate the trust, ignoring the wishes of the manager (and the trustee). A simple example can illustrate this. After the

---

[306] This rule originated from the practice of the ecclesiastical courts as a rule of legacy: Chesterman, 'Family Settlements on Trust: Landowners and the Rising Bourgeoisie' in Rubin and Sugarman (eds.), *Law, Economy and Society, 1750–1914: Essays in the History of English Law*, Professional Books, 1984, p. 153–4, citing *Lord Pawlet*'s case (1685) 2 Ventris. 366.

[307] As explained by Chesterman, ibid., the rule should be seen in the light of the successful parallel development of assignability of beneficiaries' interests: if attempts to impose conditional restraints by settlors on alienation were ineffective, assignments by beneficiaries in return for capital sums were likely to defeat any particular aims which the trust founder had in mind in seeking to postpone the receipt of benefit. It was only a logical step from there for judges to hold that the beneficiary or beneficiaries should be able to obtain the appropriate capital sum by simply calling on the trustees to transfer the trust property to them and abdicate their position as trustees. Support can be found in the dictum of Lord Langdale MR in *Curtis* v. *Lukin* (1842) 5 Beav. 147 at 156: '[The beneficiary] has the legal power of disposing of it, he may sell, charge, or assign it, for he has an absolute, indefeasible interest in a thing defined and certain; the Court, therefore, has thought fit . . . to say, that since the legatee has such the legal right and power over the property, and can deal with it as he pleases, it will not subject him to the disadvantage of raising money by selling or charging his interest, when the thing is his own, at this very moment.'

[308] A new sentence is added to art. 72 (above cited) by the learned editor of the 15th edn., of *Underhill and Hayton*: 'The equitable proprietors of the trust property are entitled to claim it for themselves even if the settlor wants the trustees to manage it for them for particular purposes of his own.' (*Underhill and Hayton*, p. 710.)

[309] Strictly speaking, in a Hohfeldian sense, the rule in *Saunders* v. *Vautier* does not give beneficiaries any right. By terminating the trust, the beneficiaries are not compelling the performance of any duty but putting the office of the trustee to an end. The rule gives the beneficiaries a 'power' correlating to a 'liability' on the part of the trustee, not a 'right' correlating to a 'duty': Harris, 'Trust, Power and Duty' (1971) 87 *LQR* 31 at 63.

[310] *Re Nelson* (1918), appearing as a note to *Re Smith* [1928] 1 Ch. 915 at 920, per Swinfen Eady MR (at 921).

execution of the unit trust deed between the manager and the trustee, a person subscribes for units and becomes the first unitholder. Before any new unitholder joins, can he terminate the unit trust as a sole beneficiary? The answer is no. He can only redeem his units as stipulated in the trust deed. After his redemption, the unit trust scheme is back to its initial stage with no subscriber. This is because the unit trust is constituted by the trustee and the manager as contracting parties. The trust of assets is only part of the contractual scheme and is also subject to the contractual provisions governing redemption and cancellation.

By reason of the contractual nature of the unit trust deed, it naturally follows that in the absence of a unanimous agreement for variation amongst all parties (the manager, the trustee, and all unitholders), they are all bound to observe the termination provisions in the unit trust deed. But in *Re AEG Unit Trust (Managers) Ltd.'s Deed*,[311] Wynn-Parry J said:

> It is true that there are express provisions setting out circumstances in which the trust will come or be brought to an end, and there are express provisions for modification of the trust deed by resolution of a specified majority of the certificate holders at meetings convened for the purpose. But it cannot be doubted that, if at any time the whole of the certificate holders required the trust to be terminated or altered in a specific request, effect would have to be given to their requirements. Equally, if in any given year all the certificate holders required that the balance of the amount available for distribution should not be added to capital as contemplated, effect would have to be given to their requirement. The court would not enforce that provision against their unanimous wish, with the result that section 164 of the Law of Property Act, 1925, has no application: *Wharton* v. *Masterman*.

It will be recalled that Wynn-Parry J not only recognized the contractual nature of the unit trust, but in fact used such nature to support his position that the rule against accumulation has no application to unit trusts.[312] If the contractual nature is recognized, the second sentence of the above quotation cannot be supported. Presumably, his Lordship's predominant motive was to assemble all the arguments[313] that could destroy any suggestion of the applicability of the rule against accumulation in the unit trust context. His concern was to lead into the sentence immediately following. *Wharton* v. *Masterman*,[314] in which Lord Davey had stated the principle as a rule against accumulation,[315] was cited. In the course of doing so, the inherent contradictions between the contractual nature of the

---

[311] [1957] 1 Ch. 415 at 422.                    [312] S. 3B(2), *ante*.

[313] The passage quoted was his Lordship's third ground for the non-applicability of the rule against accumulation. He had already ruled that there was no settlement within s. 164 of the Law of Property Act, the provision against accumulation, and that the accumulation under the unit trust deed before him also did not fall within the mischief of that provision.

[314] [1895] AC 186.                    [315] Text accompanying fn. 294, *supra*.

trust and the right of premature termination under *Saunders* v. *Vautier* may not have occurred to him. In any event, he was not called upon to decide if a unitholder can terminate the trust contrary to the express provisions of the unit trust deed. His observations about termination must be obiter.

The broader rule of *Saunders* v. *Vautier* has also been explained as a choice within 'a basic paradox at the heart of a property system operating within the tenets of liberalism: where a donor of an interest tries to restrict a donee's freedom to dispose of that interest, then the legal system must choose between competing freedom, that of the donor or that of the donee'.[316] The rule is a choice in favour of the donee.[317] It is a choice based on public policy. If the rationale behind the rule is a choice between the settlor's intention and the beneficiaries' freedom of alienation, the need for that choice simply does not have to be made where a settlor does not exist. The freedom of alienation is inherent in the unit trust mechanism that gives units the character of securities. The interest of a unitholder in the unit trust is at any moment of time his property. There is no question of gift because the trust has not been utilized as a mechanism to effect a gift. Without the policy justification behind the broader rule of *Saunders* v. *Vautier*, why should this rule apply to unit trusts?

In *Berry* v. *Geen*,[318] Lord Maugham reminded us that 'the rule has no operation unless all the persons who have any present or contingent interest in the property are *sui juris* and consent'.[319] Translated to the unit trust context, a unit trust scheme cannot be terminated unless all persons with interests in the scheme consent. The trustee and the manager do have interests as promisees under various contractual promises that make up the scheme.[320] Putting it in another way, a contracting party's consent is

---

[316] The words of Moffat, 'Trusts Law: A Song Without End?' (Review Article) (1992) 55 *MLR* 123 at 129.

[317] In Harris's terms, under the rule of *Saunders* v. *Vautier*, 'fidelity to the settlor's intention ends where equitable property begins'. (*Variation of Trusts*, Sweet and Maxwell, London, 1975, p. 2.)      [318] [1938] AC 575.      [319] Ibid., at 582.

[320] As noted before, the manager has a monetary interest arising from dealing of units. Both the trustee and the manager do have rights to remuneration as a matter of contract. The cases of *Re Pooley* (1888) 40 Ch. D 1, *Re Thorley* [1891] 2 Ch. 613 and *Re Duke of Norfolk's Settlement Trust* [1982] 1 Ch. 61 recognized trustees' remunerations as interests in the trust fund for the purposes of treating them as legacies and of paying taxes. However, this type of interest is regarded as of a special kind. For example, as *Re Duke of Norkfolk's Settlement Trust* suggests, it will not be subject to the rule in *Chapman* v. *Chapman* [1954] AC 429 that the court will only alter the terms of the trust, under its inherent jurisdiction, in cases of salvage, emergency, maintenance, and compromise. It will be very surprising if a court will keep alive a private trust, whose beneficiaries purport to terminate it under *Saunders* v. *Vautier*, solely for the purpose of paying the trustee's remuneration. But in a unit trust, there is no reason why the trustee and the manager cannot insist to continue the unit trust to earn their remuneration. Unitholders are contractually bound to follow the provisions for redemption. Therefore, for the purpose of the rule of *Saunders* v. *Vautier*, it is preferable to consider the right to remuneration as a right conferred by the contract contained in the trust deed.

necessary if other parties to the contract want to terminate the contract not in accordance with its terms.

The rule in *Saunders* v. *Vautier* has many facets but its primary character as a rule relating to gifts has not changed in its application to the trust. It necessarily follows that it cannot apply to contractual situations where no gifts are involved and where the mutual rights under a contract, not the unilateral wish of a donor, are in question.

### D. Frustration, Resulting Trust, and Property Rights

If the unit trust is founded on contract, the contract imports into the unit trust context, at least presumptively, the doctrine of frustration, which hitherto is regarded as a concept foreign to trusts. The nearest analogy in the law of trusts is the automatic resulting trust which arises from a settlor's failure to dispose of the trust property or interests in it exhaustively.[321]

### (1) Frustrating Events in Unit Trusts[322]

A likely instance of frustration of a unit trust scheme is where the purpose of the trust can no longer be achieved.[323] For example, an embargo or an enactment of a law may make investment in a foreign country contemplated by a country fund not viable.[324] Similarly, changes in tax law may frustrate tax driven trusts. Specialized funds that exploit opportunities of new technologies or inventions may face the possibility that such technologies and inventions cease to be viable. Company law's approach is to permit shareholders to petition for the winding up of the company when its whole substratum has disappeared. The court may then dissolve the company if it is just and equitable to do so.[325]

Apart from events affecting objectives of trusts, an arguable frustrating event will be the winding up of the manager. If the manager is acknowledged to be the entrepreneur of the scheme and what is involved is a matter of services in which the personal qualities of the manager are

---

[321] *Re Vandervell's Trusts (No. 2)* [1974] Ch. 269 at 294; *Underhill and Hayton*, art. 29, pp. 301 *et seq.*

[322] On frustration generally, see *Chitty*, Vol. 1, ch. 23.

[323] Cf. *Braithwaite* v. *Attorney General* [1909] 1 Ch. 510.

[324] Cf. *Codelfa Construction Pty. Ltd.* v. *State Rail Authority of NSW* (1982) 149 CLR 337; *Maine* v. *Lyons* (1913) 15 CLR 671; *RS Howard & Sons Ltd.* v. *Brunton* (1916) 21 CLR 366; *Re de Garis & Rowe's Lease* [1924] VLR 38. On supervening illegality under a foreign law, see *Chitty*, Vol. 1, para. 23–020.

[325] *Re German Date Coffee Co.* (1882) 20 Ch. D 169.

crucial,[326] its dissolution must change the scheme in a fundamental way.[327] On the other hand, most trust deeds, the Financial Services Act 1986,[328] and the Financial Services (Regulated Schemes) Regulations 1991[329] contemplate that the trustee may in an appropriate case dismiss the manager and select a new manager in its place. If such are the provisions, the personal nature of the office of the manager is debatable. In any event, if there is an express provision dealing with dissolution or insolvency of the manager,[330] that event is no longer a frustrating event.

Obviously, examples of frustration in the unit trust context are a matter of conjecture. What can be said is that frustration occurs when without default of a party a contractual obligation has become incapable of being performed because the circumstances in which performance is called for would render it a thing radically different from that which was undertaken by the contract.[331] If the event in question is an event that falls within the termination provision of the trust deed that may give rise to the secondary trust, it is an event within the contemplation of the parties; it follows that it cannot be characterized as a frustrating event. On the other hand, under the doctrine of frustration, once a frustrating event happens, it will terminate the contract automatically without the need for calling any meeting of unitholders or any resolutions by them.[332] What are the consequences of termination of a unit trust scheme by frustration?

## (2) Consequences of Frustration

The consequences of frustration under contract law are that the contract is terminated and all contractual obligations nullified as from the occurrence of the frustrating event.[333] Contractual obligations that were due to be

---

[326] Such as investment experience in the industry and the financial background. As Hope JA has said of the manager in *Parkes Management Ltd.* v. *Perpetual Trustee Co. Ltd.* (1977–1978) ACLC 29,545 at 29,554: 'Its position in the whole scheme was central to that scheme and its removal in a very real sense changed in an important way the character of the scheme.'

[327] A contract that requires personal participation is frustrated by illness or death: *Boast* v. *Firth* (1868) LR 4 CP 1; *Egg Stores (Stamford Hill) Ltd.* v. *Leibovici* [1977] ICR 260; *Notcutt* v. *Universal Equipment Co. (London) Ltd.* [1986] 1 WLR 641; *Whim Well Copper Mines Ltd.* v. *Pratt* (1910) 12 WAR 166; *Carmichael* v. *Colonial Sugar Refining Co. Ltd.* (1944) 44 SR (NSW) 233.                    [328] S. 82.

[329] The Financial Services (Regulated Schemes) Regulations 1991, reg. 7.17.1(d).

[330] Ibid., reg. 7.17.1(a)–(c).

[331] *Davis Contractors Ltd.* v. *Fareham UDC* [1956] AC 696 at 729, per Lord Radcliffe; *Tsakiroglou & Co. Ltd.* v *Noblee Thorl,GmbH* [1962] AC 93; *National Carriers Ltd.* v. *Panalpina (Northern) Ltd.* [1981] AC 675; *Pioneer Shipping Ltd.* v. *BTP Tioxide Ltd. (The Nema)* [1982] AC 724.

[332] Frustration terminates the whole contract without election by any party: *Aurel Forras Pty. Ltd.* v. *Graham Karp Developments Pty. Ltd.* [1915] VR 202.

[333] *Hirsch* v. *Zinc Corporation Ltd.* (1917) 24 CLR 34; *Appleby* v. *Myers* (1867) LR 2 CP 651; *Stubbs* v. *Holywell Ry. Co.* (1867) LR 2 Ex. 311.

performed before frustration remain valid. Money paid prior to frustration is not recoverable unless there is total failure of consideration. Work done after frustration may, however, be recovered on a restitution basis.[334] This common law position may be altered by legislation relating to frustration.[335]

Deductions from the unit trust fund to pay the service charges of the manager and the trustee are not recoverable generally. If such charges are paid in advance, it appears that they will be recoverable on the basis that there is a total failure of consideration.

The remaining concern is the consequences of frustration for the unit trust assets.

## (3) Resulting Trusts

A resulting trust[336] arises in favour of the settlor if the trust which he attempts to constitute fails; if an intending gift cannot be achieved, it will result back to the donor.[337] This is the main thrust of the doctrine of resulting trusts.

There will however be no resulting trust if a person transfers property in exchange for some contractual benefit (whether for himself or a third party), and that contractual benefit is obtained. A finding of a contract therefore excludes the doctrine of resulting trusts.

In *Cunnack* v. *Edwards*,[338] a society was established to raise funds by subscriptions to provide annuities for the widows of deceased members. On the death of the last widow, it was held by the Court of Appeal that there would be no resulting trust in favour of the estates of members because each member had parted with his subscription money absolutely in return for contractual benefits for his widow.[339]

*Cunnack* v. *Edwards* was applied by Goff J in *Re West Sussex Constabulary's Widows, Children & Benevolent Fund Trusts*.[340] His Lordship also held that no resulting trust can arise in respect of proceeds of entertainments and sweepstakes raised in fund-raising activities after the

---

[334] *Davis Contractors Ltd.* v. *Fareham Urban DC* [1956] AC 696.

[335] See s. 3D(5), *post.*

[336] The term 'resulting trust' is used here in the sense of an automatic resulting trust. For other aspects of resulting trusts, *Re Vandervell's Trusts (No. 2)* [1974] Ch. 269 at 294; *Underhill and Hayton*, arts. 29–32.

[337] Assuming that there is no gift over.                    [338] [1896] 2 Ch. 679.

[339] Rigby LJ's judgment was explicit: 'The members were not cestuis que trust of the funds or of any part thereof, but persons who, under contracts or quasi-contracts with the society, secured for valuable consideration certain contingent benefits for their widows which could be enforced by the widows in manner provided by the [Friendly Societies] Acts.' (Ibid., at 689.) Lord Halsbury in similar tone regarded the transaction as a 'bargain' by a member (ibid., at 681). It was held that the surplus fund passed to the Crown as *bona vacantia.*

[340] [1971] Ch. 1.

purpose of such raising activities failed to exhaust such proceeds. This was because 'the relationship is one of contract and not of trust. The purchaser of a ticket may have the motive of aiding the cause or he may not. He may purchase a ticket merely because he wishes to attend the particular entertainment or to try for the prize, but whichever it be he pays his money as the price of what is offered and what he receives.'[341]

The incompatibility of the contract and the resulting trust is summed up in the *obiter dicta* of Brightman J in *Re William Denby & Sons Ltd., Sick and Benevolent Fund*:[342]

> . . . It is accepted by all counsel that a fund of this sort is founded in contract and not in trust. That is to say, the right of a member of the fund to receive benefits is a contractual right and the member ceases to have any interest in the fund if and when he has received the totality of the benefits to which he was contractually entitled. In other words, there is no possible claim by any member founded on a resulting trust.

Despite the consistency in these cases, it is submitted that the contract and the resulting trust are not necessarily mutually exclusive. Express trusts have a long history of coexistence with contracts, despite some reluctance to accept this phenomenon. It is questionable whether resulting trusts should form an exception, bearing in mind that a resulting trust arises upon the failure of an express trust. If A contracts with B to settle A's properties upon trust for the benefit of C and the trust fails on the ground of perpetuities or uncertainties, the logical answer is that a resulting trust arises in favour of the settlor A. Whether A will be in breach of A's contract with B is a separate matter that depends on the terms of their contract. What happened in the benevolent fund cases was that there was a finding of a pure contractual relationship amongst members so that the obtaining of the contractual benefit ended their rights.[343] If the finding had been that there was a trust relationship, a resulting trust may arise.[344]

---

[341] Ibid., at 11. Golf J's judgment was criticized by Walton J in *Re Bucks. Constabulary Widows' and Orphans' Fund Friendly Society (No. 2)* [1979] 1 All ER 623. But this dictum was not affected by the criticism.

[342] [1971] 1 WLR 973 at 978; the facts of this case were similar to *Cunnack* v. *Edwards, supra* and *Re West Sussex Constabulary's Widows, Children & Benevolent (1930) Fund Trusts, supra*, except that Brightman J held that the original trusts had not been terminated. His comment was therefore obiter. The same conclusion regarding contract and resulting trust can also be found in the judgment of Megarry J in *Re Sick and Funeral Society of St John's Sunday School, Golcar* [1973] Ch. 51 at 59–60. See also the dicta of Scott J in *Davis* v. *Richards & Wallington Ltd.* [1990] 1 WLR 1511 at 1530–42 on the application of resulting trust to pension fund surpluses.

[343] As Golf J explained in *Re West Sussex Constabulary's Widows, Children and Benevolent (1930) Fund Trusts, supra*.

[344] *Tierney* v. *Tough* [1914] 1 IR 142; *Re Printers and Transferrers Amalgamated Trades Protection Society* [1899] 2 Ch. 184; *Re Lead Co.'s Workmen's Fund Society* [1904] 2 Ch. 196; *Re Customs and Excise Officers' Mutual Guarantee Fund* [1917] 2 Ch. 18.

An automatic resulting trust, by definition, arises when the express trust fails to dispose of all or some of the equitable interests. It follows that, in a unit trust, whether a resulting trust will arise depends on whether the express trust created by the unit trust deed fails to dispose of the equitable interests on the happening of a frustrating event. The heart of the problem is the fact that unitholders are not disposing of their assets, the subscription moneys, to someone else; the trust is used as a holding device.

If the primary trust is construed as a purpose trust of a *Re Denley* type[345] a frustrating event implies discontinuance of the contractual arrangement and hence also the impossibility of achieving the purpose of the unit trust scheme.[346] Frustration is therefore always paralleled by a resulting trust in favour of the investors. Thus, the assets are always protected against any creditors of the trustee.

If the primary trust is construed as a trust for unitholders subject to the contractual terms,[347] prima facie, frustration of the contract means there will be no contractual terms to which the express trust will be subject and therefore a resulting trust will arise. However, it is possible that a so-called 'frustrating' event may in fact be an event that triggers off the secondary trust. In this situation, the secondary express trust will operate and there will be no resulting trust.

A problem arising from a resulting trust analysis is the position of past unitholders. The conventional doctrinal position of a resulting trust is that the beneficial interest in the trust property will revert back to where it originally comes from. A possible analysis is that frustration applies to terminate the contract from the moment of the frustrating event. The contract remains valid in respect of all past transactions. Accordingly, all rights of past unitholders must have been extinguished contractually once their units have been redeemed or bought back in accordance with the unit trust deed. There is no injustice to past unitholders who have got what they contracted for. This should accord with the reality that the express trust has subsisted for a period of time.

(4) Statutory Allocation of Risks

The Law Reform (Frustrated Contracts) Act 1943 ameliorates the common law position on the consequence of frustration.[348] In principle, this Act applies to frustration of unit trust schemes. However, the main aims of this

---

[345] See s. 2A(1), *ante*.

[346] Even the winding up of the manager may be construed as a failure of the objective: see s. 3D(1), *ante*. Presumably, at the time of frustration, the three certainties of the trust still exist and no questions of perpetuities arise.                              [347] S. 2A, *ante*.

[348] Under this Act, the court is empowered to give compensation not exceeding the 'valuable benefit' received by the other party.

statute are to enable parties to recover money paid and to make adjustment or compensation for partial performance. These will give the manager and the trustee rights to recover for their services in appropriate cases. But rights under the statute are presumably rights *in personam*[349] and would not enable them to claim out of the trust fund.


## E. Remedies: Law and Equity

In spite of the fact that more than a century has elapsed since the passing of the Judicature Act 1873, its effect on substantive common law rules and equitable principles is a matter of debate. The orthodox school of thought is summed up by the famous metaphor of Ashburner:[350]

[T]he two streams of jurisdiction, though they run in the same channel, run side by side and do not mingle their waters.

Thus, the effect of the Act is exclusively procedural and administrative and it is a fallacy that there is any impact on substantive law. The new school is represented by the equally metaphorical dictum of Lord Diplock[351] made in 1977:

My Lords, by 1977 this metaphor [of Ashburner] has in my view become both mischievous and deceptive. The innate conservatism of English lawyers may have made them slow to recognise that by the Judicature Act 1873 the two systems of substantive and adjectival law formerly administered by Courts of Law and Courts of Chancery were fused. As at the confluence of the Rhône and Saône, it may be

---

[349] The statutes are meant to alter the consequence of frustration of a contract. Their remedial provisions logically are meant to alter contract remedies.

[350] Ashburner, *Principles of Equity* 2nd edn., by Browne, Butterworths, 1933, p. 18. This is also supported by Jessel MR: '. . . it was not any fusion, or anything of the kind; it was the vesting in one tribunal the administration of Law and Equity in every case, action, or dispute which should come before that tribunal'. *Salt* v. *Cooper* (1880) 16 Ch. D 544 at 549. See also *Clements* v. *Matthews* (1883) 11 QBD 808 at 814, per Cotton LJ; *Bank of Boston Connecticut* v. *European Grain & Shipping Ltd.* [1989] 1 AC 1056 at 1109, per Lord Brandon; *GR Mailman & Assc. Pty. Ltd.* v. *Wormald International (Aust.) Pty. Ltd.* (1991) 24 NSWLR 80 at 99, per Meagher J. On this issue generally, see Meagher, Gummow and Lehane, *Equity: Doctrines and Remedies*, 3rd edn., Butterworths Australia, 1992, paras. 220–59; *Snell*, p. 19; Pettit, pp. 9–11; *Hanbury and Martin*, p. 24. Baker, 'The Future of Equity' (1977) 93 *LQR* 529, esp. at 536; Evershed, 'Reflections on the Fusion of Law and Equity after 75 Years' (1954) 70 *LQR* 326; Holdsworth, 'Equity' (1935) 51 *LQR* 142; Martin, 'Fusion, Fallacy and Confusion; a Comparative Study' [1994] *Conv.* 13; Burns, 'The "Fusion Fallacy" Revisited' (1993) 5 *Bond LR* 152.

[351] *United Scientific Holdings Ltd.* v. *Burnley Borough Council* [1978] AC 904, at 924–5, criticized by Baker, *supra*. In *Her Majesty's Attorney-General* v. *Wellington Newspapers Ltd.* [1988] 1 NZLR 129 at 172, Cooke P said: 'As law and equity are now mingled . . . it does not seem to me to matter whether the duty be classified as equitable or not. The full range of remedies deriving historically from either common law or equity should be available. They include injunction, damages and account of profits.'

possible for a short distance to discern the source from which each part of the combined stream came, but there comes a point at which this ceases to be possible. If Professor Ashburner's fluvial metaphor is to be retained at all, the waters of the confluent streams of law and equity have surely mingled now.

It is outside the scope of this work to suggest which view is tenable or preferable. However, since the trust in the unit trust is a creation of the contract and is also an integral part of it, it is a point where the waters of law and equity meet. It is also a context where doctrines and theories are confronted by practical problems. Below are some observations.

First, the dual nature of the unit trust means that contractual remedies and trust remedies may be available concurrently to the appropriate parties. Concurrent remedies are recognized in a number of cases[352] and do not contradict the conservative school's doctrinal position. They are striving for doctrinal purity. They are not against legal and equitable remedies being administered at the same time. They are against 'the administration of a remedy, for example, common law damages for breach of fiduciary duty, not previously available either at law or in equity, or the modification of principles in one branch of the jurisdiction by concepts which are imported from the other and thus are foreign, for example, by holding that the existence of a duty of care in tort may be tested by asking whether the parties concerned are in fiduciary relations'.[353]

Secondly, it follows that the trustee and the unitholders should seek contractual remedies or trust remedies according to whether the issues are derived from contractual or trust principles. But this is more easily said than done. We have already seen how easy it is to characterize wrongly the source of the trustee's remuneration.[354] It is likely that there will be other instances of similar difficulties. But difficulties *per se* will not supplant the need for doctrinal clarity.

Thirdly, one particular problem, by way of example, is the scope within which the trustee is entitled to seek the court's advice and directions. An executor or trustee is always entitled to take the opinion of the court as to the course of action that it should adopt if it is in doubt.[355] Apparently, this stems from the court's jurisdiction over the execution of trusts.[356] It is

---

[352] See s. 2E of this ch., *ante*.

[353] Meagher, Gummow and Lehane, *Equity: Doctrines and Remedies*, 3rd edn., Butterworths Australia, 1992, pp. 46–7.

[354] *Application of Trust Company of Australia re Barclays Commercial Property Trust*, unreported, NSWSC (Eq. Div.) No. 1033 of 1993, 19 Mar. 1993, Waddell CJ in Eq., discussed in s. 2D(4) of this ch., *ante*.

[355] Ford and Lee, para. 1703, citing *Re Atkinson* [1971] VR 612 at 615.

[356] This is derived from recognized rules of court as well as statutes: *Underhill and Hayton*, art. 90.

obvious that no such course is available to parties to a contract on questions of performance of its terms.

The complex and novel nature of unit trusts means that the situations where advice may be sought may be numerous. Thus, advice has been sought on such matters as the effect of differentiation in tax law between resident and non-resident unitholders on distribution to unitholders,[357] the effect of the interaction between the Financial Services Act 1986, the regulations made under section 81, the trust deed, and the scheme particulars,[358] an out of court settlement with creditors of the unit trust and the implementation of such settlement,[359] the trustee acting as the manager in the interim period between the retirement of a manager and the appointment of a substitute,[360] the desirability of removal of a manager,[361] and the desirability of suing former solicitors acting for a trust.[362] No doubt, there are other applications in chambers that do not appear even as unreported judgments.

In none of these judgments, however, did the court consider its jurisdiction to hear the matter. There is no attempt to distinguish whether the matter raised by the trustee is a trust issue or a question on the performance of contractual terms contained in the unit trust deed. This could probably be attributed to the *ex parte* nature of the applications and the commonly believed extensive jurisdiction on giving advice and directions. However, if the office of the manager is contractual in origin, as acknowledged in *Parkes Management Ltd.* v. *Perpetual Trustee Co. Ltd.*,[363] any advice given by the court to the trustee on its appointment or removal must be an advice on contractual relationships.

Fourthly, the problem will be more acute if the position of the manager as a plaintiff or applicant is considered. If its status rests on contract, it follows that it does not have the *locus standi* to invoke equitable remedies regarding trusts. As just illustrated, a trustee administering investment of a trust can seek the court's direction thereby avoiding any subsequent liability. A manager administering investment of the unit trust cannot apply to the court for direction because its authority is derived from

[357] *Re Liberal Petroleums Trust* (1985) 64 Alberta Reports 243.
[358] Cf. *Re Australia Wide Property Trust* (1992) 8 ACSR 611.
[359] *Application of Murphy and Allen (Estate Mortgage Trusts)*, unreported, NSWSC (Eq. Div.) No. 3905 of 1992, 10 Aug. 1992, McLelland J.
[360] *The Application of Permanent Trustee Nominees (Canberra) Ltd.*, unreported, NSWSC (Eq. Div.) No. 4216 of 1985, 24 June 1985, Young J. It appears that the same problem of a time gap between the removal of a manager and the appointment of a substitute can also exist under reg. 7.17.1 and reg. 7.17.2.
[361] *Burns Philp Trustee Co. Ltd.* v. *Estate Mortgage Managers Ltd.*, unreported, Vic. SC, No. 2253 of 1990, 15 June 1990, Smith J.
[362] *Re Murphy*, unreported, Vic. SC, No. 9132 of 1991, 2 Apr. 1993, Smith J.
[363] (1977–1978) ACLC 29,545.

contract. Similarly, doubts can also be expressed on any disputes on the rights of the manager *vis-à-vis* the trustee or the manager. It is simply a question whether the court has jurisdiction to hear the manager.

In *Global Funds Management (NSW) Ltd.* v. *Burns Philp Trustee Co. Ltd. (in prov. liq.)*,[364] the manager, by summons, sought leave to remove the trustee which was in liquidation and to appoint an individual to act as the trustee of the unit trust. The liquidator of the trustee cross-claimed that a receiver should be appointed for the unit trust. Rolfe J held that two natural persons should be appointed trustees and the cross-claim was dismissed. It is not clear from the report on what basis the manager was allowed to invoke the court's jurisdiction to appoint trustees. It is not mentioned whether the manager is exercising its authority under the unit trust deed. It seems that the manager's authority has been assumed. But, one would have thought that the appropriate applicant should be a unitholder. If *Global Funds Management (NSW) Ltd.* v. *Burns Philp Trustee Co. Ltd. (in prov. liq.)* is correct, one wonders whether the manager has standing to ask the court to grant an order for general administration of the unit trust.

Fifthly, the issues raised have significant consequences in terms of remedies for any of the parties to a unit trust. Ultimately, the court will be influenced by the two schools of thought. The court may, if it wishes, at one stroke brush aside any contractual issues and deny the standing of the manager to invoke equity's jurisdiction. Doctrinal purity thus may be maintained. On the other hand, the contractual and trust elements in the administration of unit trust schemes are so interwoven that one wonders whether it is a correct response of law and equity to social and economic demands to insist on fine distinctions that may not produce coherence. It is against water's natural property that it can run side by side and yet does not mingle. Indeed, in unit trust cases, whether knowingly or unknowingly, the court has already enlarged its equitable jurisdiction to cover some contractual matters within unit trust schemes. There is no reason why equity cannot develop or be fertilized by principles of law. Perhaps, the real need is for issues to be positively identified so that coherent principles can develop.

[364] (1990) 3 ACSR 183.

# 3

# *The Character of Unit Trust Relationships*

The foregoing chapter has argued that the trust cannot, but the contract can, explain the tripartite relationships found in the unit trust; that the unit trust has its genesis in the contract; and that the trust is simply part of the contract creating the unit trust. The conclusions that follow must be that the parties' rights and liabilities fall primarily within the domain of contract law and that, insofar as a trust relationship has been created by the unit trust contract between particular parties, trust law also operates.

Once the contractual ingredient is recognized, there are the questions whether the contract has the effect of associating the parties to it and whether the relationship or any of the relationships created can be characterized as one of partnership or agency. If a partnership or an agency is established, rights and obligations flowing from that relationship will follow. These rights and obligations will be in addition to the express terms of the contract. They may be implied by law or may flow from the fiduciary character of the relationship. Further, it is always possible for equity to characterize a contracting party as a fiduciary without characterizing that party as a partner, an agent or a trustee. Thus, the manager may be a fiduciary of the unitholders, although it is not a partner, agent or trustee of the unitholders. Characterization is important in determining the contents of the rights and obligations of the parties to the unit trust as well as the extent of their liabilities to third parties dealing with them.

This chapter will examine the unit trust as a single multipartite relationship and then the key relationships: between the trustee and the manager, the trustee and the unitholders, the manager and the unitholders, and the unitholders *inter se*. It concludes with a note on the implications of characterization for the external liabilities of unitholders.

## 1. THE STRUCTURAL CHARACTER OF THE UNIT TRUST

The contract is a very flexible institution. It is a tool for establishing a host of commercial relationships, such as employment, agency, and partnership.

The historical account in chapter 1 has demonstrated how the deed of settlement—through the powerful tools of the trust and the contract—broke into the duopoly of the partnership and the chartered company, forced the state to recognize the joint stock company as a legal institution, and became the parent of the unit trust. A partnership was then regarded, in law, as a kind of commercial association.[1] A deed of settlement company was perceived as a large partnership with transferable shares. Logically, therefore, it was an association: and this proposition was implicit in the judgment of Brett LJ in *Smith* v. *Anderson*.[2] Thus, the element of association was a common denominator of all these institutions.

This part examines the unit trust as a single 'entity' and examines whether it has any associative character. The starting-point will be the seminal decision of *Smith* v. *Anderson*, which held that a unit trust, modelling on the deed of settlement, was not an association infringing the provisions of section 4 of the Companies Act 1862. The discussion will suggest the following propositions.

(1) An 'association' is a body of persons based on a contract under which those persons' mutual rights and obligations with regard to their common object are regulated and enforced. If the unit trust deed constitutes a single multipartite contract, the manager, the trustee, and unitholders are therefore 'associating' together for the purpose of investing the capital of the unitholders.

(2) As a form of association, a unit trust of twenty persons or more is ordinarily outside the Companies Act provision prohibiting large unincorporated business association.

(3) A partnership is a relationship with three elements: namely, a relationship which subsists between persons (i) carrying on business (ii) in common and (iii) with a view of profit. In applying this definition to unit trusts, a distinction has to be made between the concept of 'investment', which generates property gain and the notion of 'carrying on business' which generates profits. If the activities of a particular unit trust are investment only, none of the three elements is satisfied. If the trust does carry on business, elements (i) and (iii) will be established, but not (ii), since the business is carried on by the trustee, as trustee, under the direction of the manager and not by the unitholders in common.

---

[1] This was clear from the judgment of James LJ in *Re Agriculturist Cattle Insurance Co.* (1870) LR 5 Ch. 725 at 733: ch. 1, fn. 57.

[2] *Smith* v. *Anderson* (1880) 15 Ch. D 247. Brett LJ said: 'I confess I have some difficulty in seeing how there could be an association for the purpose of carrying on a business which would be neither a company nor a partnership, but I should hesitate to say that, by the ingenuity of men of business, there might not some day be formed a relation among twenty persons which, without being strictly either a company or a partnership, might yet be an association. But according to all ordinary rules of construction, if the association mentioned in sect. 4 is not, strictly speaking, a company or a partnership, it must be something of a similar kind.' (At 277.) James LJ also said: 'I cannot understand what the difference is between a company and an association' and assumed '[a] company or association . . . to be synonymous terms' (at 273).

## A. *Smith* v. *Anderson*

In *Smith* v. *Anderson*, a fixed trust was constituted by the initial vesting of a fixed block of shares in the trustees. The trustees executed a trust deed with a unitholder representing all other unitholders. The trustees had a discretion to sell and to reinvest subject to stringent restrictions in terms of unanimity amongst trustees and approval by resolutions of a meeting of unitholders. Meetings of unitholders were also held for receiving reports from the trustees, for appointing auditors, and for appointing substitute trustees. The unitholders were more than twenty in number.

The Court of Appeal held that the unitholders did not form an association within the meaning of section 4 of the Companies Act 1862. That section provided that '[n]o company, association, or partnership consisting of more than twenty persons shall be formed . . . for the purpose of carrying on any . . . business that has for its object the acquisition of gain by the company, association, or partnership, or by the individual members thereof, unless it is registered'.

There were three alternative reasons for the decision. The first was that the trust deed did not constitute any association between unitholders as there were no mutual rights or obligations. James LJ said:

I cannot find that this deed constitutes any association whatever between the persons who are supposed to be *socii*. One man goes with £90 in his hands and buys from the trustees a £100 certificate with all the chance of profit attaching to it. Another man goes the next day and takes his £90 to the same people and gets from them another certificate, by which he gets a right to share in the funds which they have in their hands. The first man knows nothing of the second, and the second knows nothing of the first; they have never come into any arrangement whatever as between themselves. *There never has been anything creating any mutual rights or obligations between those persons.* They are from the first entire strangers who have entered into no contract whatever with each other, nor has either of them entered into any contract with the trustees or any trustee on behalf of the other, there being nothing in the deed pointing to any mandate or delegation of authority to anybody to act for the certificate holders . . . *Persons who have no mutual rights and obligations do not, according to my view, constitute an association* because they happen to have a common interest or several interests in something which is to be divided between them.[3]

Secondly, if there was any association, it was not formed 'for the purpose of carrying on any . . . business'. It was for the purpose of investment. James LJ said:

But supposing that the certificate holders do constitute an association, it appears to me that it cannot, in any practical sense of the word 'business,' in any sense in which any man of business would use that word, be said that the association was

---

[3] *Smith* v. *Anderson* (1880) 15 Ch. D 247 at 274–5; emphasis supplied.

formed for the purpose of carrying on any business, either by themselves or by any agent.[4]

Brett LJ said:

The trustees were not, as I construe the deed, to enter upon a series of acts which, if successful, would obtain a gain. *They were joined together for the purpose of once for all investing certain money which was delivered into their hands*, and not for the purpose of obtaining gain from a repetition of investments. In other words, they were not associated together for the purpose of speculating in shares. That was not their business . . . I now come to the case of the certificate holders. It seems to me that even if what had to be done under the deed was to be done by them by means of the trustees as their agents, nevertheless they were not associated for the purpose of carrying on such a business as is contemplated by the 4th section, inasmuch as what was to be done under the deed did not constitute such a business.[5]

Cotton LJ also said:

If it appeared that the real object of the deed was that the trustees should speculate in investments, even though confined to this particular class, the case would have stood in a very different position. In my opinion there is nothing of that sort. This is not a provision that they shall make a profit by selling and buying again securities of this class whenever, in their opinion, the turn of the market makes it advisable so to do. *The deed is in substance a trust deed, providing how they are to hold as trustees specified securities* of a large amount with provisions enabling them in certain events to sell some of the securities, and enabling them when that is done, but only under special circumstances, to reinvest, not to speculate. In my opinion that is not a deed providing for carrying on a business within the meaning of the Act, it is a deed providing for the holding trust property . . .[6]

Thirdly, if there was any business, it was not carried on by the unitholders; it was carried on by the trustees who were less than twenty in number. James LJ said:

. . . if there is any business at all it is to be carried on by the trustees. Whatever is to be done is to be done by the trustees.[7]

Brett LJ said:

. . . the certificate holders, even if they were associated at all, were not associated for carrying on the business. It was not their business . . . They could not have been made liable for contract made by the trustees . . . Therefore, even if there be here a business within the meaning of the section, yet *it is not carried on by the certificate holders*, who are of a larger number than twenty, *but by the trustees*, who are not of the number of twenty or more . . .[8]

[4] *Smith* v. *Anderson* (1880) 15 Ch. D 247 at 275.
[5] Ibid., at 279–80; emphasis supplied.
[6] Ibid., at 283; emphasis supplied.
[7] Ibid., at 275.
[8] Ibid., at 280; emphasis supplied.

Cotton LJ said:

So far as there is any contract here to be entered into by the trustees it is only a change of investment; *so far as there is any business to be carried on it is the business of the trustees*, not as agents for principals behind, but their own business, that is to say, a business in which they contract as solely liable to outsiders, whatever may be their rights as against those for whom they are trustees. In my opinion, therefore, in this case the only alleged association of more than twenty, being the persons who have contributed their money, stand in this position, that they are not by themselves or their agents carrying on any business whatever. Therefore, in my opinion, this cannot be said to be an association prohibited by the Act. Of course if the trustees are carrying on a business for the purpose of profit, as they are not twenty in number there could be no objection under the Act to their doing so.[9]

An initial observation is that the unit trust deed used in the Submarine Cables' Trust in *Smith* v. *Anderson* was in form a deed of settlement. The intention in a deed of settlement company was to make the vehicle as similar as possible to the company incorporated by charter. Properties were meant to be held not for individual corporators but for the company as a quasi-entity for an indefinite period.[10] However, the properties in the unit trust in the Submarine Cables' Trust were intended to be disposed of, with the proceeds shared among certificate holders.[11] The intention was not one of trading but of investment. This point was emphasized by both Brett and Cotton LJJ on the basis that investment connotes acquisition of properties rather than doing business.

[9] *Smith* v. *Anderson* (1880) 15 Ch. D 247 at 285; emphasis supplied.

[10] A typical provision provides: 'That the trustees of the company, in whom any of the funds or property of the company shall for the time being be vested, shall stand possessed of the same *in trust for the company*, and shall apply and dispose of the same in such manner, for the benefit of the company, as the board of directors shall, conformably to the duties imposed on them by these presents, form time to time order or direct.' (Collyer, *A Practical Treatise on the Law of Partnership*, Sweet, Stevens and Maxwell, 1832, App. No. IX, pp. 734–59, cl. 98; emphasis supplied.) The intention to make the company a quasi-legal person holding properties was clear. In *Re Agriculturist Cattle Insurance Co.* (1870) LR 5 Ch. 725 at 733, cited at ch. 1, fn. 57, James LJ described deed of settlement companies as 'large societies on which the sun of royal or legislative favour did not shine . . . and the whole aim of the ablest legal assistants they could obtain, was to make them as nearly a corporation as possible . . .'. His Lordship also observed in *Re European Assurance Society* (1875) 1 Ch. D 307 at 320 that 'it is quite clear that, as between all the parties to these deeds of settlement, it was their intention to make themselves for all practical purposes as like a corporation as in the then state of the law was possible to be done by a mere contract'.

[11] Cl. 13 of the Submarines Cables' Trust in *Smith* v. *Anderson* provides: 'So soon as all the certificates shall in manner hereinbefore provided have been redeemed, the securities then remaining subject to the trusts of this deed shall be realized under the directions of the trustees, and the net proceeds thereof shall be divided between the holders for the time being of the coupons of reversion in the proportion of the nominal value of the said coupons held by them respectively.' (*Supra*, at 251.)

## B. The Associative Character

The first limb of the *Smith* v. *Anderson* decision was that there was no association of certificate holders. This was a view of James LJ alone and his explanation was that there were no mutual rights and obligations amongst certificate holders.[12] If his Lordship's reasoning is followed, a unit trust would constitute an 'association' whenever mutual rights and obligations under contract are found in that unit trust. As has been suggested in chapter 2,[13] the existence or non-existence of mutual rights and obligations only determines whether there is a contract. If this is correct, *Smith* v. *Anderson* cannot be regarded as having settled the issue. More specifically, two questions remain unanswered. Do all the unitholders, the trustee, and the manager together constitute an association? Do all the unitholders themselves constitute an association of investors?

What is an association then? Defining this expression is not easy for it embraces a wide range of bodies of persons that may be of different nature.[14] The difficulty is best summed up in the words of James LJ:

The word 'association', in the sense in which it is now commonly used, is etymologically inaccurate, for 'association' does not properly describe the thing formed, but properly and etymologically describes the act of associating together, from which act of associating there is formed a company or partnership.[15]

He continued to give his version of the definition:

But I believe that according to the vernacular we use on these subjects the difference which the Act intended to draw between a company or association and an ordinary partnership is this : An ordinary partnership is a partnership composed of definite individuals bound together by contract between themselves to continue combined for some joint object, either during pleasure or during a limited time, and is essentially composed of the persons originally entering into the contract with one another. *A company or association* (which I take to be synonymous terms) *is the result of an arrangement by which parties intend to form a partnership which is constantly changing*, a partnership today consisting of certain members, and tomorrow consisting of some only of those members along with others who have come in, so that there will be a constant shifting of the partnership, a determination of the old and a creation of a new partnership, and *with the intention that, so far as the partners can by agreement between themselves bring about such a result, the new partnership shall succeed to the assets and liabilities of the old partnership.*[16]

---

[12] See text accompanying fn. 3, *supra*.

[13] See ch. 2, s. 2B(5)&(6).

[14] For example, social clubs, unincorporated charitable organizations, partnerships, mutual societies, etc.

[15] *Smith* v. *Anderson* (1880) 15 Ch. D 247 at 273.

[16] Ibid., at 273–4; emphasis supplied.

Subsequently, speaking of the same section in the Companies (Consolidation) Act 1908, Clyde, the Lord President in the Scottish Court of Session said:

It is not, I think, open to doubt that the fundamental and essential characteristic of the whole class of bodies described in the Act as companies, associations, and partnerships, is that they are bodies constituted by some species of contract of society, and founded on the contractual obligations thus undertaken by the members, or *socii, inter se.* . . . No doubt the word 'association' is by itself capable of including a wide variety of much more loosely and irregularly constituted bodies of persons; but looking to the context in which it appears . . . I see no reason to doubt that *what is meant is a society (whatever its object) based on a consensual contract among its constituent members whereby their mutual relations inter se with regard to some common object are regulated and enforced.*[17]

*The Shorter Oxford English Dictionary* defines the term as:

a body of persons associated for a common purpose

The term has also been variously defined in other contexts.[18]

All the definitions appear to share the twin elements of mutual rights and obligations[19] and a common object pursued by those associated. In a

---

[17] *Twycross* v. *Potts* (1928) SC 633 at 635; emphasis supplied.

[18] An association is a legal relationship arising between members giving rise to joint rights or obligations or mutual rights and duties.' (*Re Commonwealth Homes and Investment Co. Ltd.* [1943] SASR 211, per Mayo J.) 'Before one can find an association, there must be some rules, either written or oral, by which those who are supposed to be members of it are tied together. I think that they would probably be written rules. There must be some constitution.' (*Re Thackrah* [1939] 2 All ER 4 at 6, per Bennett J.) 'If an unincorporated association is a "group of people defined and bound together by rules and called by a distinctive name" (*Re Macaulay's Estate, Macaulay* v. *O'Donnell* [1943] Ch. 435 at 436, per Lord Buckmaster) there must have been a moment in time when the first members agreed expressly or impliedly to be bound by the rules.' (*Conservative and Unionist Central Office* v. *Burrell* [1980] 3 All ER 42 at 58, per Vinelott J.) 'I infer that by "unincorporated association" in this context Parliament meant two or more persons bound together for one or more common purposes, not being business purposes, by mutual undertakings, each having mutual duties and obligations, in an organisation which has rules which identify in whom control of it and its funds rests and on what terms and which can be joined or left at will. The bond of union between the members of an unincorporated association has to be contractual.' (*Conservative and Unionist Central Office* v. *Burrell* [1982] 2 All ER 1 at 4, per Lawton LJ.) An unincorporated association has also been defined as 'an association of persons bound together by identifiable rules and having an identifiable membership'. (*Re Koeppler Will Trusts* [1985] 3 WLR 765 at 771, per Slade LJ.) 'In the modern idiom the term association has come to be regarded as attaching to a body of persons associated for a common purpose; the organisation formed to effect their purpose; a society (*Shorter Oxford Dictionary*). It may be incorporated or unincorporated and, usually, this appellation is attached to a society of a non-trading or commercial type—whereas the term company is normally associated with a commercial, profit oriented, undertaking.' (*Quinton & Quinton* v. *South Australian Psychological Board* (1985) 38 SASR 523 at 531.

[19] That mutual rights and obligations may be purely consensual and not contractual in the case of unincorporated associations of social nature and not involving property rights: Fletcher, *The Law Relating to Non-profit Associations in Australia and New Zealand*, Law Book Co., 1986, pp. 67 *et seq.*

unit trust, the unit trust deed provides the source of mutual rights and obligations.[20] Accordingly, whether the parties are associating turns on whether they have a common objective. Unlike the beneficiaries of a private trust, unitholders in a unit trust are not objects of benefaction of the settlor. They own the beneficial interests and rights in the unit trust through their conscious acts of contracting with other parties. They have the requisite contractual intention, while ordinary beneficiaries under a private trust do not.

If one accepts this approach of defining an association, the conclusion is that unitholders are associating together by pooling their resources for a common purpose, namely, management of their investment capital by the manager and the trustee in accordance with the terms of the unit trust deed.[21] Of course, such terms reflect their mutual expectations about the level of risk and gain associated with their investment. In this particular respect, it is hard to distinguish the unit trust from the deed of settlement company and the partnership (though there are other differences). If the unit trust deed constitutes a single multipartite contract,[22] there seems no reason why the trustee and the manager cannot be regarded as members of this association with different roles to play.

To sum up, it is submitted that all the parties—the trustee, the manager, and all unitholders—are 'associated', contractually, by the unit trust deed. This conclusion may not be in conflict with James LJ's approach in *Smith* v. *Anderson*.[23] It is just that his Lordship did not consider the unit trust in the case to involve mutual contractual rights and obligations.

## C. Prohibited Large Unincorporated Business Association

The Companies Acts have since 1844 imposed a general prohibition on the formation of unincorporated business associations of more than twenty persons. The significance of this provision in the development of the concept of the unit trust has been shown in the historical introduction of this work.

This provision now appears as section 716(1) of the Companies Act 1985. Section 716(1) provides that:

[n]o company, association, or partnership consisting of more than 20 persons shall be formed for the purpose of carrying on any business that has for its object the acquisition of gain by the company, association, or partnership, or by its individual members, unless it is registered as a company under this Act, or is formed in pursuance of some other Act of Parliament, or of letters patent.

---

[20] Ch. 2, s. 2, *ante*.
[21] And in the case of an authorized unit trust, regulations made under s. 81 of the Financial Services Act 1986.          [22] S. 2B(6), *ante*.          [23] (1880) 15 Ch. D 247.

Exceptions are made by subsections (2)–(5) of this section, principally for professional partnerships.

On the face of it, the decision of *Smith* v. *Anderson*[24] has settled that a unit trust will not infringe this section. For several reasons, there is a danger of this assumption. First, the decision of the Court of Appeal in this case, despite being a unanimous one, is not without its critics.[25] Criticism is not totally unjustified given the coherent judgment of the court below and the fact that the trust deed in *Smith* v. *Anderson* was modelled on those commonly used by deed of settlement companies, which by definition were 'companies' within the meaning of this statutory provision prohibiting large unincorporated associations. Secondly, even accepting the correctness of this decision, one has to admit that the judgments rested on very fine and narrow arguments. It is not hard to distinguish[26] a particular modern unit trust from the unit trust litigated in *Smith* v. *Anderson*. As a matter of form, the unit trust deed in *Smith* v. *Anderson* was one executed between a trustee and a unitholder on behalf of all others, not between a manager and a trustee. As a matter of substance, the trust was a fixed trust that contemplated passive holding by the trustee rather than active management by the manager. Whether a particular modern unit trust infringes section 716 has to be examined on its own facts.

In order for a particular unit trust to infringe this section, it must be established that:

(1) it is a 'company, association, or partnership', 'formed for the purpose of carrying on any business';
(2) it consists of 'more than 20 persons'; and
(3) the business has 'for its object the acquisition of gain' by it or by its members.

## (1) 'Company, Association, or Partnership'

It is worth emphasizing that before the introduction of registered companies, partnerships had been regarded as a kind of business

---

[24] (1880) 15 Ch. D 247.

[25] *Smith* v. *Anderson supra*, was labelled in Palmer as a 'strange' decision and its current editors suggest 'it is doubtful whether this decision of the Court of Appeal is correct, overruling as it did, the decision of Jessel MR'. (*Palmer's Company Law*, 25th (looseleaf) edn. by Morse, Sweet and Maxwell, 1992, para. 1.213, fn. 45.) It was also doubted in *Re Siddall* (1885) 29 Ch. D 1 at 6 where Bagallay LJ said: 'I must confess that, if I had had to decide *Smith* v. *Anderson*, I possibly should not have entirely agreed with all that was decided in it.'

[26] See the distinction drawn by Cave J in *Re Thomas* (1884) 14 QBD 379 at 385, discussed in s. 1D(2)(b), *post*.

association. Unincorporated joint stock companies, using the deeds of settlement as their constitutive instruments, were in turn being regarded as large partnerships with transferable shares.[27] When the registered company was introduced, the then Parliament must have intended (through the predecessor of section 716) to compel these business associations, whether they were large or small partnerships, with or without shares, to organize themselves as registered companies if they exceeded the stated number of persons. As explained by James LJ in *Smith* v. *Anderson*, the prohibition was:

to prevent the mischief arising from large trading undertakings being carried on by large fluctuating bodies, so that persons dealing with them did not know with whom they were contracting, and so might be put to great difficulty and expense, which was a public mischief to be repressed.[28]

There are important ramifications flowing from this background.

First, the expression 'company, association, or partnership' used in section 716 is intended to refer to the same or similar type of entities carrying on business. The word 'company' apparently refers to an unincorporated company, a large partnership with shares. The meaning of 'association' is not an easy one but in this context it cannot mean any form of association but an association similar to a company. This *ejusdem generis* interpretation is supported by Brett LJ. His Lordship said:

I confess I have some difficulty in seeing how there could be an association for the purpose of carrying on a business which would be neither a company nor a partnership, but I should hesitate to say that, by the ingenuity of men of business, there might not some day be formed a relation among twenty persons which, without being strictly either a company or a partnership, might yet be an association. But according to all ordinary rules of construction, if the association mentioned in sect. 4 is not, strictly speaking, a company or a partnership, *it must be something of a similar kind*.[29]

This also explains why James LJ also said: 'I cannot understand what the difference is between a company and an association.' It also explains why he assumed '[a] company or association . . . to be synonymous terms'.[30]

Of course, this purposive interpretation is also justified on the simple ground that if the word 'association' in this section includes all forms of association, unincorporated charitable or non-profit-making associations with more than twenty members will almost certainly infringe section 716

---

[27] See the explanation of James LJ in *Re Agriculturist Cattle Insurance* (1870) LR 5 Ch. 725 at 733, cited in ch. 1, fn. 57.

[28] *Smith* v. *Anderson*, (1880) 15 Ch. D 247 at 273.

[29] Ibid., at 277; emphasis supplied.

[30] See fn. 2, *supra*.

by having 'as its object'—even though it may be a subsidiary or ancillary one—the acquisition of gains. Any unincorporated charitable organization invariably must through investment or appeals for donation acquire gain before any charitable work can be done.

While Brett LJ may have difficulty in finding a business association which is neither a company nor a partnership, subsequent cases provide the needed examples, namely, mutual assurance clubs[31] and building and loan societies.[32]

It follows from this discussion that the 'company, association, or partnership' in section 716 actually refers to an association that has its origin in a partnership. A partnership, by definition, is a relationship between persons carrying on business. Thus, only large associations formed for the purpose of carrying on business, 'so that persons dealing with them did not know with whom they were contracting, and so might be put to great difficulty and expense', fall within the mischief to be repressed by this section. Clearly, the subsequent requirement in this section that the company, association or partnership has to be 'formed for the purpose of carrying on any business' merely clarifies and does not add anything to the scope of operation of this section.

Because of the historical context in which this prohibition is enacted, the reference to carrying on business in this section should bear the same meaning as the term is used in the definition of a partnership in the Partnership Act 1890. Accordingly, the question whether unitholders are carrying on business through a unit trust will be dealt with in the discussion of whether a unit trust constitutes a partnership. That discussion will suggest that, in the majority of cases, there is only investment but no business in a unit trust. If there is carrying on of a business in a particular case, the business is the business of the trustee, as a trustee, carried on under the direction of the manager; there is no business in common amongst unitholders.

## (2) 'Consisting of More Than 20 Persons'

Section 716 applies only if the number of persons constituting the company, association, or partnership carrying on business exceeds twenty. If there is any carrying on of business by the trustee of a unit trust, there is only one trustee. There cannot be a partnership or association. Even if the manager is considered as a partner, the number is less than twenty. Later

---

[31] *Re Padstow Total Loss Association* (1882) 20 Ch. D 137; see also *Re Arthur Average, etc., Association* (1875) 10 Ch. App. 542.
[32] *Shaw* v. *Benson* (1883) 11 QBD 563; *Greenberg* v. *Cooperstein* [1926] 1 Ch. 657.

in this chapter, it will also be submitted that there is no partnership constituted between the trustee and the manager.

Therefore, it is unlikely that section 716 will be infringed.

### (3) 'Acquisition of Gain'

The third condition for section 716 to apply is that the company, association, or partnership has for its object the acquisition of gains by it or any of its members. It should be noted that the acquisition of gain by members is sufficient to attract the operation of this section.

The expression 'acquisition of gain' has been broadly interpreted and is not restricted to the profit of a business. Thus, it covers a unit trust that invests in shares and stocks, even though the trust does not have an object of gaining profit from the trafficking of securities on the Stock Exchange but only aims at dividend income. The term is wide enough to cover both capital appreciation as well as income produced by the underlying investments, such as rental income and interest on deposits.

This interpretation is supported by *Re Arthur Average Association for British, Foreign, and Colonial Ships*.[33] Jessel MR said:

The 4th section [of Companies Act 1862] applies to companies or associations having for their object the acquisition of gain either by the company or association or the individual members thereof. Now, if you come to the meaning of the word 'gain,' it means acquisition. It has no other meaning that I am aware of. Gain is something obtained or acquired. It is not limited to pecuniary gain. We should have to add the word 'pecuniary' so to limit it. And still less is it limited to commercial profits. The word used, it must be observed, is not 'gains' but 'gain,' in the singular. Commercial profits, no doubt, are gain, but I cannot find anything limiting gain simply to a commercial profit. I take the words as referring to a company which is formed to acquire something, or in which the individual members are to acquire something, as distinguished from a company formed for spending something, and in which the individual members are simply to give something away or to spend something, and not to gain anything.[34]

Jessel MR's definition was accepted by Mayo J in the South Australian case of *Re Riverton Sheep Dip*[35] where his Honour also added:

'Gain' was said by Simonds J to be a word that was 'not susceptible of precise or scientific definition.' He thought the test, for such a purpose as the present, was 'whether that which is being done is what ordinary persons would describe as the carrying on of a business for gain' (*Armour* v. *Liverpool Corporation*).[36] The most appropriate definition to be found in a dictionary may be 'increase in resources or business advantages resulting from business transactions or dealings.' In s. 9(2) the

---

[33] (1875) LR 10 Ch. 545n.                    [34] Ibid.
[35] [1943] SASR 344 at 348.          [36] [1939] Ch. 422 at 437.

word is not limited to pecuniary gain, or confined to commercial profits. It means something obtained, the acquisition of something not before available (*Ian Waing v. Bo Hein*[37]).[38]

The outcome, therefore, is that the purpose of every unit trust for investment purposes will fall within the above description.

## (4) Consequence

If a unit trust is held to have infringed section 716, it is illegal. Two consequences follow. First, as regards a contract with an outsider, it will be invalid if it 'is made directly for the purpose of carrying on the business of the association'[39] but it will be valid if it is merely incidental to that business unless the contracting party has notice of the illegality.[40] Secondly, as regards unitholders constituting the illegal association, it appears that they will be protected by an order for an account of moneys received.[41]

## D. Partnership

Whether a unit trust relationship constitutes a partnership is important for the purpose of section 716 of the Companies Act 1985. It is also important in determining the liability of unitholders as a finding of a partnership means that they will be liable jointly and severally to third parties for matters done in the course of the partnership business. By contrast, a trust beneficiary may only incur several liability in the particular circumstances covered by the principle of *Hardoon v. Belilios*.[42]

A partnership is defined in the Partnership Act 1890 as:

the relationship which subsists between persons carrying on a business in common with a view of profit.[43]

---

[37] (1932) ILR 10 Man. 490.

[38] *Riverton Sheep Dip*, *supra*, at 347.

[39] *Jennings* v. *Hammond* (1882) 9 QBD 225 at 229.

[40] Thus, an illegal loan association cannot recover on a promissory note given as security for a loan (*Jennings* v. *Hammond* (1882) 9 QBD 225; *Shaw* v. *Benson* (1883) 11 QBD 563). But a stationery supplier can recover the price of stationery if it does not have knowledge of the illegality (*Re One and All Sickness and Accident Assurance Association* (1909) 25 TLR 674).

[41] *Re London Marine Insurance Association* (1869) LR 8 Eq. 176; *Greenberg* v. *Cooperstein* [1926] 1 Ch. 657.

[42] [1910] AC 118. In s. 6B and C of this ch., *post*, it will suggest that the principle established in this case only applies to a bare trust; it is a principle that an absolute beneficial owner who gets all the benefit of the property should bear the burdens unless he can show some good reason why the trustee should bear them.

[43] Partnership Act 1890, s. 1(1).

And in determining whether a partnership subsists, the Act also requires that regard must be had to three rules[44] which essentially are:

(1) 'Joint tenancy, tenancy in common, joint property, common property, or part ownership does not of itself create a partnership . . .';
(2) 'The sharing of gross returns does not of itself create a partnership'; and
(3) 'The receipt by a person of a share of profits of a business is prima facie evidence that he is a partner . . . but the receipt of such a share . . . does not of itself make him a partner . . .'

The enquiry as to whether a unit trust is a partnership involves the process of examining whether it has the three elements of 'carrying on business', 'in common', and 'with a view of profit' in the statutory definition of a partnership.

## (1) Carrying on Business

The conventional wisdom is that a private trust is a mechanism for preserving the capital for the beneficiaries,[45] which is done through the investment of that capital. Ordinarily, this is the activity that a trustee of a private trust will engage in. Partners in a partnership, on the other hand, are carrying on business.

In a modern unit trust, the portfolio may consist of a few major assets, as in the case of some authorized unit trusts constituted as property funds, or it may be very diversified, as in the case of trusts that invest in securities or in international markets. The manager may also cause the trustee to invest in futures contracts, derivatives or other hedging instruments for the purpose of efficient portfolio management.[46] The volatility and internationalization of investment markets may also require the manager to diversify and to review constantly the portfolio of underlying assets.[47] This may be dictated by the unit trust deed or statutory regulations or may simply be part of the fiduciary obligation of care.[48] Are all these activities merely investment, or do they constitute a business—an investment business—of the unitholders?

---

[44] Partnership Act 1890, s. 2.

[45] Even in 1992, the Court of Appeal stated that 'the importance of preservation of a trust fund will always outweigh success in its advancement'. *Nestle* v. *National Westminster Bank plc* [1994] 1 All ER 118 at 142, per Leggatt LJ.

[46] Subject to any restriction in the trust deed or in the scheme particulars, the Financial Services (Regulated Schemes) Regulations 1991 permit the manager of an authorized unit trust (other than a feeder fund) to enter into derivative transactions and forward transactions in currency for the purpose of efficient portfolio management: reg. 5.49 *et seq.*

[47] In *Nestle* v. *National Westminster Bank plc* [1994] 1 All ER 118, the Court of Appeal held that a trustee was under a duty to 'conduct regular reviews of the investments' (at 133, per Staughton LJ).            [48] See ch. 4, s. 2B(2), *post.*

In *Smith* v. *Anderson*, the second ground for holding that the unit trust in question did not infringe the outsize association provision was that no business was carried on.[49] The emphasis by all of their Lordships was that the trustees 'were joined together for the purpose of once for all investing certain money which was delivered into their hands, and not for the purpose of obtaining gain from a repetition of investments'.[50] If 'the real object . . . was that the trustees should speculate in investments, . . . the case would have stood in a very different position'.[51] This view was taken apparently because in their Lordships' opinion, 'carrying on' connotes repetition.[52]

The Partnership Acts define the term 'business' as including every trade, occupation or profession[53] but an inclusive definition does not give a definitive meaning of the term. Courts are prepared to accept a dictionary meaning of 'a commercial enterprise as a going concern'.[54]

It is not easy to conclude whether a unit trust can be regarded as a commercial enterprise. Prima facie, the parties do not have any intention to use the unit trust for the purpose of carrying on any trade by themselves or their agent. When an investor acquires units, he considers himself to be acquiring investment assets rather than participating in a business. It is a feature which clearly distinguishes the unit trust from the deed of settlement company although both have a deed of covenant incorporating a trust. From this angle, it is arguable that there is no 'commercial enterprise' in the very sense of these two words.

Perhaps, the real difficulty lies with the views on business and investment expressed in *Smith* v. *Anderson*. Their Lordships in this case took a very broad conception of what a business was and a very narrow interpretation of the ambit of 'investment'. Presumably, in their view, if a trust required its trustees to constantly monitor the portfolio and to constantly buy some properties and to dispose of others in order to meet certain investment criteria[55] or restriction laid down in the trust deed, the

---

[49] S. 1A, *ante*.

[50] Per Brett LJ, text accompanying fn. 5, *supra*.

[51] Per Cotton LJ, text accompanying fn. 6, *supra*.

[52] 'The expression "carrying on" implies a repetition of acts, and excludes the case of an association formed for doing one particular act which is never to be repeated.' ( (1880) 15 Ch. D 247 at 278, per Brett LJ.)          [53] Partnership Act 1890, s. 45.

[54] This is a meaning given in the *Shorter Oxford Dictionary*, accepted by Mason J in *Hope* v. *Bathurst CC* (1980) 144 CLR 1 at 8 on the interpretation of the Local Government Act 1919 (NSW). The courts in both *Canny Gabriel Jackson Advertising* v. *Volume Sales (Finance) Pty. Ltd.* (1971) 157 CLR 321 at 326–7 and in *United Dominions Corporation Ltd.* v. *Brian Pty. Ltd.* (1985) 157 CLR 1 at 11 also found the existence of a partnership on the basis that the parties are 'joint venturers in a commercial enterprise with a view to profit'.

[55] A simple illustration will be a fixed percentage of the total value of the portfolio is required to be in blue chip stocks. Any movement in total value of the trust portfolio will require a corresponding action in its blue chip composition.

trustees will be regarded as carrying on a business under that trust instrument. This approach is in line with the very limited definition of the word 'invest' given by Lawrence J in *Re Wragg*.[56] In this case, his Lordship considered the word to mean:

to apply money in the purchase of some property from which interest or profit is expected *and which property is purchased in order to be held for the sake of income which it will yield.*[57]

Investment for the purpose of capital gain appears to be excluded from his Lordship's definition. This definition may be compared with that given in *The Shorter Oxford English Dictionary* which defines the term as:

to employ money in the purchase of anything from which interest or profit is expected.

This dictionary meaning does not restrict investment to activities for the purpose of producing income.

It is questionable whether today's courts should take the restrictive approach of Lawrence J. His Lordship did not explain why this word cannot bear its ordinary meaning. In any event, *Re Wragg*[58] is distinguishable as a case on interpretation of a trust instrument. The court was ascertaining the subjective intention of the settlor, not determining the existence of a partnership.

Investment is a fast changing concept. It must have now acquired a more 'active' signification than in the days when *Smith* v. *Anderson*[59] and *Re Wragg*[60] were decided. Perhaps, the reality is that investment, like an elephant, is more easily recognized than defined.[61] Pennington gives the following description of investment:

If resources are invested, . . . they are used to acquire 'things' which are retained for a longer or shorter period in the expectation that while retained they will yield an income to the owner, or that they will eventually be disposed of at a price exceeding the cost of acquiring them, or that they will achieve both these results. On the other hand, if 'things' are acquired in order to be used (eg fuel or the raw materials used in a manufacturing business) or to be disposed of as quickly as possible after acquisition (eg the stock in trade of a wholesale or retail business), no investment is involved.[62]

Thus, according to this view, the acquisition of assets by itself does not determine whether there is a business. It is the intention of how those assets are going to be used that is important. Therefore, if the objective of

---

[56] [1919] 2 Ch. 58.                                      [57] Ibid., at 64; emphasis supplied.
[58] [1919] 2 Ch. 58.          [59] (1880) 15 Ch. D 247.          [60] [1919] 2 Ch. 58.
[61] The words of Pennington, *The Law of the Investment Market*, Blackwell Law, 1990, p. 1.
[62] Pennington, *The Law of the Investment Market*, Blackwell Law, 1990, p. 1.

a unit trust is to speculate in shares and the shares are acquired as stock in trade, there may well be a business carried on by that unit trust. The majority of unit trusts, however, are vehicles for diversifying risks. Like an ordinary individual, the unit trust acquires assets for the purpose of retention—with an expectation of income or capital gains. A unit trust may have a variety of assets but this merely reflects the intention to diversify risks. It is the same thing that an individual will do, if he had the same financial resources.

If a narrow conception of investment is taken, as in the case of *Re Wragg*, a unit trust that acquires assets for purposes of producing capital gains as well as income will be regarded as carrying on a business. If a popular conception of investment is subscribed to, a unit trust that buys and sells securities from time to time, aiming at diversification of risks rather than speculative gains, is likely to be regarded as within the realm of investment.

In any event, there is no impediment preventing a unit trust from carrying on a business and generating profits by trafficking in securities or other assets. It is a question of the terms of the relevant unit trust deed.

## (2) 'In Common'

If the participants in a unit trust are to be characterized as partners, the requirement that they carry on business 'in common' can be satisfied by arguing either (a) that the trustee, the manager, and the unitholders carry on business together as principals and agents for each other or (b) that the unitholders carry on business in common by the trustee and/or the manager as their agents.

Before these two situations are canvassed, the leading case of *Cox* v. *Hickman*[63] has to be considered. This case is interesting for its factual similarity with a unit trust. In this case, the partners of a debtor firm executed a deed whereby they assigned all properties of the firm to trustees of their creditors with powers to carry on business and to divide the net income amongst the creditors in rateable proportion. Under the deed, the majority of creditors in a meeting might make rules for conducting the business or to put an end to it altogether. The question was whether the creditors were, by the execution of the deed, partners both with the trustees and *inter se*, in carrying on the business.[64] The House of Lords held that there was no partnership involved, despite the sharing of profits. In view of the bearing of this case on the unit trusts, it may well be useful to quote *in extenso* the reasons given by Lord Cranworth:

---

[63] (1860) 8 HL Cas. 268.     [64] Ibid., at 295, per Wightman J.

It is often said that the test, or one of the tests, whether a person not ostensibly a partner, is nevertheless, in contemplation of law, a partner, is, whether he is entitled to participate in the profits. This, no doubt, is, in general, a sufficiently accurate test; for a right to participate in profits affords cogent, often conclusive evidence, that the trade in which the profits have been made, was carried on in part for or on behalf of the person setting up such a claim. But the real ground of the liability is, that the trade has been carried on by persons acting on his behalf. When this is the case, he is liable to the trade obligations, and entitled to its profits, or to a share of them. It is not strictly correct to say that his right to share in the profits makes him liable to the debts in trade. The correct mode of stating the proposition is to say that the same thing which entitles him to the one makes him liable to the other, namely, the fact that the trade has been carried on on his behalf, i.e., that he stood in the relation of principal towards the persons acting ostensibly as the traders, by whom the liabilities have been incurred, and under whose management the profits have been made.[65]

*Cox* v. *Hickman* therefore explains the degree of relevance of sharing of profits in the determination of the existence of a partnership. It establishes that partners are mutual agents of each other. Mutual agency, thus, is both a test and a consequence of a partnership.

### (a)  The Manager, the Trustee, and the Unitholders as Partners

In *Smith* v. *Anderson*, this notion was not considered. Under *Cox* v. *Hickman*, the construction of any unit trust deed is unlikely to give rise to any general mutual agency. While it is arguable that the manager and the trustee can be the unitholders' agents, there is simply no intention that the unitholders, whether collectively or individually, have the power to act as the agents of the trustee, the manager or both. A fundamental element of a unit trust is the non-participation of the unitholders who provide the capital. If there is any agency intended at all, it is only a one-sided matter, that is, the trustee or the manager will act for the unitholders.

This finding renders a characterization of a partnership relationship amongst the trustee, the manager, and unitholders very unlikely.

### (b)  Unitholders as Partners

It remains to be decided whether the unit trust as a whole constitutes a partnership of unitholders *inter se* acting through the trustee-manager as their agents.

In *Smith* v. *Anderson*, the view expressed was that if there was any business, it was the business of the trustees in their capacity as trustees and not as agents of the certificate holders. In a modern unit trust, the situation

---

[65] (1860) 8 HL Cas. 268 at 306.

is complicated further by the presence of one more party, the manager. But, in principle, the trustee and the manager can be agents carrying on business for unitholders. There are two elements involved in this, (i) a carrying on of business in common by the unitholders and (ii) an agency of the trustee-manager.

In relation to element (i), there is of course the factual difference between *Cox* v. *Hickman* and a modern unit trust. The creditors in *Cox* v. *Hickman* arguably were not the persons receiving the benefit of the trade carried on by the trustees. In truth, it was the debtors who received the benefit in the form of reduction of their indebtedness. Nevertheless, this difference does not affect the point established in this case that there must generally be a mutual agency amongst the partners in a partnership. There are ample grounds for saying that this element is non-existent in a unit trust.

In the first place, underlying the mutual agency in a partnership is the mutual trust and confidence amongst partners. This has its manifestation in the principles that interests of a partner are not transferable and admission of new partners requires unanimous consent. Free transferability of units in a unit trust—and a ready market-place for them—were and still are essential ingredients of a unit trust. Transferability means that the personal identities of unitholders are irrelevant to their relationship. It should also follow that in such a relationship there is no element of mutual confidence such as that exists between partners.

Moreover, different investors become unitholders at different times. Each regards himself as purchasing a bundle of rights in the form of a unit and each unit may have contractual rights in addition to any right in the portfolio of assets.[66] All unitholders have several, not joint, interests.

With regard to element (ii), that the trustee and the manager are carrying on business as agents of the unitholders, it may be noted that in *Smith* v. *Anderson*, there were provisions for meeting of certificate holders annually to 'be conducted in the manner prescribed in Table A to the Companies Act, 1862'[67] and to consider the trustees' report, to appoint an auditor, and to elect new trustees.[68] Such meetings could sanction reinvestment as well.[69] Despite these provisions, Brett LJ observed that it was 'obviously not true'[70] that the certificate holders were undisclosed principals. Cotton LJ explained that the power to sanction reinvestment was 'the power to give such assent as cestuis que trust usually give for a change of securities when they are not incapacitated by infancy or

[66] Ch. 5, s. 3, *post*.
[67] Cl. 25: (1880) 15 Ch. D 247 at 253.
[68] Cl. 26 of the deed: (1880) 15 Ch. D 247 at 253.
[69] Cl. 20 of the deed: (1880) 15 Ch. D 247 at 252.
[70] (1880) 15 Ch. D 247 at 280.

otherwise' and the number of cestuis que trust made it necessary to have rules for those certificate holders present in meetings to bind those absent and for the majority to bind the minority. 'They meet as cestuis que trust to give their assent, not as members of the partnership joining to carry on and control the business of the partnership.'[71]

Several years later, *Smith* v. *Anderson* was followed in *Crowther* v. *Thorley*,[72] where the Court of Appeal had to decide whether a society constituted by a deed of trust made between the trustees and the members and incorporating the rules of the society infringed section 4 of the Companies Act 1862, the same provision as in *Smith* v. *Anderson*. It was established that the trustees carried on the business of mining. It was held that the business was carried on by the trustees as trustees, and not as agents for the members. Brett MR explained the position:

Now, what is the principle which is to determine whether such trustees are trustees only, or trustees and agents as well for their cestuis que trust. An agent for a principal is a person who, having no interest of his own, *is bound to observe and obey the orders of his principal*. Were these trustees in such a position? Most decidedly not. They carried on the business in their own way, they might do so without any authority from or even in defiance of the wishes of the other members of the association.[73]

Shortly after *Crowther* v. *Thorley* came the case of *Re Thomas*.[74] The rules of a money club provided that 'the business of the society should be carried on by a committee of seven members, that all the property and assets of the society should be vested in a trustee, and that the committee should be empowered to make such by-laws and regulations for the conduct of the business of the society as they might deem necessary . . .'. Cave J distinguished *Crowther* v. *Thorley* in the following terms:

The main object of the society in *Crowther* v. *Thorley* was to buy freehold land and divide it amongst the members; and in my opinion the judgment proceeds upon the fact that the trustees carried on business in their own names and were themselves responsible. In this case the committee do not carry on the business in their own names, and are not themselves responsible in any way except that they are bound to carry on the business honestly . . .[75]

His Lordship held (*inter alia*) that the association was illegal, infringing section 4 of the Companies Act.

In another Court of Appeal decision, *Re Siddall*,[76] an association was formed for the purpose of purchasing land and reselling it in allotments to

---

[71] (1880) 15 Ch. D 247 at 284, per Cotton LJ.                    [72] (1884) 50 LT 43.
[73] Ibid., at 46; emphasis supplied.
[74] (1884) 14 QBD 379, decided eight months after the judgment in *Crowther* v. *Thorley* was given.                    [75] Ibid., at 385.                    [76] (1885) 29 Ch. D 1.

its members. The property was vested in the trustees but the management was vested in a committee. The trustees had power to borrow and the committee had power to make roads and drains etc. on the land. It was held that the association did not infringe section 4 of the Companies Act. The court felt obliged to follow *Crowther* v. *Thorley*[77] but *Re Thomas*[78] was not cited. There was no discussion of general principles or of whether the committee with management power could be regarded as an agent.

*Crowther* v. *Thorley*[79] suggests that a trustee can be an agent of the beneficiaries if the trustee is 'bound to observe and obey the orders' of the beneficiaries and *Re Thomas*[80] suggests that a separate committee can be an agent of the beneficiaries. Translated into the modern unit trust context, these two cases may suggest an argument that the unitholders are carrying on business in common through the manager as the agent and the trustee as their trustee. But is this necessarily the position? Several observations can be made.

In the first place, much can be said about Brett MR's view in *Crowther* v. *Thorley*[81] on the existence of control. It is true that in an ordinary private trust, beneficiaries collectively or individually do not have any right to direct or control the trustee in the administration of the trust.[82] At best, they can direct the termination of the trust if all are *sui juris* and absolutely entitled. But it does not follow that the presence of control will negate the existence of a pure trust relationship. The trust principle that beneficiaries cannot control their trustees on issues of management is established in the context where the trust is used as a means to carry out the donative wishes of the settlor: the principle simply gives primacy to the wish of the settlor. Where the trustee and the beneficiary are contracting parties, this element of gift of the settlor does not exist. In this respect, the unit trust deed has to be construed like any other ordinary contract in which the court is asked to consider whether the parties are principals and agents.

A principal has control over the acts of an agent but it does not follow that whenever there is control by a party over the other, the relationship is an agency. Control is also an incident of an employment relationship and may also exist with different intensity in other contractual relationships such as those between a bailor and a bailee, a supplier and a distributor (with no agency relationship established), a client and a solicitor, a lessor and a lessee, and a lender and a borrower. Thus control, by itself, is only one of the many incidents of agency. It is also pertinent to ask for what

---

[77] (1884) 50 LT 43.
[79] (1884) 50 LT 43.
[81] (1884) 50 LT 43 at 46, text accompanying fn. 73, *supra*.
[78] (1884) 14 QBD 379.
[80] (1884) 14 QBD 379.
[82] *Re Brockbank* [1948] Ch. 206; *Stephenson* v. *Barclays Bank Trust Co.* [1975] 1 All ER 625 at 637; *Holding & Management Ltd.* v. *Property Holding plc* [1990] 1 All ER 938 at 948.

purpose is control given or retained. The general principle to establish an agency is that an agency between two parties 'may be implied in a case where each has conducted himself towards the other in such a way that it is reasonable for that other to infer from that conduct consent to the agency relationship'.[83] It is simply a question whether a reasonable man will infer an agency contract on the facts. No special rules of law peculiar to agency are involved. This principle simply represents the obvious proposition that contractual terms are often inferred by the court from the circumstances.[84]

Secondly, in a unit trust, powers of investment do not originate from any settlor but from a deed in which the holder of the powers is one of the constituting parties. This differs from delegation of responsibilities to an investment agent where the power is granted primarily by the investor. Although it can be argued that this is a matter of form and is the same as the position where an investor appoints an agent in a contract prepared by that agent, it has to be acknowledged that when a unitholder acquires units, he is not asking the manager to manage his moneys separate from those of the other unitholders. The unitholder considers himself to be acquiring a bundle of rights in a portfolio of assets that are already held in the hands of the trustee.[85] His intention is to acquire beneficial interests in an existing trust fund and other rights incidental to the units. The process of acquisition of units thus demonstrates that unitholders, individually, do not intend the manager and the trustee to invest as their specific agents. They intend to acquire a share of a trust fund together with a bundle of contractual rights.

Thirdly, relevant in this context are the powers given to a meeting of unitholders. A unitholder's meeting of an authorized unit trust may be convened under regulation 11.07 of the Financial Services (Regulated Schemes) Regulations 1991. In respect of such a meeting, regulation 11.08 provides (emphasis supplied):

A meeting of holders duly convened and held in accordance with this part of these regulations shall be competent by extraordinary resolution to require, authorise or approve any act, matter or document in respect of which any such resolution is required or expressly contemplated by these regulations, *but shall not have any other powers.*

The powers of such a meeting are limited to matters that are 'required or expressly contemplated by [the] regulations' to be resolved by members. A perusal of other parts of the Regulations indicates that such matters are

---

[83] *Bowstead and Reynolds on Agency*, 16th edn., Sweet and Maxwell, 1996, art. 8.
[84] Comment to art. 8 of Bowstead, *supra*, at p. 42.
[85] Even for the first unitholder subscribing for units, the intention is the same. He intends to be joined in by other unitholders who contribute to the trust fund as well. This is their expectation of diversification.

limited to the removal of the manager,[86] modification of trust deed,[87] change of scheme particulars,[88] amalgamation,[89] and reconstruction.[90]

Similar, but often wider, powers are given to unitholders of non-authorized unit trusts.

In respect of unitholders of an authorized unit trust, the Regulations do not actually give a power to unitholders to convene a meeting for regulation 11.07 only provides that '[t]he trustee shall, on request in writing of holders registered as holding not less than one-tenth (or any proportion below one-tenth specified . . . in the trust deed) in value of the units . . . convene a meeting . . .'. Thus, unitholders only have a power to make a request. It is the trustee who is being vested with the power to convene a unitholders' meeting. If the trustee defaults, the proper remedy will be an action against the trustee. The unitholders cannot proceed to convene a meeting themselves and resolve the matters covered by the Regulations.

The powers of unitholders' meetings are a question of construction of the relevant covenants or regulation. However, they share some important common characteristics. Unlike companies, it is seldom provided for annual or periodic meetings of unitholders. Meetings of unitholders are usually confined to changes to the scheme that are of a fundamental nature and are not foreseen at the time when investors acquire their units. Examples are changes in investment policy, the manager or the institutional structure of the scheme. For an authorized unit trust, the Financial Services (Regulated Schemes) Regulations 1991 put it beyond doubt that unitholders 'shall not have any other powers' beyond those stated in the Regulations.

It is submitted that the powers of giving directions by unitholders in their meetings are not powers for the purpose of carrying on the business in common of the unitholders. The meetings can hardly be described as business meetings. The meetings convened and the directions given are for the purpose of protecting the interest of the unitholders as owners of units.

This interpretation is analogous to Cotton LJ's view that the power of certificate holders to sanction reinvestment by the trustees in *Smith* v. *Anderson* was 'the power to give such assent as cestuis que trust usually give for a change of securities when they are not incapacitated by infancy or otherwise'.[91] It may also be compared with the power of the creditors in *Cox* v. *Hickman*[92] to direct the trustees as to the management of the firm. Lord Cranworth explained:

[86] Reg. 7. 17.   [87] Reg. 11.02.   [88] Reg. 11.04.   [89] Reg. 11.05.
[90] Reg. 11.06.   [91] (1880) 15 Ch. D 247 at 284.
[92] (1860) 8 HL Cas. 268.

. . . I am aware that in this deed special powers are given to the creditors, which it was said, showed that they had become partners, even if that had been the consequence of their concurrence in the previous trust. The powers may be described briefly as, first, a power of determining by a majority in value of their body, that the trade should be discontinued, or, if not discontinued, then, secondly, a power of making rules and orders as to its conduct and management.

These powers do not appear to me to alter the case. The creditors might, by process of law, have obtained possession of the whole of the property. By the earlier provisions of the deed, they consented to abandon that right, and to allow the trade to be carried on by the trustees. *The effect of these powers is only to qualify their consent. They stipulate for a right to withdraw it altogether; or, if not, then to impose terms as to the mode in which the trusts to which they had agreed should be executed . . .*[93]

Thus, control exerted through unitholders' meetings is control exercised for the purpose of protection of the interests of unitholders as owners of units. It is not control of a general nature such as might create an agency relationship.

The position therefore is that unitholders in a unit trust do not carry on business in common through the agency of the trustee and the manager. Following the third reason of decision of James, Brett, and Cotton LJJ in *Smith* v. *Anderson*, if there is any business being conducted by a particular unit trust, it is the business of the trustee and the manager.

### (3) 'With a View to Profit'

Profit, or perhaps the accounting of it, is also a key element in the understanding of the conceptual difference between a partnership and a unit trust. As Brett LJ has explained in *Smith* v. *Anderson*, the gain by a joint stock company or corporation is that of the company, not the individual shareholders; but the gain in a partnership will not belong to the partnership as a whole but to the individual partners.[94]

In the partnership context, 'profit' is something that exists in a business for '[b]y profit is meant the net gain amount remaining after paying out of the *receipts of a business* all the expenses incurred in obtaining those receipts'.[95]

In the case of a unit trust, if there is any carrying on of a business, it will be with a view of profit. If the trustee and the manager are merely investing

---

[93] (1860) 8 HL Cas. 268 at 307; emphasis supplied.

[94] (1880) 15 Ch. D 247 at 278.

[95] *Lindley & Banks on Partnership*, 17th edn. by I'Anson Banks, Sweet and Maxwell, 1995, para. 2–05; emphasis supplied. Fletcher Moulton LJ said in *Re The Spanish Prospective Company Limited* [1911] 1 Ch. 92 at 98, ' "Profits" implies a comparison between the state of a business at two specific dates usually separated by an interval of a year. The fundamental meaning is the amount of gain made by the business during the year. This can only be ascertained by a comparison of the assets of the business at the two dates.'

without carrying on business, there is no profit at all in the sense used in the Partnership Act 1890; what is generated is property gain. In a sense, a unitholder owning units in a unit trust is analogous to a property owner receiving rental income as well as capital appreciation.

It is true that the accounting treatment of modern unit trusts takes the trust as a business entity but the primary objective of accounts is to ascertain the value of underlying assets and hence the value of each unit. No goodwill is accounted for. This view of the concept of profit as well as the accounting of unit trust gains distinguishes a unit trust from not only a partnership but also a company.

### E. Conclusion: Purpose of Associating

This analysis suggests that the trustee, the manager, and the unitholders are associating under a single multipartite contract but they are not carrying on any business in common with view to profit. What then is the purpose of their associating?

The conclusion that the parties are associating is made in the light of the liberal view given by the law to the concept of association. Primarily, the parties are associating together for the purpose of investment, with the unitholders providing the capital and the trustee and the manager providing the management services. Investment is by nature the utilization of properties to generate gains, be they income or capital appreciation. When all unitholders assemble together in unitholders' meetings, they do so in order to make a collective decision as property owners, i.e. owners of units, and not for the purpose of directing the investment management which, under the unit trust deed and the Financial Services (Regulated Schemes) Regulations 1991, is the exclusive province of the manager and the trustee.

### 2. THE TRUSTEE-MANAGER RELATIONSHIP

### A. Partnership

It cannot be denied that by entering into the trust deed, both the manager and the trustee are entering into a venture that provides services to their 'customers' and that produces their income. This is cooperation in business, but is unlikely to constitute them a partnership. Basically, the test of the existence of a partnership is by reference to the definition of a partnership discussed and also by reference to the statutory rules regarding co-ownership of assets, sharing of gross return, and also sharing of profit.[96]

---

[96] See s. 1D, *ante.*

There is no business in common. The demarcation of functions under the unit trust deed draws the line of business between them. In essence, the trustee is carrying on the business as a professional trustee and the manager is carrying on the business of investment management. They have different contractual obligations under the unit trust deed, the trustee as a trustee of properties, a registrar of unitholders,[97] and also as a supervisor of the manager and the manager as a dealer in units and as a fund manager.[98] In the unit trust deed, the trustee and the manager are making covenants severally rather than jointly and severally. There is clearly no intention to constitute themselves mutual agents so as to give rise to any inference of a business 'in common'.

Sharing of profit provides prima facie evidence of the existence of a partnership. Sharing of gross return is also a factor. Each party receives its service fees for the services rendered to the unit trust. The manager may receive additional income in the process of buying and selling units. These are gross returns rather than profits. Whether the manager or the trustee makes any profit will depend on whether there is any amount remaining after payment out of this income of all the expenses incurred by it as a separate business unit. In any event, there is no sharing of these returns between the trustee and the manager. There is also no sharing of profit between them.

Both therefore are acting as principals on their own account.

## B. Agency

The manager and the trustee are not in any relationship of agency at a general level.[99] Agency is the result of a grant of power by the principal and the assumption of obligations by the agent. At the inception of a unit trust, the manager and the trustee are contracting as principals to constitute the unit trust that enables both to act for investors according to their divided responsibilities.

The trustee cannot be regarded as the agent of the manager. It is not an agent holding properties for its principal; the properties in a unit trust do not belong to the manager. If it is an agent of the manager, it will be under an obligation to obey the order and directions of the principal. It is true that, in the majority of cases, the manager's management powers are to be exercised in the form of directions to the trustee as regards the buying and

---

[97] For an authorized unit trust, the trustee is under an obligation to maintain a register, but the manager shares the duty to ensure that the register's information is correct as it is possessing all the information through its own dealing of units: the Financial Services (Regulated Schemes) Regulations 1991, reg. 6.02.

[98] Ch. 4, s. 1B(1), *post.*

[99] *Parkes Management Ltd.* v. *Perpetual Trustee Co. Ltd.* (1977) ACLC 29,545.

selling of assets in the portfolio.[100] This does not mean that the trustee has to obey every direction. The trustee owes the unitholders a duty to supervise the manager.[101] As part of this duty, the trustee is not bound to follow the direction if the directed exercise is a matter within the trustee's discretion or if the direction involves a breach of the manager's fiduciary duty, the terms of the trust deed, or the provisions of any statute.[102]

Equally, the manager cannot be regarded as the agent of the trustee. If the manager can direct the trustee as to investments, it can hardly be regarded as the agent of the person that is subject to its direction. Moreover, in a commercial sense, the unit trust is a financial product of the manager and is often only a part of the manager's financial services. The manager is in truth 'the source and origin of the trust'[103] and also 'the entrepreneur of an investment scheme'.[104] The manager has interests in its own right and not merely subordinate interests as an agent.[105]

This position is recognized by the Financial Services (Regulated Schemes) Regulations 1991. A juxtaposition of regulation 7.02 and regulation 7.09 reveals this. Regulation 7.02 provides:

1. It is the duty of the manager to manage the scheme in accordance with: (a) the trust deed, and (b) these regulations, and (c) the most recently published scheme particulars.
2. . . . it is the manager's *right and* duty to make decisions as to the constituents of the property of the scheme in such a way as appears to him likely to secure that the objectives of the scheme are attained . . .[106]

And regulation 7.09 provides:

1. It is the duty of the trustee to take reasonable care to ensure—(a) except in relation to Part 5, that the scheme is managed by the manager in accordance with regulation 7.02.1, and (b) in relation to Part 5, that decisions about the constituents of the property of the scheme do not exceed the powers conferred on the manager.

Regulation 7.02 applies to the manager. It has two limbs, one dealing with the management of the scheme in general and the other dealing with investment of scheme property in particular. The duty of supervision of the trustee specified in regulation 7.09 mirrors this two-limb structure.

In respect of the investment of the property of the unit trust, regulation 7.02.2 spells out clearly that it is not only a duty but also 'a right' of the manager to make decisions. Correspondingly, regulation 7.09 is drafted in

---

[100] See ch. 4, s. 3A, *post*.      [101] See ch. 4, s. 1B(1), *post*.
[102] See ch. 4, s. 3C, *post*.
[103] Ibid., at 29,551, per Hope JA. His judgment was agreed to by Moffitt P and Mahoney JA.
[104] *Elders Trustee and Executor Co. Ltd.* v. *EG Reeves Pty. Ltd.* (1987) 78 ALR 193 at 228, per Gummow J.      [105] See ch. 2, s. 2D(3), *ante*.
[106] Emphasis supplied.

negative terms so as to leave no doubt that the trustee's obligation does not extend to a positive consideration on the merits of particular investments. In other words, the trustee has no 'right' to make an investment decision as its counterpart in an ordinary private trust. This is also echoed by regulation 7.03.1 which provides that '[t]he manager may without the specific authority of the trustee give instructions to agents as to the acquisition or disposal of property of the scheme'. But at the same time, regulation 7.03 requires the manager to restore the trust portfolio to its status quo if the trustee forms the opinion that the manager exceeds its power in a particular transaction.

Thus, in an authorized unit trust, both the manager and the trustee cannot be regarded as a subordinate of the other.

The position appears to be the same for other unit trusts. In *Parkes Management Ltd.* v. *Perpetual Trustee Co. Ltd.*,[107] the manager of a unit trust sought to challenge the certificate by the trustee that it would be in the interest of the unitholders for the manager to retire. It was argued (*inter alia*) by the trustee that an injunction[108] should not be granted to continue a personal relationship. This was rejected by Hope JA on the ground that the manager was neither the agent nor employee of the trustee:

It was then submitted that no injunction would be granted in a case such as the present because of the principle that injunctions will not be granted to continue a personal relationship . . . I do not think that this principle is to be applied to the present case. *The Manager is in no sense to be regarded as an employee or agent or in some analogous relationship with the Trustee*, or as seeking to ensure the continuance of such a relationship. It is entitled to ensure, in the interests of itself and of the unitholders, that the Trustee properly performs its functions and duties. Its position in the whole scheme was central to that scheme and its removal in a very real sense changed in an important way the character of the scheme.[109]

The absence of an agency at a general level does not preclude the finding of an agency relationship in some specific transactions of a trust's operation. The Financial Services (Regulated Schemes) Regulations 1991 clearly contemplates the possibility of the manager of an authorized unit trust selling and buying units as an agent of the trustee, rather than the manager acting as a principal.[110] It also requires the trustee to appoint the manager or the manager's nominee as an agent in exercising the voting rights of underlying assets.[111] These are not the only matters permitted by the

---

[107] (1977) ACLC 40–354.

[108] Presumably, the relief sought was to restrain the trustee from issuing the certificate. The terms of the injunction sought by the manager are not clear from the report.

[109] Ibid., at 29,554; emphasis supplied.

[110] The Financial Services (Regulated Schemes) Regulations 1991, reg. 4.22. This regulation is not commonly used.                    [111] Ibid., reg. 7.11.3.

Regulations. Under regulation 7.15, delegation between the trustee and the manager is generally permitted, except that the trustee's functions of oversight and custody cannot be delegated to the manager or its associate. A trust deed may expressly provide that the manager shall be the trustee's agent on specific matters. Little has been written on the way the day-to-day business of a trust is conducted but it is conceivable that delegation is inevitable in some circumstances and an agency may therefore arise from a course of conduct. For example, in an offshore trust that invests in the share markets, the manager, after making the choices for its portfolio, may simply instruct the broker to buy shares in the name of the trustee.[112] It is simply acting on behalf of the trustee in giving instructions to the broker. Likewise, a manager in a property trust[113] may be collecting rents and paying rates and other outgoings for the trustee as part of its daily management of the properties.[114]

The possibility of specific agency situations, such as those above discussed, does not undermine the basic proposition that there is no general agency relationship between the trustee and the manager.

### C. Fiduciary Character of the Trustee-Manager Relationship

### (1) Importance of Fiduciary Principles to the Relationship

The conclusion from the foregoing discussion is that the trustee and the manager are not in partnership or in a general agency relationship. They are independent contracting parties to the unit trust deed. An examination of the terms of a typical trust deed of a non-authorized unit trust in detail

---

[112] This is a scenario contemplated by reg. 7.03(1) of the Financial Services (Regulated Schemes) Regulations 1991. Arguably, that regulation constitutes the manager an agent to purchase or dispose of unit trust property in the name of the trustee. It is a statutory one but is confined to this specific type of matter. Cf. *YSF Pty. Ltd.* v. *Elders Trustee and Executor Co. Ltd.*, unreported, NSWSC (Eq. Div.) No. 5021 of 1987, Young J , 22 Apr. 1991 upheld on appeal (*Austrust Ltd. (formerly known as Elders Trustee and Executor Co. Ltd.)* v. *YSF Pty. Ltd.*, NSW Court of Appeal, No. CA 40274 of 1991, 26 May 1993). In this case, a unit trust was set up in the operation of a pig farm from which the proceeds would be distributed to the unitholders. The plaintiff supplied pig food to the manager who subsequently went into liquidation. The plaintiff sued the trustee as the principal of the manager. Under the deed, the manager was to ensure that the investments were kept in good repair. The court held that the pig food was not an investment in itself but something necessary to keep the investment, the pig, intact. On construction of the trust deed, the trustee owned the pigs and was obliged to pay the bills for expenditure and the manager was organizing the purchase of the pig food as an agent for the trustee.

[113] Be it a non-authorized one or a single property trust.

[114] Cf. *Telford Property Fund* v. *Permanent Trustee Co. Ltd.*, unreported, NSWSC (Eq. Div.) No 4026 of 1985, Kearney J, 28 Feb. 1985, where the court had to decide if the trustee had by a course of conduct displaced the duty of the manager under the trust deed to collect rent of a property of the trust.

reveals that the majority of the provisions are covenants made by either of them with unitholders or are provisions conferring powers or discretions on them by unitholders. When the regulations of the Financial Services (Regulated Schemes) Regulations 1991 are incorporated expressly into the trust deed of an authorized unit trust, it appears that they may be construed in the same manner. There are not many provisions that can operate as promises between these two parties.

Where provisions in the deed embody covenants made with unitholders, they can be enforced by unitholders as promisees. In respect of an exercise of power or discretion by the trustee which is without good faith or otherwise wrongful, unitholders can sue the trustee for breach of trust. In the case of the manager, unitholders may bring an action for an abuse of power on the basis of a breach of fiduciary duty.[115] Thus, there is no problem of standing to sue for aggrieved unitholders.

As between the manager and the trustee, the position is less clear if a claim cannot be based on contract. There are numerous situations where this may happen. Both the trustee and the manager may exercise powers as fiduciaries of unitholders. The exercise of some of these powers by one fiduciary may cause damage or injury to the other fiduciary. For example, the trustee of an authorized unit trust may abuse the power under the Financial Services (Regulated Schemes) Regulations 1991 that enables it to give notice in writing to the manager to remove the manager if for good and sufficient reason it is of the opinion that a change of the manager is desirable in the interests of unitholders.[116] The trustee may also take actions claimed to be pursuant to its duty to take all reasonable care and to exercise all due diligence . . . 'to exercise such degree of supervision of the manager's operation of the scheme as is appropriate'.[117] The trustee may also use its power to require the manager to furnish information concerning the management and administration of the scheme[118] for its own ulterior motive. The trustee may convene a unitholders' meeting[119] not for the purpose contemplated by the Regulations or the trust deed but with a view to embarrass the manager. This type of action by itself will at least cause disruption to the business of the manager. Likewise, the manager may abuse its powers. For example, it may refuse to approve an increase of remuneration where the terms of the trust deed require its approval as a condition.[120]

---

[115] For the characterization of the manager as a fiduciary, see s. 4B of this ch., *post*.

[116] Reg. 7.17. The removal will be subject to the approval of the Secretary of State (now the Treasury): s. 82 of the Financial Services Act 1986.

[117] Ibid., reg. 7.14.2.          [118] Ibid., reg. 7.08.          [119] Ibid., reg. 11.07.

[120] The Financial Services (Regulated Schemes) Regulations 1991 do not provide for increase of the trustee's charges. These are matters to be provided by the trust deed and disclosed in the scheme particulars: reg. 8.03 and Sch. 2, item 13.

In the exercise of these powers, the power holder stands in a fiduciary relation to the unitholders and any abuse can give rise to a cause of action by the unitholders based on fiduciary principles. Since the manager and the trustee are independent contractors standing at arm's length to each other, the question arises whether any abuse of such power by one of them to the detriment of the other will give the other party victimized the right to sue.

In *Parkes Management Ltd.* v. *Perpetual Trustee Co. Ltd.*,[121] the Court of Appeal of the Supreme Court of New South Wales held that such a right did exist on the particular facts of the case. The issue was seen as one of contractual construction of the particular unit trust deed and the construction adopted by their Honours was strained. It is submitted that their Honours could have framed the issue as one of fiduciary duties between co-fiduciaries, i.e., the trustee and the manager.

The question in this type of situation is whether the manager and the trustee, as fiduciaries of unitholders, could also be fiduciaries between themselves. If the answer is yes, in what particular circumstances will this situation arise? Before *Parkes Management* is examined, it may be instructive to consider the principles under which one of two persons may be characterized as a fiduciary of the other.

## (2) Principles of Characterization

It is important, first of all, to define a fiduciary. Despite voluminous literature,[122] there is no ready answer and the fiduciary relationship remains 'a concept in search of a principle'.[123] In general terms, it is

---

[121] [1977–1978] ACLC 29,543.

[122] For example, Finn, *Fiduciary Obligations*, Law Book Co., 1977; Shepherd, *The Law of Fiduciaries*, Carswell, Toronto, 1981; Sealy, 'Fiduciary Relationships' [1962] *Camb. LJ* 69; Gautreau, 'Demystifying the Fiduciary Mystique' (1989) 68 *Can. BR* 1; Finn, 'Contract and the Fiduciary Principle' (1989) 12 *UNSWLJ* 76; Finn, 'The Fiduciary Principle' in Youdan (ed.), *Equity, Fiduciaries and Trusts*, Carswell, Toronto, 1989, pp. 31 *et seq.*; Finn, 'Fiduciary Law and the Modern Commercial World' in McKendrick, *Commercial Aspects of Trusts and Fiduciary Obligations*, Clarendon Press, 1992, pp. 7–42; Flannigan, 'The Fiduciary Obligations', (1989) 9 *OJLS* 285; Sealy, 'Fiduciary Obligations, Forty Years On' (1995) 9 *JCL* 37.; Law Commission, *Fiduciary Duties and Regulatory Rules: a Consultation Paper*, HMSO, 1992; Law Commission, *Fiduciary Duties and Regulatory Rules* (Report No. 236), HMSO, 1995; *Special Lectures of the Law Society of Upper Canada 1990: Fiduciary Duties*, De Boo, 1991; Glover, *Commercial Equity: Fiduciary Relationships*, Butterworths Australia, 1995; Bean, *Fiduciary Obligations and Joint Ventures: the Collaborative Fiduciary Relationship*, Clarendon Press, 1995.

[123] The words of his Honour Mason CJ in his extra-judicial comment in 'Themes and Prospects' in Finn (ed.), *Essays in Equity*, Law Book Co., 1985, p. 246 which was cited with approval by Wilson J in the Supreme Court of Canada in *Frame* v. *Smith* (1987) 42 DLR (4th) 81 at 98.

possible to divide fiduciaries into two categories, status-based fiduciaries and fact-based fiduciaries.[124]

The status-based category includes a core of well established relationships such as trustee-beneficiary, guardian-ward, director-company, principal-agent, solicitor-client, employer-employee, and partner-partner. They are relationships which are regarded by equity as fiduciary *per se*. It is debatable as to what is the common denominator behind these relationships but it is not a matter of concern here.

The fact-based category is of more immediate interest as it may embrace the trustee-manager relationship. This category must have derived from the view that the category of cases of fiduciary relationships is no more closed than the categories of negligence at common law.[125] Unfortunately, the law is fluid and it is a category that defies definition. There are three possible bases or tests, which are not mutually exclusive,[126] according to which the court may find the existence of a fiduciary relationship.

The first test is trust and confidence. This is generally regarded as the conventional basis of the status-based fiduciary relationships. As Sealy has pointed out, breach of trust or confidence is one of the traditional heads of Chancery's jurisdiction from which the more technical concept of the trust is derived.[127] The general principle is that if confidence is reposed, and that confidence is abused, a court of equity will grant relief whether or not there is any trust of property.[128] This traditional test is best summed up in the words of McMullin J in *Farrington* v. *Rowe McBride & Partners*:[129]

A fiduciary relationship exists whenever there is a relationship of confidence such that equity imposes duties or disabilities upon the person in whom the confidence is reposed in order to prevent the possible absence of confidence.[130]

---

[124] This is the terminology of the Law Commission in *Fiduciary Duties and Regulatory Rules: a Consultation Paper* (Consultation Paper No. 124), HMSO, 1992, para. 2.4.3 and in *Fiduciary Duties and Regulatory Rules* (Report No. 236), HMSO, 1995

[125] 'The category of cases in which fiduciary duties and obligations arise from the circumstances of the case and the relationship of the parties is no more "closed" than the categories of negligence at common law.' *Laskin* v. *Bache & Co. Inc.* (1972) 23 DLR (3d) 385 at 392 per Arnup JA.                                                      [126] See discussion below.

[127] Sealy, 'Fiduciary Relationships' (1962) *CLJ* 69.

[128] *Gartside* v. *Isherwood* (1783) 1 Bro. CC 558 at 560; *Tate* v. *Williamson* (1866) 2 Ch. App. 55 at 61; *Coleman* v. *Myers* [1977] 2 NZLR 225; *Farrington* v. *Rowe McBride & Partners* [1985] 1 NZLR 83; *Standard Investments Ltd.* v. *Canadian Imperial Bank of Commerce* (1983) 5 DLR (4th) 452. It is also stated in the 2nd edn. of Meagher, Gummow and Lehane, *Equity: Doctrines and Remedies*, Butterworths Australia, 1984 that 'a fiduciary relationship exists, giving rise to obligations of that character, where the relationship is one of confidence, in which equity imposes duties upon the person in whom confidence is reposed in order to prevent the abuse of confidence' (para. 501). In the 3rd edn., the authors take the view that 'actual trust or confidence is not a necessary feature of all relationships which are undoubtedly fiduciary' (para. 501), apparently accepting Gibbs CJ's criticism of this test in the *Hospital Products* case: *supra*, at 61.          [129] [1985] 1 NZLR 83.          [130] Ibid., at 94.

The second is the undertaking test. The major proponent appears to be Scott, who states in the *California Law Review* that:

A fiduciary is a person who undertakes to act in the interests of another person. It is immaterial whether the undertaking is in the form of contract. It is immaterial that the undertaking is gratuitous.[131]

It has received its refinement by Finn in his book, *Fiduciary Obligations*:

[A fiduciary] is, simply, someone who undertakes to act for or on behalf of another in some particular matter or matters. That undertaking may be of a general character. It may be specific and limited. It is immaterial whether the undertaking is or is not in the form of a contract. It is immaterial that the undertaking is gratuitous. And the undertaking may be officiously assumed without request.[132]

This test was subsequently applied by the New South Wales Court of Appeal in the seminal case of *Hospital Products Ltd.* v. *United States Surgical Corporation*[133] and was accepted by some of their Honours in the High Court—with qualifications,[134] modifications[135] or extensions.[136]

The third can be labelled as the 'vulnerability' test. It emphasizes the vulnerable position of the objects of the fiduciary power. The leading statement is the dissenting judgment of Wilson J in the Supreme Court of Canada in *Frame* v. *Smith*,[137] which was approved in the leading Canadian case on fiduciary law, *LAC Minerals Ltd.* v. *International Corona Resources Ltd.*[138] Wilson J said:

[T]here are common features discernible in the contexts in which fiduciary duties have been found to exist and these common features do provide a rough and ready guide to whether or not the imposition of a fiduciary obligation on a new relationship would be appropriate and consistent. Relationships in which fiduciary obligation has been imposed seem to possess three general characteristics:
(1) The fiduciary has scope for the exercise of some discretion or power.
(2) The fiduciary can unilaterally exercise that power or discretion so as to affect the beneficiary's legal or practical interests.
(3) The beneficiary is peculiarly vulnerable to or at the mercy of the fiduciary holding the discretion or power.[139]

---

[131]  Scott, 'The Fiduciary Principle' (1949) 37 *Cal. LR* 539 at 540.
[132]  Finn, *Fiduciary Obligations*, Law Book Co., 1977, para. 467.
[133]  The New South Wales Court of Appeal decision was reported as *United States Surgical Corporation* v. *Hospital Products International Pty. Ltd.* [1983] 2 NSWLR 157 at 208–9.
[134]  Gibbs CJ, with whom Wilson J agreed, said the test 'cannot be accepted without qualification' but was 'not inappropriate in the circumstances' (ibid., at 72). He considered factors such as a relationship of trust and confidence, a requirement to perform some duty, and inequality of bargaining power as relevant (ibid., at 69, 70, 72).
[135]  Deane J considered that a fiduciary relationship arises in circumstances where one party was required to subordinate his or her interests to the interests of another (ibid., at 123).
[136]  Mason J (dissenting) regarded these as 'critical features' and other factors had to be considered: see texts accompanying fn. 151, *infra*.                    [137]  (1987) 42 DLR (4th) 81.
[138]  (1989) 61 DLR (4th) 14 at 27 (per La Forest J) and at 62–3 (per Sopinka J).
[139]  *Supra*, at 98–9.

This test is also supported by the judgment of Dawson J in the *Hospital Products* case:

There is, however, the notion underlying all the cases of fiduciary obligation that inherent in the nature of the relationship itself is a position of disadvantage or vulnerability on the part of one of the parties which causes him to place reliance upon the other and requires the protection of equity acting upon the conscience of that other . . .[140]

The trust and confidence test has been regarded by Gibbs CJ in the *Hospital Products* case as 'neither necessary for nor conclusive of the existence of a fiduciary relationship'.[141] His Honour gave the example of a trustee not trusted by his beneficiaries. Dawson J also suggested that business persons might have misplaced confidence in others and this did not make the relationship a fiduciary one.[142] Yet it may be argued that the trust and confidence in the fiduciary flows from the weak, disadvantaged, and vulnerable position that the beneficiary is in. The vulnerability test is, in substance, the other side of the same equation.

The undertaking test has been received in Australia with enthusiasm. However, it is submitted that, as the litigation in the *Hospital Products* case demonstrates, all commercial contracts for services have the 'undertaking' element and the test by itself cannot distinguish those that create a fiduciary relationship from those that do not. Further criteria must therefore be admitted in the identification of the existence of a fiduciary relationship. Even its main proponent, Finn, has moved away from his earlier position that the test is 'an accurate and a workable one for the purposes of the conflict rule'[143] to the suggestion that '[a]t best, all one can give is a description of a fiduciary—and one which, if it expresses the fiduciary idea, is no more precise than a description of the tort of negligence'.[144] Indeed, there are signs that the learned author is also placing less emphasis on the 'undertaking' element.[145] In 'Fiduciary Law and the Modern Commercial World', Finn defined a fiduciary in the following terms:

A person will be a fiduciary in his relationship with another when and in so far as that other *is entitled to expect that he will act* in that other's interests or (as in a

---

[140] *Supra*, at 41; approved in the Supreme Court of Canada in *LAC Minerals Ltd.* v. *International Corona Resources Ltd.* (1989) 61 DLR (4th) 14 at 63, per Sopinka J.

[141] (1984) 156 CLR 41 at 69.                                    [142] (1984) 156 CLR 41 at 147.

[143] Finn, *Fiduciary Obligations*, Law Book Co., 1977, para. 467.

[144] Finn, 'Fiduciary Law and the Modern Commercial World' in McKendrick (ed.), *Commercial Aspects of Trusts and Fiduciary Obligations*, Clarendon Press, 1992, p. 9.

[145] Finn, 'The Fiduciary Principle' in Youdan (ed.), *Equity, Fiduciaries and Trusts*, Carswell, Toronto, 1989, p. 46; Finn, 'Fiduciary Law and the Modern Commercial World' in McKendrick (ed.), *Commercial Aspects of Trusts and Fiduciary Obligations*, Clarendon Press, 1992, a paper presented in the Oxford Law Colloquium in 1991.

partnership) in their joint interests, to the exclusion of his own several interests.[146]

In this definition, the fiduciary's undertaking has been replaced with the beneficiary's entitlement to maintain an expectation. That entitlement, as explained in a footnote, 'may arise from what one party undertakes or appears to undertake . . . for the other; from what actually is agreed between the parties; or, for reasons of public policy, from legal prescription'.[147] There appears to be a shift from the act of the fiduciary to the 'right'[148] or expectation of the beneficiary. In a way, perhaps a subtle one, this is in line with the vulnerability test and the trust and confidence test which look at the beneficiary's position in the transaction. Indeed, other proponents of an undertaking definition have found it necessary to embrace the elements of confidence reposed in the fiduciary, reliance and vulnerability.[149] Even Mason CJ's description of a fiduciary relationship in the *Hospital Products* case embraces all elements of the three theories:

The accepted fiduciary relationships are sometimes referred to as relationships of *trust and confidence* or confidential relations; cf. *Phipps* v. *Boardman*,[150] viz., trustee and beneficiary, agent and principal, solicitor and client, employee and employer, director and company, and partners. The *critical feature* of these relationships is that the fiduciary *undertakes or agrees to act* for or on behalf of or in the interests of another person in the exercise of a *power or discretion* which will affect the interests of that other person in a legal or practical sense. The relationship between the parties is therefore one which gives the fiduciary a special opportunity to exercise the *power or discretion* to the detriment of that other person who is accordingly *vulnerable* to abuse by the fiduciary of his position. The expressions 'for', 'on behalf of' and 'in the interests of' signify that the fiduciary acts in a 'representative' character in the exercise of his responsibility . . .'[151]

---

[146] Ibid., p. 9; author's fn. omitted and emphasis supplied.     [147] Ibid., fn. 18.

[148] The word 'entitled' used by Finn has such a connotation.

[149] e.g., Gautreau (a Canadian judge), in 'Demystifying the Fiduciary Mystique' (1989) 68 *Can. BR* 1 at 7 gives the following definition: 'A fiduciary relationship will occur where a person undertakes, either expressly or by implication, to act in relation to a matter in the interests of another, in a manner that is defined or understood by them, and is entrusted with a power to affect such interests. The other person relies on or is otherwise dependent on this undertaking, and, as a result, in a position of vulnerability to the exercise of such power; and the first person knows, or should know, of such reliance or vulnerability.'

[150] [1967] 2 AC 46 at 127.

[151] (1984) 156 CLR 41 at 96–7; emphasis supplied. Cf. the definition given by his Honour in his paper presented at the Second International Symposium on Trusts, Equity and Fiduciary Relationships: 'A fiduciary relationship will arise . . . when one party undertakes to act in the interests of the other party rather than in his or her own interests in relation to a particular matter or aspect of their arrangement and that other party, being unable to look after his or her own interests in that matter or aspect of the arrangement, is basically dependent upon the first party acting in conforming with his or her undertaking.' ('The Place of Equity and Equitable Doctrines in the Contemporary Common Law World: an Australian Perspective' in Waters (ed.), *Equity, Fiduciaries and Trusts*, Carswell, Toronto, 1993, p. 11.)

Perhaps, the truth is that no single definition is possible or desirable. All we can do is to give 'a description of a fiduciary'[152] or describe 'the critical feature of'[153] or 'common features discernible in'[154] a fiduciary relation. Of these three tests, therefore, none should be read as exclusive of the others; they should be considered as 'factors' to be weighed up in identifying a relationship that would give rise to fiduciary obligations.[155]

### (3) *Parkes Management Ltd.*: A Case in Search of a Principle?

In *Parkes Management Ltd.* v. *Perpetual Trustee Co. Ltd.*,[156] the manager of a unit trust was aggrieved by the trustee's issue of a certificate that it was in the interest of the unitholders that the manager should be dismissed. On the question of the manager's *locus standi*, Hope JA said:

It is submitted for the Trustee that it is only a beneficiary who can challenge the exercise by a trustee of a power . . . There would appear to be three answers to this submission. Firstly, that the Manager was a beneficiary; secondly, that the provisions of cl. 20(1) of the Deed entitled the Manager to ensure that the Trustee exercised any power under the Deed bona fide without indirect motive, and with a fair consideration of the issues; and thirdly that being a party to the Deed the Manager was entitled to challenge the certificate . . .[157]

While this judgment supports the contractual nature of the unit trust, the discussion in the foregoing chapter[158] suggests that the three grounds given by his Honour are open to criticism. His Honour did not cite any authority to support his conclusion that the manager was a beneficiary. Some trusts cases discussed in chapter 2 suggest that for some purposes trustees' remuneration constitutes an interest in the trust funds. It is unsure if his Honour was relying on these cases and if so what would constitute the basis for extending them to a manager. If a manager's remuneration is contractual in nature, this ground is not a valid one. The second ground involves implying a new term without reference to precedents or principles on contractual implied terms. The third ground is the weakest of all. The fact that the manager is a party does not automatically give rise to a cause of action. The court should establish that the manager was the promisee of the relevant covenant. In the case of an authorized unit trust, it is not clear

---

[152] Words of Finn: see text accompanying fn. 144, *supra*.
[153] Words of Mason CJ: see text accompanying fn. 151, *supra*.
[154] Words of Wilson J: see text accompanying fn. 139, *supra*.
[155] The Law Commission interpreted the courts in *Hospital Products Ltd.* v. *United States Surgical Corporation*, *supra*, and *LAC Minerals Ltd.* v. *International Corona Resources Ltd.*, *supra*, as considering factors rather than applying particular tests: para. 2.4.6.
[156] [1977–1978] ACLC 29,543.
[157] [1977–1978] ACLC 29,543 at 29,553.          [158] Ch. 2, s. 2D(3), *ante*.

who is the promisee when the Financial Services (Regulated Schemes) Regulations 1991 are incorporated into the trust deed. There are strong grounds to construe the unitholders as the covenantees.[159] There is therefore a possibility that the factors, such as the second and third grounds, considered by his Honour may not be present in other unit trusts.

It is submitted that fiduciary principles offer a better theoretical basis if similar situations were to arise.

At a general level, the trustee-manager relationship is not a fiduciary one. The relationship *per se* certainly is not an established class of status-based fiduciary. There is no question that the trustee and the manager act as principals in their negotiation of the terms of the unit trust. The result of this negotiation is that both 'undertake' to act for the unitholders, not for the other party to the transaction. Invariably, there are no elements of trust and confidence, reliance and vulnerability in the relationship itself.

However, a person 'may be in a fiduciary position *quoad* a part of his activities and not *quoad* other parts: each transaction, or group of transactions must be looked at'.[160] It is possible for the trustee or the manager to be characterized as fiduciary of the other in limited matters. In this context, it is important to bear in mind that both the trustee and the manager are dealing at arm's length. The court will not find the existence of a fiduciary relationship that would alter the intended operation of the contract terms according to their true construction or merely for the purpose of providing proprietary remedy or of achieving priority over general creditors.[161]

In a unit trust, there are specific matters in which the manager or the trustee will act as an agent for the other.[162] That agency status will trigger the flow of fiduciary obligations incidental to that transaction. The scope of fiduciary relationship may be very limited and the fiduciary elements in it may be less intense than those arising in their respective relationships with unitholders.

In the situation of an abuse of power by a co-fiduciary exemplified by *Parkes Management*, there is no element of an undertaking. The trustee does not undertake to exercise its powers contained in the trust deed 'for',

---

[159] Provision to the effect that each unitholder is deemed a party to the deed is mandatory for an authorized unit trust (the Financial Services (Regulated Schemes) Regulations 1991, Sch. 1, Part I). This is a ground for saying that the unitholders are intended to be covenantees: see ch. 2, s. 2B(6).

[160] *New Zealand Netherlands Society 'Oranje' Inc.* v. *Kuys* [1973] 2 All ER 1222 at 1229–30, per Lord Wilberforce.

[161] *Hospital Products Ltd.* v. *US Surgical Corporation* (1984) 156 CLR 41; *Kelly* v. *Cooper* [1993] AC 205; *Re Goldcorp Exchange Ltd.* [1994] 2 All ER 806; *Westdeutsche Landesbank Girozentrale* v. *Islington LBC* [1996] 2 WLR 802; *Target Holdings* v. *Redferns* [1996] 1 AC 421.                                                              [162] S. 2B of this ch., *ante*.

'on behalf of' or 'in the interests of' the manager. Nor does the manager undertake anything in the interest of the trustee. The 'undertaking' is an undertaking to act for the benefit of the unitholders.

Arguably, it can be said that there is an expectation that each of them will take into account the interest of the other in the exercise of a power that will cause damage or injury to that other. In the second formulation of Finn's definition of a fiduciary,[163] the learned author's focus is on the 'entitlement' to an expectation that one will act in the interest of the other. That entitlement may arise from an undertaking, which does not exist between the manager and the trustee. It also cannot be regarded as a contractual term between them. There is also no public policy reason for equity to impose such a fiduciary obligation. It would seem that a fiduciary relationship cannot be supported on an undertaking theory.

The existence of a fiduciary duty can, however, be justified in terms of the 'vulnerability' test, as the relationship has the three characteristics described by Wilson J in *Frame* v. *Smith*.[164] This can be illustrated by using the factual circumstances of *Parkes Management*. A trustee certifying that it is in the interest of unitholders to dismiss the manager is exercising some form of discretion or power. This exercise satisfies the second characteristic of her Ladyship's formulation, as the trustee can 'unilaterally' exercise the power to affect 'the beneficiary's legal or practical interests'. There is no doubt that the manager, as the person who initiates the unit trust scheme, has 'practical' interests in the scheme. It is particularly vulnerable because any abuse can be made under the cloak of protection of the unitholders.

Perhaps, the position can be better understood if the content of the obligations that may arise from this fiduciary finding is also examined. A finding of a fiduciary relationship between the manager and the trustee must imply that the fiduciary, be it the manager or the trustee, has the duty to consider the interest of its co-fiduciary in addition to that of the unitholders. Is it in breach of the undivided loyalty rule? The answer appears to be no. As Fletcher Moulton LJ has reminded us, it is absurd 'that every kind of fiduciary relation justifies every kind of interference . . . The nature of fiduciary relationship must be such that it justifies the interference.'[165] Fiduciary relationships may take a variety of forms and may give rise to a wide variety of obligations.[166]

In the context of the unit trust, the trustee or the manager 'undertakes' to exercise the powers 'for', 'on behalf of' or 'in the interests of' the unitholders. That undertaking is part of the covenants in the unit trust deed

---

[163] Text accompanying fn. 146, *supra*.
[164] Text accompanying fn. 139, *supra*.
[165] *Re Coomber* [1911] 1 Ch. 723 at 728.
[166] *Chan* v. *Zacharia* (1984) 154 CLR 178 at 195, per Deane J.

and the co-fiduciary, as a party to that deed, must have consented to such an arrangement. The character of the venture dictates that the interests of the unitholders must be paramount.[167] There is no question that the trustee and the manager cannot be regarded as in a position of 'vulnerability' on all matters of the unit trust.

Vulnerability occurs only when (1) honesty and good faith are missing in relation to an exercise of a particular power of a fiduciary which affects the 'legal or practical interests' of the co-fiduciary and (2) that power is exercised under the cloak as an exercise for the benefit of unitholders.[168]

Therefore, it is submitted that when the trustee or the manager exercises a power in the interest of unitholders which prejudicially affects the interest of its co-fiduciary, it has a duty towards that co-fiduciary to exercise that power 'without indirect motive, with honesty of intention and with a fair consideration of the issues'.[169] This is the same conclusion as was reached in *Parkes*. However, this is not reached on the basis that the manager is a beneficiary of a unit trust. It is reached by resorting to first principles of fiduciary law. A fiduciary analysis offers a consistent basis for actions for breaches of other fiduciary duties owed by the trustee where the manager can establish a fact-based fiduciary relationship between them. It also enables the trustee to sue the manager in a converse situation on the same theoretical foundation.

### 3. THE TRUSTEE-UNITHOLDERS RELATIONSHIP: CUSTODIAL AGENCY, BARE TRUST OR ACTIVE TRUST?

A unit trust deed typically has provisions for (a) a primary trust to the effect that whilst the unit trust is a going concern the trustee will hold the unit trust assets for the unitholders 'subject to the terms and conditions of the trust deed' and, in the case of an authorized unit trust, 'all regulations made under section 81 of the Financial Services Act 1986' and (b) a

---

[167] 'The subject matter over which the fiduciary obligations extend is determined by the character of the venture or undertaking for which the partnership exists, and this is to be ascertained, not merely from the express agreement of the parties, whether embodied in written instrument or not, but also from the course of dealing actually pursued.' *Birtchnell* v. *Equity Trustee, Executors and Agency Co. Ltd.* (1929) 42 CLR 384 at 408, per Dixon J. Although this dictum was made in a partnership context, its principle is of general application: Lord Wilberforce in *New Zealand Netherlands Society 'Oranje' Inc.* v. *Kuys* [1973] 2 All ER 1222.

[168] The emphasis here is on the vulnerability. Apparently, the manager and the trustee are also in a collaborative fiduciary relationship in Bean's analysis (*Fiduciary Obligations and Joint Ventures: the Collaborative Fiduciary Relationship*, Clarendon Press, 1995, pp. 139 *et seq.*) so that mutual trust and confidence as well as good faith are important considerations.

[169] This is stated in Jacobs, *Law of Trusts in Australia*, 4th edn., 301 to be the duty owed to beneficiaries of a trust by the trustee in his exercise of a discretion. This was cited in *Parkes Management* v. *Perpetual Trustee Co. Ltd.* [1977–1978] ACLC 29,543 at 29,551.

secondary trust for realization of assets and division of its proceeds upon the termination of the trust by the trustee.[170] There is thus no question that the trustee holds the assets in the capacity as a trustee of an express trust. However, it has often been said that the trustee's function in a unit trust is merely to hold the trust assets for the unitholders and that it does not actively manage them like ordinary trustees. The question therefore is in what character does the trustee hold assets: a custodial agent, a bare trustee or an active trustee?[171]

The answer to this question is important in determining the liabilities of unitholders. If the trustee holds properties as a custodial agent, the unitholders may be personally liable to third parties for all acts done within the scope of agency. If on the other hand the unitholders are not principals, but are merely beneficiaries of a trust, they cannot be liable for acts of the trustee who is acting as a principal. However, as beneficiaries, they may be under an obligation to personally indemnify the trustee under the principle of *Hardoon* v. *Belilios*.[172] The basis of *Hardoon* v. *Belilios* is not entirely clear, and it will be submitted in section 6 of this chapter that this principle applies only when the trustee is a bare trustee.

The term 'custodial agent' is in itself ambiguous. It may mean an agent having possession *simpliciter*, without legal title; it may mean an agent with the title of the property of the principal vested in it. In the former sense, the agent is a bailee.

If legal title to property belonging to another is vested in an agent, this fact alone is sufficient for courts of equity to characterize the trustee of a unit trust as a trustee. The question which then arises is simply whether the trustee has the additional character of an agent. An agent is under an obligation to obey the instructions of its principal. As indicated earlier,[173] the unit trust deed, as a contract of all the parties, denies the existence of any entitlement of the unitholders to question the trustee's dealing of the trust fund. There is no agency relationship in addition to the trust relationship. Therefore, the remaining question is whether the trustee is a 'bare trustee' or an 'active trustee'.

There are two possible meanings of the term 'bare trust'. In *Christie* v. *Ovington*,[174] Hall VC defined a bare trustee as:

a trustee to whose office no duties were originally attached, or who, although such duties were originally attached to his office, would, on the requisition of his cestuis, be compellable in equity to convey the estate to them, or by their direction.

---

[170] Ch. 2, s. 2A, *ante*.

[171] A bare trustee is also called a passive trustee. The trust administered by the active trustee is called a special trust: *Underhill and Hayton*, art. 4.

[172] [1910] AC 118. It will be suggested that a bare trust is a basis of application of the principle in this case: see s. 6 of this ch., *post*.

[173] S. 1D(2) of this ch., *ante*.                    [174] (1875) 1 Ch. D 279.

In short, it is a mere nominee or dummy for the true owner.[175] This view is supported by cases such as *Re Cunningham and Frayling*[176] and *IRC* v. *Silverts*.[177]

In *Morgan* v. *Swansea Urban Sanitary Authority*,[178] Jessel MR criticized the view expressed by Hall VC and took the view that a bare trustee was a trustee with no personal beneficial interest in the trust property. His view had support in the case of *Re Blandy Jenkins' Estate*.[179]

A third view combines both elements of the two. This is the approach taken in the fourth edition of *Halsbury's Laws of England* which states:

A bare trustee is a person who holds property in trust for the absolute benefit and at the absolute disposal of other persons who are of full age and *sui juris* in respect of it, and who has himself no present beneficial interest in it and no duties to perform in respect of it except to convey or transfer it to persons entitled to hold, and he is bound to convey or transfer the property accordingly when required to do so.[180]

This approach has support in the judgment of Gummow J in the recent Australian case of *Herdegen* v. *FCT*.[181]

Jessel MR's definition is simply that of a trustee who happens to be not one of the beneficiaries. His Lordship's view does not appear to serve any analytical purpose or to enlighten the duty aspect of the trust. The former view of Hall VC is preferred by standard trusts texts.[182]

In a unit trust, the manager is the centre of activities. It makes the investment decisions, issues and redeems units, and performs a range of administrative tasks. However, an active manager does not imply a 'duty-less' trustee. The Financial Services (Regulated Schemes) Regulations 1991 contemplate the trustee of an authorized unit trust to act in two capacities, as a custodian of properties and also a supervisor of the manager.[183] Under the Regulations, the trustee has responsibility to oversee that the manager will manage the scheme in accordance with the Regulations, the trust deed, and the scheme particulars, to ensure that the manager's investment does not exceed its power, to ensure that the unit pricing arrangement is proper, and to report to the unitholders annually

---

[175] *IRC* v. *Silverts* [1951] 1 Ch. 521 at 530.　　　　[176] [1891] 2 Ch. 567.
[177] [1951] 1 Ch. 521.　　　　[178] (1878) 9 Ch. D 582 at 585.
[179] [1917] 1 Ch. 46.　　　　[180] Vol. 48, para. 641.
[181] (1988) 84 ALR 271. His Honour defined bare trustees: 'those trustees who have no interest in the trust assets other than that existing by reason of the office and the legal title as trustee and who never have had active duties to perform or who have ceased to have those duties, such that in either case the property awaits transfer to the beneficiaries or at their direction'.
[182] *Underhill and Hayton*, art. 4; Ford and Lee, para. 9780; Waters, p. 27; *Lewin* 16th edn., p. 6; Keeton and Sheridan, *Law of Trusts*, 12th edn. by Sheridan, Barry Rose, 1993, p. 38.
[183] See ch. 4, s. 1B(1), *post*.

the conduct of the manager in the management of the unit trust.[184] In respect of a non-authorized unit trust, similar supervisory functions of the trustee have been recognized by courts.[185] Moreover, it can also be said that the office of the trustee carries with it residual powers and duties[186] that will enable it to seek directions and remedies from the court for the benefit of unitholders.

In *IRC* v. *Silverts*,[187] the Court of Appeal held that a custodian trustee who was bound by the provisions of the Public Trustee Act 1906 to give effect to the directions of the managing trustee was not a bare trustee. The reason for the court's decision was that the custodian trustee had a duty not to obey directions that involved a breach of trust. *A fortiori*, a trustee such as the trustee of a unit trust with active duties to perform cannot be characterized as a bare trustee.

It follows from the above analysis that the trustee in a unit trust is neither a custodial agent with mere possession nor a bare trustee with no duties to perform. It is a paid trustee with active duties to perform.[188]

4. THE MANAGER-UNITHOLDERS RELATIONSHIP

### A. Is the Manager a Trustee?

In crude terms, in a unit trust, the manager performs all the functions of management of the trust assets that would have been carried out by the trustee if the trust were a private trust used as a means of disposition of properties. This leads to the question whether the manager can be considered as a trustee, by analogy to the statutory scheme contained in the Public Trustee Act 1906[189] that allows the simultaneous appointment of a custodian trustee and a managing trustee. A custodian trustee under this Act is one who gets in and holds the title to the trust property. The management of the trust property and the exercise of any power or discretion are vested in the managing trustee. As between the custodian trustee and the managing trustee, a custodian trustee has the custody of all securities and documents of title relating to the trust property, but the

---

[184] See reg. 7.03.2, 7.09–7.14, and 10.06.
[185] *Parkes Management Ltd.* v. *Perpetual Trustee Co. Ltd.* (1977–1978) ACLC 29,545; *The Application of Permanent Trustee Nominees (Canberra) Ltd.*, Unreported, NSWSC (Eq. Div.) No. 4216 of 1985, 24 June 1985, Young J; *Telford Property Trust* v. *Permanent Trustee Co. Ltd.*, Unreported, NSWSC (Eq. Div.), No. 4026 of 1985, 28 Feb. 1985, Kearney J.
[186] See ch. 4, s. 7, *post*.                        [187] [1951] 1 Ch. 521.
[188] The content of those duties will be examined in ch. 4, especially ss. 3 and 4, *post*.
[189] S 4.

managing trustee is permitted free access to them and is entitled to take copies or extracts. A custodian has to concur in and perform all acts.[190]

One is therefore tempted to conclude that the manager is a managing trustee as it resembles the managing trustee created by the statute. But one has to recognize that a trust with a custodian and a managing trustee is a statutory class of its own. The office of a managing trustee is a creature of an enabling statute.[191] In order to be so considered all the requirements of the relevant statute have to be complied with. What a private trust instrument can achieve depends on equitable principles, not on an inapplicable statute. Furthermore, law reports do contain examples of powers of investment being reserved to the settlor, to one of the beneficiaries or to a third party.[192] None suggests that power, without more, can make a person a trustee. This is because trusts are fastened upon the property of legal owners, the trustees. There is no trust without property.[193] Powers may be fiduciary in nature but it does not follow that their holder is a trustee. Moreover, in a unit trust, the manager may have powers that are not fiduciary in nature.

It follows from the above analysis that a manager is not a trustee in the strict sense of the word.

## B. The Manager as a Fiduciary

When the first unit trust schemes appeared in the 1860s, they were used as alternatives to the registered company. It is not surprising that they were marketed in the same manner as shares. The manager, as the entrepreneur of the unit trust, inevitably involved itself in the promotion of the unit trust. Such activities accord the manager the status of a promoter for 'the term promoter is a term not of law, but of business'.[194] It has been held to cover not only persons who get up a company but also persons inviting people to join in partnerships.[195]

---

[190] Generally, see Maurice, 'The Office of Custodian Trustee' (1960) 24 *Conv.* 196; Stephenson, 'Co-trustees or Several Trustees?' (1942) 16 *Temple ULQ* 249 at 250–5.

[191] *Arning* v. *James* [1936] Ch. 158 implicitly recognizes that the offices of custodian and managing trustees are statutory creations so that any appointment that does not strictly follow the statutory provisions will be void. In this case, it was held that an appointment of a bank, as both custodian trustee and managing trustee, was ineffective for the statute contemplated two offices by two persons. The court would not construe the appointment as one appointing an ordinary trustee and the original trustee who attempted to retire through the appointment of the bank was not discharged.

[192] *Beauclerk* v. *Ashburnham* (1854) 8 Beav. 322; *Cadogan* v. *Earl of Essex* (1854) 18 Jur. 782; *Re Hurst* (1892) 67 LT 96; *Re Hotham* [1902] 2 Ch. 575; *Re Hart's Will Trusts* [1943] 2 All ER 557. These cases are discussed in ch. 4, s. 3C, *post*.

[193] *Re Barney* [1892] 2 Ch. 265 at 272, per Kekewich J.

[194] *Whaley Bridge Calico Printing Co.* v. *Green* (1879) 5 QBD 109 at 111, per Bowen J.

[195] *United Dominions Corporations* v. *Brian Pty. Ltd.* (1985) 157 CLR 1.

In *Elders Trustee and Executor Co. Ltd.* v. *EG Reeves Pty. Ltd.*,[196] Gummow J held that a manager of a unit trust was also a promoter and, as such, fell into the status-based category of fiduciary. He also held that as a consequence the manager owed fiduciary duties to unitholders.[197] It ought to be stressed, however, that this fiduciary status should be confined to promotional activities such as issuing the prospectus or scheme particulars and contracting to purchase properties on the unit trust's behalf.[198] Beyond that, the question whether the manager is a fiduciary or not depends on the nature of activities in which it may engage. In considering the significance of the *Elders Trustee* case, it should be noted that in cases involving company promoters, the duties recognized are owed to the company to be formed, not to the shareholders in it. In a unit trust situation, it is the relationship with the unitholders that is in issue.

When the manager manages the investment of the unit trust, it assumes functions analogous to that of a managing trustee under statute. Whilst it cannot be characterized as a trustee, its activities as a fund manager are most likely to be accepted by the court as establishing a fact-based fiduciary.[199] The manager has control of properties belonging to others, although it does not hold their title. It is undertaking activities in the interest of other persons, the unitholders. It is a holder of power that can unilaterally affect the interest of the unitholders. In a commercial sense, the unitholders are in a vulnerable position for they have no right to interfere with the management of their own money. In most cases, the speed with which transactions have to be done preclude them from having any knowledge at all. Moreover, it is their confidence in the manager's investment expertise that attracts investors to become unitholders. These common factors alone should satisfy all tests for establishing a fiduciary relationship in the management activities of the manager.

Apart from investment management, however, there are businesses of the unit trust that cannot be regarded as undertaken by the manager in the interests of unitholders. In the majority of unit trusts, for example, the manager acts as a dealer of the units. In deciding whether to cancel units redeemed from unitholders, the manager can hardly be regarded as a fiduciary. The manager is entitled to retain units purchased from an outgoing unitholder if it considers profitable to do so. Likewise, the

---

[196] (1987) 78 ALR 193.

[197] Cf. *Hichens* v. *Congreve* (1828) 4 Russ. 562 which held that a promoter of a deed of settlement company was a fiduciary of its members.

[198] It is common for a manager to arrange the purchase of properties for a property trust under a contract conditional upon the unit trust scheme being materialized. A fiduciary relationship can exist before the formal creation of a unit trust: *Galmerrow Securities Ltd.* v. *National Westminster Bank plc*, unreported, Harman J, 20 Dec. 1993; see also *Swain* v. *Law Society* [1981] 3 All ER 797 at 805–6.          [199] See s. 2C(1), *ante*.

manager is not accountable to unitholders as a whole or any particular unitholder for the profits the manager makes through buying and selling units.[200]

In conclusion, in a unit trust, the manager does not have title to the trust property but has control over its investment. Without title, it cannot be a trustee. However, its control over the trust assets and the management duties it has undertaken are major factors which may lead the court to characterize it as a fiduciary of the unitholders.

### 5. THE RELATIONSHIP OF UNITHOLDERS *INTER SE*

In an earlier part of this chapter,[201] it has been concluded that unitholders cannot be characterized as partners. Actions done and decisions made by them through meetings can be regarded as the acts of owners of the rights constituted by the units. They are analogous to assents by beneficiaries of trusts.

Of course, as in companies, in order for actions to be taken by a large aggregate of individuals, meetings and rules for majority decisions are necessary. Voting rights simply are parts of the rights constituting units. Once the majority in a meeting is given the power to bind the minority, there emerges the tension between voting powers as property rights and the notion of fairness in the exercise of those powers.

The starting-point is that when unitholders vote in a unitholders' meeting, they vote in respect of their units, which are their property, and the right to vote is attached to a unit as an incident of property to be enjoyed by its owner.[202] There is no reason why, in the absence of other factors, an owner of units in the course of enjoying this property right should be under a duty to other unitholders. This was the conclusion reached by the Full Court of the Supreme Court of Western Australia in *Gra-ham Australia Pty. Ltd.* v. *Perpetual Trustees WA Ltd.*[203] by relying on leading cases concerning shareholders of companies.[204] In this case, the

---

[200] There is a statutory obligation for the manager of an authorized unit trust to disclose prominently in the scheme particulars a statement to this effect: the Financial Services (Regulated Schemes) Regulations 1991, reg. 8.05.3.

[201] S. 1D of this ch., *ante.*

[202] 'The units are a species of property created by the deed. . . . They are trust interests, derive their existence from the trust and are conditioned by whatever conditions the trust imposes on them.' Per Bryson J, *Elkington* v. *Moore Business Systems Australia Ltd.* (1994) 13 ACSR 342 at 350 approved on appeal (1994) 15 ACSR 292 at 296. His Honour was commenting on the burden created by the unit trust deed, but arguably the same reasoning applies to rights conferred by the trust deed: cf. *Peters' American Delicacy Co. Ltd.* v. *Heath* (1939) 61 CLR 457 at 504.          [203] (1989) 1 WAR 65.

[204] *Allen* v. *Gold Reefs of West Africa Ltd.* [1900] 1 Ch. 656 and *Peters' American Delicacy Co. Ltd.* v. *Heath* (1939) 61 CLR 457.

redemption price provided in the trust was based on the value of underlying assets seven days before the redemption request. Immediately after the collapse of the stock market in October 1987, the manager made no payment until after a meeting of unitholders had resolved that redemption should be made on the basis of current asset value. It was held that the power of a majority of unitholders to amend the trust deed was wide enough to make amendments that would defeat the vested or accrued rights of a unitholder.

In coming to this conclusion, Malcom CJ stated that the following propositions from the judgment of Latham CJ in *Peters' American Delicacy Co. Ltd.* v. *Heath*[205] '*apply equally to a trust deed for a unit trust as they did to a deed of settlement of the kind under which limited companies were once established*'.[206] In *Peters'* case, Latham CJ said:

. . . (ii) The contract between members of the company and between the company and its members which is constituted by the articles must be regarded as containing among its terms a provision that articles may be altered in the manner provided by the Act. An alteration in a particular case may constitute a breach of contract with a shareholder, but such a breach does not invalidate the resolution to alter the article.

(iii) Where the rights of members of the company depend only upon the articles, it is possible to alter the rights of members or of some only of the members by altering the articles. The fact that an alteration prejudices or diminishes some of the rights of the shareholders is not, in itself, a ground for attacking the validity of an alteration. Any other view would, in effect, make unalterable and permanent any articles which conferred rights upon a class of shareholder, or possibly upon any shareholder, if they or he desired that those rights should continue to exist unchanged. It is plainly not the law that the fact that an alteration of articles alters the rights or prejudices the rights of some shareholders is sufficient to prevent the alteration from being validly made.

(iv) The power to alter articles must be exercised bona fide. *It is generally said that the power must be exercised bona fide for the benefit of the company as a whole.*

 (v) When the validity of a resolution of shareholders is challenged, the onus of showing that the power has not been properly exercised is on the party complaining. The court will not presume fraud or oppression or other abuse of power.[207]

In upholding the validity of the amendment, the court in *Gra-ham* must have impliedly held that the majority had exercised their power properly. Thus, at one stroke, the court both recognized the voting rights incident to units and admitted into the law of unit trusts the company law principle

---

[205] (1936) 61 CLR 457.                    [206] *Supra*, at 81; emphasis supplied.

[207] This passage was cited at ibid., 80–1 (emphasis supplied). Proposition (i) of Latham CJ was regarded as not applicable as it related to the statutory power of the relevant Companies Act. In relation to the power of a company's general meeting to amend its articles, this passage has to be read in the light of *Gambotto* v. *WCP Ltd.* (1995) 182 CLR 432.

that the power to alter articles 'must be exercised bona fide for the benefit of the company as a whole'. This principle arguably[208] has two requirements: (1) that the alteration should be made bona fide and (2) that it should tend to benefit the company as a whole. It has its origin in the equitable doctrine of fraud on a power, rather than fiduciary principles.[209]

The application of this principle to unit trusts was justified by Malcom CJ on analogy with the deed of settlement company. This may perhaps be questioned. It is clear from *Smith* v. *Anderson*[210] that certificate holders were not considered as 'associating' for the purpose of carrying on business despite the use of a deed of settlement. The deed of settlement company for trading purposes was regarded as a large partnership with transferable shares. The court in *Smith* v. *Anderson* must have impliedly made a distinction between unit trusts (using deeds of settlement as their constitutions) and deed of settlement companies themselves which later evolved into the registered company. That distinction could possibly be between the carrying on of investment activities by trustees and the carrying on of business by agents of shareholders. The court could of course have concluded that this distinction was unimportant but the issue was not addressed at all in *Gra-ham*.

By now, the law must have developed a distinct body of company law. The fact that two institutions have the same origin should not *per se* lead to the conclusion that the same body of principles applies. Brothers, despite their common parents, are not twins automatically. Directors' duties, despite their origin in the trust, are not trustees' duties. Latham CJ stated that 'the power [to alter articles] must be exercised bona fide for the benefit of the company as a whole'.[211] Malcom CJ said: 'It cannot be said that the alteration was made otherwise than bona fide for the benefit of the unitholders as a whole.'[212] The apparent similarity of these two formulations is deceptive. If the unitholders are not associating, as *Smith* v. *Anderson* has suggested, is it right to look at all unitholders as a whole? The very notion of units, as investments, has strong connection with underlying assets. Unlike shareholders, unitholders are acquiring rights rather than participating in a business, which, even if there is any in a particular unit trust, is conducted by the trustee, as trustee.[213] A company

---

[208] In *Brown* v. *British Abrasive Wheel Co. Ltd.* [1919] 1 Ch. 290, Astbury J treated the principle as having a twofold requirement but Scrutton LJ in *Shuttleworth* v. *Cox Bros. & Co. (Maidenhead) Ltd.* [1927] 2 KB 9 regarded the principle as having one requirement that 'the shareholders must act honestly having regard to and endeavouring to act for the benefit of the company' (at 23).

[209] Ford and Austin, *Principles of Corporations Law*, 7th edn., Butterworths Australia, 1995, paras. 11.030–11.040.     [210] (1880) 15 Ch. D 247.

[211] Text accompanying fn. 207, *supra*.     [212] (1989) 1 WAR 65 at 81.

[213] Subject to such direction of the manager as the trust deed or the relevant regulation may provide.

is a separate legal entity whilst a unit trust is not. 'The company as a whole', even in the commercial sense rather than in the legal sense,[214] connotes a body with perpetual existence and limited liability. As a result, the term 'the company as a whole' has almost attained the status as a term of art of company law. For example, it has been suggested that the term covers not only present members but also future members of a company.[215] Although this is explained in textbooks as a balancing of the short-term and long-term interests of the company (as a whole), [216] the inclusion of future members into the concept is probably attributable to the fact that the company is a continuing body. Recently, in the context of directors' duty to act in good faith for the benefit of the company as a whole, the term has also been said to include present and future creditors.[217] The justification is 'the enjoyment by members of limited liability and the inability of creditors to look beyond the assets of the company in the normal case'.[218] Therefore, 'the company as a whole' is a concept evolving around characteristics of registered companies which may not be shared by unit trusts.

If the above arguments are valid, it is submitted that the direct import of the company law formula on the power to alter articles is not justified. Does it then follow that there is no limitation on the exercise of voting powers by the majority in a unit trust? The answer is probably no. It is most likely that the court will intervene if a majority of unitholders votes for a purpose outside the scope of purposes for which the voting power is conferred. This can be justified on either or both of the following grounds.

The first ground is the equitable doctrine of fraud on a power. The company law formulation that the power must be exercised bona fide for the benefit of the company as a whole is best to be regarded as a specific application of the broader doctrine of fraud on a power. Dixon J in *Peters'* case itself saw the company law rule as a formula to invalidate any apparently regular exercise of voting power which is really 'a means of securing some personal or particular gain, whether pecuniary or otherwise, which does not fairly arise out of the subjects dealt with by the power and *is*

---

[214] There is authority in company cases that the phrase 'the company as a whole' does not mean the company as a commercial entity, distinct from the corporators: *Greenhalgh* v. *Arderne Cinemas* [1951] Ch. 286 at 291; *Ngurli* v. *McCann* (1953) 90 CLR 425 at 438.

[215] *Provident International Corporation* v. *International Leasing Corporation Ltd.* [1969] 1 NSWLR 424 at 440; *Darvall* v. *North Sydney Brick & Tile Co. Ltd.* (1989) 15 ACLR 230; *Dawson International plc* v. *Coats Patons plc* [1989] BCLC 233.

[216] e.g., Ford and Austin, *supra*, para. 8.090.

[217] *Walker* v. *Wimborne* (1976) 137 CLR at 7 and *Kuwait Asia Bank EC* v. *National Mutual Life Nominees Ltd.* [1990] 3 WLR 297.

[218] Ford and Austin, *supra*, para. 8.100, citing *Walker* v. *Wimborne, supra*, and *Kuwait Asia Bank EC* v. *National Mutual Life Nominees Ltd., supra*.

*outside and even inconsistent with the contemplated objects of the power*.[219]
If a specific formula cannot be applied, it is most likely that the court will
resort to first principles.

The doctrine is a broad one. It applies not only to voting powers but also
to other powers as well.[220] It guards against any abuse of power and not
merely fraud in the narrow sense of dishonesty. In *Duke of Portland* v.
*Topham*,[221] Lord Westbury said:

The settled principles of the law upon this subject must be upheld, namely, that the
donee, the appointor under the power, shall at the time of the exercise of that
power, and for any purpose for which it is used, act with good faith and sincerity,
and with an entire and single view to the real purpose and object of the power, and
not for the purpose of accomplishing or carrying into effect any bye or sinister
object (*I mean sinister in the sense of its going beyond the purpose and intent of the
power*) which he may desire to effect in the exercise of the power.[222]

As emphasized by Lord Parker in a later case, *Vatcher* v. *Paull*,[223] '[t]he
term fraud in connection with frauds on a power does not necessarily
denote . . . any conduct which could be termed dishonest or immoral. It
merely means that the power has been exercised for a purpose, or with an
intention, beyond the scope of or not justified by the instrument creating
the power.'

Thus, the width of the doctrine should enable the court to set aside a
majority resolution where there is any abuse. An apparent difference of
this approach is that there is no 'for the benefit of the unitholders as a
whole' requirement suggested by Malcom CJ.[224] Another possible difference, which may not be immediately apparent, is that the equitable
doctrine is operating in a negative manner by 'negativing' an exercise of a
power which may otherwise be valid but the company law formulation is
more in the nature of a positive duty.

The second ground is that the majority in particular circumstances is a
fact-based fiduciary of the minority. This may sound novel. But if the 'trust
and confidence', 'undertaking' or 'vulnerability' test is satisfied, there is no
reason why fiduciary duties may not be imposed. Indeed, the departure
from the ruling in *Percival* v. *Wright*[225] in the leading company law case of
*Coleman* v. *Myers*[226] must suggest that such a possibility cannot be

[219] *Peters' American Delicacy Co. Ltd.* v. *Heath* (1939) 61 CLR 457 at 511; emphasis
supplied.
[220] e.g. powers of appointment of beneficial interests. See *Hanbury and Martin*, pp. 180 *et
seq*; Maclean, *Trusts and Powers*, Law Book Co., 1989, pp. 85 *et seq*.
[221] (1864) 11 HLC 32.          [222] Ibid., at 54; emphasis supplied.
[223] [1915] AC 372 at 378.          [224] (1989) 1 WAR 65 at 81.
[225] [1902] 2 Ch. 421, which is cited for the general proposition that a director owes fiduciary
duties to the company as a whole, not individual shareholders.
[226] [1977] 2 NZLR 225, which held that a director owed fiduciary duties to the shareholders
of a company on the particular facts of the case.

precluded. Thus, where the court establishes that a majority of unitholders in a particular unit trust is a fiduciary of the minority on the facts, the majority may be under a duty to act in good faith in its exercise of its voting power.


6. IMPLICATIONS: LIABILITIES OF UNITHOLDERS

## A. Characterization and Liabilities

Characterizing the internal relationships of a unit trust has important implications for the parties, as the nature of the relationship between parties ultimately affects their liabilities towards each other as well as to outsiders dealing with them. From an investor's point of view, it is of immense importance whether his investment carries liabilities with it. Two types of liabilities need to be considered: liability to indemnify parties *inter se* and liability towards third parties dealing with the trustee or the manager.

There are three elementary principles which may be restated before unitholders' liabilities are considered.

(1) Trusts law: The starting-point is that a trustee acts as a principal on its own account, not as an agent for the settlor or for the beneficiaries. The trustee is liable personally to third parties at common law for common law ignores the trust. A settlor is not liable to indemnify the trustee by reason only of having requested the trustee to act as the trustee of the trust.[227] *A fortiori*, a beneficiary, who has not made any request to the trustee, is not liable to indemnify the trustee. Any principle of beneficiaries' liabilities to trustees must rest on some principle other than the mere existence of the trust itself.

(2) Agency: The agent acts for the principal. An act done within its scope of agency is that of the principal. Accordingly, the principal is liable to indemnify the agent. The principal is also liable to an outsider dealing with the agent for the principal is the true party to the transaction.

(3) Partnership: All partners are mutual agents. A partner is acting collectively for himself or herself as well as an agent for other partners. Partners have joint and several liabilities towards outsiders and may be liable to indemnify co-partners proportionate to their interests in the partnership.

---

[227] 'The trustee voluntarily accepts the trust, and can only incur liability in consequence of his own act in so accepting; . . . he must be taken to accept the trust relying on the trust funds.' (*Fraser* v. *Murdoch* (1881) 6 App. Cas. 855 at 872–3, per Lord Blackburn.)

Although the transferability of shares was recognized as a feature that distinguished deed of settlement companies from partnerships, there was no question that partnership principles apply to them.[228] In particular, persons dealing with deed of settlement companies were considered to be in the same position as persons dealing with partnership firms. Consequently, common[229] provisions in deeds of settlement limiting the personal liabilities of members to the amount of their subscriptions were finally settled in the 1854 case of *Re Sea, Fire & Life Assurance Co.*[230] to be ineffective as against persons dealing with the company even though they had notice of the terms of the deed of settlement.[231] In order to be effective, the limitation of liability had to be part of the terms of the contract.[232] Such provisions were, however, effective as amongst members themselves.[233]

In *Smith* v. *Anderson*, the Court of Appeal held that the certificate holders were not associating for the purpose of carrying on business. The trustees were investing as ordinary trustees. The court did not consider the similarity of the trust deed in question with a deed of settlement. Presumably, the inference from the finding that the trust in question was not a company must be that trust principles applied to questions of certificate holders' (beneficiaries') liabilities.

The position reached is interesting. At the risk of oversimplification, it is almost true to suggest that the liabilities of unitholders to outsiders are governed by trust law principles whereas liabilities of members of deed of settlement companies were governed by partnership principles. But the position is complicated by the fact that the general propositions on beneficiaries' liabilities stated above are subject to the exceptions of the principle in *Hardoon* v. *Belilios*.[234]

### B. *Hardoon* v. *Belilios*: A Principle of Absolute Owners' Liability

The principle of *Hardoon* v. *Belilios* has been stated by McGarvie J in *JW Broomhead (Vic.) Pty. Ltd. (in liq.)* v. *JW Broomhead Pty. Ltd.*[235] as follows:

---

[228] *Hallett* v. *Dowdall* (1852) 21 LJQB 98; *Re Agriculturist Cattle Insurance Co.* (1870) LR 5 Ch. 725 at 733, per James LJ. Part of his Lordship's judgment on this point is extracted in ch. 1, fn. 57, *supra*.

[229] Hunt, *The Development of the Business Corporation in England 1800–1867*, Harvard UP, 1936, pp. 33–4, 72, and 99–101. [230] (1854) 3 De GM & G 459.

[231] Ibid., at 475–7. Such a clause was held 'to militate against the principle of partnership as hitherto understood in this country . . . that every person engaged in partnership is liable solidarily, as they say upon the Continent, for everything'. Hunt, *supra*, p. 99. This in effect restricted the earlier decision of *Hallet* v. *Dowdall* that it was of no effect in respect of third parties without notice.

[232] *Hallett* v. *Dowdall* (1852) 21 LJQB 98. (Hunt, *supra*, pp 33–4, 72, and 99–101).

[233] *Hallett* v. *Dowdall* (1852) 21 LJQB 98 at 107, per Martin B.

[234] [1910] AC 118. [235] [1985] VR 891.

[The] general principle is that a trustee is entitled to an indemnity for liabilities properly incurred in carrying out the trust and that right extends beyond the trust property and is enforceable in equity against a beneficiary who is *sui juris*. The basis of the principle is that the beneficiary who gets the benefit of the trust should bear its burdens himself.[236]

In the same case, his Honour held that:

the general principle in *Hardoon* v. *Belilios* applies where there are several beneficiaries[237]

and that:

where there are several beneficiaries entitled to separate benefits, a beneficiary who gets a proportion of the benefit of the property should bear that proportion of its burdens unless he can show why the trustee should bear that proportion of them himself.[238]

*Broomhead* is generally regarded as important to unit trusts because the beneficiaries' interest in that trust was expressed as units. The trust was in fact used to carry on business. It was however more in the nature of a fixed trust than the type of unit trust used for collective investment that is under discussion.

Apart from this, if the principle in *Hardoon* v. *Belilios* is as wide as is stated by McGarvie J (and also in major texts),[239] it would be a general rule rather than an exception. This is because, apart from discretionary trusts, all beneficiaries holding vested interests under trusts have benefits from their trusts and therefore will fall within the rule if they are adults or upon their reaching majority. Trusts used for investment purposes will in the ordinary course of events be caught.

This rule of indemnity is important to third parties dealing with trustees because authorities recognize that creditors of trustees have the right of subrogation to the indemnity of the trustees themselves.[240] This right is wholly derivative; if it cannot be established that the rule is applicable or if

---

[236] [1985] VR 891 at 936.

[237] Ibid., at 937: his Honour took the view that it was irrelevant whether the beneficiaries requested the trustee to act.

[238] Ibid., at 939.

[239] Ford and Lee, para. 14030; Pettit, p. 462; Jacobs, para. 2105.

[240] *Re Johnson* (1880) 15 Ch. D 548; *Re Blundell* (1889) 44 Ch. D 1; *Re Frith* [1902] 1 Ch. 342; *Vacuum Oil Pty. Ltd.* v. *Wiltshire* (1945) 72 CLR 319. Ford and Lee, para. 1410, however, question whether this right of subrogation is confined to the right against trust assets and does not extend—logically—to right of personal indemnity from beneficiaries. This is because the right of subrogation stems from a practice of the Court of Chancery in administration actions in the distribution of a fund under administration by the court. If this right of subrogation does not extend to right of personal indemnity, the creditors have to petition for the winding up or bankruptcy of the trustee and the right of indemnity becomes the general assets available to general creditors.

the facts fall within the rule's exceptions, the trustees do not have a claim to indemnity and third party creditors cannot therefore assert any claim against beneficiaries.

The *Hardoon* principle also runs counter to the basic idea that the trustee is the principal. The general rule that the trustee alone is liable certainly has its origin in the fact that the trust was not an institution recognized by common law. It is also consistent with equity's rule in *Re Brockbank*[241] that beneficiaries are not entitled to direct the trustee in the management of the trust. If beneficiaries cannot direct the trustee how to act, they should not be liable for acts for which they have no responsibility. If beneficiaries can instruct the trustee how to act, liabilities on their part are justified on agency principles; a new principle is not necessary.

There is accordingly an underlying discomfort with *Hardoon* v. *Belilios*. Perhaps, it is this discomfort that leads Ford and Lee to offer a justification based on the requirement of the rule that the beneficiaries have to be *sui juris*:

An earlier statement in the opinion that 'the plainest principles of justice require that the cestui que trust who gets all the benefit of the property should bear its burden unless he can show some good reason why his trustee should bear them [sic] himself' must be taken to be limited to cases where the beneficiaries are all *sui juris*, entitled to the same interest and absolutely entitled.

When that is the case, the relationship between the trustee and the beneficiaries could be ended at any time by the beneficiaries calling for the legal title. Because the beneficiaries have that power there can be inferred a continuing request by them to the trustee to incur liabilities in the course of the administration of the trust even if the beneficiaries have made no express request. If this rationalisation is valid, it should extend to cases where all the beneficiaries are *sui juris* and are, between them, absolutely entitled but they have successive rather than concurrent interests.[242]

What then does *Hardoon* v. *Belilios* represent? Perhaps the gist of *Hardoon* can be found in the sentence before 'the plainest principles' quoted by McGarvie J from the judgment of Lord Lindley in *Hardoon*:[243]

The next step is to consider on *what principle an absolute beneficial owner of trust property can throw upon his trustee the burdens incidental to its ownership.* The plainest principles of justice require that the cestui que trust who gets all the benefit of the property should bear its burdens unless he can show some good reason why his trustee should bear them himself . . . [W]here the only cestui que trust is a person *sui juris*, the right of the trustee to indemnity by him against liabilities incurred by the trustee by his retention of the trust property has never been limited

---

[241] [1948] Ch. 206; *Stephenson* v. *Barclays Bank Trust Co.* [1975] 1 All ER 625 at 637; *Holding & Management Ltd.* v. *Property Holding plc* [1990] 1 All ER 938 at 948.
[242] Ford and Lee, para. 14030.    [243] [1910] AC 118.

to the trust property; it extends further, and imposes upon the cestui que trust a personal obligation enforceable in equity to indemnify his trustee.[244]

*Balsh* v. *Hyham*[245] was then cited by Lord Lindley as establishing that '*absolute beneficial owners* of property must in equity bear the burdens incidental to its ownership and not throw such burdens on their trustees'.[246]

The following comments can be made:

(1) If the true principle is one of benefit and burden, logically, a beneficiary should not be liable beyond the benefit that he obtains from the trust. In other words, he should not be exposed to personal liability: all the trustee should be able to obtain is an indemnity from the trust assets.

(2) It appears that Lord Lindley was enunciating a principle of property law. His Lordship repeatedly emphasized that he was looking for the incidents of 'an absolute beneficial owner' of trust property. The case of *Hardoon* itself was about the incident of calls attached to shares that were not fully paid up.

(3) In some sense, therefore, it is a misdirected enquiry to ask whether the principle of *Hardoon* v. *Belilios* is extended to multiple beneficiaries. The proper question that has to be addressed is who is an absolute owner of trust property within this principle? The number of beneficiaries is simply not an issue.

(4) It is implicit in Ford and Lee's analysis that the learned authors would regard the case of *Saunders* v. *Vautier*[247] as providing the answer. The logic seems to be that if all the beneficiaries, who are all *sui juris* and together absolutely entitled to the trust property, can terminate the trust, they collectively are absolute owners for the purpose of the principle of *Hardoon* v. *Belilios*. This argument, attractive[248] as it may be, ignores the fact that at best the rule in *Saunders* v. *Vautier* gives beneficiaries only a 'power' to terminate the trust. They may respect the wishes of the settlor and decide not to exercise this power. If the learned authors' rationalization is correct, the rule in *Saunders* v. *Vautier* creates a 'liability' for the beneficiaries, not a power, since from the moment when all beneficiaries attain majority, they become liable to indemnify the trustee automatically. It would also follow from this view that silence will create liability. Perhaps, more damaging to this argument is the fact that the termination of

---

[244] [1910] AC 118 at 123–4; emphasis supplied.            [245] (1728) 2 P Wms. 453.
[246] *Supra*, at 124; emphasis supplied.                         [247] (1841) 4 Beav. 115.
[248] This is 'attractive' because the rule in *Saunders* v. *Vautier* gives an 'ownership right' not intended by the settlor, a rule representing the point where fidelity to the settlor's intention ends and equitable property begins. (Harris, *Variation of Trusts*, Sweet and Maxwell, 1975, p. 2.) For the basis of this rule, see ch. 2, s. 3C, *ante*.

a trust under *Saunders* v. *Vautier* requires the unanimous consent of all beneficiaries. If one beneficiary alone does not want there to 'be inferred a continuing request . . . to the trustee to incur liabilities', he is powerless because the trust cannot be terminated without the others' consent. Liabilities beyond his benefit in the trust assets can hardly be fair.

(5) Perhaps, it is not preferable to divorce a judicial pronouncement from the facts behind it. The question facing the court in *Hardoon* v. *Belilios* was quite simple. It was whether the beneficial owner of unpaid shares should be liable to indemnify his nominee shareholder for calls.[249] Encountering this question, a layman may quickly jump to the conclusion: 'of course'. It is ironic that lawyers have to search for a principle. It is in this context that Lord Lindley raised the issue of liability of 'an absolute beneficial owner' of trust properties. The absolute beneficial owner in his case was a beneficiary of a bare trust. Indeed, it is hard to describe someone as an 'absolute' beneficial owner except in the case of a beneficiary under a bare trust.

(6) It is therefore submitted that the test of applicability of the principle of *Hardoon* v. *Belilios* is whether the trustee is a bare trustee with no obligation to perform other than to transfer the properties to the beneficiaries on demand. Support from this approach may be found in *Underhill and Hayton* where both *Hardoon* v. *Belilios* and *JW Broomhead (Vic.) Pty. Ltd. (in liq.)* v. *JW Broomhead Pty. Ltd.*[250] are cited as authority for the principle of '[p]ersonal indemnity by beneficiary under a simple trust'.[251] And the learned editor further says: '[t]he above decisions, however, only relate to the case of simple trusts in favour of a person or persons absolutely entitled who created the trust themselves or who accepted a transfer of the beneficial ownership in the trust property with full knowledge of the facts'.[252]

(7) As a unit trust deed is a contract, a party cannot terminate a unit trust unilaterally unless there is provision in it that empowers such a party to do so. The right of termination under *Saunders* v. *Vautier* is a rule of gift, not a rule of contract. As is submitted above, it should not be applicable to unit trusts.[253] If this is the position, there is no liability of personal indemnity under Ford and Lee's analysis of *Hardoon* v. *Belilios*.

(8) Whilst the unit trust is operating as a going concern, unitholders do not have rights in underlying assets but rather a right to redemption at a price

---

[249] The first sentence of Lord Lindley's judgment states that: 'The question raised by this appeal is whether the plaintiff, who is the registered holder of some shares in a banking company which is being wound up, is entitled to be indemnified by the defendant who is the beneficial owner of those shares, against calls made upon them in the winding-up of the company.' (*Supra*, at 121.)  [250] [1985] VR 891.
[251] *Underhill and Hayton*, p. 798.    [252] *Underhill and Hayton*, p. 800.
[253] Ch. 2, s. 3C, *ante*.

calculated by a contractual formula that takes into account the value of underlying assets. They can hardly be regarded as the beneficial owners of underlying assets. It is when the unit trust is terminated that a trust for sale arises;[254] only in this circumstance will *Broomhead* be relevant. If the 'bare trust' theory in (6) is accepted, it follows that there will be no personal liability to indemnify the trustee until all the trustee's obligations relating to winding up the unit trust scheme have been performed. Only when all such obligations have been performed can the trustee be regarded as a bare trustee.

## C. Exceptions to the Principle of *Hardoon* v. *Belilios*

The principle of *Hardoon* v. *Belilios* is not one of universal application. There are two exceptions to it. The first is that the right of personal indemnity may be excluded by the trust instrument. This was recognized by Lord Lindley[255] and was consistent with cases on deed of settlement companies. In *McLean* v. *Burns Philp Trustee Co. Pty. Ltd.*,[256] an application was made by a unitholder for (*inter alia*) an order for general administration. One of the grounds was that a proposed transaction by the trustee might expose beneficiaries to liabilities to outsiders. In rejecting this ground, the court held that a clause in a unit trust purporting to exempt unitholders from liability 'incurred in connection with any investment or in respect of any action taken by [the trustee and the manager] hereunder' was effective to deny the trustee any right of indemnity so that there was no right for which the creditor of the trustee can be subrogated.

The second exception to the principle in *Hardoon* v. *Belilios*[257] is 'where the nature of the transaction excludes it'. This was established by the Privy Council in *Wise* v. *Perpetual Trustee Co. Ltd.*[258] two years after *Hardoon* v. *Belilios*[259] was decided. It was held in this case that the principle has no application to trustees of clubs. Lord Lindley explains:

In *Hardoon* v. *Belilios* this Board had to consider the right of trustees to be indemnified by their cestuis que trustent against liabilities incurred by the trustees by holding trust property. The right of trustees to such indemnity was recognised as well established in the simple case of a trustee and an adult cestui que trust. But, as was then pointed out, this principle by no means applies to all trusts, and it cannot be applied to cases in which *the nature of the transaction excludes it*.

---

[254] See discussion in ch. 2, s. 2A, *ante*.

[255] When his Lordship said: '[i]t is quite unnecessary to consider in this case the difficulties which would arise if these shares were held by the plaintiff . . . upon special trusts limiting the right to indemnity. In those cases there is no beneficiary who can be justly expected or required personally to indemnify the trustee against the whole of the burdens incident to his legal ownership . . .' (at 127).                     [256] (1985) 2 NSWLR 623.

[257] [1910] AC 118.          [258] [1903] AC 139.          [259] *Supra*.

Clubs are associations of a peculiar nature. They are societies the members of which are perpetually changing. They are not partnerships; they are not associations for gain; and the feature which distinguishes them from other societies is that no member as such becomes liable to pay to the funds of the society or to anyone else any money beyond the subscriptions required by the rules of the club to be paid so long as he remains a member. It is upon *this fundamental condition*, not usually expressed but understood by everyone, that clubs are formed; and this distinguishing feature has been often judicially recognised.[260]

The 'nature of a transaction' that will have the effect of excluding the principle of *Hardoon* v. *Belilios* is a matter of conjecture. It seems that his Lordship was saying that it was a fundamental condition of club members' payment of subscription money that they would not be liable. If this was the principle of *Wise*, it could be argued that unitholders of unit trusts are making investments 'on condition' that they have no responsibility for those investing. This condition can be implied from the fact that the 'nature of the transaction' involved in the acquisition of units is the acquisition of assets, and not 'carrying on of a business'.

The lessons therefore are twofold. On a theoretical basis, it cannot be doubted that the combination of the contract and the trust has produced associations, partnerships, companies, and unit trusts. The line to be drawn between them is very thin. Their intimacy is a story of history. At a pragmatic level, care must be exercised in drafting provisions of a unit trust deed that will affect the characterization of the parties' relationship, as liabilities depend on the nature of their relationship. Whilst declaratory provisions excluding partnership or association of any kind are by no means undesirable, it must be recognized that the court will always examine the nature of the contract and relationship as a whole. The cloud surrounding the basis of *Hardoon* v. *Belilios* requires that this issue should be confronted. If it is desired that unitholders should not be liable to outsiders, there should be an express provision excluding their liabilities and stating that their subscription money is paid on the condition that liability is excluded. Indeed, Schedule 1 of the Financial Services (Regulated Schemes) Regulations 1991 requires a trust deed of an authorized unit trust to state that:

a holder is not liable to make any further payment after he has paid the purchase price of his units and that no further liability can be imposed on him in respect of the units which he holds.[261]

---

[260] Ibid., at 149; emphasis supplied.
[261] This is an obligatory item in Part I of Sch. 1.

# 4

## *Trusteeship in the Unit Trust*

### 1. INTRODUCTION: SPLIT OF TRUSTEESHIP

The trust has achieved a separation of the legal and equitable ownership by imposing on the legal owner, the trustee, an obligation to hold the trust properties for the benefit of the beneficiaries. That obligation is a characteristic feature of the trust. The unit trust involves a split of that trust obligation into the custody of the trust corpus and the management of that corpus. If the trust is a manipulation of the facets of ownership[1] resulting in a two-party relationship, the unit trust is a furtherance of that manipulation which results in a tripartite relationship.[2]

This manipulation is a product of a contract that incorporates the trust. This contractual element signifies a service dimension of the trusteeship[3]— one which is about engagements of the professional services of the trustee, the manager, advisers, and experts that may be involved in the management of unit trust assets. It also signifies a business use of the trust institution for the purpose of active generation of wealth, a move away from its conventional use as a means of passive preservation of assets or their value. It is a move that requires those managing the trust assets to take risks rather than to avoid them. It is a situation where they will be judged not only in terms of honesty and loyalty but also in terms of skill and performance.

By vesting the management powers in the hands of the manager, the trustee as a legal owner may be subject to the directions of the manager when such powers are exercised or will have to obtain the manager's consent in some circumstances. At the same time, there are numerous instances where the manager is required to obtain the consent of the

---

[1] Moffat, pp. 5–11.

[2] The function of a private trust's manipulation of facets of ownership is to achieve a 'downward' transfer to the beneficiaries. The unit trust utilizes the 'holding' function of the trust: the beneficiaries make 'upward' transfers to the trustee to achieve a collective ownership—a combination of capital to generate wealth. See ch. 2, s. 3A, *ante*.

[3] In *Burns Philp Trustee Co. Ltd.* v. *Estate Mortgage Managers Ltd.*, unreported, Vic. SC, No. 2253 of 1990, 8 June 1990, Smith J accepted that the trust deed could be a service contract but it was 'no ordinary contract of service' and a mandatory injunction to perform the covenant relating to making books available for inspection by the trustee or the auditor appointed by it was granted. See s. 1A(3)(b) and 2C(2) of ch. 2, *ante*.

trustee. The trust deed, ancillary contracts, and the Financial Services Act 1986 and its regulations may also allocate duties and powers to other parties. The ways that powers and responsibilities may be shared and the complexity that may be involved depend on the construction of the provisions of the trust deed and on how the relationships of the parties are structured.

The purpose of this chapter is to examine various types of splitting of powers in a unit trust and the consequences for the trustee and the manager. Before this examination is proceeded to, the management power structure of the unit trust and the duty context of management powers will be discussed.

## A. Split of Trusteeship in Private Trusts

The nature of trusteeship has undergone a gradual evolution which is tied closely with the nature of the trust corpus and with changes in social conditions. The trust was a product that originated from the medieval use of land. It was a device that enabled landowners to evade taxes, to avoid forfeiture in civil wars, to circumvent mortmain statutes, to create separate estates for married women, and to make provisions for family members generally. With land as the predominant type of trust property and with trustees essentially being friends and relatives amongst the landowning class, the powers and duties of trustees were essentially administrative in character.[4] Once economic life became more complex,[5] there were more demands on trustees' abilities to manage trust assets. This might be difficult for trustees who did not possess either the ability or the time to look after affairs of their friends.

The inevitable result was for the powers of the trustee to be shared by those who had the necessary expertise. One development was the enactment of section 23 of the Trustee Act in 1925. This permitted the delegation to agents and those qualified without any liability to the trustee acting in good faith. Of course, this was not the only development. There was a growing demand for more trustees as a result of the general growth of wealth in the population, the widespread use of wills by them, complexity of modern investments, and also the emerging problems of

---

[4] The rule that trusteeship is gratuitous reflected these conditions in which the trust was originally developed.

[5] By mid-nineteenth century, business activities prospered in England and the typical trustee was a man of business who might sit upon one or two boards of directors: see Keeton, *Modern Developments in the Law of Trusts*, Northern Ireland Legal Quarterly, Belfast, 1971, pp. 18–19.

fraud and incompetence amongst some private trustees. This led to the emergence of corporate trustees.[6] As observed by Keeton,[7] the emergence of corporate trusteeship has tended to bring about a differentiation in functions between trustees. The enactment of the Public Trustee Act of 1906[8] to facilitate the simultaneous appointments of a custodian trustee and a managing trustee for a trust was a full recognition of the need for specialization. The provisions of this Act have not been widely used by settlors of private trusts. However, its idea of specialization is found in many modern forms of trust. Thus, a trustee of a charity may be subject to directions of a committee, an occupational superannuation fund may have an investment board, a trustee of partnership assets may be subject to majority decisions of managing partners, a trustee of an unincorporated body may be subject to the directions of the governing committee, and a trustee of a private trust may be required to obtain the consent or approval of a protector in the exercise of dispositive or administrative powers.[9]

## B. Splitting Powers of Management in the Unit Trust

### (1) Statutory Allocation of Powers and Duties

Against this background, a structure of dual administration in the unit trust is a logical step in the functional specialization of the powers and responsibilities previously found in the single person of the trustee. The unit trust was in the forefront of this development. The first regulation of unit trusts in the United Kingdom in 1939[10] made the trustee-manager structure a model for the management of unit trusts. This model was adopted by many statutes of common law countries and was followed closely by unregulated schemes.

Under the Financial Services Act regime, the distribution of management powers of an authorized unit trust is regulated by regulations under the Act and supplemented to a lesser extent by the trust deed. Any

[6] Marsh, *Corporate Trustees*, Europa Publications, 1952, pp. 67–9.
[7] Keeton, *Modern Developments in the Law of Trusts*, Northern Ireland Legal Quarterly, Belfast, 1971, p. 16.
[8] Generally, see Maurice, 'The Office of Custodian Trustee' (1960) 24 *Conv.* 196; Stephenson, 'Co-trustees or Several Trustees?' (1942) 16 *Temple ULQ* 249 at 250–5.
[9] Stephenson, 'Co-trustees or Several Trustees?' (1942) 16 *Temple ULQ* 249 at 255, points out that in a private trust, separate trustees may be appointed by reason of the location or different nature of assets. Generally, it can be said that settlors nowadays reject the 'legal list' as the range of permitted trustee investments and wide investment clauses are common. One safeguard that has been adopted is for the trustee to obtain the consent of certain persons, often called 'protectors', whose appointment is also provided in the trust instrument. On protectors, see *Underhill and Hayton*, pp. 23–5.
[10] Prevention of Fraud (Investments) Act 1939; see ch. 1, s. 4C, *ante*.

provision in the trust deed that is inconsistent with the regulations will not be valid. For a non-authorized unit trust, the power distribution is determined by the trust deed.

The statute itself is silent as to whether the manager is subordinate to the trustee. Similarly, a trust deed of a non-authorized unit trust is also silent as to this position. In the ordinary case, one is not the subordinate or agent of the other.[11]

In respect of the trustee, the following functions and duties are conferred expressly or implicitly by the statutory provisions or trust deeds:

(1) Custody of title. Under the Financial Services (Regulated Schemes) Regulations 1991, the trustee must take into its custody or under its control all the capital property of the scheme, collect any income thereof and hold the same in trust for the unitholders in accordance with the trust deed and the Regulations.[12] It is a function not delegable to the manager or its associate.[13] For every unit trust deed, there is always a declaration of trust clause that the trustee will hold upon trust all properties for the unitholders. Trustees' obligations necessarily follow from this very fact of holding properties belonging to others. In *Bank of New South Wales* v. *Vale Corporation (Management) Ltd. (in liq.)*,[14] it was said that the trustee of a unit trust has the fundamental duty of getting in and holding the moneys constituting the trust fund.

(2) Oversight of the manager. As observed in chapter 3,[15] regulation 7.09.1 of the Financial Services (Regulated Schemes) Regulations 1991 imposes a general duty on the trustee to use reasonable care to oversee the management of an authorized unit trust and a specific duty to use such care to ensure that the manager will not exceed its investment power. That specific duty does not extend to second-guessing the merit of an investment decision. The trustee also has the duty to oversee the 'procedures and methods for the calculation of prices at which units are issued and redeemed'.[16] These oversight functions are again not delegable to the manager.[17] This oversight duty is a new kind of trustees' duties not encountered by a trustee of a private trust. In a private trust, a trustee is

---

[11] The Financial Services (Regulated Schemes) Regulations 1991, reg. 7.02 and reg. 7.09; *Parkes Management Ltd.* v. *Perpetual Trustee Co. Ltd.* (1977–1978) ACLC 29,545. But it is possible for one to be the agent of the other in specific matters: ibid., reg. 7.15.4 and reg. 7.15.5 and reg 7.11.3; *YSF Pty. Ltd.* v. *Elders Trustee and Executor Co. Ltd.*, unreported, NSWSC (Eq. Div.) No. 5021 of 1987, Young J, 22 Apr. 1991, upheld on appeal (*Austrust Ltd. (formerly known as Elders Trustee and Executor Co. Ltd.)* v. *YSF Pty. Ltd.*, NSW Court of Appeal, No. CA 40274 of 1991, 26 May 1993); *Telford Property Fund* v. *Permanent Trustee Co. Ltd.*, unreported, NSWSC (Eq. Div.) No. 4026 of 1985, Kearney J, 28 Feb. 1985. See ch. 3, s. 2B, *ante*.     [12] Ibid., reg. 7.10.1–7.10.3.     [13] Ibid., reg. 7.15.2.
[14] Unreported, NSW Court of Appeal, CA No. 428 of 1979, 21 Oct. 1981.
[15] S. 2B, *ante*.     [16] Ibid., reg. 7.09.2.     [17] Ibid., reg. 7.15.2.

under an obligation to supervise its agents or delegates, but not someone who is not its delegate.

For a non-authorized unit trust, arguably, this oversight duty is part of the equitable fiduciary duties of skill, care, prudence, and diligence applicable to all trustees. The general duty of supervision may be said to be implied from a common trustee's covenant that it will take reasonable steps to become informed by the exercise by the manager of its powers, and the performance of its functions, under the deed and also from some common manager's covenants to inform the trustee about any proposal to vary its investment policy, to make available to the trustee such details as it requires relating to the unit trust, to give the trustee statements by the manager's auditor as to whether the manager's accounting and other records for the scheme comply with the trust deed, to make available to the trustee records of the unit trust for inspection, to advise the trustee if an associate is a party to a disposal or acquisition of trust assets, and to retire from office at the request of the trustee in the event of insolvency or if in the reasonable opinion of the trustee the manager has not remedied a breach or if the trustee reasonably believes that it is in the best interests of the unitholders. It is a question of construction for each trust deed but such duty of supervision has been recognized by case-law.[18]

(3) Registrar of units. This is provided by regulation 6.02 of the Financial Services (Regulated Schemes) Regulations 1991 which requires the trustee of an authorized unit trust to establish and maintain a register of holders. As a general principle, any trustee of a fixed trust is under an obligation to hold trust assets for the benefit of beneficiaries and to distribute to them their respective shares. Such an obligation cannot be performed unless a list of them can be drawn up. In a unit trust, the allocation of this registrar function to the trustee is therefore a natural step. However, if the manager is buying and selling units, the trustee may not have the information necessary for the keeping of a register of unitholders. Consequently, the Financial Services (Regulated Schemes) Regulations 1991 impose on the manager the obligation to ensure that the information on the register is at all times complete and up to date,[19] and to supply information to the trustee on new unitholders and on changes of particulars of existing unitholders.[20] In practice, it is simpler for the manager to maintain the register and the trustee's duty of maintaining the register is often delegated

---

[18] *The Application of Permanent Trustee Nominees (Canberra) Ltd.*, unreported, NSWSC (Eq. Div.) No. 4216 of 1985, 24 June 1985, Young J (citing *Parkes Management Ltd.* v. *Perpetual Trustee Co. Ltd.* (1977–1978) ACLC 29,545); *Telford Property Trust* v. *Permanent Trustee Co. Ltd.*, unreported, NSWSC (Eq. Div.), No. 4026 of 1985, 28 Feb. 1985, Kearney J.        [19] Reg. 6.02.4, which imposes the same obligation on the trustee as well.
[20] Reg. 6.02.5.

to the manager. Alternatively, a separate registrar may also be appointed by the trustee. For a non-authorized unit trust, it is common practice for the manager to be allocated with the registrar's function by the trust deed.

In respect of the manager, the following functions and duties are conferred explicitly or implicitly by the statutory provisions or trust deeds:

(1) Dealer in units. One of the attractions of a unit trust is liquidity. The manager has since the early days of the unit trust been the provider of a ready market for the acquisition and disposal of units of schemes under its management. Under the Financial Services (Regulated Schemes) Regulations 1991, the manager must at all times during the dealing day be willing to issue units[21] and be willing to redeem units.[22] Similar provisions may also be found in trust deeds of non-authorized unit trusts.

(2) Trust fund manager. This is the most important function for the manager. It would be the responsibility of the trustee if the trust were a private trust. Under the Financial Services (Regulated Schemes) Regulations 1991, it is the duty of the manager of an authorized unit trust to manage the scheme in accordance with the regulations, the trust deed, and the most recently published scheme particulars.[23] The Regulations also state clearly that it is the manager who has 'the right' to decide the composition of the unit trust portfolio.[24] Of course, the range of investments, investment objectives and restrictions will be prescribed by the trust deed[25] and the scheme particulars.[26] The same management function will be allocated to the manager by the trust deed of a non-authorized unit trust. However, it is not difficult to find trust deeds which fail to demarcate clearly supervisory and management powers between the trustee and the manager.

### (2) Types of Shared Powers

It is clear that the Financial Services Act 1986 and its regulations lay down a dual management structure and specify the respective duties of the manager and the trustee. Within this broad framework, under the Financial Services (Regulated Schemes) Regulations 1991, there will be matters that require their joint decisions or matters where a party's

---

[21] Reg. 4.15; some limited exceptions are permitted by this regulation.
[22] Reg. 4.18; some limited exceptions are permitted by this regulation.
[23] Reg. 7.02.          [24] Reg. 7.02.2; see ch. 3, s. 2B, *ante*.          [25] Reg. 5.02.3.
[26] Restrictions included in the scheme particulars have to be observed as if they are part of the Financial Services (Regulated Schemes) Regulations 1991: reg. 5.02.4.

decision is subject to the approval or consent of the other. Below this dual structure of trust management, registrar, investment adviser, custodian or property manager may be appointed to share some of the functions through a series of contractual or trust arrangements. For the purpose of analysis, shared powers can be divided into four categories.

(1) Directory power. This is the power given to a person to direct another person to perform some of the duties of that other person. The basic tenet of the unit trust concept is that investment decisions will be made by the manager. Once a decision is made as to acquisition or disposal of trust assets, it is the trustee that will carry out that decision. The trustee is therefore subject to the directions of the manager. Directory powers in the hands of the manager are thus a prominent characteristic of unit trusts.

(2) Veto power. A person exercising a particular power may by the terms of the trust deed be required to obtain the consent or approval of another person. In this sense, that other person has a power to veto a particular decision. In the unit trust, it is very common to specify matters that require the manager to obtain the consent or approval of the trustee or vice versa.[27]

(3) Delegation. A unit trust deed may require the trustee or the manager to delegate some of its responsibilities in certain circumstances. Such a requirement is power sharing in effect. Delegation will be mandatory if the trustee or the manager has no discretion in deciding whether to delegate or not. Common examples include the appointment of a custodian of foreign assets and the appointment of an investment adviser in some markets, such as the options or futures market.

Delegation by the trustee or the manager may, however, be permissive. This is delegation in the conventional sense.

(4) Advisory power. Valuers, investment advisers, lawyers, and other experts may be appointed by the trustee or the manager to provide advice or opinion which the trustee or the manager has to consider but is not obliged to follow. Again, appointments may be mandatory or permissive.

These power splits in unit trusts are less common in private trusts. Despite the view that a dual structure of management 'contains fundamental legal and commercial contradictions' and '[t]he fact of split responsibility is a problem',[28] it is submitted that serious contradictions have not been proved to exist. Existing case-law is capable of producing a logical and coherent analysis of the consequence of the split of trusteeship. Of course,

---

[27] For illustrations, see s. 3 of this ch., *post.*

[28] Australian Law Reform Commission, *Collective Investments: Other People's Money,* Report No. 65, Vol. 1, 1993, paras. 12.3 and 12.4.

like any other legal principles, its actual application depends on particular factual situations. The rest of this chapter is devoted to such an analysis.

## (3) Duties, Rights, and Powers

In a conventional analysis, not only has the trust been defined in terms of the trustee's obligations,[29] but a trustee's exercise of powers is treated by equity as circumscribed by the duties of trustees.[30]

In the unit trust, the contract is the medium through which duties and powers are carved out of conventional trusteeship. The contract inevitably involves mutuality of promises and gives rise to contractual rights on the part of the trustee, the manager, and other parties.[31] Powers may be given to a party for the furtherance or protection of its own rights as well as for the carrying out of duties of that party. Whilst cases are relatively few, it is established in our trust jurisprudence that a distinction can be drawn between a beneficial power and a fiduciary power,[32] with the former being exercisable for the interest of the power holder. Because of the element of contractual rights in unit trusts, it is submitted that this distinction assumes prime importance in the interpretation of any particular power. The presence of parties other than the trustee calls into question the status of a party exercising a particular power. As explained in chapter 3, the manager is a fiduciary in respect of most but not necessarily all aspects of the administration of the unit trust; there are matters in which it does not stand in the position of a fiduciary. Thus, a manager is not accountable to unitholders for profits made through buying and selling units because it is the manager's right and it is not dependent on any term of the trust deed or regulation excluding fiduciary duty in this regard. Parties such as investment advisers and valuers are in the same position. The status of

---

[29] Notably, by *Lewin* and *Underhill and Hayton*: see ch. 2, s. 2C(1), *ante*.

[30] As Ford and Lee observe: 'The duty of the trustee is to perform her or his trust, however simple or complex it may be. *The trustee's powers as trustee exist for that purpose and for no other.* The trustee is therefore under a duty, in the performance of the trust, consciously to exercise as well as consciously to refrain from exercising her or his powers as the circumstances of the trust from time to time warrant. . . . Particular powers are often found in the context of a particular duty. For instance a power to appoint agents and delegates is found in the context of a duty to act personally, and where there is more than one trustee, unanimously.' (Para. 12060; emphasis supplied.) It has long been established that even for uncontrollable authorities there is a duty to act bona fide, i.e., not to act 'oppressively, corruptly, spitefully or with other improper motive, or for reasons which can be said to be irrational, perverse, or irrelevant to any sensible expectation of the settlor, or failed or refused to consider whether or not to exercise the power'. (*Underhill and Hayton*, p. 667, citing *Re Lofthouse* (1885) 29 Ch. D 921 at 930, *Re Manisty's Settlement* [1973] 2 All ER 1203 at 1210, *Klug* v. *Klug* [1918] 2 Ch. 67.) [31] Ch. 2, s. 1A(3), *ante*.

[32] See s. 3B(1) of this ch., *post*.

each in a particular context is relevant to the determination whether a particular power is beneficial or fiduciary.

## A. Loyalty

There is no question that under trusts law, a trustee's powers are given to him for the purpose of performing the trust for the benefit of beneficiaries and the core of a trust invariably is the preservation of its assets or their value. Proscriptive duties of loyalty are imposed on a trustee in relation to the exercise of his powers: he 'is not, unless otherwise expressly provided, entitled to make a profit; he is not allowed to put himself in a position where his interest and conflict'.[33] Stated more comprehensively, he:

(a) cannot misuse his position, or knowledge or opportunity resulting from it, to his own or to a third party's possible advantage; or (b) cannot, in any matter falling within the scope of his service, have a personal interest or an inconsistent engagement with a third party—unless this is freely and informedly consented to by the beneficiary or is authorised by law.[34]

Under this formulation,[35] the 'no-profit' rule, as stated in point (a), is wide enough to cover both the obligation not to profit from properties belonging to the beneficiary and the obligation not to profit from information or opportunities obtained. Point (b) extends the 'no-conflict' rule to cover the situation where two masters are being served and the duty owed to one conflicts with that owed to the other.[36] Thus, equity seeks not to tell what

[33] *Bray* v. *Ford* [1896] AC 44 at 51–2, per Lord Herschell.
[34] This is the formulation of a fiduciary's loyalty duties based on the judgment of Deane J in *Chan* v. *Zacharia* (1984) 154 CLR 178 at 198–9 by Finn, 'Fiduciary Law and the Modern Commercial World' in McKendrick (ed.), *Commercial Aspects of Trusts and Fiduciary Obligations*, Clarendon Press, 1992, p. 9, which is equally applicable to a trustee. Deane J's formulation is in terms of the liability of a fiduciary to account. His Honour said: 'Stated comprehensively in terms of the liability to account, the principle of equity is that a person who is under a fiduciary obligation must account to the person to whom the obligation is owed for any benefit or gain (i) which has been obtained or received in circumstances where a conflict or significant possibility of conflict existed between his fiduciary duty and his personal interest in the pursuit or possible receipt of such a benefit or gain, or (ii) which was obtained or received by use or by reason of his position or of opportunity or knowledge resulting from it.'
[35] This formulation in substance divides the loyalty duty into two rules, the 'no-profit' rule and the 'no-conflict' rule. For a discussion of the analytical danger in breaking down the general principle into two rules, see Shepherd, *The Law of Fiduciaries*, Carswell, Toronto, 1981, pp. 147–51.
[36] This is similar to the four-point formulation of The Law Commission, *Fiduciary Duties and Regulatory Rules: a Consultation Paper* (Consultation Paper No. 124), HMSO, 1992,

the trustee should do to preserve the trust assets—that is the province of the trust instrument—but to tell him what is prohibited. These duties have been seen as duties complementing the trustees' duty to preserve assets. As Ford and Lee have observed:

With respect to the economic well-being of the trust the trustee's duty of loyalty complements the duty to preserve the trust assets by disabling the trustee from taking any unauthorised profit, from allowing any conflict to arise between the duty the trustee has undertaken and any interest he or she has, from undertaking any duty which may conflict with the duty he or she has undertaken, and from setting up the rights of others against those of the beneficiaries.[37]

The trustee in a unit trust will automatically be subject to these loyalty duties by reason of its holding the unit trust assets. Of course, these duties have been extended by the courts to persons in fiduciary positions vigorously as 'an inflexible rule of a Court of Equity'.[38] Once a particular aspect of the manager's relationship is characterized as fiduciary,[39] the manager is subject to the same duties as the trustee. Compared with a private trust, although the 'trusteeship' is shared between two persons— the trustee and the manager—it can fairly be said that the content of loyalty duties owed by those managing the trust to the beneficiaries remain the same. If there is any difference from a private trust, it is not in the content of those duties but in their factual applications.

In the application of existing principles to a new situation, there may be uncertainty or ambiguity that needs clarification or, where justified,

---

para. 2.4.9 which summarizes the duty as '(i) the "no conflict" rule. A fiduciary must not place himself in a position where his own interest conflicts with that of his customer, the beneficiary. There must be a "real sensible possibility of conflict"; (ii) the "no profit" rule. A fiduciary must not profit from his position at the expense of his customer, the beneficiary; (iii) the undivided loyalty rule. A fiduciary owes undivided loyalty to his customer, the beneficiary, and therefore must not place himself in a position where this duty towards one customer conflicts with a duty that he owes to another customer. A consequence of this duty is that a fiduciary must make available to a customer all the information that is relevant to the customer's affairs; (iv) the duty of confidentiality. A fiduciary must use information obtained in confidence from his customer, the beneficiary, for the benefit of the customer and must not use it for his own advantage or for the benefit of any other person.'

[37] Ford and Lee, para. 9100.

[38] *Bray* v. *Ford* [1896] AC 44 at 51–2, per Lord Herschell. The rule is also said to be 'inflexible . . . and must be applied inexorably by [the] court' (*Parker* v. *McKenna* (1874) LR 10 Ch. 96 at 124–5, per James LJ).

[39] It must be emphasized that the term 'fiduciary' covers different varieties of factual relationships and the exact ambit of the loyalty duty in any particular case depends on its own facts. This is particularly true of the manager who may not be a fiduciary of the unitholders in some aspects of the trust operation: see ch. 3, s. 2C(2), *ante*. See also Sealy, 'Fiduciary Relationships' [1962] *Cam. LJ* 69 at 73, citing *Re Coomber* [1911] 1 Ch. 723 where Fletcher Moulton LJ said: '. . . in some minds there arises the idea that if there is any fiduciary relation whatever any of these types of interference is warranted by it. They conclude that every kind of fiduciary relation justifies every kind of interference. Of course that is absurd. The nature of fiduciary relation must be such that it justifies the interference.' (At 728.)

exclusion. There may also be circumstances where additional investor protection may be justified. In respect of an authorized unit trust, this is what regulation 7.16 seeks to achieve. In general, this regulation seeks to extend the fiduciary duties owed by the trustee and the manager to cover activities of investment advisers and associates of the manager and the trustee. At the same time, it also seeks to exclude the operation of equitable rules from an otherwise invalid transaction when investors are adequately protected. The duties imposed on the trustee and the manager by the Regulations are in addition to and not in derogation from the duties imposed by equity.[40] However, equitable duties may be qualified or restricted by the Regulations.[41] It should be emphasized that regulation 7.16 does not apply to non-authorized unit trusts. The positions in equity and under the statute are examined below.

## (1) The 'No-Conflict' Rule

'It is a rule of universal application that no one having [fiduciary] duties to discharge shall be allowed to enter into engagements in which he has or can have a personal interest conflicting or which possibly may conflict with interests of those to whom he is bound to protect.'[42] Thus, the trustee or the manager is under a duty not to place itself in a position where there is an actual conflict of interests or where such conflict may potentially exist.

It follows from this general rule[43] that a trustee or a manager must not enter into 'self-dealing' transactions.[44] Except where market usage permits,[45] the courts have never permitted a fiduciary, in the course of the same transaction, to approbate and reprobate on its undertaking by acting as a fiduciary on the one side, and as an undisclosed principal in its private capacity on the other.[46] Thus, a manager cannot direct the trustee to use

---

[40]  The Financial Services (Regulated Schemes) Regulations 1991, reg. 7.12.1.

[41]  Ibid., reg. 7.12.4.

[42]  *Aberdeen Railway Co.* v. *Blaikie Brothers* (1854) 1 Macq. 462 at 471; of the same effect is Lord Cranworth's dictum in *Broughton* v. *Broughton* (1855) 5 De GM & G 160 at 164.

[43]  'The self-dealing rule is founded on and exemplifies the wider principle that "no-one who has a duty to perform shall place himself in a situation to have his interests conflicting with that duty." ' (*Movitex Ltd.* v. *Bulfield* [1988] BCLC 104 at 117 per Vinelott J, citing Lord Cranworth in *Broughton, supra.*)

[44]  It is a long established rule that trustees cannot self-deal: *Webb* v. *Earl of Shaftesbury* (1802) 7 Ves. 480; *Ex p. Lacey* (1802) 6 Ves. 625; *Ex p. James* (1803) 8 Ves. 337; *Wright* v. *Morgan* [1926] AC 788; *Underhill and Hayton*, art. 61, pp. 646 *et seq*. This rule is equally applicable to other fiduciaries: *Rothschild* v. *Brookman* (1831) 2 Dow. & Cl. 188; *De Bussche* v. *Alt* (1878) 8 Ch. D 286; *McPherson* v. *Watt* (1877) 3 App. Cas. 254; *Nugent* v. *Nugent* [1908] 1 Ch. 546; *Silkstone & Haigh Moor Coal Co.* v. *Edey* [1901] 1 Ch. 167; *Queensland Mines Ltd.* v. *Hudson* (1978) 18 ALR 1; *Re Thompson's Settlement* [1985] 2 All ER 720.

[45]  e.g., futures markets permit an agent to deal with the principal: *Limako BV* v. *Hentz & Co.* [1972] 2 Lloyd's Rep. 24; *SNW Commodities* v. *Falik* [1984] 2 Lloyd's Rep 224.

[46]  Finn, *Fiduciary Obligations*, Law Book Co., 1977, p. 222.

the trust fund to buy assets from itself or through its associate companies. Similarly, where the manager is an associate of an underwriter of a share issue, the manager may not direct the trustee to subscribe for the new shares when the sign of under-subscription occurs. Nor may it direct the trustee to buy from the underwriter when the subscription is unsuccessful if the purpose is to 'dump' unwanted securities to the unit trust. On the same basis, the trustee must not allow a loan to the manager itself. It is submitted that the trustee can refuse to use trust funds to buy shares of a related company of the manager which is a takeover target, where the motive of the manager's direction to the trustee is solely to assist that company's defence of the takeover bid.

In applying this self-dealing rule to a sale of trust property, the cases appear to draw a distinction between a trustee and other fiduciaries.[47] A disposition of trust property to a trustee[48] is automatically voidable by any beneficiary *ex debito justitiae*,[49] irrespective of whether the disposition was by way of auction[50] or at a price fixed by an independent valuation.[51] This is 'because no court is equal to the examination and ascertainment of the truth'.[52] A purchase by a fiduciary, on the other hand, is valid if the fiduciary 'can show that, in fact, he did not abuse his position, i.e. he gave the best price after making full disclosure of all material facts'.[53] If these principles are applied blindly, it would produce the absurd result that, after disclosure to unitholders, the manager could direct the trustee to sell unit trust properties to itself at a fair price, while the trustee would be forbidden to buy trust properties despite the fact that it is the manager who alone can decide on a disposition.

The answer to the manager's position is that disclosure and payment of a fair price alone may not suffice. Ultimately, it is a question whether the

[47] This distinction is emphasized in Goff and Jones, *The Law of Restitution*, 4th edn. by Jones, Sweet and Maxwell, 1993, p. 648.
[48] Purchase by a trustee cannot be done through a partnership in which the trustee is a partner (*Re Thompson* [1985] 2 All ER 720) or a company in which he is a majority shareholder (*Silkstone & Haigh Moor Coal Co.* v. *Edey, supra*) or can influence its decision (*Movitex* v. *Bulfield* [1988] BCLC 104 at 122 per Vinelott J).
[49] *Tito* v. *Waddell (No. 2)* [1977] 3 All ER 129 at 241, per Megarry V-C.
[50] *Ex p. Lacey* (1802) 6 Ves. 625; *Whichcote* v. *Lawrence* (1798) 3 Ves. 740.
[51] *Williams* v. *Scott* [1900] AC 499; *Wright* v. *Morgan* [1926] AC 788.
[52] Per Lord Eldon, *ex p. James* (1803) 8 Ves. 337 at 345 and *ex p. Lacey* (1802) 6 Ves. 625 at 627.
[53] *Underhill and Hayton*, p. 18, citing *Dunne* v. *English* (1874) LR 18 Eq. 524 at 533; *Spencer* v. *Topham* (1856) 22 Beav. 573; *Gibson* v. *Jeyes* (1801) 6 Ves. 266; *Johnson* v. *Fesemeyer* (1858) 3 De G & J 13; *Edwards* v. *Meyrick* (1842) 2 Hare 60. (These cases are cited in *Underhill and Hayton*, p. 651.) This, in effect, is the 'fair-dealing' rule applied to trustees purchasing the beneficial interest: 'if a trustee purchases the beneficial interest of any of his beneficiaries, the transaction is not voidable *ex debito justitiae*, but can be set aside by the beneficiary unless the trustee can show that he has taken no advantage of his position and has made full disclosure to the beneficiary, and that the transaction is fair and honest'. (*Tito* v. *Waddell (No. 2)* [1977] 3 All ER 129 at 241, per Megarry V-C.)

manager has abused its position. If it has, the trustee may refuse to follow its direction.

As far as the trustee of the unit trust is concerned, if the decision in *Holder* v. *Holder*[54] is an indicator, it is possible that the court may depart from the strictness of the rule. In this case, the Court of Appeal held that an executor, who purported to renounce his executorship in circumstances where (on admission of counsel) such renunciation would be ineffective, was not in breach of trust when he purchased the trust property. The reasons of Harman LJ's decision were 'that the beneficiaries never looked to [the renouncing executor] to protect their interests[,] . . . that the price paid was a good one. . . . Further, the [other executors] were not influenced by the [renouncing executor] in connexion with the sales.'[55] Sachs LJ went further:

> . . . I agree with Danckwerts LJ[56] in his comments on that part of the foundation of the rule which stems from the alleged inability of a court to ascertain the state of mind of a trustee: and am inclined to the view that an irrebuttable presumption as to the state of his knowledge may no longer accord with the way in which the courts have now come to regard matters of this type. Thus the rigidity of the shackles imposed by the rule on the discretion of the court may perhaps before long be reconsidered as the courts tend to lean more and more against such rigidity of rules as can cause patent injustice . . .[57]

Apart from *Holder* v. *Holder*, there is also authority to suggest that the rule is not an absolute one. *Underhill and Hayton* take the view that:

> [t]he rule as to selling to himself only applies where the express or constructive trustee is substantially an active trustee. He may purchase where he is the mere depository of the legal estate without any duties, and without ever having had any
> . . .[58]

The example given in the footnote of this statement is a trustee to preserve contingent remainders and the authority is the old case of *Sutton* v. *Jones*.[59] Unfortunately, the issue in this case was whether a trustee to preserve contingent remainders might be appointed to a remunerative position, not whether he might purchase. Perhaps, a stronger authority is *Re Boles and British Land Co.'s Contract*,[60] which was not cited in *Holder*. In this case, Buckley J permitted a trustee who had retired for twelve years to purchase, despite the fact that the self-dealing rule had been applied to retiring trustees.[61] His Lordship explained:

---

[54] [1968] Ch 353.                                                 [55] Ibid., at 394–5.
[56] Danckwerts LJ took the view that 'it is a matter for the discretion of the judge' (ibid., at 398).               [57] Ibid., at 402–3.               [58] *Underhill and Hayton*, p. 653.
[59] (1809) 15 Ves. 584.                                          [60] [1902] 1 Ch. 244.
[61] *Spring* v. *Pride* (1864) 4 De GJ & Sm. 395; *Wright* v. *Morgan* [1926] AC 788; *Re Mulholland's Will Trusts* [1949] 1 All ER 460.

The principle that lies at the root of this matter is that a trustee for sale owes a duty to his cestuis que trust to do everything in his power for their benefit, and is therefore absolutely precluded from buying the trust property, irrespective of questions of undervalue or otherwise, *because he may be thus induced to neglect his duty.* Beyond that, if he retires with a view to becoming a purchaser so as to put himself in a position to do what would otherwise be a breach of trust, that will not do. But if he has retired and there is nothing to shew that at the time of the retirement there was any idea of a sale, and in fact there is no sale for twelve years after his retirement, is there anything to prevent him from becoming a purchaser? I think not.[62]

There is no question that the distinction between this case and those cases where the retirement of trustees was with a view to purchase is a valid one. Implicit in this judgment is the recognition that there is no absolute rule against self-dealing. The willingness of his Lordship to look at the reality is consistent with the approach of the court in *Holder* and the recent application of the no-conflict rule in other contexts.[63]

If the broader approach of *Holder* is adopted, it must be a question of fact whether a trustee in a unit trust can purchase. The court may take into account the fact the trustee does not participate in the decision to make the sale.[64]

On the other hand: '[i]t is debatable whether the observations of Danckwerts and Sachs LJJ, although sensible and pragmatic, will be followed. They are not easy to reconcile with the old law which has stood for over 200 years.'[65] Moreover, it is not hard to confine the case to its own special facts: '[the renouncing executor] had never acted . . . in a way which could be taken to amount to acceptance of a duty to act in the interests of the beneficiaries'.[66] Indeed, it is still arguable that on the facts there was a renunciation by conduct.[67] An authority that renunciation may be by conduct, *Stacey* v. *Elph*,[68] was not cited in *Holder*.

---

[62] Ibid., at 246–7; emphasis supplied.

[63] In *Re Drexel Lambert Holdings Ltd.'s Pension Plan* [1995] 1 WLR 32 where the court authorized four member-trustees of a pension scheme in the process of being wound up to apply surplus funds as proposed by the trustees for the benefit of members—which would result in benefits being vested in them. See also *Jones* v. *AMP Perpetual Trustee Co. NZ Ltd.* [1994] 1 NZLR 690 and *British Coal Corporation* v. *British Coal Staff Superannuation Scheme Trustees Ltd.* [1995] 1 All ER 912.

[64] Of course, the trustee is not a bare trustee (ch. 3, s. 3, *ante*) and cannot fit into the statement of *Underhill and Hayton* stated above.

[65] Goff and Jones, *The Law of Restitution*, 4th edn. by Jones, Sweet and Maxwell, 1993, p. 650.

[66] Per Vinelott J in *Re Thompson's Settlement* [1985] 2 All ER 720 at 730.

[67] In *Holder* v. *Holder*, counsel for the defendant, the renouncing executor, admitted that the formal renunciation was ineffective. The wisdom of that admission had been questioned by their Lordships: [1968] Ch. 353 at 392 (per Harman LJ), at 397 (per Danckwerts LJ), and at 401 (Sachs LJ).

[68] (1833) SC 2 LJ Ch. (NS) 50. The headnote of this report reads: 'A person, named as executor and trustee under a will, did not formally renounce probate until after the death of

The no-conflict rule also prohibits any 'scalping' by the manager. Scalping is the practice of effecting personal transactions of the fiduciary before effecting transactions in the same or related properties for the beneficiary, followed by further personal transactions to profit from the resultant market activity.[69] One simple example is for the manager to acquire a sizeable position of an obscure stock on the stock exchange, then direct the trustee to invest in such stock. The manager then sells in the market—presumably at a higher price as a result of the acquisition activities of the trustee.

The no-conflict rule also prohibits any 'churning' activities. Churning is the abuse where a fiduciary, without regard to the interest of its beneficiary, encourages or deliberately leads it to trade excessively and thereby gains from the excessive trading activities.[70] This is primarily a broker-type of abuse since a broker earns commissions and more trades mean more income. As a unit trust manager's fees are usually a percentage of the total assets of the trusts, churning should not be common. However, this may exist where the manager is associated with brokers in the financial markets and excessive trading of the trust assets, such as jogging between shares of the same risk profile, will generate more income for its associated companies. Any such activity will involve a breach of the manager's fiduciary duty to the unitholders.

Under this rule, in the absence of authorization, the manager may not invest in companies or businesses in which it is interested.[71]

The most obvious application of the no-conflict rule is that the fiduciary must not compete with the beneficiary.[72] If the manager is investing its own money while at the same time managing the unit trust assets, the manager may be competing with the trust for opportunities. In a stock

the acting executrix, nor did he ever disclaim by deed the trust of the real estate; but he purchased a part of the real estate, and took the conveyance from the widow, who was tenant for life, and the heir, to whom the estate must have descended upon the disclaimer of the trust. During the life of the acting executrix, however, he interfered in the disposition of the testator's property, as her friend or agent. Held, that he was not, under the circumstances, chargeable as executor or trustee. . . . A deed of disclaimer is the best evidence of the renunciation of a trust, but the conduct of the party, desirous of renouncing a trust, may amount to a disclaimer.'

[69] This is a type of malpractice of stockbrokers documented in the Securities Exchange Commission, *Report of the Special Study of Securities Markets*, HR Doc. No. 95, 88th Cong., 1st Sess., pt. 1, 372, 1963, quoted in Frankel, *The Regulation of Money Managers*, Little, Brown & Co., 1978, Vol. 2, p. 387.          [70] Frankel, ibid., Vol. 2, pp. 390–1.

[71] For investment by an authorized unit trust in other schemes managed by the manager or its associates, see the Financial Services (Regulated Schemes) Regulations 1991 reg. 5.15 and reg. 5.69.

[72] *Re Thomson* [1930] 1 Ch. 203; *Hivac Ltd.* v. *Park Royal Scientific Instruments Ltd.* [1946] Ch. 169; *Mordecai* v. *Mordecai* (1988) 12 NSWLR 58; *Rosetex Co. Pty. Ltd.* v. *Licata* (1994) 12 ACSR 779; *McPearson's Ltd.* v. *Tate* (1993) 35 AILR 285.

market boom, the manager may want to allocate good stock with limited supply to itself rather than to the trust. When the market is losing its strength, the question is: who goes out first? It seems that in such circumstances this rule requires the manager, as a fiduciary, not to compete with the trust, and therefore to give priority to the trust. In relation to the trustee, if it is merely executing the direction from the manager, there seems no reason why the trustee cannot enter into a competing transaction in circumstances where there is never any conflict of duty and interest.[73]

Perhaps, a more serious problem is where the competition comes from another person or trust for whom the manager or the trustee acts as well. The fact that the unit trust is a medium of investment services inevitably means that the manager or the trustee will operate in more than one type of unit trust to cater for different demands of the market. It is unheard of that a manager should manage only one unit trust.[74]

Two forms of conflict can result when the manager or the trustee serves two masters. The first is where two unit trusts compete for the same 'undivided' loyalty owed by the manager. If two unit trusts' investment criteria demand the acquisition of the same stock, the stockbroker instructed by the manager may acquire the bulk for the two trusts at different prices and the manager must decide how to allocate the shares with different prices to these two trusts. Conversely, in a falling market, the manager must decide which bulk of shares is sold first if its stockbroker can only do trades at different price levels. Presumably, all unitholders who acquire units with knowledge of the fact that the manager is managing a number of trusts must have impliedly given the requisite consent.[75] Thus, the manager is not in breach of any duty by acting for more than one trust. But it does not follow that the manager may not be in breach of loyalty by favouring a particular trust in specific transactions. Indeed, it is known that sometimes a manager, for marketing reason, may 'boost' the performance of a particular trust at a particular time by allocating to that trust stocks or investments whose prices rise during the interval between acquisition and allocation. A speculative answer to the allocation problem posed here is that the manager must act on the principle that equality is equity and must make a pro-rata allocation of investments of different prices.

The second type of competition occurs when the fiduciary acts for both parties in one transaction. In principle, the rule forbids a situation where

---

[73] Cf. *Holder* v. *Holder, supra.*

[74] A manager of an authorized unit trust is not permitted to engage in activities other than acting as a manager of a unit trust, an open-ended investment company, or an investment trust company (s. 83 of the Financial Services Act 1986).

[75] *Kelly* v. *Cooper* [1993] AC 205.

the fiduciary, acting for the seller, would be obliged to obtain the highest price from itself acting as a fiduciary of the purchaser, who would expect the lowest possible price.[76] In normal circumstances this is unlikely to occur for two unit trusts which the manager manages because the manager should have a consistent economic outlook of a particular sector of the economy. However, it is possible it is intended that a particular trust is to maintain a more liquid position while another trust has funds to invest. In such circumstances, the manager cannot 'marry' the transaction for both trusts.[77]

## (2) The 'No-Profit' Rule

Under this rule, a fiduciary has to account for all gains obtained by reason of its position, or through an opportunity or information resulting from it.[78]

A fiduciary may not obtain and retain secret gains. Thus, in a transaction that would be effected between a unit trust and a third party, the manager cannot interpose a nominee to deal with the trust first and arrange for this nominee to consummate the transaction with the third party at a profit. Any such profits must be accounted for.[79] A fiduciary also cannot take any bribe or secret commission.[80]

This no-profit rule forbids any profiting from the unit trust properties unless the profit is both disclosed and assented to.[81] A trustee of a unit trust may have within its control investment assets of the trust. It is possible

---

[76] As a matter of agency law, an agent cannot act for both parties unless he discloses all material facts and obtains their informed consent: *Bowstead and Reynolds on Agency*, 16th edn., Sweet and Maxwell, 1996, para. 6–060; *Fullwood* v. *Hurley* [1928] 1 KB 498; *Anglo-African Merchants Ltd.* v. *Bayley* [1970] 1 QB 311 at 323; *Dargusch* v. *Sherley Investments Pty. Ltd.* [1970] Qd. R 338 at 347; *Eagle Star Insurance Co. Ltd.* v. *Spratt* [1971] 2 Lloyd's Rep. 116 at 133; *North and South Trust Co.* v. *Berkeley* [1971] 1 WLR 470; *Farrington* v. *Rowe, McBride & Partners* [1985] 1 NZLR 83; *McDonnell* v. *Barton Realty Ltd.* [1993] 3 NZLR 418.

[77] Unless custom in a particular market permits it. For example, there is a market usage to marry buy-sell orders in stock transactions (*Jones* v. *Canavan* [1972] 2 NSWLR 236) but the price must be the market price.

[78] *Chan* v. *Zacharia* (1984) 154 CLR 178 at 198–9, per Deane J: fn. 34, *ante*.

[79] Cf. *Turnbull* v. *Garden* (1869) 38 LJ Ch. 331 where an agent who obtained a rebate but charged his principal the full price was held liable to account for it despite the fact that he did not charge any commission. See also *North American Land and Timber Co. Ltd.* v. *Watkins* [1904] 1 Ch. 242; *Hippisley* v. *Knee Brothers* [1905] 1 KB 1; *De Bussche* v. *Alt* (1878) 8 Ch. D 286.

[80] *Metropolitan Bank* v. *Heiron* (1880) LR 5 Ex. D 319; *Williams* v. *Barton* [1927] 2 Ch. 9; *Att.-Gen.* v. *Goddard* (1929) 98 LJKB 743; *Reading* v. *R* [1949] 2 KB 232; *Mahesan S/O Thambiah* v. *Malaysia Government Officers' Co-operative Housing Society Ltd.* [1979] AC 374; *Att.-Gen. for Hong Kong* v. *Reid* [1994] AC 324.

[81] *Brown* v. *IRC* [1965] AC 244; cf. *Re Oatway* [1903] 2 Ch. 356; *Shallcross* v. *Oldham* (1862) 2 J & H 609.

for it to use them to make a gain in some circumstances. For example, assets in its hands may be used to consummate a *de facto* short sale. If the trustee expects the market to fall, it will sell the assets; when the asset price does actually fall, it will acquire them again for the unit trust. Any gains so made must be accounted for.[82] Under this rule, the manager or the trustee may not use the voting rights of the shares to vote themselves into office of directors of companies issuing such shares and gain directors' remunerations.[83] They can be directors if such positions are obtained not by reason of the use of such shares.[84]

This rule also forbids any diversion of opportunities.[85] This was the classic position of the trustee in *Keech* v. *Sandford*,[86] a case which has been extended to a fiduciary in *Chan* v. *Zacharia*.[87] Presumably, a manager of a property trust negotiating a property transaction cannot have the transaction consummated by itself or through its nominee.[88]

This rule also forbids any use of insider information.[89] Both the manager and the trustee are in the best position to know the actual asset value of the unit trust they manage. It is not difficult for them to know or estimate in advance both the offer and bid prices of the units of the trust before the next valuation point. A malpractice is for them to purchase units through nominees if the prices are going to rise and to sell if the prices are going to fall. Such practices would be a breach of the no-profit rule.

The above illustrations demonstrate some unfamilar dimensions of application of the loyalty duty to unit trusts. This apparently flows from two features of the unit trust.

The first is what was mentioned earlier. The unit trust deed is a contract

---

[82] Cf. *Re Oatway* [1903] 2 Ch. 356; *Shallcross* v. *Oldham* (1862) 2 J & H 609.

[83] *Re Francis* (1905) 92 LT 77; *Re Macadam* [1946] Ch. 73; *Re Gee* [1948] Ch. 284.

[84] *Re Dover Coalfield Extension Ltd.* [1908] 1 Ch. 65 as distinguished by Harman J in *Re Gee*, ibid., at 294.

[85] *Regal (Hastings) Ltd.* v. *Gulliver* [1942] 1 All ER 378; *Industrial Development Consultants Ltd.* v. *Cooley* [1972] 1 WLR 443; *Cook* v. *Deeks* [1916] 1 AC 554; *Peso Silver Mines Ltd.* v *Cropper* (1966) 58 DLR (2d) 1.

[86] (1726) Sel. Cas. Ch. 61, where a lessor refused to renew a lease to the trust but allowed the trustee to renew in his personal capacity and the trustee was held to be accountable.

[87] (1984) 154 CL 178 (partner diverting a lease liable).

[88] Cf. *Walden Properties Ltd.* v. *Beaver Properties Pty. Ltd.* [1973] 2 NSWLR 815. In this case, three parties to a joint venture agreed that one venturer would negotiate for the purchase of shares of a company owning a property and if the purchase was successful that venturer would sell all such shares to all parties in equal proportion. One party's shares were in fact offered to a related party of the negotiating venturer. It was held that both the negotiating venturer and its related party were liable to account.

[89] *Robb* v. *Green* [1895] 2 QB 315; *Boardman* v. *Phipps* [1967] 2 AC 46; *Surveys and Mining Ltd.* v. *Morrison* [1969] Qd. R 470; *Att.-Gen.* v. *Guardian Newspapers Ltd. (No. 2)* [1990] 1 AC 109 (the 'Spycatcher' case). The insider trading provisions of Part V of the Criminal Justice Act 1993 do not apply to unit trusts as they apply only to securities specified in Sch. 2 of that Act, which do not include unit trusts (s. 54).

for services—trustee services and investment services. The trustee and the manager are providing specialized financial services. It is inevitable that each of them may provide similar services to other persons. There will be more opportunities for conflicts arising from acting for multiple masters.

The second feature is the predominance of managers in the management of unit trust assets. This means that, in the unit trust context, the fiduciary duties of a person without legal title are of greater importance. This in turn generates unfamiliar issues relating to the role of the legal owner, the trustee, in relation to the exercise of powers by this fiduciary. This will be the subject of the discussion in the remaining parts of this chapter.

## (3) The Financial Services Act Provisions

Under section 83 of the Financial Services Act 1986, a manager of an authorized unit trust is not permitted to engage in activities other than acting as a manager of a unit trust, an open-ended investment company, a 'body corporate whose business consists of investing its funds with the aim of spreading investment risk and giving its members the benefit of the results of the management of its funds',[90] or a collective investment scheme. The Act does not restrict the activities of the trustee of a unit trust and its position is governed by equitable principles above discussed.

As noted earlier, dealing in units is the contractual right of the manager. Any gain by the manager from issuing and redeeming units is not a secret profit and therefore is not accountable to anyone. This is the position of the manager of an authorized unit trust if it discloses prominently in the scheme particulars a statement to this effect.[91]

Further, in the exercise of the manager's investment power, the manager must not invest or dispose of units in another collective investment scheme managed by the manager or its associates unless the manager reimburses the unit trust with any charge or mark-up arising on the issue or redemption of units in those schemes.[92] This provision therefore claws back into the trust the 'secret profit' in the form of charges payable to the manager (or its associate) in its capacity of a manager of the scheme to be invested.

The main provision supplementing the loyalty duty is regulation 7.16 of the Financial Services (Regulated Schemes) Regulations 1991 which imposes on the manager and the trustee of an authorized unit trust the obligation to take reasonable steps to ensure that 'affected persons', i.e.,

---

[90] i.e., an investment trust company.
[91] The Financial Services (Regulated Schemes) Regulations 1991, reg. 8.05.3.
[92] Ibid., reg. 5.69.

the manager, the trustee, an investment adviser, and their respective associates, will comply with that regulation.

An affected person may not accept deposit from or make loan to the unit trust unless it is an eligible institution and the deposit or loan satisfies the arm's length requirement. Any stock-lending transaction entered into with an affected person and any service contract by associates of the manager, the trustee or an investment adviser have to satisfy the arm's length requirement as well. The arm's length requirement is that the arrangement must be 'at least as favourable' as that effected 'on commercial terms negotiated at arm's length between two independent parties'.

An affected person may not sell property[93] to or purchase property[94] from the unit trust scheme unless an independent valuation has been obtained and the trustee is of the opinion that the terms of the transaction are not likely to result in any material prejudice to unitholders. In the case of an approved security or an approved derivative, the transaction is also valid if there is best execution through a member of the relevant exchange under the rules of the exchange. Where an independent valuation cannot reasonably be obtained, the transaction is valid if the trustee has reliable evidence that the transaction satisfies the arm's length requirement.

This regulation extends the duties of the trustee and the manager to cover activities of their associates. The manager and the trustee may be vicariously liable for breaches of this regulation by their associates unless it can be proved that 'reasonable steps' have been taken to ensure compliance. Under the Financial Services Glossary 1991, in relation to a person, an associate means (a) an undertaking in the same group as that person; (b) an appointed representative of the first person or of any undertaking in the same group; or (c) any other person whose business or domestic relationship with the first person or its associate might reasonably be expected to give rise to a community of interests between them which may involve a conflict of interest in dealings with third parties.[95] A group is, in turn, defined in the Act to include 'a body corporate in which a member of the group holds a qualifying capital interest',[96] which is 'an interest in the relevant shares of the body corporate which the member holds on a long-term basis for the purpose of securing a contribution to its

[93] Including vesting property in the trustee in exchange for issue of units in the unit trust unless upon a unitization: reg. 7.16.5. A unitization is an arrangement for a newly formed scheme under which property of a body corporate or a collective investment scheme becomes the first property of the newly formed scheme and the holders of the wound up scheme become the first participants (reg. 4.05).

[94] Except for an *in specie* redemption effected under reg. 4.28.

[95] Applied to the Financial Services (Regulated Schemes) Regulations 1991 by Sch. 4, para. (1) of the Regulations.

[96] Financial Services Act 1986, Sch. 1, para. 30(1), applied by the Financial Services (Regulated Schemes) Regulations 1991, Sch. 4, para. (1).

own activities by the exercise of control or influence arising from that interest'.[97] A holding of 20 per cent or more of the nominal value of the voting shares of the body corporate is presumed to be a qualifying capital interest.[98] Thus, the reach of the regulation is very extensive.

At the same time, regulation 7.16 lessens the strictness of the equitable rules by validating transactions that are effected on arm's length terms, by best execution on exchange or with independent valuation.


## B. Skill and Care


### (1) The Trustee

Given that the primary obligation of a trustee is to hold properties belonging to others and to preserve them for the benefit of the beneficiaries, it is no surprise that trustees are generally expected 'to use such due diligence and care as men of ordinary prudence and vigilance would use in the management of their own affairs'.[99] When investing, they are expected 'to take such care as an ordinary prudent man would take if he were minded to make an investment for the benefit of other people for whom he felt morally bound to provide'.[100] This focus on integrity rather than ability ties in with the conventional wisdom that '[t]he importance of

---

[97] Financial Services Act 1986, Sch. 1, para. 30(2).

[98] Ibid., para. 30(3)&(4).

[99] *Underhill and Hayton*, art. 54, p. 545 citing *Brice* v. *Stokes* (1805) 11 Ves. 319, *Massey* v. *Banner* (1820) 1 Jac. & W 241, *Bullock* v. *Bullock* (1886) 56 LJ Ch. 221, *Speight* v. *Gaunt* (1883) 9 App. Cas. 1, *Austin* v. *Austin* (1906) 3 CLR 516 at 525, *Fouche* v. *Superannuation Fund Board* (1952) 88 CLR 609, *Re Lucking's Will Trusts* [1967] 3 All ER 726 at 734, and *Bartlett* v. *Barclays Bank Trust Co.* [1980] Ch. 5; Paling, 'The Trustee's Duty of Skill and Care' (1973) 37 *Conv.* 48, fn. 12, where *Underhill and Hayton's* statement is questioned. An error of judgment may not be negligence. Thus, in *Galmerrow Securities Ltd.* v. *National Westminster Bank plc*, unreported, 20 Dec. 1993, Harman J held that it was not negligent for a trustee of a non-authorized unit trust not to remove the property fund manager whose investment strategy failed in the London property market crash of 1974.

[100] *Re Whiteley* (1886) 33 Ch. D 347 at 355, per Lindley LJ; *Cowan* v. *Scargill* [1985] Ch. 270 at 288, per Megarry V-C; *Nestle* v. *National Westminster Bank plc* [1994] 1 All ER 118. In *Learoyd* v. *Whiteley* (1887) 12 App. Cas. 727 at 733, Lord Watson also said: 'As a general rule the law requires of a trustee no higher degree of diligence in the execution of his office than a man of ordinary prudence would exercise in the management of his own private affairs. Yet he is not allowed the same discretion in investing the moneys of the trust as if he were a person *sui juris* dealing with his own estate. Business men of ordinary prudence may, and frequently do, select investments which are more or less of a speculative character; but it is the duty of a trustee to confine himself to the class of investments which are permitted by the trust, and likewise to avoid all investments of that class which are attended with hazard. So, so long as he acts in the honest observance of these limitations, the general rule already stated will apply.'

preservation of a trust fund will always outweigh success in its advancement'.[101]

When investment has become a sophisticated business, with the objective of the trust moving away from the preservation of assets towards the preservation of the capital value, managerial skill has become more prominent and equity has developed a second standard for those who profess to be professional trustees or with special skill. They are expected to possess a higher standard of diligence and knowledge. As Brightman J explained:

I am of opinion that a higher duty of care is plainly due from someone like a trust corporation which carries on a specialised business of trust management. . . . With a specialist staff of trained trust officers and managers, with ready access to financial information and professional advice, dealing with and solving trust problems day after day, the trust corporation holds itself out, and rightly, as capable of providing an expertise which it would be unrealistic to expect and unjust to demand from the ordinary prudent man or woman who accepts, probably unpaid and sometimes reluctantly from a sense of family duty, the burdens of a trusteeship.[102]

What is the general nature of these duties? An undisputed answer is that these standards of care are part of equity's trust jurisprudence. The duties of skill and prudence in the implementation of the trust are part of the fiduciary duties of the trustee.[103] Proceedings against trustees for negligence are equity proceedings for breach of trust.[104] There is no question that in a private trust, the relationship between the trustee and the beneficiaries is generally not a contractual one and accordingly there is no implied contractual duty of care between them.

Logically, it might be possible to fit the trustee-beneficiary relationship into the sort of neighbourhood principle enunciated in *Donoghue* v.

---

[101] *Nestle* v. *National Westminster Bank plc* [1994] 1 All ER 118 at 142, per Leggatt LJ. See also *Learoyd* v. *Whiteley* (1887) 12 App. Cas. 727 at 732, per Lord Halsbury; *Bartlett* v. *Barclays Bank Trust Co.* [1980] Ch. 515.

[102] *Bartlett* v. *Barclays Bank Trust Co. Ltd.* [1980] Ch. 515 at 534 but see the observation of Thomas J in *Jones* v. *AMP Perpetual Trustee Co. NZ Ltd.* [1994] 1 NZLR 690. It is still not clear if the difference in standard is to be based on the professing of specialist expertise, remuneration or professional trusteeship. In *Re Waterman's Will Trusts* [1952] 2 All ER 1054, Harman J considered a higher duty on the basis of remuneration as well as the advertising of skills. See Moffat, pp. 368–70; Paling, 'The Trustee's Duty of Skill and Care' (1973) 37 *Conv.* 48 at 55; Shindler, 'Note of Recent Cases' (1980) 44 *Conv.* 155 at 158.

[103] Contra, Meagher, Gummow and Lehane, *Equity: Doctrines and Remedies*, 3rd edn., Butterworths Australia, 1992, para. 502: '. . . a trustee's duty to exercise reasonable care, though equitable, is not specifically a fiduciary obligation'. (Approved in *Permanent Building Society (in liq.)* v. *Wheeler* (1994) 14 ACSR 109 at 157 which in turn was approved in *Bristol and West Building Society* v. *Mothew* [1996] 4 All ER 698 at 711.) Meagher, Gummow and Lehane, perhaps, are conceiving care and honesty as distinct but as Waters has observed, p. 750, the issue is: 'At what point does inability pale into dishonesty?'

[104] *Learoyd* v. *Whiteley* (1887) 12 App. Cas. 727.

*Stevenson.*[105] Doctrinally, however, short of a revolution at common law, this is impossible. This is because common law does not recognize the trust; nor does common law recognize equitable ownership or equitable interests. A legal owner, the trustee, therefore cannot owe any common law duty of care to equitable owners.[106] In *Fletcher* v. *National Mutual Life Nominees Ltd.*,[107] a money market operator invited deposits from the public. Pursuant to statutory requirement in New Zealand, a trust deed was executed between the operator and a trustee for the depositors which imposed certain duties on the trustee as trustee of the debts. On a preliminary question of law whether the liability of the trustee arose only from the breach of duty as trustee and not in tort, Henry J answered in the positive. On the question of negligence, Henry J observed:

The relationship between the parties is one which exists only by reason of [the trustee] having entered into the trust deed. It is the trust deed which defines the duties of the trustee, and it also confines those duties to those which are therein expressed or can properly be implied . . . The position is that [the trustee's] liability to the depositors rests only on its breach of what are express provisions of the trust deed. The deed apart, [the trustee] has no relationship to any depositor which could give rise to a duty of care . . . The proposition that the general law requires a party to a deed (or a trustee) to exercise care to see it observes the term of the deed (or of the trust), breach of which would constitute the tort of negligence, is in my view conceptually unsound. The terms of the deed or trust impose the duty— nothing else. Historically a trustee's liability for lack of diligence has been classed as breach of trust, and under the control of the Courts of equity, not as constituting the tort of negligence under the jurisdiction of the common law.[108]

The trust arrangement in *Fletcher* is no different from a unit trust. Henry J's decision is highly persuasive.

In a unit trust, the trustee will however be liable in contract as well as under trust law,[109] as the trust relationship with unitholders is created by the contract.[110] The content of the trustee's obligation may be modified by the contract.[111] Where a question is covered by the terms of the unit trust deed, it is a question of construction. Where the trust deed is silent, the court may have to consider whether a particular incident is an implied term or an equitable duty. Where necessary, there is no reason to deter the court from reaching a conclusion that there are concurrent duties in trust

[105] [1932] AC 562.
[106] Cf. *Wickstead* v. *Browne* (1992) 30 NSWLR 1 at 17; *Downsview Nominees Ltd.* v. *First City Corporation Ltd.* [1993] AC 295.
[107] [1990] 1 NZLR 97.          [108] Ibid., at 104.
[109] Cf. *Nocton* v. *Lord Ashburton* [1914] AC 932; *Hospital Products Ltd.* v. *US Surgical Corporation* (1984) 55 ALR 417 at 454, per Mason J.
[110] Ch. 2, s. 2B(4), *ante*.          [111] *Kelly* v. *Cooper* [1993] AC 205.

and in contract. For example, under trust principles, a professional trustee is liable to maintain the higher standard of skill that it professes to have.[112] Equally, as a matter of contract, a professional person who possesses a particular skill is liable for breach of contract if he or she neglects to use that skill as other reasonably competent members of the profession. The test is not by reference to the reasonable man on the Clapham omnibus.[113] The unit trustee is such a professional person.[114]

## (2) The Manager

As the manager is in a contractual relationship with the unitholders, it may have a contractual duty of care under the express or implied terms of the contract as contained in the unit trust deed. Historically, the court has chosen the contract as a medium of control over the conduct of people giving professional services.[115] Invariably, the court will imply a duty of skill·and care into a contract for professional services.[116] However, as Deane J in *Hawkins* v. *Clayton*[117] has reminded us, the preconditions for implying a term into a contract include that the term must be necessary for the efficacy of the contract, and the term must have been intended by the parties to form part of the contract.

Deane J's reasoning does not preclude a duty in tort. Thus, there is no

---

[112] *Bartlett* v. *Barclays Bank Trust Co. Ltd.* [1980] Ch. 515 at 534, discussed in s. 2B(1), *ante*; *Re Waterman's Will Trusts* [1952] 2 All ER 1054; *Nestle* v. *National Westminster Bank plc* [1994] 1 All ER 118 at 140.

[113] Of course the unresolved question is whether the standard is that which other professionals actually do or whether the standard is that they ought to do in the eyes of the court. The better view is the latter as the 'extent of the legal duty in any given situation must . . . be a question of law for the court' (per Oliver J, *Midland Bank Trust Co. Ltd.* v *Hett, Stubbs & Kemp* [1979] 1 Ch. 384 at 402); see *Jackson & Powell on Professional Negligence*, 3rd edn., Sweet and Maxwell, 1992, para. 1–68.

[114] Whether a person is a professional is a question of fact (*Robbins Herbal Institute* v. *Federal Commissioner of Taxation* (1923) 32 CLR 457 at 461; *Currie* v. *Commissioners of Inland Revenue* [1921] 2 KB 332 at 340–1). In general, a profession involves the idea of an occupation requiring either purely intellectual skill or of manual skill controlled by the intellectual skill of the operator (*Commissioners of Inland Revenue* v. *Maxse* [1919] 1 KB 647). Ultimately one has to ask: would the ordinary reasonable man say now, in the time in which we live, of any particular occupation, that it is properly described as a profession (per Du Parcq LJ, *Carr* v. *Inland Revenue Commissioners* [1944] 2 All ER 163). If a distinction is drawn between lay and professional trustee by our trusts law, it would be illogical if a professional trustee, such as a unit trust trustee, is not a professional at common law.

[115] Notably, *Groom* v. *Crocker* [1939] 1 KB 194. Originally, the law regarded obligation as arising out of professional status. But status relationships were 'eventually largely swallowed by the expansive concept of contract': Atiyah, *The Rise and Fall of Freedom of Contract*, Clarendon Press, 1979, p. 416.

[116] *Midland Bank Trust Co. Ltd.* v. *Hett, Stubbs & Kemp* [1979] 1 Ch. 384.

[117] (1988) 164 CLR 539 at 582–7, with whom Mason CJ and Wilson J agreed in this respect.

reason why the manager may not also be liable under the principle in *Hedley Byrne & Co. Ltd.* v. *Heller & Partners Ltd.*[118] if it advises a potential unitholder in the selection of unit trusts or if any statement made in the scheme particulars is wrong and made with negligence.[119] If any positive intention to deceive is established, it may also be liable for the tort of deceit.[120] Of course, these tortious liabilities may be concurrent with those under contract.[121]

A further question is whether the manager as a fiduciary has a third head of liability in equity for breach of duty of care, just as in the case of trustees. This is important from the perspective of relief available to unitholders. In general, the proof of a breach of fiduciary duty means that the plaintiff will have made available to it a host of equitable remedies such as injunction, rescission of transactions, account for profits, tracing of property, and enforcement of a constructive trust in respect of assets acquired in breach of duty. Directly relevant to the breach of the duty of skill and care is the difference between equitable compensation and common law damages.[122] At law, the quantum of damages is circumscribed by rules of foreseeability, causation, mitigation, contributory negligence, and remoteness.[123] In equity, the remedy of equitable compensation is restitutionary in nature and the defendant may be required to compensate the plaintiff by putting him in as good a position as he was in before the

---

[118] [1964] AC 465.

[119] Cf. *Elders Trustee and Executor Co. Ltd.* v *EG Reeves Pty. Ltd.* (1987) 78 ALR 193; *Famel Pty. Ltd.* v. *Burswood Management Ltd.* (1989) 15 ACLR 572.

[120] In *Derry* v. *Peek* (1889) 14 App. Cas. 337.

[121] The literature is voluminous: see generally, Free, 'Can Parties in Contractual Relations be Liable to Each other in Tort?' (1978) 3 *Auckland ULR* 243; Morgan, 'The Negligent Contract-Breaker' (1980) 58 *Can BR* 299; Smillie, 'Negligence & Economic Loss' (1982) 32 *U of Toronto LJ* 231; French, 'The Contract/Tort Dilemma' (1983) 5 *Otago LR* 236; Reynolds, 'Tort Actions in Contractual Situations' (1985) 11 *NZULR* 215; Mason, 'Contract & Tort: Looking Across the Boundary from the Side of Contract' (1987) 61 *ALJ* 228; Swanton, 'The Convergence of Tort and Contract' (1989) 12 *Syd. LR* 40; Partlett, *Professional Negligence*, Law Book Co., 1985, ch. 6. The House of Lords in *Henderson* v. *Merrett Syndicates Ltd.* [1994] 3 All ER 506 recognized the existence of the concurrent liability both in contract and in tort of an agent in the Lloyds market.

[122] In *Galmerrow Securities Ltd.* v. *National Westminster Bank plc*, unreported, 20 Dec. 1993, Harman J emphasized that 'damages' was not an appropriate term on the question whether equitable compensation should be paid by a trustee of a non-authorized unit trust. See generally, Gummow, 'Compensation for Breach of Fiduciary Duty' in Youdan (ed.), *Equity, Fiduciaries and Trusts*, Carswell, Toronto, 1989, pp. 57 *et seq*; Davidson, 'The Equitable Remedy of Compensation' (1982) 13 *Melb. ULR* 349; McCamus, 'Remedies for Breach of Fiduciary Duty' in *Special Lectures of the Law Society of Upper Canada 1990: Fiduciary Duties*, De Boo, Ontario, 1991; Tilbury, 'Equitable Compensation' in Parkinson (ed.), *The Principles of Equity*, LBC Information Services, 1996, pp. 781–815.

[123] See Gummow, *supra*, at 75–87.

injury. In general, factors affecting damages do not apply.[124] Limitations of actions may also be different.[125]

Ultimately this resolves into the question whether there is a fiduciary duty of care. The leading case is *Nocton* v. *Lord Ashburton*.[126] A client was induced by his solicitor to enter into a mortgage in which the solicitor had a financial interest. Subsequently, he was also advised to release part of the mortgage properties and the security was rendered insufficient. In respect of the original transaction, it was barred by the Statute of Limitations, at law, and by acquiescence, in equity. In respect of advice for release, the trial judge found that no intention to defraud was proved. The House of Lords agreed and their Lordships also held[127] that the pleading and the conduct of the case precluded a finding of negligence. However, their Lordships found that the client succeeded on the footing that there was a breach of a duty arising from a fiduciary relationship. The interrelation between contractual, tortious, and fiduciary duty of care was explained by Viscount Haldane VC:

My Lords, the solicitor contracts with his client to be skilful and careful. For failure to perform his obligation he may be made liable at law in contract or even in tort,[128] for negligence in breach of a duty imposed on him. In the early history of the action of *assumpsit* this liability was indeed treated as one for tort. There was a time when in cases of liability for breach of a legal duty of this kind the Court of Chancery appears to have exercised a concurrent jurisdiction. That was not remarkable, having regard to the defective character of legal remedies in those days. But later on, after the action of assumpsit had become fully developed, I think it probable that a demurrer for want of equity would always have lain to a bill which did no more than seek to enforce a claim for damages for negligence against a solicitor. . . .

---

[124] *Nocton* v. *Lord Ashburton* [1914] AC 932 at 958, per Viscount Haldane VC; *Re Dawson (deceased)* [1966] 2 NSWLR 211 at 216, per Street J; *Commonwealth Bank of Australia* v. *Smith* (1991) 102 ALR 453 at 479–80. However, this restitutional basis may not be applied strictly. In *Target Holdings Ltd.* v. *Redfern* [1996] 1 AC 421, it was held that the specialist rules as to compensation for breach of traditional trusts were not necessarily applicable to bare trusts arising in commercial situations. In the New Zealand case of *Day* v. *Mead* [1987] 2 NZLR 433 it was said that assessment was subject to 'what the justice of the case requires according to considerations of conscience, fairness and hardship and other equitable features such as laches and acquiescence' (at 462 per Somers J). In the Canadian case of *Canson Enterprises Ltd.* v *Boughton & Co.* (1991) 85 DLR (4th) 129, causation was considered. Further, equitable compensation may not necessarily be the exclusive remedy for breach of fiduciary duties. It appears that the remedy of damages was also available in equity, despite the general belief that it is a common law remedy: McDermott, 'Jurisdiction of the Court of Chancery to Award Damages' (1992) 108 *LQR* 652; Spry, *Equitable Remedies*, 4th edn., Law Book Co., 1992, p. 608.

[125] As recognized by Viscount Haldane VC in *Nocton* v. *Ashburton* [1914] AC 932 at 957: text accompanying fn. 129, *infra*.                    [126] [1914] AC 932.

[127] By all of their Lordships except Lord Parmoor.

[128] This case predated *Hedley Byrne & Co. Ltd.* v. *Heller & Partners Ltd.* [1964] AC 465.

This, however, does not end the matter. When, as in the case before us, a solicitor has had financial transactions with his client, and has handled his money to the extent of using it to pay off a mortgage made to himself, or of getting the client to release from his mortgage a property over which the solicitor by such release has obtained further security for a mortgage of his own, a Court of Equity has always assumed jurisdiction to scrutinise his action. It did not matter that the client would have had a remedy in damages for breach of contract. Court of Equity had jurisdiction to direct accounts to be taken, and in proper cases to order the solicitor to replace property improperly acquired from the client, or to make compensation if he had lost it by acting in breach of a duty which arose out of his confidential relationship to the man who had trusted him. This jurisdiction, which really belonged to the exclusive jurisdiction of the Court of Chancery, had for the client the additional advantage that . . . the Statute of Limitations would not apply when the person in a confidential relationship had got the property into his hands.

My Lords, since the Judicature Act any branch of the Court may give both kinds of relief, and can treat what is alleged either as a case of negligence at common law or as one of breach of fiduciary duty.[129]

It is not entirely clear from this passage whether his Lordship found in favour of the client on the basis that the solicitor had placed himself in a position where his duty conflicted with his interest[130] or that the solicitor was in breach of a fiduciary duty of care.[131] *Nocton* v. *Lord Ashburton*[132] has not assumed much long-term significance in the context of negligent misstatement. This is because the utility of this case is overshadowed by the wider principle based on 'special relationship' enunciated in *Hedley Byrne & Co. Ltd.* v. *Heller & Partners Ltd.*[133] Interestingly, *Nocton* was used as a springboard by the House of Lords in *Hedley Byrne* to develop the common law concept of 'special relationship' in a negligence action.[134] Not only did *Hedley Byrne* support an interpretation that *Nocton* did in fact establish a fiduciary duty of care, Viscount Haldane's judgment in a Scottish appeal also lent support to this interpretation. In *Robinson* v. *Bank of Scotland Ltd.*,[135] he said:

. . . I wish emphatically to repeat what I said in advising this House in the case of *Nocton* v. *Lord Asburton*, that it is a great mistake to suppose that, because the principle in *Derry* v. *Peek* clearly covers all cases of the class to which I have referred, therefore the freedom of action of the courts in recognising special duties arising out of other kinds of relationship which they find established by the

---

[129] *Hedley Byrne & Co. Ltd.* v. *Heller & Partners Ltd.* [1964] AC 465 at 956–7.

[130] The second paragraph of the passage cited.

[131] The first paragraph of the passage cited.

[132] [1914] AC 932.                                                          [133] [1964] AC 465.

[134] See especially judgments of Lord Morris, ibid. at 502–3, and Lord Hodson, ibid. at 508. Before the decision of *Hedley Byrne*, Sealy has argued that the true basis of liability for negligent misstatement was not in tort but in equity. ('Some Principles of Fiduciary Obligations' [1963] *Camb. LJ* 119 at 137.) *Nocton* and *Woods* v. *Martins Bank Ltd.*, discussed below, were cited in support.                                      [135] 1916 SC (HL) 154.

evidence is in any way affected. I think, as I said in *Nocton's* case, that an exaggerated view was taken by a good many people of the scope of the decision in *Derry* v. *Peek*. The whole of the doctrine as to fiduciary relationships, as to the duty of care arising from implied as well as express contracts, *as to the duty of care arising from other special relationships which the courts may find to exist in particular cases*, still remains, and I should be very sorry if any word fell from me which should suggest that the courts are in any way hampered in recognising that the duty of care may be established when such cases really occur.[136]

Further support of the existence of a fiduciary duty of care can be found in *Woods* v. *Martins Bank Ltd.*[137] Salmon J held that a bank was liable in tort for negligent investment advice. His alternative reasoning was that the bank was a fiduciary in breach of its duty of care[138] but *Nocton* was not cited. This decision was approved by the House of Lords,[139] without any adverse comment on the alternative reasoning. In the recent House of Lords decision in *White* v. *Jones*,[140] Lord Browne-Wilkinson also accepted a duty of care as part of fiduciary duties. His Lordship said:

The paradigm of the circumstances in which equity will find a fiduciary relationship is where one party, A, has assumed to act in relation to the property or affairs of another, B. A, having assumed responsibility, *pro tanto*, for B's affairs, is taken to have assumed certain duties in relation to the conduct of those affairs, *including normally a duty of care*. Thus, a trustee assumes responsibility for the management of the property of the beneficiary, a company director for the affairs of the company and an agent for those of his principal. By so assuming to act in B's affairs, A comes under fiduciary duties to B. Although the extent of those fiduciary duties (*including duties of care*) will vary from case to case some duties (*including a duty of care*) arise in each case.[141]

In two Canadian cases, *Laskin* v. *Bache & Co. Inc.*[142] and *Maghun* v. *Richardson Securities of Canada Ltd.*,[143] customers suing their brokers were able to rely on *Nocton* to obtain higher compensation on the basis of breach of fiduciary duty and not breach of contract. Dicta in support can also be found in the Australian case of *Bennett* v. *Minister of Community Welfare*.[144]

The notion that a fiduciary owes its beneficiary a duty of care is not

---

[136] 1916 SC (HL) 154 at 157; emphasis supplied.　　　　　[137] [1959] 1 QB 55.

[138] *Supra*, at 72, where his Lordship said: 'In my judgment, a fiduciary relationship existed between the plaintiff and the defendants. No doubt the defendant Johnson could have refused to advise the plaintiff, but, as he chose to advise him, the law in these circumstances imposes an obligation on him to advise with reasonable care and skill.'

[139] *Hedley Byrne & Co. Ltd.* v. *Heller & Partners Ltd.* [1964] AC 465 at 510.

[140] *White* v. *Jones* [1995] 2 WLR 208.

[141] Ibid., at 209–30, emphasis supplied. See also *Henderson* v. *Merrett Syndicates Ltd.* [1994] 3 All ER 506 at 543 (criticized by Heydon, (1995) 111 *LQR* 1.)

[142] [1972] 1 OR 465.　　　　　[143] (1986) 58 OR (2d) 1.

[144] (1992) 176 CLR 408 at 557, per McHugh J.

universally accepted. It has been rejected on the basis that this approach is a perversion of words.[145] In an action by a building society against its directors for negligence in certain transactions in *Permanent Building Society (in liq.)* v. *Wheeler*,[146] the Full Court of Western Australia rejected the claim that the directors were liable for breach of fiduciary duty. Ipp J explained:

There are indeed many difficulties inherent in the concept of 'fiduciary wrongs'. It seems to me that many of those difficulties stem from equating an equitable duty to exercise care with a fiduciary duty to take care. It is essential to bear in mind that the existence of a fiduciary relationship does not mean that every duty owed by a fiduciary to the beneficiary is a fiduciary duty. In particular, a trustee's duty to exercise reasonable care, though equitable, is not specifically a fiduciary duty. Similarly, in my opinion, a director's duty to exercise reasonable care, though equitable (as well as legal) is not a fiduciary obligation.[147]

The difficulty with this reasoning is the source of the equitable duty of care asserted is not entirely clear. It seems correct to say that there is no tort of negligence in equity parallel to common law negligence.

If a manager can be characterized as a fiduciary in equity, it follows that there may be a duty of care owed to unitholders as part of its fiduciary duties. It depends on which school of thought may be accepted. This may be important to unitholders because they would be given equitable remedies against a contracting party. Moreover, cases on trustees' investment duties can in appropriate circumstances be precedents on managers' duties of care.

## C. Exculpatory Provisions

Some of the most important provisions of a unit trust deed are exemption clauses. By exempting the trustee or the manager from liability for breach of trust or fiduciary duty or from the performance of any duties, they may

---

[145] 'The word "fiduciary" is flung around now as if it applied to all breaches of duty by solicitors, directors of companies and so forth. But "fiduciary" comes from the Latin "*fiduciara*" meaning "trust". Thus, the adjective, "fiduciary" means of or pertaining to a trustee or trusteeship. That a lawyer can commit a breach of the special duty of a trustee, e.g., by stealing his client's money, by entering into a contract with the client without full disclosure, by sending a client a bill claiming disbursements never made and so forth is clear. But to say that simple carelessness in giving advice is such a breach is a perversion of words. . . . those who draft pleadings should be careful of words that carry such a connotation.' *Gerardet* v. *Crease* (1987) 11 BCLR (2d) 361 at 362, per Southin J.

[146] (1994) 14 ACSR 109.

[147] (1994) 14 ACSR 109 at 157; approved in *Bristol and West Building Society* v. *Mothew* [1996] 4 All ER 698 at 711. In *Breene* v. *Williams* (1995) 138 ALR 259 at 274 it was emphasized that the concern of fiduciary law is not negligence; cf. *McInerney* v. *MacDonald* (1992) 93 DLR (4th) 415.

in effect negate any positive terms that appear in other parts of the trust deed.[148] They are commonplace in unit trust deeds. As a matter of interpretation, trusts law has taken an approach which is different from contract law. As the unit trust deed is a contract that incorporates a trust,[149] the interaction of the two approaches must be considered.

## (1) Contract Law Approach and the Manager

Doctrinally, the position of the manager in questions involving exemption clauses is straightforward enough: it is a matter of contract law.

Since the House of Lords decisions in *Suisse Atlantique Société d'Armement Maritime* v. *NV Rotterdamsche Kolen Centrale*[150] and *Photo Production Ltd.* v *Securicor Transport Ltd.*,[151] it is clear that there is no rule of law by which an exemption clause may be eliminated, or deprived of effect, regardless of its terms.[152] The question whether an exemption clause is applicable where there is a fundamental breach of contract, or a breach of a fundamental term or any term, is one of construction of the contract.[153] It follows that it is possible for a unit trust deed to exempt the manager from liabilities for breaches of fiduciary duties or of duties of care and skill implied by the contract or founded in tort. Of course, in any particular case, the efficacy of any provision will be subject to various interpretative devices developed in various cases. Thus, the *contra proferentem* rule[154] requires a construction against the manager, as the party who inserts the provision, if the exemption clause is ambiguous.[155] The law also requires clear words for negligence to be excluded.[156]

---

[148] Matthews, 'The Efficacy of Trustee Exemption Clauses in English Law' [1989] *Conv.* 42 at 43 for a discussion of the types of exemption clauses.

[149] Ch. 2, s. 2, *ante*.      [150] [1967] 1 AC 361.      [151] [1980] 1 All ER 556.

[152] *Photo Production Ltd.* v. *Securicor Transport Ltd.* [1980] AC 827 at 841, per Lord Wilberforce.

[153] It is a construction of the whole contract, not merely the exclusion clause alone: ibid., per Lord Wilberforce. The House of Lords position was reached by the High Court of Australia in 1965 in *Sydney City Council* v. *West* (1965) 114 CLR 481; see also *Thomas National Transport (Melbourne) Pty. Ltd.* v. *May and Baker (Australia) Pty. Ltd.* (1966) 115 CLR 353; *Van der Sterren (Hand E)* v. *Cibernetics (Holdings) Pty. Ltd.* (1970) 44 ALJR 157. For the distinction between a fundamental breach and a breach of a fundamental term, see Greig and Davis, pp. 636, 641, and 651.

[154] *Davis* v. *Pearce Parking Station Pty. Ltd.* (1954) 91 CLR 642 at 649. It is not entirely clear if this rule is the same as 'the principle of strict interpretation': Greig and Davis, pp. 622–3.

[155] The court will not give an interpretation to pervert the meaning of clear language: *Van der Sterren* v. *Cibernetics (Holdings) Pty. Ltd.* [1970] ALR 751; *Darlington Futures* v. *Delco Australia Ltd.* (1986) 161 CLR 500; *Nissho Iwai Australia Ltd.* v. *Malaysian International Shipping Corporation, Berhad* (1989) 167 CLR 219.

[156] *Davis* v. *Pearce Parking Station Pty. Ltd.* (1954) 91 CLR 642; *Commissioner for Railways (NSW)* v. *Quinn* (1946) 72 CLR 345 at 372; *Wilson* v. *Darling Island Stevedoring & Lighterage Co. Ltd.* (1956) 95 CLR 43 at 71; *Port Jackson Stevedoring Pty. Ltd.* v. *Salmond & Spraggon (Aust.) Pty. Ltd.* (1978) 139 CLR 231 at 258.

Under the Unfair Contract Terms Act 1977, a contract term cannot exclude or restrict liability for loss or damage resulting from negligence unless it satisfies the requirement of reasonableness laid down in the Act.[157] Further, where a person deals with the other party as consumer or on the other's standard terms of business, the other party cannot exclude or restrict its liability for breach of contract, or claim to be entitled to render a contractual performance substantially different, or claim to be entitled to render no performance, unless the relevant term also satisfies the requirement of reasonableness.[158] However, it seems that the Unfair Contract Terms Act 1977 may not apply to the provisions of a unit trust deed. This is because the Act does not apply to 'any contract so far as it relates to the creation or transfer of securities or of any right or interest in securities'.[159] A trust deed is an instrument that creates units of a unit trust and provides for their transfer and redemption. Units are in the nature of securities.[160]

## (2) Trust Law Approach and the Unit Trust Trustee

There is as yet no judicial pronouncement in England that an exculpatory clause in a trust is to be interpreted in the same manner as a contract. Instead, it has been assumed in all trusts texts that there are trust obligations which can never be excluded as a matter of law. This will be the position of a trustee of a non-authorized unit trust. A trustee of an authorized unit trust will also be subject to section 84 of the Financial Services Act 1986.

### (a) Equity's Position

In theory a settlor can insert whatever provisions he or she wishes, including one that excludes any action against the trustee for breach of trust. Courts are, however, reluctant to uphold the literal wording of a widely drawn exemption clause at its face value. It is not surprising that exemption clauses are construed strictly against trustees relying on them. Ultimately, the court must resolve the reach and scope of such clauses. Academic commentators are not entirely in agreement regarding the general principles to be deduced.

As a broad proposition, it has been said that '[t]he position so far as English law is concerned is . . . that an express exculpation clause may relieve a trustee from liability where it is relied upon for a purpose within

---

[157] S. 1(2). A contract cannot exclude liability for negligence resulting in death or personal injury and the reasonableness requirement is inapplicable: s. 1(1).                    [158] S. 3.
[159] S. 1 and Sch. 1, para. 1(e); *Micklefield* v. *SAC Technology Ltd.* [1990] 1 WLR 1002.
[160] This is the subject of discussion of ch. 5, *post*.

the settlor's contemplation provided the loss was not occasioned by intentional wrongdoing, gross negligence or fraud on the trustee's part'.[161] Thus, under this view, an exemption clause is inoperative not only where there is deliberate misconduct by the trustee but where there is gross negligence.

Arguably, this view is supported by three Scottish appeals[162] to the House of Lords. These cases are *Knox* v. *Mackinnon*,[163] *Rae* v. *Meek*,[164] and *Clarke* v. *Clarke's Trustee*.[165] In the first case, Lord Watson said:

It is settled in the law of Scotland that such a clause is ineffectual to protect a trustee against the consequences of *culpa lata*, or gross negligence on his part or any conduct which is inconsistent with bona fides. I think it is equally clear that the clause will afford no protection to trustees, who from motives however laudable in themselves act in plain violation of the duty which they owe to the individuals beneficially interested in the funds which they administer.[166]

Lord Watson's statement was adopted by Lord Herschell in *Rae* v. *Meek*.[167] In the third case, Lord President Clyde stated:

It is difficult to imagine that any clause of indemnity in a trust settlement could be capable of being construed to mean that the trustees might with impunity neglect to execute their duty as trustees, in other words, that they were licensed to perform their duty carelessly.[168]

However, both *Knox* and *Rae* are cited as authorities for a narrower proposition by *Underhill and Hayton*[169] in their discussion of liability for acts of co-trustees:

. . . it would seem that an exculpatory clause cannot protect a trustee who commits a breach of trust in bad faith or intentionally or with reckless indifference to the beneficiaries' interests.

This proposition apparently does not see exemption clauses as ineffective to exempt liabilities for negligence or 'gross negligence'. Interestingly, the rationale is supplied by the learned editor of the ninth edition of Hayton and Marshall:[170]

---

[161] Cockburn, 'Trustee Exculpation Clauses Furnished by the Settlor' [1993] *ABR* 163 at 170; Matthews, 'The Efficacy of Trustee Exemption Clauses in English Law' [1989] *Conv.* 42.
[162] The degree of diligence required of the trustee is the same both under English and Scottish laws: *Rae* v. *Meek* (1889) 14 App. Cas. 558 at 569, per Lord Herschell.
[163] (1888) 13 App. Cas. 753.    [164] (1889) 14 App. Cas. 558.
[165] 1925 SC 693.    [166] *Supra*, at 765.
[167] *Supra*, at 572.    [168] *Supra*, at 707.
[169] p. 902; similarly, Ford and Hardingham, 'Trading Trusts: Rights and Liabilities of Beneficiaries' in Finn (ed.), *Equity and Commercial Relationships*, Law Book Co., 1987, pp. 48–88 at p. 57.
[170] Hayton and Marshall, *Cases and Commentary on the Law of Trusts*, 9th edn., Sweet and Maxwell, 1991, p. 716, fn. 48. The editor of Hayton and Marshall, Professor Hayton, is also the editor of the 15th edn. of *Underhill and Hayton*.

Some cases like *Wyman* v. *Paterson*[171] and *Re Poche*[172] suggest an exemption clause cannot excuse gross negligence falling short of reckless indifference but it is difficult to justify this. Indeed, the *Re Vickery*[173] view that 'wilful default' in the statutory exemption clause in Trustee Act 1925, s. 30(1) extends only to deliberate or reckless conduct means that s. 30(1) can excuse gross negligence. Only where a trustee has *mens rea* (a guilty mind) should he be prevented from relying on an exemption clause.

Thus, *Re Vickery* provides the authority for the position of *Underhill and Hayton*. Further, in a recent Court of Appeal decision in Jersey, *Midland Bank Trustee (Jersey) Ltd.* v. *Federated Pension Services Ltd.*,[174] the court reviewed the three Scottish decisions and came to the conclusion that the comments cited above were 'clearly reached as a matter of construction' and that the judges could not be 'taken to be expressing the view that no trustee could ever be permitted to exclude liability for negligence or gross negligence'. The court concluded that '[t]here is no general principle . . . preventing a trustee from protecting himself against liability for breach of trust by clear words, save in the case of fraud' and that clauses relied on by trustees as exculpating them from liability for breach of trust are to be construed narrowly and strictly. Thus, under this view, apart from fraud, an exemption clause will be given effect to. However, it is not entirely clear if 'fraud' in this formulation carries the same meaning as 'wilful default' in the *Vickery* sense.[175]

The *Midland Bank Trustee* case therefore is a clear rejection of the wider proposition that intentional wrong, gross negligence, and fraud of a trustee cannot be excluded or modified. Before accepting this narrower formulation or the wider proposition or indeed either of the two propositions one must question the theoretical basis of each of these propositions.

It seems that even under the narrower view, an exemption clause cannot effectively exclude wilful default. The difference between the two views is a question of degree. Both views seem to be premised on the idea that the fiduciary character of a trustee and the right of the beneficiary against the trustee for due administration cannot be taken away; otherwise, the relationship is not a trust relationship at all.[176] If this idea is correct—and there is no reason to suggest otherwise—it should follow that if an exemption clause denies all duties incident to a trust, the proper conclusion is not that the exemption clause is invalid but that on construction the

---

[171] [1900] AC 271 at 286.

[172] 6 DLR (4th) 40 at 55.

[173] [1931] 1 Ch. 572 at 583.

[174] [1996] Pen. LR 179.

[175] The Court in *Midland Bank Trustee (Jersey) Ltd.* did not find it necessary to decide on the meaning of fraud in this context.

[176] Matthews, *supra*, at 47; Waters, pp. 756–7.

intention is not to create a trust relationship.[177] In the unit trust situation, if the conclusion in respect of a clause is that it exempts the trustee from all duties of a trustee, the court should hold that the relationship is one of creditor-debtor and the unit trust deed is merely a contract. The clause should be given effect to, rather than ruled invalid. In any event, a distinction can be drawn between trustees' loyalty duties and duties to exercise skill and care. In respect of the latter, a clause that exempts a trustee's liability to perform such duties will not strip the trustee of its essential character as a trustee.

Another justification given is public policy.[178] But it is acknowledged that a settlor has a right to determine the level of loyalty expected of its trustee. A settlor may, for example, permit the trustee to profit from its position or to place itself in a position where its duty and interest may conflict. It may, likewise, determine the level of care and skill.[179] There is no public policy reason for saying that a settlor cannot make such decisions. Logically, there is no public policy reason for denying a settlor the right to make a decision for excluding all duties of fidelity and skill and care, if that is the true wish of the settlor. The true question is, 'What is the wish of the settlor?' This is a question of interpretation and depends upon the precise meaning of the words used by the settlor read in the context and circumstances. It is not for the court to say whether the settlor can exempt the trustee from liabilities in question; the proper question for a court is whether the settlor has done so.[180] Of course it is improbable that in normal circumstances a settlor would desire a clause that expressly excludes the liability of the trustee for fraud, bad faith or gross misconduct. At best, this can raise a presumption, but it cannot be a matter of law that a settlor cannot exclude such liabilities.

The argument against a public policy justification is surely stronger for unit trusts. Here, the trust is created by a contract and a contract, by nature, involves mutuality of rights.[181] There is no policy reason why the court should adopt an approach different from contractual construction. It is not for the court to say that a unit trust beneficiary may not contract out

---

[177] Cf. *MacRobertson Miller Airline Services* v. *Commissioner of State Taxation (WA)* (1975) 133 CLR 125 where a clause printed on a ticket negated all obligations of an airline company. The High Court of Australia held that there was no contract of carriage in existence and hence no stamp duty was attracted. If words of trust have been used, the court will have to decide whether in all the circumstances of the case there is certainty of intention to create a trust. The use of the word 'trustee' or 'trust' is not conclusive: *Commissioner of Stamp Duties (Qld.)* v. *Jolliffe* (1920) 28 CLR 178; *Tito* v. *Waddell (No. 2)* [1977] Ch. 106.

[178] Waters, p. 756; *McLean* v. *Burns Philp Trustee Co. Pty. Ltd.* (1985) 2 NSWLR 623 at 640–1, per Young J.

[179] *Hayim* v. *Citibank* [1987] AC 730.

[180] Cf. Windeyer J's comment on a contractual exemption clause in *Sydney City Council* v. *West* (1965) 114 CLR 481 at 503.       [181] Ch. 2, s. 1A(3), *ante*.

of the right of recourse against the trustee for due administration; the question is whether the beneficiaries have done so.

Whatever may be the position in relation to other types of trust, two conclusions regarding unit trusts can be drawn from the above discussion. First, it seems difficult to support a rule of equity that an exemption clause will be invalid if it excludes liability for gross negligence. Secondly, it is also illogical that a unit trust deed cannot exclude some or all trustees' liabilities. This is particularly so since the unit trust deed is a contract. It must be a question of construction whether a particular breach is exempted. If this second conclusion is not accepted by the court, the position of the trustee and the manager as regards exemption clauses will be different.

### (b) Statutory Position of Authorized Unit Trusts

Section 84 of the Financial Services Act 1984 provides:

Any provision of the trust deed of an authorised unit trust scheme shall be void in so far as it would have the effect of exempting the manager or trustee from liability for any failure to exercise due care and diligence in the discharge of his functions in respect of the scheme.

This section only applies to authorized unit trusts. Exemption clauses in non-authorized unit trusts are not affected.

Under this section, an exemption clause is not void in its entirety. It is only void 'in so far as' it would have the effect of exempting the manager or the trustee from liability for any failure to exercise due care and diligence. Thus, this statutory provision itself does not render void a clause excluding or modifying the fiduciary duties of a manager or a trustee. Whether such a clause is effective or the extent of its effectiveness will be governed by the case-law discussed above. It seems clear that such a clause will be construed strictly and it may not be effective if it purports to exclude liability for wilful default or fraud.

Further, in respect of a clause that does not exclude fraud or wilful default but excludes some fiduciary duties, it would seem that such a clause cannot conflict or be inconsistent with any provision of the Financial Services (Regulated Schemes) Regulations 1991, in particular, Part 7 which provides for the duties of the manager and the trustee. This is because such provisions are 'binding on the manager, trustee and participants independently of the contents of the deed'[182] and any breach on the part of the manager or the trustee shall be deemed a breach by it of

---

[182] Financial Services Act 1986, s. 81(3).

the rules of the recognized self-regulating organization.[183] The consequence is that civil actions may lie against the manager or the trustee.[184]

This section does not preclude the trust deed from defining the 'functions' of the manager or the trustee so that it may not have responsibility in particular matters. The line between a provision that defines responsibility and one that has the 'effect' of exempting liability is not easy to draw. Any possibility to define responsibility of a manager or a trustee of an authorized unit trust is circumscribed by the extensive provisions of the Financial Services (Regulated Schemes) Regulations 1991.

This section only applies to a 'provision in the trust deed'. It does not stop the unitholders holding a meeting to pass a resolution to sanction or waive a breach of duty on the part of the manager or the trustee. However, it is doubtful if such an avenue is open to unitholders of an authorized unit trust. This is because such a resolution is beyond the power of such a meeting. Under regulation 11.08 of the Financial Services (Regulated Schemes) Regulations 1991, a 'meeting of holders duly convened and held' shall be 'competent . . . to . . . approve any act . . . in respect of which any such resolution is . . . expressly contemplated by these regulations, *but shall not have any other powers*' [emphasis supplied]. Relieving a manager or a trustee from breach is not a matter expressly contemplated by the Regulations.

It also appears that enlarging the power of a unitholders' meeting in the trust deed would not be possible. Regulation 2.02.1 provides that '[a] unit trust scheme does not qualify to be authorised . . . unless the scheme is constituted by a deed which . . . (a) conforms with Schedule 1 below, and (b) (subject to (a) above) makes no provision for matters which are dealt with elsewhere in these regulation'. Powers of a meeting of unitholders are matters dealt with by Part 11 of the Regulations—regulation 11.08 of which spells out clearly that such a meeting shall not have any powers other than those provided by regulation 11.08. The Regulations do not provide for the consequence if a scheme were able to obtain authorization despite the trust deed containing provisions contravening regulation 2.02.1. The authorization order may be revoked.[185] Until revocation, arguably, those terms are overridden by regulation 2.02.1—which by virtue of section 81(3) of the Act is binding on the parties 'independently of the contents of the deed'.

As this section only applies to provisions in a trust deed, it does not override any provisions in other statutes. Under section 61 of the Trustee Act 1925, the court may on an application by the trustee relieve it from

---

[183] Financial Services Act 1986, s. 95(1).
[184] Ibid., ss. 62 and 62A.
[185] Ibid., s. 79.

liability for any breach of trust on the ground that the trustee acted honestly and reasonably and ought fairly to be excused. This statutory relief is available to any trustee, whether it is a trustee of an authorized unit trust or a non-authorized unit trust. However, it is not available to the manager.

3. DIRECTORY POWERS AND INVESTMENT DECISIONS

## A. Investment Decision Structure in a Unit Trust

As explained in chapter 2,[186] the trust in a unit trust is a trust with two limbs, a primary trust and a secondary trust. The primary trust is a trust whilst the scheme is a going concern. It may be interpreted as a trust of the *Re Denley's* type or as a trust subject to the contractual provisions of the trust deed and, in the case of an authorized unit trust, the regulations made under section 81 of the Financial Services Act 1986. The secondary trust only arises at the very moment when the trust scheme is terminated. It is a trust for sale and distribution.

The provisions to which the primary trust is subject depend on whether the unit trust is an authorized unit trust or non-authorized unit trust. The most important of these provisions will be those along the line of regulation 7.02.2 and regulation 7.09.1. Regulation 7.02.2 provides:

Subject to paragraph 1,[187] it is the manager's right and duty to make decisions as to the constituents of the property of the scheme in such a way as appears to him likely to secure that the objectives of the scheme are attained and that any particular objectives specified in the scheme particulars are achieved.

And regulation 7.09.1 provides:

It is the duty of the trustee to take reasonable care to ensure . . . that decisions about the constituents of the property of the scheme do not exceed the powers conferred on the manager.

Under these provisions, the manager has 'a right' to make an investment decision but the trustee does not. The trustee's obligation is one of oversight and does not extend to consider the merit of particular investments. In practice, since the trustee is the title holder of all scheme property, it has to execute all documents and implement the investment decision of the manager. And since it has no right to second-guess a particular investment decision, it means that it has to execute the directions given by the manager. In respect of an authorized unit trust, regulation

---

[186] S. 2A, *ante*.
[187] Which imposes an overall duty of management of the scheme on the manager.

7.10.1 accordingly provides that the trustee must take all steps and execute all documents which are necessary to secure that acquisitions, disposals, and loans properly made by the manager are completed.

Further provisions in the trust deed may limit the power to direct investment to certain descriptions of assets or may impose percentage restriction on certain investments or lay down some conditions which the manager must satisfy before making a particular investment.[188] For example, an authorized unit trust constituted as a property fund is subject to percentage restriction on investment in approved immovables.[189] Investment in approved immovables is also on condition that the manager obtains a report of an independent valuer[190] stating that the immovable would be capable of being disposed of reasonably expeditiously at the valuation made by him.[191] In a non-authorized property trust, where a single investment may constitute a substantial proportion of the trust fund, the trust deed may stipulate a detailed procedure for valuation and for submission of an investment proposal to the trustee.

In practice, any investment decision structure of an authorized unit trust must also be assessed with the knowledge that a manager is a company that manages a stable of unit trusts, investment trust companies, and other collective investment schemes.[192] It is possible for a manager of a non-authorized unit trust or an offshore unit trust to perform investment advisory services for individuals, pension funds, or private trustees on a contractual basis. In fact, this is very common for managers offshore. This may affect the loyalty duties of the manager in directing the trustee to make any investment.[193] It may also affect the trustee's decision whether to follow a particular direction.

In general, a research department of the manager will prepare research reports on the economic climate, prospect and outlook of an economic sector or of particular industries, assets or companies. The research will be utilized by many teams or individuals within the manager's organization that are responsible for investment decisions. Even within a team, there

---

[188] The Financial Services (Regulated Schemes) Regulations 1991, reg. 5.02; restrictions may also be contained in scheme particulars of an authorized unit trust: reg. 5.02.4.

[189] In general, investment in approved immovables is to be within a band of 20%–80% and the requirements of reg. 5.33 of the Financial Services (Regulated Schemes) Regulations 1991 must be satisfied.

[190] The valuer must satisfy the requirements of reg. 5.33.10, ibid.

[191] Ibid., reg. 5.33.3.

[192] S. 83 of the Financial Services Act 1986 prohibits the manager of an authorized unit trust to engage in activities other than acting as a manager of a unit trust, an open-ended investment company, an investment trust company, and a collective investment scheme and activities 'for the purposes of or in connection with' acting as such manager. It seems that a manager can only act as a plan manager of a Personal Equity Plan which wholly invests in schemes that it manages: Securities and Investments Board, *Unit Trust Only Personal Equity Plan* (Consultative Paper 22), 1989. [193] S. 2A of this ch., *ante*.

may be allocated responsibilities for several unit trusts. Once a decision is reached, it will be communicated to the trustee for execution.[194] Of course this only describes what may happen generally. The day-to-day process may vary with particular trust deeds or the course of dealing between a particular manager and a particular trustee.[195]

Apart from investment decisions, there may be administrative matters where responsibilities may likewise be split between the trustee and the manager so that one is subject to the direction of the other. Depending on the terms of the trust deed, and (in the case of an authorized unit trust) the regulations, a manager may direct the trustee to create or cancel units,[196] to exercise votes of shares forming part of the trust portfolio in a particular manner,[197] to borrow money for the use of the scheme on terms that the borrowing is to be repayable out of scheme property,[198] to insure trust assets, to distribute income to unitholders, and to make reimbursement of administrative expenses, and to pay out remuneration to the trustee and the manager and the fees of valuers, auditors, solicitors, experts or agents engaged. A trustee may direct the manager to rectify any incorrect pricing of units,[199] to cancel any transaction that exceeds the manager's investment power,[200] to suspend the issue and redemption of units 'if there is good and sufficient reason to do so having regard to the interests of participants or potential participants',[201] and to procure additional valuation of the properties of a property fund by the standing independent valuer.[202]

## B. Position of the Manager

Although the manager has extensive control over the ways that the trust assets are to be invested or dealt with, it is not a trustee. This is because the title to assets does not vest in it.[203]

---

[194] It is also possible for the manager to give instructions to agents to acquire or dispose of unit trust assets directly: reg. 7.03.

[195] Even in the case of a non-authorized unit trust, it is usual that the manager instructs relevant dealers or agents directly. This should be done under an express power, but the court will have no difficulty to find that the manager is the agent of the trustee: see ch. 3, s. 2B, *ante*.

[196] The Financial Services (Regulated Schemes) Regulations 1991, reg. 4.07 and reg. 4.10.

[197] Ibid., reg. 7.02.3 and reg. 7.11.1, but it cannot direct the trustee as to the exercise of voting rights of units in a collective scheme.

[198] Ibid., reg. 5.62.

[199] Ibid., reg. 7.02.5.

[200] Ibid., reg. 7.03.

[201] The suspension is not to exceed a period of 28 days: ibid., reg. 13.02. For a property fund, the trustee may also require the manager to suspend dealings in units if the trust is having a liquidity problem to meet likely request for redemption: ibid., reg. 12.10.

[202] Ibid., reg. 12.06.                                    [203] See ch. 3, s. 4A, *ante*.

## (1) Fiduciary or Beneficial Power Distinction

The first question is whether the manager's power is a fiduciary power or a beneficial power for its own benefit. Scott[204] and the *American Restatement*[205] draw a clear distinction between such powers in the discussion of a private trustee being subject to directory or veto powers of others. It has been questioned if such a distinction exists in English cases.[206] Indeed, judges in early English cases did not appear to be particularly concerned with enunciating such a principle. However, there is no reason to doubt that Scott's position represents the English position as well. The early case *Discconson* v. *Talbot*[207] supports such a proposition. So do cases on veto powers[208] and some cases on powers of appointment.[209]

In practice such a distinction may not be easy to draw.[210] For example, it is not easy to decide if an express power to invest in other unit trusts managed by the same manager is a beneficial power or a fiduciary power. It may be a beneficial power because it enables the manager to generate income as a manager selling the units of the unit trust to be invested[211] and also because cross-investment can boost fund sizes of the manager's funds and hence its goodwill in the industry. It may be fiduciary in nature because all investment powers are to be exercised for the benefit of unitholders.[212]

If a particular manager's power is held to be fiduciary in nature, a consequence is that the court will impose fiduciary duties as outlined in section 2 of this chapter.[213] In the absence of an express power, the

---

[204] Scott, s. 185.  [205] *American Restatement of the Law: Trusts 2d*, 1959, s. 185.
[206] Pearce, 'Directing the Trustee' (1972) 36 *Conv. (NS)* 260 at 264.
[207] (1870) LR 6 Ch. 32, discussed at fn. 210, *infra*. All their Lordships in the Court of Appeal in this case regarded this point as settled by *Howard* v. *Ducane* (1823) T & R 81.
[208] e.g., *Re Callen* (1918) 18 SR (NSW) 219.
[209] In *Re Triffitt's Settlement* [1958] Ch. 852, where a power of appointment to be exercised in favour of 'such person or persons other than and except T and any wife of his and in such manner generally as the wife [the power holder] shall from time to time or at any time by deed revocable or irrevocable with the consent in writing of the trustees for the time being hereof . . . which consent such trustees may withhold or give at their absolute discretion without being in any way liable for the exercise of such discretion appoint' was held to be beneficial in nature and was therefore a power that could be delegated.
[210] In *Discconson* v. *Talbot, supra*, a power of sale and exchange was exercisable 'at the request' of the tenant for life, and it was held that the tenant for life stood in no fiduciary position towards the remainderman. However, in *Re Massingberd's Settlement* (1890) 63 LT Rep. 296, on a similar provision, the Court of Appeal held that the tenant for life was a fiduciary. In *Re Wise's Settlement*, an unreported case noted in (1954) 218 LT 116, Wynn-Parry J regarded these two cases as not reconcilable and followed *Discconson*.
[211] For an authorized unit trust, this aspect is regulated by reg. 5.69 which 'claws' back (by requiring the manager to pay) into the unit trust all issue and redemption charges of the scheme to be invested.  [212] Ch. 3, *ante*.
[213] Both in terms of loyalty and skill and care.

manager cannot place itself in a position where its duties conflict with its own interests or duties owed to other unit trusts under its management. Thus, the manager must not obtain financial benefit from a third party in return for a particular direction to the trustee.[214]

Another consequence of the fiduciary characterization is that the manager, as a fiduciary, is not entitled to delegate any investment decisions in the absence of any express provision to the contrary.[215] If the power is beneficial, it is delegable without any express provision. Thus, any draftsman must consider an express provision in a unit trust deed if it is intended that the manager may delegate some part of its management power—which by nature will be fiduciary.[216] In the case of an authorized unit trust, the manager is given the power to delegate all its functions to any person, including the trustee.[217] However, if the delegate is the trustee or an associate of the manager or the trustee, the manager will be vicariously liable for all acts and omissions of the delegates. For other delegates, the manager can avoid liability by showing that it was reasonable for the agent to be employed for the function delegated, the agent was and remained competent, and the manager had taken reasonable care to ensure the function was undertaken by the agent in a competent manner.

## (2) Contractual and Tortious Duties

If a power is not fiduciary in nature, it legally follows that the manager holds no fiduciary duty in respect of its exercise. But, it does not necessarily follow that it may not be in breach of its contractual duties or tortious duties.[218] Thus, if a non-authorized property trust is formed for the purpose of, and authorizes, the acquisition of two buildings previously

---

[214] *Perpetual Trustee Co. Ltd.* v. *Cowan (No. 2)* (1900) 21 LR (NSW) Eq. 278; *Nissen* v. *Grunden* (1912) 14 CLR 297 at 318–19.

[215] *Re Triffitt's Settlement* [1958] Ch. 852, discussed at fn. 209, *supra*. Also, in *Re Callen, supra*, where the trustee was given power of sale subject to the consent of the life tenant, it was held that the power of consent of the life tenant was beneficial in nature and the life tenant might give consent by his attorney.

[216] In practice, the delegation clause is very extensively drafted—including the power to permit the delegate to sub-delegate: 'The manager may subject to the prior written approval of the trustee by power of attorney appoint any person to be attorney or agent of the manager for such purposes and with such powers and authorities as it thinks fit with power for the attorney or agent to subdelegate any such powers and authorities and also to authorise the issue in the name of the manager of documents bearing facsimile signatures of the manager or of the attorney or agent either with or without proper manuscript signatures of its officers thereon.' (*Australian Ency. F & P*, Vol. 3, p. 1015, cl. 7(8).)

[217] *Supra*, reg. 7.15.

[218] *Nocton* v. *Lord Ashburton* [1914] AC 932. See also the discussion at s. 2 of this ch., *ante*.

owned by an associated company of the manager, the manager is not in breach of its fiduciary duties in the acquisition, but it is still bound by the provisions on borrowing limits if the acquisition requires any finance.

A manager assumes overall investment responsibility of a unit trust under some express provisions of a trust deed. For an authorized unit trust, this is provided by regulation 7.02 of the Financial Services (Regulated Schemes) Regulations 1991. As the trust deed is a contract constituting the scheme, whether a particular exercise of power is fiduciary or not, the manager has to fulfil the contractual duty of management expressly provided in it. This duty, it is submitted, is positive in nature and requires the manager to take actions to initiate investment decisions. For the trustee, this positive duty on the part of the manager means that the trustee is not under any obligation to initiate a decision.[219]

## (3) Standard of Skill and Care

As to the standard of skill and care expected of a private trustee, it has been held that this depends on whether the trustee is a professional trustee or not. If it is not, the standard expected is no more than that of 'businessmen of ordinary prudence' so long as the trustee confines its investment to what is authorized and not attended with hazard. A professional trustee, on the other hand, will be 'liable for breach of trust if loss is caused to the trust fund because it neglects to exercise the special care and skill which it professes to have'.[220] These duties are equitable duties recognized in trust cases; they are not contractual in nature.[221] If the analysis of *Nocton*[222] in this chapter is accepted, by analogy, managers will be subject to the same principle regarding standards of care of trustees. As professional managers, the higher of the two standards is expected of them. If a court holds that *Nocton* does not apply to managers in unit trusts, then as the office of the manager is contractually created, the court has to reason from the implied term theory. Any implied term has to be justified on the basis of business efficacy and the intention of the parties.[223] Arguably, a professional standard of care may be implied from the investment expertise which managers usually profess to have.

---

[219] There is no direct authority but this implication should be apparent and is supported by the *American Restatement of the Law: Trusts 2d*, 1959, s. 185. Cf. approval power. If the intention is for the trustee to initiate a direction from the manager, the provisions would be for the trustee to seek the direction, just as consent, of the manager.

[220] *Bartlett* v. *Barclays Bank Trust Co. Ltd.* [1980] 1 All ER 139 at 152, per Brightman J; *Nestle* v. *National Westminster Bank plc* [1994] 1 All ER 118 at 140.

[221] S. 2B(1), *ante.*                                                    [222] [1914] AC 932.

[223] See *Hawkins* v. *Clayton* (1988) 164 CLR 539 at 582–7: discussed in s. 2B(2), *ante.*

In practice, at least for a non-authorized unit trust,[224] these standards of care will be subject to express provisions in the unit trust deed that may lower such standard. Such express provisions are contractual in nature. However, a contractual analysis may not always work in favour of the manager. For example, if a statement is made in the scheme particulars regarding the future profitability of the unit trust, the court may construe this as a warranty given by the manager. Liability may arise for breach of warranty even though the manager has exercised a high degree of care.[225] Alternatively, any such statement may be construed as a misrepresentation.

## (4) Deviation, Variation, and Ratification

The court has both equitable and statutory jurisdictions to sanction variations of powers of trustees.[226] If the office of the manager is contractual, it appears that any variation cannot be sanctioned by the court but must be sanctioned by other contracting parties. This is so notwithstanding that such a power could be fiduciary in nature, for the court has no jurisdiction to sanction variations of powers of fiduciaries.

If the manager does actually exceed its authority and directs the trustee to invest in unauthorized investments, it appears that it will be liable for all losses. In the case of an authorized unit trust, the trustee has the power to require the manager to reverse the transaction at the manager's expense.[227] Theoretically, breaches can be ratified by unitholders. In a non-authorized trust, this can often be done by a meeting of unitholders. In the case of an authorized unit trust, a unitholders' meeting does not have the power to ratify any breach on the part of the manager or the trustee.[228] However, it does have the power to approve modification of the trust deed[229] and the scheme particulars.[230] It seems that a modification can take retrospective effect so as to ratify a breach.[231] Further, all parties to a

---

[224] S. 84 of the Financial Services Act 1984 avoids any provision in a trust deed of an authorized unit trust that has the effect of exempting the manager from liability for 'any failure to exercise due care and diligence'. It is uncertain as to the standard of due care and diligence required by that section. Arguably, it refers to the standard that would be implied by common law, i.e. in the case of a professional, a higher standard that it professes to have.
[225] Cf. *Eyre* v. *Measday* [1986] 1 All ER 644; *Thalce* v. *Maurice* [1986] QB 644 (medical practitioner, warranting result liable even not negligent).
[226] *Underhill and Hayton*, art. 49(2), pp. 468 *et seq*.
[227] The Financial Services (Regulated Schemes) Regulations 1991, reg. 7.03.
[228] Ibid., reg. 11.08, discussed in ch. 3, s. 1D(2)(b), *ante*.
[229] Ibid., reg. 11.02.
[230] Ibid., reg. 11.04.
[231] In *Gra-ham Australia Pty. Ltd.* v. *Corporate West Management Pty. Ltd.* (1990) 1 ACSR 682 a retrospective modification of a trust deed affecting rights of unitholders was held to be valid.

contract can waive a breach by a party. There is no reason why all unitholders cannot waive a breach if they are unanimous.

## C. Position of the Trustee

As a general rule, directions given in a trust deed must be followed by the trustee.[232] It follows that if the unit trust deed directs the trustee to follow the decision of the manager in the making or disposal of investments, the direction is imperative. But is this always the case?

Several cases in which third parties were given powers to direct the trustees have bearing on this point. Three aspects emerged. First, in all these cases, the courts approached this as a question of construction of the particular power involved.[233]

Secondly, if on true construction of the trust provision, a direction from a third party is mandatory, the trustee has no discretion to depart from it.[234] *Beauclerk* v. *Ashburnham*[235] was regarded[236] as establishing this. In this case, the trustees were 'authorised and required', 'by and with the consent and direction' of the tenant for life, to lay out the trust monies on 'leasehold hereditaments' 'in some convenient place'. Lord Langdale MR held that it was imperative on the trustees, on the requisition of the tenant for life, to invest in leasehold.

In *Cadogan* v. *Earl of Essex*,[237] a deed of settlement provided that 'it should be lawful for the said trustees . . . and they . . . were thereby required, at any time or times during the lives or life of the said Lord Cadogan and Lady Cadogan . . . with their . . . approbation in writing' to invest in freehold, copyhold or leasehold. Kindersley VC purported to apply *Beauclerk* and held that the trustees had no discretion when they were called upon to invest in leaseholds by the tenants for life. He said:

These words evidently meant something more than a mere authority to do it, . . . the trustees being required to do a certain act, that must necessarily signify that it was imperative on them, if required by the tenants for life so to do[238]

In *Re Hurst*[239] a testator gave his sons in succession an option to purchase

---

[232] *Underhill and Hayton*, art. 49.

[233] This was clear from the judgment of Bennett J in *Re Hart's Will Trusts* [1943] 2 All ER 557, especially at 558.

[234] *Beauclerk* v. *Ashburnham* (1854) 8 Beav. 322; *Cadogan* v. *Earl of Essex* (1854) 2 Drew. 227, (1854) 18 Jur. 782; *Re Hurst* (1890) 63 LT 665, aff'd. (1892) 67 LT 96.

[235] (1854) 8 Beav. 322.   [236] In *Cadogan* v. *Earl of Essex*, *supra*.

[237] (1854) 18 Jur. 782. The report in the Jurist, which contained the full wording of clause in question as well as a fuller judgment, is to be preferred to that in Drewry Reports (2 Drew. 227) reproduced in the English Reports.

[238] Ibid., at 783.   [239] (1892) 67 LT 96.

his mill business at a price determined by valuation and to pay the price by instalments on security of a bond and a mortgage to the full value of the price of the mill business. The trustees were directed accordingly. The eldest son exercised the option. Subsequently, there were defaults in the payment of the mortgage instalments. In an action for breach of trust by other beneficiaries, it was alleged (*inter alia*) that the taking of the mortgage amounted to wilful default. It was held by the Court of Appeal that the direction was mandatory and there was no breach of trust in respect of the taking of the mortgage. Lindley LJ, delivering the court's judgment, said:

The sale of the mill for £50,000 secured by the bond and mortgage was not only justifiable, but was a transaction *with reference to which the trustees had no option.*[240]

Chitty J, at first instance, also said:

A mortgage for the full value property sold would, of course, have been a breach in any ordinary case in the absence of express authority from the testator. But here there was not only an authority conferred upon the trustees, but there was an express direction of the testator to them, *with which they were bound to comply.*[241]

The third aspect is that courts were reluctant to conclude that trustees had no scope to manoeuvre. Even in *Beauclerk*, Lord Langdale did not intend to exclude the trustee's discretion altogether, for he said in respect of 'particular houses, or as to their title, situation, description . . . the trustees had a most important discretion to exercise'.[242] The reluctance was also apparent from the judgment of Kekewich J in *Re Hill*,[243] where the trustee was empowered to invest, at the request of the tenant for life, in particular land. His Lordship said:

As I understand the law, where there is a direction or power to trustees to sell or purchase at the request of the tenant for life, that means that if the tenant for life makes the request the trustees must sell or purchase, and not merely that they may do so. In my opinion, under this power, if a fit occasion arose, and there was *no objection on the score of price*, the tenant for life could in effect insist upon the trustees purchasing the unsettled moiety or any particular part of it; and, consequently, upon the request being made, there would arise a 'liability'—that is to say, an obligation on the part of the trustees—to make the purchase.[244]

In *Re Hotham*[245] the Court of Appeal held that upon a direction by a tenant for life under section 22 of the Settled Land Act 1882 to invest capital moneys upon a specified mortgage of real estate, the trustees were

---

[240] (1892) 67 LT 96 at 97; emphasis supplied.
[241] (1890) 63 LT 665 at 667; emphasis supplied.
[242] Ibid., at 328.     [243] [1896] 1 Ch. 962.
[244] Ibid., at 966; emphasis supplied.     [245] [1902] 2 Ch. 575.

not bound to invest upon the mortgage unless and until they were satisfied that the direction had been given upon a proper investigation as to title, a proper report as to the value of the proposed security, and proper advice as to the form of the mortgage. On being so satisfied the trustees were bound to make the investment. In *Re Hart's Will Trusts*,[246] trustees were required 'to invest the capital of the . . . trust fund in such investments in their names or their control as my said son may from time to time direct whether the same be investments authorised by law for the investment of trust funds or not and shall pay the income arising from such investment to my said son during his life'. Bennett J held that the son might direct the trustees to purchase shares from himself. His Lordship said:

The power is to direct the investment of the capital in such investments as the testatrix's son may from time to time direct. Upon the language of the power as a whole, in my judgment, *provided he acts in good faith*, [the son] is entitled to give directions to the trustees to realise any investments constituting the trust fund which they from time to time may hold. In my judgment, upon the language of the clause, the trustees are bound to comply with those directions save that they are to satisfy themselves, the shares not being shares in which there is a free and open market, that the price which they pay for them is a reasonable and proper price at the time they make the purchase.[247]

Thus, despite the imperative nature of some directions, the courts are prepared to say that trustees retain some discretion as to price, title, or the value of security. Apart from that, no general principle can be discerned. At best, *Beauclerk*, *Re Hill*, *Re Hotham*, and *Re Hart's Will Trusts* can be regarded as putting a strict construction on directing clauses so that in respect of matters not expressly mentioned the discretion remains with the trustee. *Re Hart's Will Trusts* is an attempt to further introduce a 'good faith' requirement. But the basis was not explained. Nor was there any clarification of the relationship between this requirement and the distinction between beneficial and fiduciary powers, which was regarded as determinative in other cases discussed above.[248]

Against this state of the case-law, several observations can be made in the unit trust context.

(1) It was recognized in *The Application of Permanent Trustee Nominees (Canberra) Ltd.*[249] and *Telford Property Trust* v. *Permanent Trustee Co. Ltd.*[250] that the trustee of a unit trust has a duty to supervise the manager. The Financial Services (Regulated Schemes) Regulations 1991 expressly

---

[246] [1943] 2 All ER 557.                    [247] Ibid., at 558; emphasis supplied.

[248] See s. 3B(1) of this ch. *ante*.

[249] Unreported, NSWSC (Eq. Div.) No. 4216 of 1985, 24 June 1985, Young J, citing *Parkes Management Ltd.* v. *Perpetual Trustee Co. Ltd.* (1977–1978) ACLC 29,545.

[250] Unreported, NSWSC (Eq. Div.) No. 4026 of 1985, 28 Feb. 1985, Kearney J.

require the trustee of an authorized unit trust to take reasonable steps to ensure that the manager manages the scheme in accordance with the Regulations, the trust deed, and the scheme particulars. They also require the trustee to take similar steps to ensure that the manager's investment decisions do not exceed its powers.[251] It is also clear that the manager's 'right' to make investment decisions is subject to its duty to manage the scheme[252] and for the purpose of securing that 'the objectives of the scheme are attained and that any particular objectives specified in the scheme particulars are achieved'.[253] Thus, whether a unit trust is authorized or not, the trustee has a duty of oversight or supervision. The subject matters of supervision are clearly various decisions of the manager (made pursuant to the powers given to the manager). Any so-called directions are decisions which, subject to the terms of the trust deed, the trustee has to supervise. It follows from *Beauclerk*, *Re Hill*, *Re Hotham*, and *Re Hart's Will Trusts* that any direction will not by itself be regarded as absolute.

(2) In determining whether a direction ought to be followed, it is submitted that the trustee should draw a distinction between the fiduciary and the beneficial powers of the manager. This is supported by *Discconson v. Talbot*,[254] *Re Massingberd's Settlement*,[255] and *Re Wise's Settlement*,[256] which are cases of private trusts where the distinction was drawn in relation to powers of direction.[257]

(3) If the power is beneficial, the manager can act in its best interest. The manager is not subject to any fiduciary duties. The trustee must observe the direction of the manager unless the manager is in breach of some contractual, tortious or statutory duties.[258] The life tenant in *Re Hart's Will Trusts* clearly was in such a position. Otherwise, the life tenant cannot direct the trustee to purchase from the life tenant himself. In a unit trust, a manager is given the duty and power to redeem units from unitholders. After redemption, it may not exercise its power to direct the trustee to cancel the units so redeemed. It may hold them in the 'box' and sell them to new participants. These powers to direct the trustee to create and cancel units are beneficial powers as they are intended to enable the manager to deal in units as a principal.[259]

---

[251] Reg. 7.09.

[252] Reg. 7.02.2 is expressed to be 'subject to paragraph 1' which imposes the duty to manage the scheme in accordance with the trust deed, the Regulations, and the scheme particulars.　　　　　[253] Ibid.　　　　　[254] (1870) LR 6 Ch. 32.

[255] (1890) 63 LT Rep. 296.

[256] An unreported case noted in (1954) 218 LT 116.

[257] Though the different conclusions were reached on similar facts: see fn. 210, *supra*.

[258] Discussed below.

[259] Under the Financial Services (Regulated Schemes) Regulations 1991, it is possible for the manager to deal as an agent of the trustee: reg. 4.22.

(4) If a power given to the manager is a fiduciary power, as with most powers relating to investment decisions, the trustee must not comply with the manager's direction if the trustee knows or ought to have known that the manager is in breach of its fiduciary duties. Examples of possible breaches of fiduciary duties include self-dealing, scalping, churning, competing with the unit trust, secret commissions, bribes, using unit trust properties or confidential information. They have been discussed.[260] In case of doubt, the trustee should apply to court for directions.[261]

An unresolved question is the extent of investigation and enquiry which a trustee is required to make in respect of every direction given by the manager. It is submitted that the trustee has no positive duty to actively investigate into the fiduciary position of the manager in the absence of any express provision in the trust deed. The trustee should only be required not to turn a blind eye to what it knows or ought to have known having regard to the facts known to it. The reason is that under the trust constituted by a typical unit trust, the manager occupies a central position and its powers are not delegated powers. The respective powers and responsibilities of the trustee and the manager are compartmentalized.[262] That compartmentalization is achieved through the unit trust deed, which is a contract between the trustee, the manager, and the unitholders. Contract law implies nothing more than is required for the business efficacy of the transaction.

(5) The trustee must not follow a direction of the manager if such direction is in breach of the express provisions of the unit trust. This is so irrespective of whether the power in question is beneficial or fiduciary. If it were otherwise, the duty of supervision would be completely hollow.

In respect of every investment proposed by the manager, this means that the trustee has to check each proposal against the letter of the unit trust deed. It is submitted that this involves a two-stage process. First, the trustee must satisfy itself that the manager's proposed investment is positively authorized by the unit trust deed or the scheme particulars. The trust deed may have an express clause dealing with what is to be invested or may do the same by way of a definition of 'authorised investments'. The authorized investments may be defined by reference to assets, such as bank or money market deposits, bonds, shares, real properties, mortgages,

---

[260] S. 2 of this ch., *ante*.

[261] The trustee should not make the decision itself because under the unit trust deed the trustee has no power of management of assets.

[262] Reg. 7.02 and reg. 7.09 of the Financial Services (Regulated Schemes) Regulations 1991, discussed earlier, illustrate this. See also *Parkes Management Ltd.* v. *Perpetual Trustee Co. Ltd.* (1977–1978) ACLC 29,545; *The Application of Permanent Trustee Nominees (Canberra) Ltd.*, unreported, NSWSC (Eq. Div.) No. 4216 of 1985, 24 June 1985, Young J; *Telford Property Trust* v. *Permanent Trustee Co. Ltd.*, unreported, NSWSC (Eq. Div.) No. 4026 of 1985, 28 Feb. 1985, Kearney J.

futures, options, and units in other unit trusts. They may also be defined by reference to countries or geographic locations, such as most international and country funds.

Even if a particular investment is an authorized investment, the trustee must satisfy itself that the negative restrictions are complied with. There are four common types of negative restrictions. First, a percentage or concentration restriction may be provided for a single asset,[263] a class of assets, the total assets in a country or a region so that exposure to a particular type of risk is limited. Secondly, a purpose restriction may apply to certain types of investments which are generally perceived to be risky. Thus, a derivative transaction, a forward transaction in currency or stocklending may only be entered into for the purpose of efficient portfolio management.[264] A purpose restriction may be accompanied by a percentage restriction, in which case the trustee must ensure that both are complied with. The third type is a gearing restriction. The trustee has to ensure that the level of borrowing is that permitted by the trust deed.[265] The fourth is a restriction on investments which may place the manager in a position of conflict of interests.[266] This is making express what would otherwise be so regarded by equity.

As the duties of a trustee are continuing ones, it is important that the trustee must monitor the total value of the portfolio as well as the value of individual assets, since most negative restrictions are expressed in terms of the relative values of particular assets to the total portfolio. Changes in market conditions and in the volume of redemption may affect compliance with such restrictions.

From this discussion, it is clear that the nature of the duties of the trustee in relation to investments is administrative in character. In practical terms, this is simply a compliance programme similar to that commonly used in-house by banks, building societies, and securities firms for regulatory compliances. In no sense does this involve the trustee second-guessing the manager's investment decision as a second-guessing involves a process of assessing the risks of an investment against its return. All trust deeds or regulations, by making the manager responsible for investments, make a clear demarcation that this is the duty of the manager, not of the trustee. (6) Similarly, the trustee should not follow a direction of the manager if

---

[263] e.g., the Financial Services (Regulated Schemes) Regulations 1991 reg. 5.14.

[264] Ibid., reg. 5.49 *et seq*. Similarly, a non-authorized unit trust may restrict investments in forward rate agreements, foreign exchange contracts, futures, options, and other derivatives to be used only for the purpose of hedging against interest rates, exchange rates, and other market risks.

[265] Reg. 5.62 and reg. 5.63, ibid., give the trustee the general power to borrow on instruction of the manager up to 10% of the value of the property of the scheme.

[266] Ibid., reg. 7.16.

to so do is in violation of any statutory provisions, such as those relating to money laundering[267] or taxation.[268]

(7) An unanswered issue is whether the trustee is under a duty to solicit directions from the manager. Following the fiduciary and beneficiary distinction, if the manager's power is a beneficial power, the trustee is not under any obligation to seek a direction. If the power is fiduciary, the position is more complicated. Given the compartmentalization of duties, the centrality of the manager in investment decisions, and the contractual relationship between the manager and each unitholder, there is no duty on the part of the trustee to initiate a decision for investment or disposal of investment in response to market conditions. This does not, however, mean that the trustee can turn a blind eye to the state of affairs of the unit trust.

It is submitted that the trustee's position in respect of any omission by the manager to give a direction is the same as with any positive direction given by the manager. If the trustee knows or ought to know that any failure to give a direction in a particular situation is a breach of duty on the part of the manager, the trustee should ask the manager to give the direction and, if it fails to direct, should seek the court's directions. An example would be that, where there is a percentage restriction on certain investments, any change in total value of the portfolio may require the manager to direct a disposal of certain investments in order to comply with the percentage restriction.[269] If the manager does not do so, the trustee should seek its direction. If the manager still does not give the required direction, it does not follow that the trustee can simply act as if the direction had been given and proceed to dispose of the investment itself. The trustee should approach the court for directions. In *Re Hart's Will Trusts*,[270] Bennet J said:

Before making any change of investment it is the duty of the trustees, in my judgment, upon the construction of this particular power to consult [the son] if they are reasonably able to consult him and to act in accordance with his directions if he gives them. If he refuses or fails to give them, then they must be free to act.[271]

Clearly, as Bennett J has observed, the question is one of construction. In a unit trust, if the manager does not give a direction, the trustee is not 'free

---

[267] The Drug Trafficking Offences Act 1986, the Criminal Justice Act 1988, the Prevention of Terrorism (Temporary Provisions) Act 1989, the Criminal Justice (International Co-operation) Act 1993, the Criminal Justice Act 1993, and the Money Laundering Regulations 1993.     [268] Unit Trust Records Regulations 1946.
[269] In the case of an authorized unit trust, this will be the type of contravention beyond the control of the manager and the trustee for the purpose of reg. 7.14 which requires the manager to take such steps as are necessary to ensure a restoration of compliance as soon as is reasonably practicable but in any event not exceeding six months or other periods applicable to the transaction in question.     [270] *Supra.*     [271] *Supra*, at 558.

to act' because by the terms of the unit trust deed, investment management power does not vest in it. The trustee should seek directions from the court.

4. VETO POWERS

Under the Financial Services (Regulated Schemes) Regulations 1991, there are many situations where the trustee has to obtain the 'consent', 'approval' or 'agreement' of the manager, and vice versa. There are also provisions that require a party not to act without 'consulting' the other party.[272]

For example, the manager 'may instruct' the trustee to create[273] and to cancel[274] units but the trustee may refuse to follow these instructions '[w]here . . . the trustee is of the opinion that it is not in the interests of participants'.[275] Similarly, the trustee may refuse to comply with the manager's instructions to create units in exchange for assets if the trustee is not satisfied that there is no 'material prejudice to the interests of participants or potential participants'.[276] The manager may, 'with the prior agreement of the trustee', suspend dealing in units for a period not exceeding twenty-eight days.[277] For the valuation of units, if the manager wishes to adopt an exchange rate other than the average rate provided by the Regulations,[278] the trustee's agreement is required.[279]

The manager may only invest in a market other than an eligible market under regulation 5.07A.1 after 'consultation' with the trustee.[280] Presumably, the trustee may veto the manager's decision if the trustee has difficulty in appointing a custodian[281] in that market or if the trustee considers that it is not in a position to discharge its oversight obligation under regulation 7.09. When the manager enters into a derivative

---

[272] The reason behind the choice of word used in a particular context of the Regulations is not entirely clear. It seems that the draftsman is not particularly meticulous in his or her selection.

[273] Unit Trust Records Regulations 1946, reg. 4.07.          [274] Ibid., reg. 4.10.

[275] Ibid., reg. 4.12. It is not clear from this regulation as to the basis on which a trustee can form such an opinion. Nor does this regulation require that the reason has to be stated in the notice of refusal to be given to the manager.

[276] Ibid., reg. 4.08.2.          [277] Ibid., reg. 13.02.

[278] S. 2 of Table 4.2 of reg. 4.29.          [279] Id.          [280] Ibid., reg. 5.07A.2.

[281] The trustee is liable for the acts of a custodian unless conditions laid down in reg. 7.15.6, ibid., are satisfied. Reg 7.03.3, ibid., provides that '[w]here the trustee is of the opinion that (a) an acquisition of property . . . involves documents of title . . . being kept in the custody of a person other than the trustee and (b) the trustee cannot reasonably be expected to accept the responsibility which would otherwise be placed upon him as a delegator, the trustee may require the manager to cancel the transaction . . .'. Thus, even for a single transaction, the trustee has power to require the manager to reverse that transaction on the basis of custody risk.

transaction or a forward transaction in currency for the purpose of efficient portfolio management, the trustee may veto it 'if its purpose could reasonably be regarded as speculative'.[282] The manager may invest in contravention of Part 5 of the Regulations if the 'reason for the contravention is beyond the control of the manager and trustee' provided the manager 'has obtained the consent of the trustee'.[283]

In respect of the accounts of the scheme, the manager is given the power to elect a particular accounting period to end seven days earlier or later than the previous accounting period chosen but the 'agreement' of the trustee is required.[284]

The manager has the powers to appoint an auditor and a standing independent valuer of a property fund and to remove them but in all cases the exercise of power has to be 'with the approval of the trustee'.[285]

In respect of the trustee, some of its powers under the Regulations are also subject to veto by the manager. Where an *in specie* redemption is to be effected under regulation 4.28, the trustee is given the power to select the property to be transferred to the redeeming unitholder but such selection has to be made 'after consultation with the manager'. If the trustee wants to distribute income of less than £1, the manager has to be 'consulted' before the distribution.[286] The trustee has the power to convene a unitholders' meeting at such time and place as it thinks fit but, again, the trustee is required to consult the manager as to the time and place of the meeting.[287]

Similar examples can also be found in unit trust deeds of other unit trusts.[288] In fact, in the negotiation stage, each will seek to protect its own interests as well as to protect against possible liabilities to unitholders.

---

[282] Ibid., reg. 5.51.4.  
[284] Ibid., reg. 9.02.7.  
[283] Ibid., reg. 7.14.

[285] Ibid., reg. 7.05 and reg. 12.05. The trustee has the power to remove the standing independent valuer without the consent of the manager; its only obligation is to 'inform' the manager of such removal: reg. 12.05.4.

[286] Ibid., reg. 9.04.2.  
[287] Ibid., reg. 11.07.

[288] A trust deed may require the manager to obtain the approval of the trustee: (a) in the formats of application for units, redemption requests, transfer forms, unit trust certificates, and other documents; (b) in making investments in options, futures, and forward currency contracts for the purpose of hedging; (c) in the selection of a consumer price index for the purpose of determining fee increases, or a reference bank for determining the exchange rate for the purpose of calculations involving foreign currencies; (d) in the appointment of property managers, valuers, investment advisers or other experts; (e) in the establishment of branch registers of unitholders; (f) in entering into insurance policies, guarantees, scrip lending agreements, underwriting agreements, and other contracts; (g) in granting powers of attorney delegating the manager's discretion; and (h) in any change of investment policy. The trustee may have to seek the consent of the manager: (a) in the appointment of custodians, valuers, and legal advisers; (b) in the delegation of its authorities; (c) in the transfer of assets *in specie* to satisfy a redemption request; (d) in changing the name of the trust; or (e) in changing the governing law of the trust.

Because the manager has assumed wide substantive powers in modern unit trusts, it is the trustee which often seeks to put a check on such powers at the negotiation stage. Consequently, it is usual for a trust deed to give more veto powers to the trustee than to the manager.

In principle, the relative positions of the holder of the veto power and the holder of the substantive power should be the same as in the case of the manager giving directions and the trustee being subject to directions. Thus, a distinction has to be made between fiduciary and beneficial powers, the exercise of the latter not being subject to fiduciary responsibilities.[289] A fiduciary power will be subject to fiduciary duties towards the unitholders.

There are however two important differences between these two types of power. First, the status of the veto power holder is important in ascertaining both the powers and the duties that may be involved. A particular veto power in the hand of the trustee is not necessarily the same as it is in the hand of the manager. The trustee is a trustee but the manager is a contractual fiduciary.[290] In the exercise of any power, a trustee is subject to trustees' duties but a manager is subject to contractual duties and, in matters where it is a fiduciary, fiduciary duties. This difference in status may have remedial implications as well. Trustees have powers to invoke the court's inherent and statutory jurisdictions over trustees such as asking the court to give advice and direction, to vary the trustees' powers, and to obtain the court's sanction for departure from the terms of the trust.[291] In *Harrison* v. *Thexton*,[292] the court authorized the exercise of a power which was subject to consent, despite the refusal of the person with consent power. By contrast, a manager cannot invoke the court's jurisdiction to vary trust powers.[293]

Secondly, the holder of a directory power is under a positive duty to initiate a decision on matters covered by the power. In making that decision, the power holder is under a duty of skill and care. A veto power, however, is a power of review that only arises when the holder of the substantive power makes a decision. From the standpoint of the substantive power holder, the seeking of consent is only a condition of an exercise of the power. As a consequence, a veto power holder is not under a primary duty to initiate a decision. For example, if the unit trust deed requires the manager to seek the consent of the trustee in any investment in a single asset that exceeds 5 per cent of the value of the portfolio, there is no duty

---

[289] *Re Callen* (1918) 18 SR (NSW) 219, discussed at fn. 215, *supra*.
[290] See ch. 3, *ante*.                            [291] *Underhill and Hayton*, art. 49(2).
[292] (1858) 4 Jur. NS 550; *Re Thompson* [1929] NZLR 88; *Re Beale's Settlement Trusts* [1932] 2 Ch. 15 and *Costello* v. *O'Rorke* (1869) IR 3 Eq. 172 at 184. These cases must be read subject to the rule that if the requisite consent is a condition precedent the court cannot dispense with it: see *Re Forster's Settlement* [1942] Ch. 199; *Re 90 Thornhill Road* [1970] Ch. 261, and the discussion below.                            [293] See s. 3B(1) of this ch., *ante*.

on the trustee to initiate the investment. The initiating obligation remains with the manager. In principle, responsibilities for decision making and for reviewing a decision are different in scope. The former is positive in nature and the power holder has greater scope of freedom. The latter is relatively negative, in the sense that the decision of another person is vetoed only if there are good reasons.

A third possible distinction between a directory power and a veto power flows from the second. If the duty of making an investment decision is in the hand of the holder of the directory power, i.e. the manager, the trustee who invests at its own initiative will be in breach of trust. It is not possible for the manager to give the direction subsequently because at the time when that direction is sought, there is a breach already. It is for the beneficiaries of that power to waive that breach.[294] The manager could only waive the breach if it had an express power to do so on behalf of unitholders.

By contrast, cases indicate that the consent of a particular person in relation to a particular exercise of power may be construed as a condition precedent or a condition which may be satisfied either before or after the decision is made. If it is a condition precedent, it must be satisfied before the power is exercisable and there is no power in the court to dispense with that consent.[295] In deciding whether a particular consent is a condition precedent or not, there is no fixed and firm rule; it is acknowledged to be a question of construction.[296] In *Greenham* v. *Gibbeson*,[297] Tindal CJ said:

Whether in all cases a consent, where necessary, must be given before the execution of a power, or whether it will in some cases be sufficient to ratify the execution of the power by a subsequent consent, it is unnecessary at present to determine. It is sufficient to lay it down, that where the nature and object of the power, and the circumstances of the case point to a previous consent, then such previous consent is necessary, although not required by the terms of the power.[298]

It can easily be understood that where the power is a fiduciary power, the prima facie construction is that it is a condition precedent. The reason is that the fiduciary's consent should be a free consent after full consideration of the interests of the beneficiaries and should not be influenced by the

---

[294] Cf. *Re Williams, deceased* [1950] Qld. SR 148, discussed below. For an authorized unit trust, a meeting of unitholders may not have the power to waive a breach: see s. 2C(2)(b), *ante*.

[295] *Re Forster's Settlement* [1942] Ch. 199; *Re 90 Thornhill Road* [1970] Ch. 261.

[296] Per Harvey J, in *Re Callen* (1918) 18 SR (NSW) 219 at 226, citing *Greenham* v. *Gibbeson* (1834) 10 Bing. 362.

[297] (1834) 10 Bing. 362. This case was applied in *Gilbey* v. *Rush* [1906] 1 Ch. 22. This passage was cited with approval in *Perpetual Trustee Co. Ltd.* v. *Cowan (No. 2)* (1900) 21 NSWR 278 at 298–9 and *Perkins* v. *Permanent Trustee Co. Ltd.* (1923) 23 SR (NSW) 358 at 363. [298] Ibid., at 374.

pressure of subsequent events. In *Bateman* v. *Davis*,[299] trustees were given power to advance money, with consent of A, to A's husband. Money was advanced and consent was given subsequently by a deed. It was held by Leach VC that the consent was invalid because:

[t]he actual advance of the money to the husband, who perhaps had spent it, created a pressure upon the plaintiff, which gave to her subsequent approbation a very different character from the free consent required by the settlement.[300]

As Stuart VC in *Stevens* v. *Robertson*[301] observed:

A consent which is not a free one is no consent at all, and if the Court thinks that the consent actually given is not free, it holds that no consent has been given. That was the principle on which *Bateman* v. *Davis* was decided, and it was in no sense determined on the footing that the consent ought to have been given previous to the advance.

Speaking of a fiduciary power of consent of a trustee, Kekewich J also said in *Gilbey* v. *Rush*:[302]

What consent is necessary? Now, in the first place, it must be a consent at the time; nothing retrospective will do. There was a passage cited from *Greenham* v. *Gibbeson,* which expresses that well. It must be a consent at the time and it must be a consent *ad hoc*, with reference to the particular transaction, not given without deliberation, not given without reference to what was proposed at the moment; but given with direct responsibility.[303]

These considerations suggest that it would be difficult not to construe a fiduciary veto power as a condition precedent. In a unit trust, the deed may, for example, provide that the manager shall not invest more than 5 per cent of the portfolio assets in futures contracts without the consent of the trustee. If the manager invests more than 5 per cent and seeks consent subsequently the trustee will be in a dilemma. If a gain is shown at the time of consent, there is no reason to disapprove. If a loss is made at the time of consent, the worry of the trustee is the extent of loss when the futures positions are liquidated in the market. Any refusal to give consent may cause a dispute or, indeed, litigation by the manager as to whether the trustee has exercised its power of consent properly. In such event, the manager may hold onto the investment and there may be further losses as a result. Perhaps, the manager may be an effective manager in the overall

---

[299] (1818) 3 Madd. 98.                                    [300] Ibid., at 99.
[301] (1868) 37 LJ Ch. 499 at 503.                          [302] [1906] 1 Ch. 1.
[303] Ibid. The same principle can be deduced from an earlier case of *Child* v. *Child* (1855) where trustees were empowered, with the consent of the wife, to lend the trust monies to the husband. The wife authorized an immediate loan as well as subsequent loans the husband might require. It was held that she might not give a prospective consent to future loans and that her consent was necessary to each loan.

performance of the trust; it may also be on good terms with the trustee. The trustee may consider the implications of refusing to give consent on the manager and on the future of the trust. It may be tempted not to jeopardize its relationship with the manager. Thus, subsequent consent is not true consent at all; the trustee is instead giving its approbation *ex post facto* to a particular conduct. In doing so, the trustee has to take into account factors extraneous to the subject matter for which a consent is sought. The consent given is 'not free';[304] the subsequent circumstances have 'created a pressure . . . which gave [the] subsequent approbation a very different character from the free consent required'.[305] A consent cannot be equated with a ratification. Therefore, a fiduciary consent has to be regarded as a condition precedent.

Where the power is a beneficial power, it is unlikely that the giving of subsequent consent will be invalid. In the first place, in the absence of any express indication, the court will not construe the consent as a condition precedent. *Stevens* v. *Robertson*[306] illustrates the point. By a settlement the trustees were authorized, with the consent in writing of the tenant for life, to alter, vary or transpose the trust fund from time to time. The trustees varied the investments without such consent but the life tenant signed receipts of income from the varied investment. It was held that the trustees had the relevant consent. Similarly, in *Perkins* v. *Permanent Trustee Co. Ltd.*[307] a settlor made a settlement of his undivided share under the will of his father. He himself was a life tenant of the settlement. The settlement provided that the trustees might with his consent in writing during his life and after his death at the discretion of the trustees make or concur in any arrangement with the executors of the will for the realization or partition of the estate of the father. Proceedings were instituted by the trustees for the partition. No formal consent was obtained from the life tenant beforehand but he was kept fully informed of the proceedings. He also expressed his satisfaction in correspondence with the trustees. Street CJ in Equity held that consent was given within the meaning of the settlement.

Where the consent is a condition precedent, the giving of a subsequent consent by the beneficiary of the power is treated by the court to be a ratification or an acquiescence which precludes any action. This was clear from the judgment of Macrossan CJ in *Re Williams, deceased*[308] where he said in relation to a power to make advances with the consent of all life tenants in a settlement:

---

[304] See Stuart VC's comment in *Stevens* v. *Robertson*: text accompanying fn. 301, *supra*.
[305] See Leach VC's comment in *Bateman* v. *Davis*: text accompanying fn. 300, *supra*.
[306] *Supra*.     [307] (1923) 23 SR (NSW) 358.
[308] [1950] Qld. SR 148.

If, as I think, the advances were not a proper exercise of the powers of the trustee when made, no subsequent consents can alter that fact. . . . Nevertheless, as the provision for consent in writing is a provision for the benefit of the persons having any prior life interest existent or contingent, I think that if all such persons consented to the advances *ex post facto* the trustee would be freed from liability for having made the advance.[309]

Thus, it may be concluded that if the power to give consent is a beneficial power, a subsequent consent is effective as a ratification or an acquiescence. This may be contrasted with the fiduciary consent required by the trust deed as a condition precedent, which cannot be given *post facto*.

### 5. DELEGATION

#### A. Delegation Without Express Provisions

#### (1) The Trustee

The contractual nature of the unit trust means that there are matters in which the trustee and the manager have interests as contracting parties. Thus, the distinction drawn by the law between beneficial and fiduciary powers is important.[310] In relation to beneficial powers, the trustee can delegate without express authorization in the unit trust deed.[311] For fiduciary powers, the trustee will be in the same position as the trustees of private trusts.

The general rule is that trustees must act personally.[312] A trustee cannot delegate its duties and powers. There are two exceptions of fairly limited nature conferred by case-law or statute. The first exception is that a trustee may delegate its discretions in respect of properties situated abroad.[313] The second enables a trustee to delegate its powers and discretions by a power of attorney for a period not exceeding twelve months but the trustee remains liable for the acts and defaults of the attorney.[314]

The power to appoint delegates to exercise the duties and powers of the trustee must be distinguished from the power to appoint agents to undertake ministerial acts to implement decisions made by trustees. Such a power, according to *Speight* v. *Gaunt*,[315] exists if the employment of an

---

[309] [1950] Qld. SR 148 at 202.      [310] S. 3B(1), *ante*.
[311] *Re Callen* (1918) 18 SR (NSW) 219; *Re Triffitt's Settlement* [1958] Ch. 852.
[312] *Underhill and Hayton*, art. 57.
[313] *Stuart* v. *Norton* (1860) 14 Moo. PC 17; *Re Dunlop* (1925) 26 SR (NSW)126; now this is provided by Trustee Act 1925, s. 23(2).
[314] Trustee Act 1925, s. 25, as amended by Powers of Attorney Act 1971, s. 9.
[315] (1883) 9 App. Cas. 1; *Re Parsons, ex p. Belchier* (1754) Amb. 218.

agent is normally necessary or in the ordinary course of affairs from the point of view of a prudent person of business. This power has been extended by section 23(1) of the Trustee Act 1925.

In the appointment of an agent, the trustee is under a twin duty of care both in the initial choice of the agent[316] and in the continuing supervision of that agent.[317] In performing these duties, the standard applicable to unit trust trustees will be that of a professional trustee.[318]

It would be very rare to find a unit trust deed that does not give additional delegation powers to the trustee. For an authorized unit trust, additional[319] powers of a unit trust trustee are provided by regulation 7.15 of the Financial Services (Regulated Schemes) Regulations 1991. It also modifies the liability of a trustee delegating its function. This will be dealt with below.

## (2) The Manager

The manager's beneficial powers are delegable whilst its fiduciary powers are non-delegable in the absence of express authorization.[320] The manager does not have the benefit of enabling provisions of the Trustee Act 1925.[321] Since legislative provisions are extensions of equitable principles, trustee cases will be relevant. However, it is important to note that the manager is a contractual fiduciary. The authority of the manager is derived from the contract contained in the trust deed. The source of authority must be interpreted on the basis of implied terms. For example, it is not difficult to conclude that a manager with an express power to invest in shares may have an implied power to appoint agents to perform ministerial acts such as the engagement of brokers to buy or sell shares in the stock market.[322] As this is a question of implied terms, cases developed at common law in relation to agents' powers to appoint sub-agents to perform ministerial

---

[316] *Fry* v. *Tapson* (1884) 28 Ch. D 268, where the trustee investing trust money on mortgage relied on his solicitor's choice of a valuer who in fact also acted for the mortgagor and the trustee was held liable.

[317] *Matthews* v. *Brise* (1843) 6 Beav. 239; *Griffiths* v. *Porter* (1858) 25 Beav. 236; *Graham* v. *Gibson* (1882) 8 VLR (Eq.) 43; *Re Weall* (1889) 42 Ch. D 674; *Wyman* v. *Paterson* [1900] AC 271; *Guazzini* v. *Pateson* (1918) 18 SR (NSW) 275; *Re Lucking's Will Trusts* [1968] 1 WLR 866. [318] S. 2B(1), *ante*.

[319] This regulation does not replace the powers of a trustee under case-law or the Trustee Act 1925: reg. 7.12.

[320] *Re Callen* (1918) 18 SR (NSW) 219; *Re Triffitt's Settlement* [1958] Ch. 852.

[321] S. 5A(1) of this ch., *ante*.

[322] It is stated in *Bowstead and Reynolds on Agency*, 16th edn., Sweet and Maxwell, 1996, comments to art. 36 (para. 5-003), that '. . . an agent may delegate the performance of purely ministerial or ancillary acts, unless there is evidence of usage not permitting this . . .'. For an authorized unit trust, this is provided by reg. 7.03.

duties, rather than the trustee cases on delegation mentioned above, offer better precedents.

## B. Permissive Delegation

This covers the situation where the trustee or the manager is given the discretion to delegate all or some of the duties and powers to a third party if it so wishes. In this sense, delegation permitted in equity or under the Trustee Act 1925 is permissive in nature.[323]

For an authorized unit trust, the position is governed by regulation 7.15 of the Financial Services (Regulated Schemes) Regulations 1991. In general, subject to two broader categories of restrictions, and also subject to any restriction in the trust deed, both the trustee and the manager are permitted to delegate any of their functions to any person, including the trustee and the manager themselves.[324] The delegation permitted by this regulation is not confined to ministerial acts but extends to any discretion.

The first category of restriction is on delegation of core functions. Under the Regulations, the trustee has two core functions, oversight of the manager and custody of trust assets. The trustee is prohibited from delegating the oversight function to the manager or its associates. It is also prohibited from delegating the custody function to the manager. In respect of delegation to any other person, regulation 7.15.3 provides that:

The trustee may not delegate to anyone the function of being a custodian of documents of title or documents evidencing title to property of the scheme unless the arrangements with the custodian prevent the custodian from releasing the documents into the possession of a third party without the consent of the trustee.

The trustee can appoint a custodian under the general power of delegation conferred by regulation 7.15 but this paragraph requires the trustee to do so on terms that the custodian cannot release title documents into the possession of a third party without the consent of the trustee. It aims at preventing any third party lien from arising. One particular concern is whether this restricts the trustee's ability to appoint a nominee for the purpose of a dematerialized clearing system such as CREST.[325] The

---

[323] This is especially true for delegation to agents under s. 23(1) of the Trustee Act 1925 which is possible irrespective of whether it is necessary or in the ordinary course of affairs: *Re Vickery* [1931] 1 Ch. 572.

[324] Reg. 7.15.1 (manager's delegation) and reg. 7.15.4 (trustee's delegation).

[325] This is an electronic system for recording and transferring securities that will dispense with the need to collect and transmit share certificates and transfer forms. It is implemented by the Uncertificated Securities Regulations 1995. For a description of the system, see *Palmer's Company Law*, 25th (looseleaf) edn. by Morse, Sweet and Maxwell, 1992, para. 6.701 *et seq.*

answer seems to be not. This is because this paragraph only applies to an appointment of 'a custodian of documents of title or documents evidencing title to property of the scheme'. While a nominee appointed for the purpose of settlement under a clearing system may have legal title to the securities or properties involved, that nominee is not given any custody of title documents. The very fact of its appointment is to avoid the need for any title document. Thus, regulation 7.15.3 does not affect any appointment of nominees for the purpose of dematerialized clearing or settlement systems.

The management function of an authorized unit trust is vested in the manager. Contrasting with the trustee's delegation, there is no prohibition on the persons to whom the manager may delegate its management function. But if the manager delegates any function concerning the management of the property of the scheme, the manager remains responsible for all acts and omissions of such delegate.[326] This is so even though the delegate may not in any way be associated with the manager. In practice, relying on regulation 7.15, a manager frequently appoints investment advisers and investment managers which are its associates and these appointments are disclosed in the scheme particulars.[327]

The second category of restriction is on delegation to associates. The regulation provides that if the manager or the trustee delegates any function to the manager, the trustee or their associates, it will remain responsible for the acts or omissions of the delegate 'as if they were acts or omissions of the manager, or as the case may be of the trustee'.[328] This in effect provides for automatic vicarious liability of the manager or the trustee. It is an absolute liability even though the manager (or the trustee) acts in good faith and it appoints and supervises the delegate with due care and diligence.[329]

Subject to these two restrictions, the trustee and the manager may delegate to any person, including the other party. It will not be vicariously liable for acts or omissions of its agent if the conditions of regulation 7.15.6 are satisfied. These conditions are:

(a) that it was reasonable for an agent to be employed for the function in question; and
(b) that the agent was and remained competent to undertake the function in question; and
(c) that the manager (or trustee) had taken reasonable care to ensure that the function in question was undertaken by the agent in a competent manner.

---

[326] Reg. 7.15.5(a).
[327] Financial Services (Regulated Schemes) Regulations 1991, Sch. 2, para. 3.
[328] Reg. 7.15.5.
[329] This is because this para. 5 provides that liability remains with the principal even though it can satisfy the conditions in para. 6, discussed below.

Thus, the manager and trustee can avoid liability if it exercises reasonable care and skill in the initial appointment of as well as in its supervision of the agent.

For non-authorized unit trusts, clauses enabling the manager and the trustee to delegate are widely drafted. In particular, without express provisions, it would seem difficult to delegate to a custodian the power of holding title to properties,[330] and also to appoint a nominee for the purpose of dematerialized clearing or settlement systems.[331] Widely drawn powers are inserted to avoid any difficulty of having to make amendments to the trust deed if such power is found subsequently to be wanting. To protect the unitholders, it is often provided that the consent of the other party (i.e. the trustee or the manager, as the case may be) is required for some delegations. In making such delegations, the trustee of a non-authorized unit trust, like a private trustee, is under the duty to act as a prudent person would do in the selection of agents and also to continue to exercise the necessary supervision.

The manager in making a delegation will have a duty of care, either under equitable principles[332] or by virtue of an implied term.[333] If trustee cases are a guide, it is likely that a court will conclude that there is a duty of care in both the selection and the continuing supervision of the agent.

## C. Mandatory Delegation

This covers the situation where the unit trust deed directs the appointment of agents or delegates in certain circumstances and the trustee or the manager is given no discretion. In some offshore unit trusts, the appointment of a custodian or investment adviser in certain markets or abroad may be made mandatory by the trust deed. Sometimes, an investment adviser's contract may have been entered into prior to units being offered to the public. Thus, a property manager may have been appointed for a property trust. It is also very common for advisers to be appointed for futures and options funds, country funds, and trusts of specialized sectors.

---

[330] Which is very common for overseas assets. A custodian of title of overseas assets can be appointed under s. 23(2) of the Trustee Act 1925. A trustee may deposit documents of title 'with any banker or banking company or any other company whose business includes the undertaking of the safe custody of documents'. If documents of title are deposited with the manager, it is debatable whether the manager's business includes the undertaking of custody of documents for the purpose of this section: see Underhill, 'Trustees and the New Financial Services Regime', (1991) 10 *The Co. Lawyer* 191.

[331] It is not entirely clear if the appointment of a nominee can be regarded as one of necessity under case-law: *Stuart* v. *Norton* (1860) 14 Moo. PC 17.

[332] See s. 2B(2) of this ch., *ante*.     [333] Ibid.

It is obvious that this so-called delegation is an indirect way of splitting the conventional trustees' responsibilities. In some sense, this is also a further sharing of the manager's responsibilities. As in other situations the trustee's duties are measured in terms of both selection and supervision of the agent. If the trustee is given no discretion in the appointment, as where a direction is laid down in the unit trust deed, there is no reason why the trustee will have liability in such matters.

It seems that provisions that purport to give mandatory directions to the trustee will be construed strictly by the courts. The cases on directions to trustees[334] demonstrate that the court jealously guards the discretion of the trustee. One implication of this is that in matters where the trustee is considered to retain a discretion, it will incur liability for its wrongful exercise or non-exercise. For example, a unit trust deed may direct the trustee to appoint a custodian in shares traded in particular overseas stock markets. Under this provision, whenever the trustee buys shares in those overseas markets, it must engage an overseas custodian. It cannot direct the overseas broker to arrange for the securities documents to be registered in its name. However, this provision will not be construed as denying the trustee the power to choose a custodian. If it has a discretion to choose a custodian, it will remain liable for selecting someone not qualified to act as a custodian.[335]

## D. Secret Delegation

Units in unit trusts are securities *per se*.[336] Thus, if so authorized by the unit trust constitution,[337] the manager may direct the trustee to invest in units of another unit trust. As an extreme example, if the manager directs the trustee to use all the unitholders' money to acquire units of another unit trust with same or similar investment objectives, the manager does not have to make any investment decision, which it is under an obligation to make. In effect, the manager secretly delegates all investment decisions to the manager of the unit trust in which it has directed the trustee to invest.

---

[334] S. 3C of this ch.

[335] This is so despite *Re Vickery* [1931] 1 Ch. 572. Even for Maugham J, the Trustee Act 1925, s. 30(1) does not automatically exempt an honest but foolish appointment: 'No doubt [a trustee] should use his discretion in selecting an agent, and should employ him only to act within the scope of the usual business of the agent' (ibid., at 581).

[336] Ch. 5, ss. 3 and 4, *post*.

[337] An authorized unit trust constituted as a securities fund may invest in units in a collective investment scheme if that scheme to be invested is also a securities fund or warrant fund or a scheme that fulfils the conditions of reg. 5.12 of the Financial Services (Regulated Schemes) Regulations 1991. For a non-authorized unit trust, this depends on the terms of the trust deed.

The end result is that the manager receives the agreed management fees without having to make any decision. In fact, this form of malpractice is sometimes used to earn 'double' fees by investing in unit trusts managed by the same manager or its associates as the manager will also receive management charges in the unit trusts to be invested. Of course, such malpractice will not take this extreme form but will be disguised by investing in a number of different unit trusts or other collective investment schemes. For an authorized unit trust, this form of inflating the management charges by cross-investment in group schemes is not possible. Regulation 5.15 requires the scheme to be invested to state that its investment will be restricted to a particular geographic area or economic sector and the constitution of the investing scheme and scheme particulars to state that the property of the investing scheme may include such units. The manager is also required to pay back to the investing scheme all manager's charges of the scheme to be invested.[338] While this regulation protects unitholders of the investing scheme in financial terms, it does not prevent the managers of group schemes from boosting their fund sizes by cross-investment. This may be done under the motive of protecting the group's goodwill where for some reason a particular fund is under-invested.

It is submitted that the propriety of this form of 'secret delegation' is not a question of interpretation of the power of delegation. It is a question of fiduciary duty in the exercise of investment powers. If the investment in unit trusts is within the express terms of an investment clause, the question is whether there is a breach of fiduciary duty of care and duty of loyalty since the manager is acting under a motive other than acting in the best interest of the unitholders. Thus analysed, the validity of secret delegation can be resolved according to established fiduciary principles.

### E. Responsibilities of Delegates and Agents to Unitholders

There are several ways in which the court may hold that delegates or agents owe duties directly to the unitholders.

In the first place, a custodian having the title of the unit trust property registered in its name is a trustee in equity. If it does not have any power to deal with the property or any other responsibility, it will be a bare trustee of the property obliged to deal with it as the trustee or the manager may direct.[339]

---

[338] Reg. 5.15(c) and reg. 5.69.

[339] *IRC* v. *Silverts* [1951] 1 Ch. 521; *Christie* v. *Ovington* (1875) 1 Ch. D 279; *Re Cunningham and Frayling* [1891] 2 Ch. 567; see ch. 3, s. 3, *ante*.

Secondly, delegates and agents of the trustee or the manager may also be liable as constructive trustees under the two categories of constructive trusteeships commonly labelled as 'knowing receipt' of, or dealing with, trust property and 'knowing assistance' in a dishonest or fraudulent design. These two categories are derived from the seminal decision of Lord Selborne in *Barnes* v. *Addy*[340] and have received refinement in a large number of recent cases.[341] For the present purpose, it suffices to quote the two paragraphs from article 38 of *Underhill and Hayton*:

(3) a person, not being a trustee, becomes personally liable to account as a constructive trustee if he assists in a dishonest breach of trust or other fiduciary duty and has actual knowledge of such dishonest breach or has suspicions that there may be some such dishonest breach but wilfully shuts his eyes to the obvious (so having 'Nelsonian' knowledge . . .) or wilfully or recklessly fails to make such inquiries as an honest and reasonable man would then make (so having 'naughty' knowledge) thereby exhibiting sufficient dishonesty on his part to justify the imposition of a secondary personal liability upon him as an accessory. Indeed, he will be liable if dishonestly assisting in an honest breach;

(4) a person, not being a trustee, becomes personally liable to account as a constructive trustee if he receives trust or other fiduciary property within the scope of his agency role and then deals with such property with such role with actual 'Nelsonian' or 'naughty' knowledge that he is acting inconsistently with the fiduciary relationship. It is immaterial that the breach of fiduciary duty for which the fiduciary is primarily liable is dishonest or not[.]

Broadly speaking, the 'knowing assistance' category is directed against unconscionable conduct of the constructive trustee and the 'knowing receipt' category is against any unconscionable enrichment. They are wide enough to apply to persons involved in any breach of trust on the part of the trustee and any breach of fiduciary duties on the part of the

---

[340] (1874) 9 Ch. App. 244 at 251–2 where his Lordship said: '. . . strangers are not to be made constructive trustees merely because they act as the agents of trustees in transactions within their powers, transactions, perhaps of which a Court of Equity may disapprove, unless those agents receive and become chargeable with some part of the trust property, or unless they assist with knowledge in a dishonest and fraudulent design on the part of the trustees'.

[341] The major issue in all recent cases is on the extent of knowledge required in order for a person to be liable as a constructive trustee. On 'knowing assistance', see *Baden Delvaux and Lecuit* v. *Société Générale* [1983] BCLC 325 (upheld on appeal: [1985] BCLC 258); *Agip (Africa) Ltd.* v. *Jackson* [1990] Ch. 265; *Eagle Trust plc* v. *SBC Securities Ltd.* [1992] 4 All ER 385; *Lipkin Gorman* v. *Karpnale Ltd.* [1989] 1 WLR 1340; *Equitable Industries Group Ltd.* v. *Hawkins* [1991] 3 NZLR 700; *Polly Peck International plc* v. *Nadir (No. 2)* [1992] 4 All ER 769. On 'knowing receipt', see *Baden*, ibid., *Re Montagu's SettlementTrusts* [1987] Ch. 264; *Polly Peck International*, ibid., *Woolwich Building Society* v. *IRC (No. 2)* [1991] 4 All ER 577; *Lipkin* v. *Karpnale Ltd.*, ibid.; *Cowan de Groot Properties Ltd.* v. *Eagle Trust plc* [1992] 4 All ER 700; *El Ajou* v. *Dollar Land Holdings plc* [1993] 3 All ER 717.

manager.[342] An accessory liability attaches to a person who dishonestly procures or assists in a breach of fiduciary obligation. It is not necessary that in addition the fiduciary was acting dishonestly.[343] It is clear now that an accessory cannot be made liable except on the basis of his own dishonesty. Dishonesty on the part of the accessory requires the taking of a risk by the accessory to the prejudice of another's rights, which risk is known to be one which there is no right to take.[344] Mere negligence on the accessory's part does not suffice.[345]

A major worry for agents or delegates of the trustee or the manager, such as solicitors, accountants, stockbrokers, custodians, and valuers, is their knowledge of the capacity of the trustee or the manager. On the one hand, as agents or delegates, they are bound simply to follow the instructions of their principals. Indeed, it does not make any commercial sense for them to enquire into the propriety of each instruction.[346] On the other hand, knowledge plays an important part when the court has to decide whether two doctrines will apply to give unitholders remedies against them.

Trust cases have demonstrated that the court is very reluctant to make an agent of a trustee liable to the beneficiaries directly on the basis of constructive trust. The agent will not be liable for merely carrying out the instructions of the trustee, even when it knows that the property is trust property.[347] There must be a want of probity on its part.[348] One cannot expect an agent to make detailed investigations to see whether or not its principal is validly appointed or whether or not its principal is properly

[342] It seems that a director of the trustee or the manager may be liable as an accessory if he dishonestly procures the breach: *Royal Brunei Airlines* v. *Tan* [1995] 3 All ER 97; *Dempster* v. *Mallina Holdings Ltd.* (1994) 15 ACSR 1; *Australian Securities Commission* v. *AS Nominees Ltd.* (1995) 18 ACSR 459; *Educational Resources Pty. Ltd. (in liq.)* v. *Poteri* (1996) 20 ACSR 628.
[343] *Royal Brunei Airlines* v. *Tan* [1995] 3 All ER 97.
[344] *Baden* v. *Société Générale* [1992] 4 All ER 161 at 234; *Royal Brunei Airlines* v. *Tan* [1995] 3 All ER 97.
[345] *Royal Brunei Airlines* v. *Tan* [1995] 3 All ER 97.
[346] The delegate will not be put on enquiry merely because a particular transaction does not fall within the power implied by law if that transaction is within powers commonly conferred on trustees: *El Ajou* v. *Dollar Land Holdings plc* [1993] 3 All ER 717 at 743.
[347] *Mara* v. *Browne* [1895] 1 Ch. 199; *Grehan* v. *Rich* (1921) 21 SR (NSW) 712; *Williams Ashman* v. *Price and Williams* [1942] Ch. 219 at 228.
[348] In the words of Bennett J in *Williams-Ashman* v. *Price and Williams* [1942] Ch. 219 at 228: 'an agent in possession of money which he knows to be trust money, so long as he acts honestly, is not accountable to the beneficiaries interested in the trust money unless he intermeddles in the trust by doing acts characteristic of a trustee and outside the duties of an agent'. Sachs LJ in *Carl-Zeiss-Stiftung* v. *Herbert Smith & Co. (a firm) (No. 2)* [1969] 2 Ch. 276 at 299 also said, '. . . professional men and agents who have received moneys as such and acted bona fide are accountable only to their principals unless dishonesty as well as cognisance of trusts is established against them'. (See also the comments to the same effect by Edmund-Davies LJ in the same case: ibid., at 303–4).

exercising its power. After the decision in *Royal Brunei Airlines* v. *Tan*,[349] it seems that the sole question is whether a person dishonestly assists in a breach of trust or fiduciary duty. An agent is not liable for negligently failing to appreciate that it is acting inconsistent with the trust or if it had forgotten about the terms of the trust that it once knew. The recent case of *Finers* v. *Miro*[350] suggests that such agents or delegates may apply to the court for directions. In the case of solicitors, the court's directions may override any clients' privilege of confidentiality where there are suspicious grounds.

It should also be noted that the agreement made between the trustee (or the manager) and the delegate or the agent may be an instrument of delegation, such as a power of attorney, or it may simply be a contract establishing rights and duties of the agent as an independent contractor. A significant question is whether the trustee or the manager contracting could be regarded as holding the benefit of such a contract on behalf of all unitholders. The consequence of such a finding would be that unitholders could sue such an agent directly by joining the trustee or the manager as a party.[351]

There is no authority on this point except *Wills* v. *Cooke*,[352] where a beneficiary sued a firm of solicitors retained by the trustees for breach of an implied term in their retainer and for negligence. In a procedural summons by the solicitors to strike out the statement of claim, Slade J took the view that the question whether the benefit of the trustees' contract with the solicitors was itself a trust asset was a question of construction of the retainer. His Lordship 'tentatively' inclined to the view that the more common contract of retainer between trustees and solicitors was one solely for the benefit of the trustees,[353] though he thought it was possible for contracts to have some characteristics of each class. The procedural summons was dismissed.

In the unit trust situation, where the contract involves the so-called agent in a capacity as an independent contractor and the contract confers benefits on the trust as a whole or on all unitholders, there are stronger grounds for saying that the trustee or the manager is holding the benefit of the contract for the unitholders. Falling into this category are contracts appointing a broker to advise as well as to execute investment decisions in futures or

---

[349] *Supra*; *Williams-Ashman* v. *Price and Williams*, *supra*; *Re Montagu's Settlement* [1987] Ch. 264; *Agip (Africa) Ltd.* v. *Jackson* [1990] Ch. 265; *Cowan de Groot Properties Ltd.* v. *Eagle Trust plc* [1992] 4 All ER 700 at 754.

[350] [1991] 1 All ER 182.      [351] Ch. 5, s. 5, *post*.

[352] Which was only briefly reported in (1979) 123 Sol. J 405.

[353] Despite the fact that the trustees had a right of reimbursement under general law and the Trustee Act 1925, s. 30(2).

other specialized markets. This is clearly different from the case of solicitors advising trustees as trustees.

6. ADVISORY POWERS

If the unit trust deed directs the trustee or the manager to obtain the advice of a certain person on certain matters, such advice will often be construed as a condition precedent to the exercise of the substantive power in question. Obvious examples are the requirements of legal advice, valuation, and actuarial advice.

The powers of appointment of such advisers are fiduciary powers and therefore not delegable.[354] However, this does not preclude the trustee from making enquiries, seeking information or asking for a character reference about a potential adviser so long as the ultimate decision is its own. In making this selection, the trustee or the manager must exercise due care and diligence.[355]

As a matter of construction, if a condition precedent requires the obtaining of expert advice, the trustee or the manager must obtain and consider such advice but it is not precluded from coming to a different conclusion. But if on a proper construction it is a direction to follow such advice, then the trustee is bound to follow the expert's determination unless it is shown that the expert has acted fraudulently or with some improper motive, has been guilty of some mistake of a substantial character, or has materially misdirected himself.[356] In *Re Imperial Foods Ltd.'s Pension Scheme*,[357] rules of a pension scheme for employees of a company and its subsidiaries provided that in the event of a subsidiary ceasing to be such the trustee was to transfer a portion to a new scheme and the portion was to be 'determined by the actuary and shall be such portion of the fund as shall in all the circumstances appear to him to be appropriate'. When two subsidiaries were sold, an actuary was appointed. In determining the amount of the portion to be transferred, the actuary made his valuation using the past service reserve method (being the amount of assets required to meet pension benefits for service rendered to date) with an allowance for future pay and pension increases. However, at

---

[354] Delegation of the selection of an adviser can hardly be described as an act 'from necessity or conformable to the common usage of mankind' within the principle of *Ex parte Belchier* (1754) Amb. 218: cf. *Robinson* v. *Harkin* [1896] 2 Ch. 415; *Fry* v. *Tapson* (1884) 28 Ch. D 268.

[355] *Fry* v. *Tapson* (1884) 28 Ch. D 268.

[356] *Collier* v. *Mason* (1858) 25 Beav. 200 at 204; *Dean* v. *Prince* [1954] Ch. 409 at 418–19; *Re George Newnes Group Pension Fund* (1969) 98 J Inst. of Actuaries 251; *Re Imperial Foods Ltd.'s Pension Scheme* [1986] 2 All ER 802.      [357] Ibid.

the time of calculation, the fund had a surplus over the actuarial liabilities. Transferring members sought to set aside the actuary's calculation and argued that he should use a share of fund method, which would give them a pro-rata entitlement of the actuarial value of the fund, including the surplus. Based on the above reasoning, Walton J held that an actuary's determination based on the past service reserve method could not be challenged.[358] However, if the circumstances since the advice was given have changed significantly, the trustee or the manager may decline to act on the advice and may seek a fresh opinion from the adviser.[359]

An adviser's position *vis-à-vis* the unitholders will be that described above in respect of an agent or delegate.

### 7. RESIDUAL MANAGEMENT POWERS OF THE TRUSTEE

It is established that the powers of the manager are not delegated powers derived from the trustee; the manager is a primary source of authority, having been responsible for the set up of the unit trust. However, despite this stated position, it is submitted that the trustee has reserve powers incidental to its status as a trustee by reason of its legal ownership of the properties and equity's imposition of duties on such an owner. The position appears to be that if the manager cannot find authority for a particular act in the express or implied powers of the unit trust deed, the manager cannot do the act. The unit trust deed is the source of the manager's authority. Doctrinally, the manager cannot go beyond that and seek the court's approval or sanction of a particular action.[360] By contrast, the status of a trustee gives the trustee the right to seek authorization or assistance from the court.[361] In *The Application of Permanent Trustee Nominees (Canberra) Ltd.*,[362] in an application for advice by the trustee under section 63 of the Trustee Act 1925 (NSW),[363] Young J held that in the unit trust where the power to manage and the 'watchdog' power were deliberately compart-mentalized, there was no scope to find 'a manifestation of intention . . .

---

[358] Walton J held, obiter, that he would choose this method if he had to make a choice.
[359] *Stannard* v. *Fisons Pension Trust Ltd.* [1992] 1 WLR 27.
[360] But in *Global Funds Management (NSW) Ltd.* v. *Burns Philp Trustee Co. Ltd. (in prov. liq.)* (1990) 3 ACSR 183, the manager applied to remove the trustee which was in liquidation and to appoint substitutes. Rolfe J granted the order but it was not clear if the application was made by virtue of the provisions of the trust deed or under the court's equitable jurisdiction: see the discussion in ch. 2, s. 3E.
[361] Ibid.
[362] Unreported, NSWSC (Eq. Div.) No. 4216 of 1985, 24 June 1985, Young J.
[363] This section is declaratory of the inherent jurisdiction of the court: Ford and Lee, para. 17030, citing *Dobson* v. *Salvation Army* (unreported, Tas. SC, No. 15 of 1983). See RSC Ord. 85, discussed in *Underhill and Hayton*, art. 90, pp. 809 *et seq*.

that the trustee may adjust his conduct to the change and act as he would not otherwise be intended to act'.[364] However, his Honour held, obiter, that the court can grant power to the trustee to act as the manager in the interim period under section 81 of the Trustee Act 1925 (NSW), which is the equivalent section 57 of the Trustee Act 1925. Two observations can be made.

First, there is no reason to question his Honour's judgment to the extent that it must be a question of construction. However, it would be too sweeping a proposition to say that in a unit trust the trustee does not have any management power at all or that the court can never find any manifestation of an intention that the trustee may act in an emergency. At the very least, when the primary trust is terminated and a secondary trust for sale and distribution arises, the trustee must have such powers to manage trust assets as may be implied from the power to sell or as are conferred by trustee statutes. Thus the requisite intention is present in the majority of trust deeds. For an authorized unit trust, regulation 7.12 of the Financial Services (Regulated Schemes) Regulations 1991 provides that 'the manager and the trustee have, by virtue of these regulations, all the powers conferred on them by the general law' unless such powers are qualified or restricted by the Regulations. While it is not entirely clear what powers have been conferred on a manager by the general law, it is clear that there is a considerable body of principles and provisions with regard to trustees' powers. Thus, the position with regard to an authorized unit trust is that if a particular power is not vested expressly or implied by the Regulations in the manager of the unit trust, the trustee's powers under general law will apply. For a non-authorized unit trust, since the Regulations do not apply, the question is one of construction of the trust deed. In the absence of any clear exclusion of powers conferred by equitable principles or statute, the very status of a trustee must imply that it will have such powers. [365]

Secondly, whatever the outcome of construction of the unit trust deed, the decision in *The Application of Permanent Trustee Nominees (Canberra) Ltd.* has two implications:

---

[364] These are words of *Scott on Trusts*, 3rd edn., p. 1268, quoted with approval by his Honour. However, no English or Australian authorities were cited.

[365] *Australian Ency. F & P*, Vol. 3, p. 1012, cl. 7(1) provides that: 'Subject to the provisions of this deed the trustee shall have all the powers over and in respect of the property and assets constituting the trust fund which it could exercise if it were the absolute and beneficial owner of such property and assets . . .'. It is not clear the extent this clause has been used in offshore unit trusts. On construction, the phrase 'subject to the provisions of this deed' means that in normal circumstances the provision giving the manager full management power overrides any management power of the trustee as conferred by equity or statute. But where the manager is dismissed or for some other reason ceases to act, this provision will mean that the trustee has 'all the powers over and in respect of' the trust property.

(1) As the application in the case itself demonstrates, the trustee of a unit trust has the same power of a private trustee to apply to court for the determination of any question or for any relief which could be determined or granted under an administration action. By itself, this is a kind of reserve power not available to the manager.

(2) The decision recognizes that the court can confer powers of management on the trustee of a unit trust in an emergency or when the circumstances justify the court's exercise of jurisdiction under section 57 of the Trustee Act 1925. Logically it follows that a trustee of a unit trust can also apply to the court for variation of the trust under the Variation of Trusts Act 1958 or inherent jurisdiction of the court. An application under the 1958 Act has the advantage that alteration of beneficial interests is also possible. In practice, this will be an open court hearing which is more expensive than a chamber hearing of a section 57 application.[366] As it is unlikely that an order for variation of beneficial interest will be sought by the trustee of a unit trust, a section 57 application is more likely. In any event, it is uncertain as to the implication on such an application of the fact that the unit trust deed is a contract between the manager, the trustee, and the participants.

---

[366] *Anker-Petersen* v. *Anker-Petersen* (1991) 88 Law Soc. Gaz. Pt. 16, 32.

# 5

# *Nature of Units*

The term unit trust carries with it the connotation that it is a species of trust. Its distinctiveness as a species is supposed to be found in the word 'unit', a word that describes the trust. An understanding of the legal features of a unit will provide us insights into the character of a unit trust. It also enables us to determine if such features are necessary components in the unit trust as a distinct legal institution. It is imperative to our understanding whether the law of unit trusts is a mere application of private trust principles in the commercial arena and whether the term unit trust is no more than a commercial description that does not have any legal signification.

At a pragmatic level, this conceptual adventure will also assist the determination of the *situs* of the units, which is important as a matter of private international law and which often features in tax planning and in questions of tax liability. It also provides guidance if the court is called upon to determine questions of priority between competing interests, particularly where units have been used as securities for loans and advances. This enquiry will also throw light on disputes with unitholders on the exercise of rights of underlying assets and on questions of the manner of disposition of the units themselves.[1] If a unit is a kind of property, then when a private trustee invests in units, the sole issue in determining whether he has acted properly is one of construction of his investment powers.[2] He cannot be regarded as in breach of his fiduciary duty on the ground that he has delegated his investment decision to the unit trustee. The nature of units in unit trusts will also determine the applicability of the Unfair Contract Terms Act 1977 to unit trust deeds.[3]

The first section of this chapter will delineate the difference in functional character of the trust corpus of a private trust and that of a unit trust. This

---

[1] Whether an asset is a unit trust used to affect transmission on death as well for on intestacy realty passed to the heir and personalty to the next of kin. Nowadays, the devolution of both realty and personalty is the same.

[2] The Trustee Investment Act 1961 considers unit trust units as items of properties. Units of an authorized unit trust will be 'wider-range' investments (Sch. 1, Part III, para. 3) and units of a gilt unit trust are 'narrow-range' investments within Part II of Sch. 1 (Trustee Investments (Additional Powers) (No. 2) Order 1994). If, which is not uncommon, the Trustee Investment Act provisions are excluded, the investment powers of a particular trust will have to be construed whether units are permitted.

[3] Ch. 4, s. 2C(1), *ante*.

difference, as demonstrated by cases on deed of settlement companies, is fundamental in determining the rights of unitholders in underlying assets, which is the subject of discussion of the second section. In this second section, deed of settlement company cases will be used to support the proposition that as a matter of construction, units in modern unit trusts operating on a cash fund principle do not confer on unitholders any interests in the underlying assets. This position does not contradict the leading case of *Baker* v. *Archer-Shee*[4]—if the true meaning of this case is understood.

The third section examines the constituent parts of rights comprising a unit. The fourth suggests that these constituent parts constitute one single indivisible chose in action. The implications of the propositions developed in this chapter are examined in the final sub-section.

### 1. THE NATURE OF THE TRUST CORPUS AND THE RIGHTS IN A UNIT

## A. The Trust Corpus and the Cash Fund Concept

The trust is by nature a relationship fastened upon the properties of the trust. Considerable debate has been focused upon the rights of a beneficiary in the trust properties.[5] In a private trust, the trust is a means of disposition of properties by way of gift. The trust corpus in the private trust, even when the settlor is one of the beneficiaries, is the subject matter of a gift. In this sense, the trust has a distributive character that makes use of equity's recognition of a multiplicity of interests within a trust. A beneficiary's interest is an interest in a gift. His interest is a matter of degree of ownership. If he is a beneficiary under a discretionary trust, he has nothing more than a right to be considered as a beneficiary.[6] If he is an

---

[4] [1927] AC 844.

[5] Maitland, *Equity*, 2nd edn., by Brunyate, 1936, pp. 23, 29–32, 106–52; Maitland, *Selected Essays*, 1936, pp. 129–34, 143–7, 170–4; Ames, *Lectures on Legal History and Miscellaneous Legal Essays*, Harvard UP, 1913, pp. 76, 269, 289; Winfield, *Province of the Law of Tort*, Cambridge UP, 1931, pp. 108–15; Hanbury, *Modern Equity, Being the Principles of Equity*, Stevens, 1935, pp. 54–62; Moffat, pp. 185–8; Ford and Lee, pp. 53–63; Scott, 'The Nature of the Rights of the *Cestui Que Trust*' (1917) *Columbia LR* 269; Stone, 'The Nature of the Rights of the *Cestui Que Trust*' (1917) *Columbia LR* 467; Hart, 'The Place of Trust in Jurisprudence' (1912) 28 *LQR* 290; Latham, 'The Right of the Beneficiary to Specific Items of the Trust Fund' (1954) 32 *Can BR* 520; Waters, 'The Nature of the Trust Beneficiary's Interest' (1967) 45 *Can BR* 219.

[6] They do not have any interest in the subject matter: *Gartside* v. *IRC* [1968] AC 553; *Re Weir's Settlement Trusts* [1971] Ch. 145; *Re Coleman* (1888) 39 Ch. D 443. Each can only release his individual interests: *Re Gulbenkian (No. 2)* [1970] Ch. 408. But all beneficiaries, if *sui juris*, may agree to terminate the trust: *Re Nelson* [1928] Ch. 920n; *Re Smith* [1928] Ch. 915; see ch. 2, s. 3C, *ante*.

adult beneficiary under a bare trust,[7] he almost has full ownership as he can at any time call upon the trustee to assign the property to him. If he is only one of several beneficiaries under a fixed trust, he has rights similar to his counterpart in a bare trust in that he and other beneficiaries collectively, if *sui juris*, can agree to terminate the trust; otherwise, each will only have an ascertainable interest.[8]

By contrast, and as demonstrated in the foregoing chapters, a unit trust does not have a distributive character; its trustee does not have dispositive power; the unitholders are not objects of a gift; the moneys in the trust corpus are not gifts. The trust corpus consists of money belonging to the beneficiaries themselves. In substance, unitholders are contributors of capital. Contributions by unitholders are for the purpose of investment, and investment by nature is the use of capital for the purpose of gain, whether in terms of income or appreciation of capital value.

Thus, functionally, the trust corpus of a unit trust is the same as the share capital of a company.[9] Their difference is a matter of form. Share capital belongs to the company as a legal person. The legal interest in the unit trust corpus is vested in the trustee subject to equitable obligations, and subject to the investment directions of the manager, but ultimately it is for the enjoyment of unitholders. The company form denies investors ownership of any form in the underlying assets.[10] The trust gives investors equitable rights in a form recognizable by our system of law, though the nature of such rights is still debatable.[11]

From the historical account in chapter 1, it is clear that the early 1930s witnessed the emergence of three forms of unit trusts, namely, (a) the fixed trust, (b) the flexible trust operating on an appropriation principle, and (c) the flexible trust operating on a cash fund principle. The modern unit trust[12] is a flexible trust operating on a cash fund principle.

The fixed trust was built upon the idea of pro rata ownership in equity of the underlying investment. Under a fixed trust, the manager purchased a

---

[7] In *Christie* v. *Ovington* (1875) 1 Ch. D 279 at 281, Hall VC defined a bare trustee as a trustee with no duty attached or, if with duty attached, one being compellable to convey the estate. Thus, a trustee with active management duties is not a bare trustee: *Re Cunningham and Frayling* [1891] 2 Ch. 567; *IRC* v. *Silverts* [1951] 1 Ch. 521; *Schalit* v. *Joseph Nadler Ltd.* [1933] 2 KB 79 at 81–2. A different view was expressed in *Morgan* v. *Swansea Urban Sanitary Authority* (1878) 9 Ch. D 582 at 585 and *Re Blandy Jenkins' Estate* [1917] 1 Ch. 46. See also *Hedegen* v. *FCT* (1988) 84 ALR 271 at 282, per Gummow J and ch. 3, s. 3, *ante*.

[8] Thus, he has an interest in possession under the trust: *Underhill and Hayton*, pp. 30–2.

[9] Ch. 3, s. 1C, *ante*.

[10] *Macaura* v. *Northern Assurance Co.* [1925] AC 619; *CSD (NSW)* v. *Millar* (1932) 48 CLR 618; *Short* v. *Treasury Commissioners* [1948] AC 534 at 545.

[11] See s. 2 of this ch., *post*.

[12] With the exception of a single property trust constituted under s. 76(4)–(6) of the Financial Services Act 1986 and the Financial Services Act 1986 (Single Property Schemes) (Exemption) Regulations 1989.

block of securities as specified in the trust deed and deposited it with the trustee. The first block was the first unit. Subsequent blocks of units were of matching composition. In effect, a unit was a group of shares and investments and the manager was initially the owner of the whole beneficial interest in the assets comprised in the unit. The trust deed provided that each unit, after the addition of expenses, should be subdivided into sub-units to be sold to investors. Each sub-unit entitled its holder to the beneficial interest in the proportion of one to the total number of sub-units. As the underlying assets were fixed and were variable only in limited circumstances, each unitholder knew in advance the exact underlying investments and the proportion that he owned.[13] To avoid confusing this type of trust with 'fixed trusts' that are not discretionary trusts, it will be called in this chapter a 'fixed investment trust', a term used by the editor of the All England Reports in *Re Whitehead's Will Trusts*.[14] Thus, a fixed investment trust is a particular type of fixed trust.

Under a flexible trust[15] the manager could vary the size, nature, and proportions of the underlying assets at its discretion subject to the terms of the trust deed. Originally, the manager proceeded on the same basis as a fixed investment trust and purchased securities which it deposited with the trustee. It then issued units to be sold to the public. The trust deed of a flexible trust usually provided that the trust corpus could be extended in size. Expansion could be made under either the appropriation principle or the cash fund principle. Under an appropriation trust, the manager had to purchase a block of investments and appropriated to the trust before it issued units. The units in substance were owned by it; when they were sold to investors, the manager was reimbursing itself. Under a cash fund trust, which was a later development, the manager accepted cash from investors and issued units without having first to purchase investments. When units were issued, the proceeds were added to the trust fund as cash for investment.

The emergence of this type of flexible cash fund trust is the most significant step in the development of the unit trust concept. Conceptually, the trust fund has become one of money. In terms of operation, it is a

---

[13] The case *Smith* v. *Anderson* (1880) 15 Ch. D 247 is an early example. In the 1930s, fixed trusts in England were modelled on American fixed trusts: see ch. 1, s. 4, *ante*, for a historical account. Merriman, *Unit Trusts and How They Work*, 2nd edn., Pitman, 1959, ch. 3 provides an excellent arithmetical illustration of the working of this type of trust. Examples of this type of unit trust in England, Australia, and Canada can also be seen in the law reports: *Re Whitehead's Will Trusts* [1959] 2 All ER 497; *Charles* v. *FCT* (1954) 90 CLR 598 and *MNR* v. *Trans-Canada* [1955] 5 DLR 576. The latter two are discussed in s. 2B, *post*.

[14] [1959] 2 All ER 497, discussed in fn. 113, *infra*. Ford, 'Unit Trusts' (1960) 23 *MLR* 129, uses the term 'fixed unit trust' to distinguish the fixed trust.

[15] See Merriman, *supra*, ch. 4 and *Australian Fixed Trusts Pty. Ltd.* v. *Clyde Industries Ltd.* (1958) 59 SR (NSW) 33.

precedent for modern open-ended trusts that permit investors to liquidate their investment by redeeming their units from the trust fund. The number of trust units, and therefore the size of the investment capital, can increase or decrease as circumstances may require. Until the introduction of the open-ended investment company recently, this is an important advantage that the company form fails to provide. This development also witnesses the change in conception of the trust corpus from a specified quantity of specified securities to a cash fund to be managed and to be made productive by the manager. This cash fund principle is the operating principle of modern unit trusts.

In managing the money of the trust fund, it is sometimes desirable for the trustee, at the direction of the manager, to exercise the borrowing power conferred by the trust deed. An overdraft or a short-term loan may be arranged to cover any sudden surge of redemption requests at a time when the manager considers it inadvisable to sell the underlying investments. This type of borrowing to provide liquidity is common for trusts that consist of buildings or assets that are not readily realizable. More often, the nature of portfolio assets may be such that it is in accordance with good management principles[16] to engage in arbitrage or hedging activities in the currency, futures or other financial markets. In such activities, liabilities such as margin calls may be involved. As an investment strategy, all items of assets and liabilities are looked at as components within a portfolio. Each component carries different risk factors and balancing different risks is the manager's management skill. It is not difficult to conclude that the trust corpus is in reality a capital sum represented by the difference between assets and liabilities.

This capital character of the trust fund is reflected in its accounting treatment. The Statement of Recommended[17] Practice relating to Authorised Unit Trust Schemes issued by the Investment Management Regulatory Organisation requires a portfolio statement, a statement of assets and liabilities (or balance sheet), and an income account for a half

---

[16] For example, efficient portfolio management under ss. K and J of Part 5 of the Financial Services (Regulated Schemes) Regulations 1991. Generally, see *Nestle* v. *National Westminster Bank plc* [1994] 1 All ER 118 and the unreported judgment at first instance (Hoffmann J, 28 June 1988); Haskell, 'The Prudent Person Rule for Trustee Investment and Modern Portfolio Theory' (1990) 69 *NCLR* 87; Halbach Jun., 'Trust Investment Law in the Third Restatement' (1992) 77 *Iowa LR* 1151; Butler, 'Modern Portfolio Theory and Investment Powers of Trustees: the New Zealand Experience' (1995) 16 *NZULR* 349; Johnson, 'Speculating on the Efficacy of "Speculation": An Analysis of the Prudent Person's Slipperiest Term of Art in Light of Modern Portfolio Theory' (1996) 48 *Stanford LR* 419.

[17] This is a misnomer: reg. 10.02.3 provides that '[a] report . . . *shall* consist of the matters required to be stated therein by the Statement of Recommended Practice relating to Authorised Unit Trust Schemes' issued by IMRO in Apr. 1991; emphasis supplied.

yearly report. It requires for an annual account a balance sheet, distinguishing between income and capital account, a portfolio statement and summary of major portfolio movements, an income account, and a statement of movements in net assets. There is also a requirement of provision of comparative figures in the balance sheet. Thus, the required accounting treatment places emphasis on disclosure to investors and is no different from accounts of a company account. The presentation of accounts of non-authorized unit trusts is the same.

To sum up, the trust fund of a unit trust has not much difference from the capital of a company. The moneys are employed to generate gain. This is a big contrast to an ordinary private trust.

## B. Rights in a Unit: A Preliminary Analysis and Three Propositions

A modern trust deed invariably provides that the trustee will hold the unit trust assets for the unitholders 'on and subject to the terms and conditions of the trust deed' and in the case of an authorized unit trust, the regulations made under section 81 of the Financial Services Act 1986.[18] It is always possible for the trust deed or the relevant regulations to contain hundreds of covenants or terms that may alter or add to the rights in the beneficial interests of the trust assets. With the varieties of unit trusts and the varieties of units in the market today, the significance of the qualifying statement 'on and subject to the terms and conditions of the trust deed' may easily be overlooked.

Units in today's unit trusts are far more complicated than mere entitlement of beneficial interests. In broad terms, modern innovations are along the path of enhancement of the inherent advantages of unit trusts: risk-minimization and liquidity.

The core purpose of unit trusts is to enable investors with small capital to spread risk in a large portfolio. Modern trusts are structured in the direction of enlarging the investment base in terms of types of assets, industrial or commercial sectors, and geographical regions that the trust can invest. The effect is more than an extension of the manager's power. It necessitates a set of valuation principles for the calculation of the value of a variety of assets. The trustee may have to enter into custodian contracts, appointing custodians to take custody of assets overseas or in some specialized markets, as well as advisory or management contracts as dictated by the specialized nature of assets. Risk-minimization is also achieved in some cases by conferring on units the benefit of a guarantee of the level of income or of the return of capital, with or without a guaranteed

---

[18] See ch. 2, s. 2A, fn. 88 and text accompanying that footnote.

appreciation.[19] The guarantee could be given by the manager, in which case the provisions can form part of the trust deed constituting the unit trust. Alternatively, where the guarantee is given by a third party, a separate guarantee may be executed by the trustee for the benefit of the unitholders.[20] A third direction is to let the unitholders assess for themselves the risks in each sector and to let them determine the necessary adjustment. This is the umbrella trust. An umbrella trust is in reality a group of different trusts, with different risk profiles or objectives, under the common management of the same trustee and manager. The trust assets are separate but they are set up under one trust deed.[21] Under the trust deed, unitholders have the right to switch between different trusts constituting the umbrella trust.

On the liquidity side, redemption arrangements have been enhanced by contractually permitting unitholders to liquidate units by means of modern communication such as telephones, facsimiles, telexes, and automatic teller machines. To facilitate this kind of arrangement, uncertificated units emerge in open-ended trusts to enable the manager to remit redemption money immediately without waiting for the return of unit trust certificates. The stock market has also been used to achieve the liquidity objective for closed-end trusts in which the number of units is fixed.[22] The single property trust is a modern example. Techniques used are similar to those of public issue of shares. Purchase of the underlying properties may have been negotiated and contracts conditional upon the subscription of a fixed

[19] A guarantee of return of capital is used mainly in a trust that invests in futures as futures by nature are perceived as risky and may deter investors. The guarantee invariably provides for the obligation of the guarantor to arise at the end of a stipulated period and any redemption during this period will not have the benefit of the guarantee. A fixed percentage of the trust fund will be invested in fixed deposits or similar financial instruments that mature at the end of the stipulated period with capital and interest equal to the total value of all units. The remainder of the fund is invested in futures contracts in manner stated in the trust deed. To enhance this feature, the fixed deposit may be pledged to the depositing bank in return for the bank issuing a bank guarantee in favour of unitholders. One of the major regulatory concerns is whether the inclusion of the word 'guaranteed' in the name of the fund is undesirable or misleading thereby contravening s. 78(5) of the Financial Services Act 1986: see Securities and Investments Board, *Regulated Collective Investment Schemes: Key Policy Issues* (Discussion Paper) 1993, paras. 5.1–5.12.

[20] In the case of an authorized unit trust, the property of the unit trust is forbidden to be used to discharge any counter-indemnity provided by the trustee or the manager: reg. 5.67 of the Financial Services (Regulated Schemes) Regulations 1991.

[21] In the case of an authorized unit trust, this position is explicitly provided by reg. 5.47: '1. . . . each of the separate parts of an umbrella fund shall be invested as if it were a single scheme . . . 2. No part of an umbrella fund may invest in units in another part, nor may any part invest in units in another umbrella fund.'

[22] This type of trust is not to be confused with the fixed investment trust. Although the number of units is fixed, it is still operating on a cash fund principle. The manager does not acquire the underlying assets. The trust deed provisions follow the open-ended trusts in terms of management of a cash fund, though the power may be more restrictive.

percentage of units are usually entered into. Underwriting contracts may also be arranged.

It appears from the above discussion that units are made up of interests in the following:

(a) all capital contributions by unitholders, income and investments for the time being representing such moneys, the value of which being the difference between assets and liabilities;
(b) the benefit of contractual promises made by third parties to the manager (or the trustee) for the benefit of individual unitholders, for example an income or capital guarantee;
(c) the benefit of contractual promises made by third parties to the manager (or the trustee) in the normal course of administration of the trust or investment of the trust fund, for example contracts appointing brokers or other agents or for sale and purchase of assets;
(d) the benefit of promises made by the manager to the trustee for the benefit of unitholders;
(e) the benefit of promises made by the trustee to the manager for the benefit of unitholders;
(f) the benefit of promises by the trustee, the manager, and other unitholders to a unitholder where that unitholder is a direct party, for example provisions relating to redemption, voting, proxies, and meetings.

In analytical terms, the interests mentioned in paragraph (a) form the trust corpus of the unit trust that the trustee holds. Interests in paragraphs (b)–(e) are interests of unitholders only when trusts of the promises are established. If the relevant promise in paragraph (b) or (c) is made to the manager, it is of the same character as those in paragraph (e), which are hybrid in nature in that the manager is in the eye of equity the trustee of that promise. There is no impediment to classifying that as a kind of trust interest. The contractual interests of paragraph (f) cannot be classified as trust interests but they are interests forming part of a unit.

Units therefore are bundles of such rights as the manager and the trustee may incorporate at the time of the drafting of the trust deed.[23] This bundling is to achieve the single objective that these units will attract investors. To

---

[23] Authorized unit trusts are subject to the Financial Services (Regulated Schemes) Regulations 1991, which may be incorporated into the trust deed. Unit trusts have been applied to mining ventures, see Ford, 'The Unit Trust as a Production Joint Venturer' [1985] *AMPLA Yearbook* 1 and Gonski, 'The Unit Trust as a Production Joint Venturer' [1985] *AMPLA Yearbook* 17; Pritchard, 'An Innovation in Unit Trusts' (1985) 23 *Law Society J* 134. The unit trust concept also has an application to the Canadian oil and gas industries: Waters, pp. 447–8. Canadians have also devised the split bond trust that splits income and capital (Waters, ibid., at fn. 45).

all investors, each unit is an item of property that is freely transferable.[24]
The common perception is that units are a kind of property analogous to
shares. And it is the submission of this work that this perception is
justified. This position is best understood from their legal attributes, which
will be examined in the rest of this chapter in terms of the following three
propositions:

(1) Unless the trust instrument provides specific interests in the underlying
assets, a unit does not confer any interest in individual assets. It only
confers a proportion of the net value of the trust fund, measured as the
difference between its assets and liabilities, calculated and realizable in
manner provided by the trust instrument. It is a kind of personal property.
(2) A unit is a chose in action comprising (a) an interest in the net value
of the trust fund as aforesaid, (b) rights to due administration by the
trustee and the manager of the trust of the underlying assets and
contractual rights amongst or between the trustee, the manager, and
unitholders, (c) benefits of contractual promises by third parties, and (d)
statutory rights for enforcing the instrument constituting the unit trust.
(3) It is an indivisible chose in action that is redeemable and transferable
in manner provided by the trust instrument.

The first proposition is a statement of the relationship between a
unitholder's right and the underlying investment assets. This proposition
produces the result that the proprietary nature of the underlying assets will
not have any bearing on the characterization of a unit as real or personal
property. The second proposition is a positive proposition as to the
component rights in a unit. The third suggests the character of a unit as a
single item of property.

## 2. THE RIGHTS OF A UNITHOLDER IN UNDERLYING ASSETS
### (THE FIRST PROPOSITION)

On the question of the rights of unitholders in the underlying assets of the
trust fund, there are two strands of authorities that may be relevant to our
understanding. In the first place, as the vast body of trust law is derived
from trusts used in family dispositions, the line of cases after *Baker* v.
*Archer-Shee*[25] will be relevant. Indeed, *Baker* has been applied in

---

[24] Free transferability of units in an authorized unit trust is provided by reg. 6.12. In
general, except for pension and charitable schemes, a transferor has right to freely transfer its
units subject to minimum holding and qualification requirements contained in the trust deed.
[25] [1927] AC 844.

commercial trusts and none of the decisions finds it necessary to distinguish the commercial from the family situations. As discussed in chapter 1, deed of settlement companies can be regarded as the origin of modern unit trusts, both in form and substance. The approaches of cases on such companies will illuminate our analysis.

## A. *Baker* v. *Archer-Shee* in Private Trusts

For almost a century, there has been a debate[26] on the nature of the rights of a beneficiary in a trust. One view is that a beneficiary's remedy is in the form of an action against the trustee and this is a right *in personam*. Another view regards beneficial interests in trusts as equitable proprietary interests and accordingly a beneficiary has a right *in rem*.

With the decision of *Baker* v. *Archer-Shee*,[27] which has been applied in common law countries such as Australia, Canada, and New Zealand, modern text writers have almost abandoned this *in rem-in personam* debate—by classifying beneficiaries' interests as 'hybrids'[28] or 'sui generis'[29] or by suggesting that a beneficiary has both real and personal rights and the question whether it is *in rem* or *in personam* depends on the context.[30] That abandonment still leaves unanswered what is the *ratio decidendi* of *Baker* and the extent of its application. In the subsequent history of *Baker*, taxation principles and private international law issues have periodic prominence. Within this complex, courts have struggled to determine the reach of *Baker*.

Two issues seem to have received particular concern. The first is the meaning of *Baker*: does it represent the elimination of the trustee, and if not what does *Baker* mean? The second is the relevance of the number of beneficiaries in applying *Baker*.

In *Baker*, the father left the residue of his estate by his will upon trust to apply 'the whole of the . . . income and profits . . . to the use of [his] daughter . . . during her life'. The trust was situate in New York and the trustee was a New York trust company appointed by the daughter pursuant to the power in the will. The trust property consisted entirely of non-British securities. The trustee had never remitted to the daughter in England the trust income, but had paid the income, less any sums required for American income tax and the trustee's fees and expenses, to her bank

---

[26] For the views of different jurists in this debate, see publications cited in fn. 5, *supra*.
[27] [1927] AC 844.
[28] Hanbury, *Modern Equity*, 8th edn., Stevens, pp. 444–6 but the editor of *Hanbury and Martin*, p. 21, accepts Pettit's term 'sui generis'.
[29] Pettit, *Equity and the Law of Trusts*, 7th edn., Butterworths, 1993, p. 76.
[30] Hayton and Marshall, *Cases and Commentary on the Law of Trusts*, 9th edn. by Hayton, Stevens, 1991, pp. 10–12.

account in New York. The husband of the daughter was assessed for income tax on the net amount of the income. Under the relevant income tax legislation, 'tax in respect of income arising from securities, stocks, shares or rents in any place out of the United Kingdom' should be computed on the full amount, but 'tax in respect of income arising from possessions out of the United Kingdom other than stocks, shares or rents' was only on the actual sums annually received in the United Kingdom. The House of Lords, by a majority of three to two, held that the daughter was specifically entitled under the will during her life to the interest and dividends of the securities, stocks, and shares comprised in the trust fund and that her husband was assessable to income tax whether such interest and dividends were remitted to the United Kingdom or not. In the course of judgment, Lord Carson, one of the majority, reserved his view if the life tenant in question was not the sole beneficiary. He said: '. . . had the residue still undetermined or had the share to which [the beneficiary] was entitled been a proportion only of the income or profits of the residue other questions would, no doubt, arise'.[31]

The majority was in effect saying that the trust beneficiary's interest was more than a right *in personam* for due administration of the trust against the trustee and that she had an interest in the trust assets. This runs against the traditional view that a beneficiary's right is to claim the assistance of a court of equity to enforce the trust and to compel the trustee to discharge it.[32] The academic response then was that *Baker* was a menace to equitable principles.[33]

Putting aside the question of doctrinal purity, it is unclear if *Baker* is suggesting the elimination of the trustee for tax purposes, let alone for any other matter. If that is the position, *Baker* can be a sword against the tax authority where the trustee is the taxpayer. This was what happened two years later in *Reid's Trustees* v. *CIR*.[34] In this case, the testator died leaving certain War Loan with interest accrued but unpaid at the time of death. For estate duty payment, the valuation included the accrued interest. When interest was subsequently received, the trustees treated it as capital for the purpose of accounting between the life and subsequent interest.

---

[31] Hayton and Marshall, at 869.

[32] [1927] AC 844 at 850, per Viscount Summer, one of their lordships in the minority.

[33] Hanbury, 'A Periodical Menace to Equitable Principles' (1928) 44 *LQR* 468 where the learned commentator said: '. . . looseness of language and forgetfulness of "Maitland's axiom" have led to another decision which, unless explicable as pure "income tax law" and therefore not to be widely construed, stands, it is submitted, as a contradiction of clear equitable principle. This decision is *Baker* v. *Archer-Shee*.' (At 469.) In a similar vein but otherwise much politer tone, the editor of Notes in the same volume of the *Law Quarterly Review* suggests that 'if there were . . . a higher tribunal then counsel for the unsuccessful respondent in *Baker* v. *Archer-Shee* could, with propriety, advise his client that a further appeal might prove successful' (at 8).                                        [34] (1929) 14 TC 512.

The question before the court was the liability of the trustee to income tax on the interest. The relevant tax legislation made no provision for the deduction of tax from payments of income out of trust estates. The trustee argued, relying on *Baker*, that the liability to tax of income received by trustees depended upon the position as regards liability of the beneficiary; that in this case the interest received was treated as capital as a matter of ordinary principles of accounting between trustees and income-beneficiaries; that the beneficiaries would never receive the interest as income and therefore no liability to tax was possible. It was held by the Scottish Court of Session that on construction of the statute the interest was income and the trustees were the persons receiving or entitled to the income.

The trustees in this case were pushing *Baker* to its logical conclusion that a trust is 'a mere agency or conduit pipe'[35] so that it is to be ignored for tax purposes. The court was concerned with tax-avoidance implications of this proposition as any income might be consumed or directed by the trust to be capitalized so that beneficiaries might never receive income as such that might have been subject to income tax.[36] Their response to *Baker* was to confine it within narrow limits. Dicta from *Baker* that pointed to the direction of elimination of the trustee would be jealously guarded. Lord Sands suggested that *Baker* was 'strictly limited to the case where the circumstances are similar, viz., where there is one beneficiary and the estate is already realised and duly invested'.[37] Lord Morison would confine *Baker* to 'cases solely to the ascertainment of the income from foreign investments chargeable'[38] to tax.

Another attempt was made by a taxpayer to apply *Baker* in his favour in *Macfarlane* v. *CIR*,[39] a decision delivered by the Court of Session on the same day as *Reid's Trustees*.[40] The beneficiary claimed repayment of income tax. The measure of his relief depended on the proportion between the amount of his income which had borne income tax and the 'amount of his total income from all sources'. Part of his income arose from two trusts that provided his entitlement after expenses had been met. The beneficiary claimed that the effect of *Baker* was that the trustee was a mere agent for the beneficiary for tax purposes and accordingly expenses incurred in the administration of the trust were incurred by the beneficiary; and that, therefore, in calculating the repayment the total income should include all expenses of the trusts which the trustees incurred before paying his life interests. The beneficiary was also relying on the fact that the revenue in

---

[35] (1929) 14 TC 512 at 529, per Lord Sands.
[36] See Lord President Clyde's judgment, ibid., at 523–4.
[37] Ibid., at 529.　　　　　　　　　　　[38] Ibid., at 531.
[39] (1929) 14 TC 532.　　　　　　　　[40] (1929) 14 TC 512.

*Baker* withdrew[41] during argument any claim to tax upon that part of the dividend income which was consumed in the administration of the trust in New York. It was not difficult for the court to reject this interpretation of *Baker*. It was not bound by a concession of a party. '[P]ayment of the expenses of administration was a prior purpose . . . and the [beneficiary] could claim or receive from the trust estates nothing until that prior purpose had been fulfilled.'[42] The expenses of the trustee therefore could not be included in the total income.[43]

The reluctance to apply *Baker* continued. In *Schalit* v. *Nadler*[44] the question was whether a beneficiary under a declaration of trust of a long lease was a 'person from time to time entitled . . . to the income . . . of the land leased' within the Law of Property Act 1925 so that he could distrain the rent reserved under a sublease. Goddard J, delivering the judgment of the court, held that the right of a beneficiary whose trustee has leased property subject to the trust was not to the rent, but to an account from the trustee of the profits received.[45] *Baker* was not cited in the judgment.[46]

The trend was reversed in *Nelson* v. *Adamson*.[47] In this case, the life tenant under an Australian will was resident in the United Kingdom. He was in the same situation as in *Baker* except that the whole of the trust income was subject to a prior annuity. No appropriation had been made. In Lawrence J's view, *Baker's ratio decidendi* is that 'the interposition of a trustee does not prevent the income of the *cestui que trust* arising, within

---

[41] See Viscount Sumner's judgment [1927] AC 845 at 849. The Lord President found the revenue's concession 'odd' (ibid., at 539). Logically, in *Baker*, all income before payment of New York tax and the trustee's expenses should be subject to English tax. His Lordship also pointed this out in *Reid's Trustees* (1929) 14 TC 512 at 522–3.

[42] Ibid., at 539.

[43] Affirming the pre-*Baker* decision of *Murray* v. *IRC* (1926) 11 TC 133; see also *IRC* v. *Lord Hamilton of Dalzell* (1926) 10 TC 406.

[44] [1933] 2 KB 79.

[45] He refused to make his decision on a narrower basis that the trustee was not a bare trustee, who had obligations towards the superior landlord for which he could recoup himself out of the rent from the subtenant: ibid., at 82–3.

[46] The doctrinal difficulty of *Baker* resurfaced with *Schalit*. *Schalit* was first hailed in the *Law Quarterly Review* as a 'salutary check on the modern tendency to treat legal and equitable interests in land as interchangeable'. (Notes (1933) 49 *LQR* 480.) But, without citing *Baker*, *Schalit* was not too soon for it to be ranked by another editor of *Law Quarterly Review* as a wrong decision: Notes, (1934) 50 *LQR* 158 (which in turn generated a reply from the editor of the 1933 note at (1934) 50 *LQR* 320). Latham, 'The Right of the Beneficiary to Specific Items of the Trust Fund' [1954] *Can BR* 520 at 537 supports this decision on the ground that it concerns the machinery for enforcing the trust whilst *Baker* is a case of economic interest of the beneficiary.

[47] [1941] 2 KBD 44. In Victoria, at about the same time as *Nelson* v. *Adamson*, Martin J in *Young* [1942] VLR 4 refused to apply *Baker* to the situation of several residuary legatees subject to a life interest. *Young* was criticized in the New South Wales case of *McCaughey* v. *CSD* but was approved by the New Zealand Court of Appeal in *Stannus* v. *CSD*. It was overruled by the Full Court in Victoria in *New Zealand Insurance Co. Ltd.* v. *CPD*.

the meaning of the Income Tax Acts, from the stocks and shares held by the trustee'.[48] Accordingly, he held that the further interposition of an annuitant made no difference. He was prepared to apply *Baker* to a trust of two beneficiaries.[49] He did not regard *Macfarlane* v. *CIR*[50] as relevant and the reservation of Lord Carson[51] was not considered.

In *Stannus* v. *CSD*,[52] a daughter was given, subject to a prior annuity, life interests in one-half of the residuary estate of the father, with power to appoint her children to her share. To this point, the facts were similar to *Nelson* v. *Adamson*.[53] The daughter, by a deed of appointment, directed the trustee to raise out of her half share a sum in favour of her son, and for this purpose, she released her life interest in this sum so that such life interest should merge with the reversionary interest of the son. This sum was raised out of assets all situated in England. The court found that the release of the daughter's life interest was a gift. The question was whether that gift was one of an interest in properties located in England or of an interest in an equitable chose in action located in New Zealand. The latter would be subject to New Zealand gift duty.

By a majority of three to one, the Court of Appeal held that, as the daughter was not the sole life tenant of an ascertained residuary trust fund, she did not have any interest in any specific investment of the trusts, but a right to have the trusts performed and to enforce its performance—which was properly described as an equitable chose in action—and the subject matter of the gift was a portion of the equitable chose in action. This conclusion was reached by the majority by supplying an answer[54] to the 'questions' that Lord Carson might have in mind if there were more than one beneficiary.[55] Finlay J summed up the argument best:

. . . If there are more than one, then the trustees have an important, if simple, function to perform—namely, to divide the available balance between the *cestuis que trust*, according to their respective interests. Those interests may be unequal. In given cases, there may, in respect of individual interests, be allowances and charges to be taken into account, which have relation to those particular interests alone, and permeating such a situation is a duty and a responsibility to the trusts with which they are charged, apart from any possible duty to individual beneficiaries.

Dealing with such a situation is a proper function of trustees in their administrative character. Until those functions are performed, no one of the *cestuis que trust* could claim to be entitled to any other than . . . a balance sum. . . .

It is true that where, as here, neither interest is in any way hypothecated or

---

[48] Ibid., at 47.                    [49] Id.                    [50] (1929) 14 TC 532.
[51] Text accompanying fn. 31, *supra*.                    [52] [1947] NZLR 1.
[53] [1941] 2 KBD 44.
[54] [1947] NZLR 1 at 24–5, per Callan J, with whom Kennedy J concurred; and at 38–9, per Finlay J.                    [55] See text accompanying fn. 31, *supra*.

charged, the function of the trustees is simple, but that does not change the inherent character of the function, for the functional possibilities are present, and might at any time be invoked.[56]

*Nelson* v. *Adamson*[57] was distinguished as a decision as to what the income arose from, within the meaning of the Income Tax Acts of the United Kingdom.[58] This is the same interpretation of *Baker* as that by Lord Morison in *Reid's Trustees*.[59]

*Nelson* v. *Adamson*[60] had its vindication in Victoria in *New Zealand Insurance Co. Ltd.* v. *CPD*.[61] In this case, at the relevant time, after distribution and administration of the will trust of the father, two daughters had life interests in the remainder of the residuary estate as tenants in common in equal shares with power of appointment in respect of the capital and income of their respective shares. The father's estate included shares in Victorian companies but the administration of the trusts of the estate was situate in New Zealand. One daughter exercised her power of appointment before her decease. The question was whether she had in Victoria 'property over or in respect of which [she] had at the time of [her] death a general power of appointment'. Such property would be subject to Victorian probate duty. The court held that she had a general power of appointment over half the undivided interest in the property the subject of the trusts that included the shares in Victorian companies; and that therefore probate duty was assessable to the extent of the value of one-half of those company shares. The court saw 'no basis in logic or reason for not applying the principles laid down in the *Archer-Shee* cases'[62] to a trust under which two or more persons are concurrently entitled to trust property as tenants in common for life. In the joint judgment of Winneke CJ and Menhennitt J, *Stannus* was distinguished but approved in the following terms:

. . . [I]n the *Stannus* case the gift related to a fund of £10,000 to be thereafter created by the trustees and which required for its creation an appropriation of assets to her share by the trustees. . . . [I]t was not possible, therefore, to say, when the gift was made, that it was in respect of any identifiable asset or assets the subject of the trust. We would respectfully agree with the conclusion that, as what was given was a specified sum to be provided out of an unidentified part of a body of assets . . . it was appropriate to say that what was given was a chose in action against the trustees. . . .[63]

---

[56] [1947] NZLR 1 at 38–9.                                      [57] [1941] 2 KBD 44.
[58] Per Callan J [1947] NZLR 1 at 26, seizing upon that part of Lawrence J's judgment which is quoted in text accompanying fn. 48, *supra*.
[59] See text accompanying fn. 38, *supra*.
[60] [1941] 2 KBD 44.              [61] [1973] VR 659.                [62] Ibid., at 665.
[63] Ibid., at 668; Smith J considered the point in question in *Stannus* to be what the donor purported to give away. If the donor did have proprietary interest in the trust assets, it was not that interest that she purported to give away, which was subject to gift duty. (Ibid., at 670.)

The survey of *Baker* in private trusts should not be concluded without a note on *CSD (Qld.)* v. *Livingston*,[64] though it is a case of unadministered estate. The issue was whether a residuary legatee in an unadministered estate of a testator who died domiciled in New South Wales, comprising assets in Queensland, has a beneficial interest in property situated in Queensland and if she has, on her death her estate will be subject to duty under Queensland's Succession and Probate Duties Acts. The facts were similar to the those appearing in cases studied so far except that the estate of the testator was in the course of administration. The Privy Council held[65] that for an estate in the course of administration, there was no trust fund consisting of any gift to any beneficiary in which he could be said to have any beneficial interest because no trust had as yet come into existence to affect the asset of the estate; that the deceased's property was vested in the personal representative in full right and no beneficial interest in any item of property belonged to any beneficiary; and that the beneficiary was only entitled to a chose in action, capable of being invoked for any purpose connected with the proper administration of the estate. There is no doubt that the Board's opinion depends on 'the peculiar status which the law accorded to an executor for the purposes of carrying out his duties of administration'.[66] Apart from that, the Board must have been influenced by the fact that an executor in the course of administration has continuing duties 'to preserve the assets, to deal properly with them, and to apply them in a due course of administration for the benefit of those interested according to that course, creditors, the death duty authorities, legatees of various sorts, and the residuary beneficiaries'.[67] Was this akin to the reasoning of *Stannus*, where the court refused to apply *Baker* to more than one beneficiary?

## B. *Baker* v. *Archer-Shee* in Unit Trusts

So far, the position is this. With regard to the number of beneficiaries, the effect of *Nelson* v. *Adamson*[68] and *New Zealand Insurance Co. Ltd.* v. *CPD*[69] is that *Baker* is not limited to trusts with one beneficiary and the existence of a number of beneficiaries, whether in succession[70] or concurrently,[71] does not affect their respective claims to proprietary interests in the subject matter of a trust. Ironically, the expansive application of *Baker* was achieved in *New Zealand Insurance* only at the price of admitting that a beneficiary may not have a proprietary interest in

---

[64] [1965] AC 694.
[65] Reaffirming the law in *Sudeley* v. *AG* [1897] AC 11.
[66] Ibid., at 707.
[67] Id.
[68] [1941] 2 KBD 44.
[69] [1973] VR 659.
[70] As in *Nelson*.
[71] As in *New Zealand Insurance*.

the trust assets in some fixed trust[72] situations, such as where the beneficial interest is 'a specified sum to be provided out of an unidentified part of a body of assets'.[73] This may be significant in assessing the true meaning of *Baker*. At this juncture this is still a matter of conjecture as the Scottish tax cases are only indicative of what *Baker* does not represent and do not define the boundaries of *Baker*. In any event, *New Zealand Insurance* has cleared the hurdle for *Baker*'s application to unit trusts, if the number of beneficiaries should ever be an issue.

In *Charles* v. *FCT*,[74] the trust was a fixed investment trust governed by a declaration of trust which limited investments to securities of specified companies. After the manager caused to be vested in the name of the trustee securities authorized for investment by the trust deed, units were issued by the trustee to certificate holders nominated by the manager. In selling the units, the manager added 7.5 per cent as a service charge, out of which it paid all expenses of administration as well as the trustee's remuneration. The trustee was not entitled to have any remuneration paid out of the trust fund. A certificate holder of a certain number of units had a right to exchange his units for a proportionate part of the underlying securities. The deed contained no power to traffic in securities. The manager could request the trustee to realize or vary some investments in certain circumstances but the trustee had absolute discretion as to the request. The evidence accepted was that at no time were securities acquired for the purpose of resale at a profit, and sales were normally made when the manager anticipated a fall in the value of shares. A certificate holder received in the tax year a sum representing (a) dividends of securities and (b) profits on the sale of securities and rights of shares held by the trustee, and profit on the distribution on a winding up of a company in which the trustee held shares. Component (a) was accepted by both the taxpayer and the Commissioner of Taxation as income from properties. The question under appeal was whether component (b) was profits from business or profits arising from the carrying on or carrying out of a profit-making scheme so that it possessed the character of income from personal exertion. The High Court of Australia held that the conclusion from the evidence accepted was that the profits from realization of securities were from transactions effected in the course of performing a fiduciary duty to preserve for beneficiaries as far as practicable the assets comprising the trust fund which might appear to be in jeopardy. Accordingly, component (b) was not taxable as income in the hands of the certificate holder.

The High Court was therefore applying *Baker* in a subtle way for it was

---

[72] The term is used in contradistinction to a discretionary trust.
[73] Text accompanying fn. 63, *supra*.          [74] (1954) 90 CLR 598.

in effect saying that in determining the character of income in the hands of a beneficiary in a fixed investment trust, the interposition of the trust can be ignored so that the beneficiary can be equated with the trustee: the trust is not a company. In the joint written judgment of Dixon CJ, Kitto J, and Taylor J, the court said:

. . . [A] unit held *under this trust deed* is fundamentally different from a share in a company. A share confers upon the holder no legal or equitable interest in the assets of the company; it is a separate piece of property. . . . [A] unit *under the trust deed before us* confers a proprietary interest in all the property which for the time being is subject to the trust of the deed: *Baker* v. *Archer-Shee*;[75] so that the question whether moneys distributed to unit holders under the trust form part of their income or of their capital must be answered by considering the character of those moneys in the hands of the trustees before the distribution is made.[76]

This statement is important for it has often been quoted for a general principle that it does not represent. *Charles* has been quoted as the authority establishing that a unitholder in a unit trust has an interest in the underlying assets. But their Honours were very careful to confine the statement to the unit under the trust deed before them, namely, a fixed investment trust. Moreover, when the case was heard, the Commissioner had already agreed to treat that portion of the distributed fund which came from dividends received by the trustee as the income of the certificate holder derived from property.[77] The question whether a unit is an item of property, and consequently income from it is indivisible, was therefore not raised. Had it been raised, the applicability of *Baker* would be a more vexed question. By accepting the dividend component to be property income, the Commissioner was admitting the effect of *Baker* in that component, i.e., that income in the hand of the trustee had the same character in the hand of the beneficiary. In respect of the remaining portion of the distribution, the court had little room to manoeuvre, as the fixed investment trust was a fixed trust with all the beneficial interest ascertained, making it very difficult to argue that *Baker* was not applicable.

Shortly after *Charles* was decided by the High Court of Australia, another fixed investment trust was the subject of taxation proceedings. This time, it was before the Supreme Court of Canada in *MNR* v. *Trans-Canada Investment Corporation Ltd.*[78] The trust was a typical fixed investment trust. Under the trust deed, an administrator (i.e. the manager) was to purchase a fixed number of predetermined shares of common stock of companies to constitute a trust unit. Upon all the shares of underlying companies of a unit being vested in the trustee, the trustee would issue shares of a trust unit. Each share of a trust unit represented an undivided

---

[75] [1927] AC 844.        [76] (1954) 90 CLR 598 at 609; emphases supplied.
[77] Ibid., at 609.                        [78] [1955] 5 DLR 576.

equal interest in the unit. The administrator was permitted to be a holder of shares in the unit. The administrator, which was a corporation, received distribution from the trust in its capacity as a holder. That income comprised dividends from underlying corporations that were resident in Canada as well as other incomes received but after all expenses had been deducted. The relevant Income Tax Act allowed certain deductions in computation of income 'where a corporation received a dividend from a [non-exempt] corporation that was resident in Canada'. The question was whether the administrator as a holder was entitled to claim those deductions as a corporation that received a dividend from the underlying corporations. The court, by a majority of three to two, affirmed the judgment of the Exchequer Court and held that the interposition of a trustee between a dividend-paying taxable corporation and the beneficial owner, being a corporation, of the former's shares did not destroy the tax exemption.

The majority focused on the interpretation of the relevant tax statute. Their judgment contained no illumination of the *Baker* principle—other than their agreement with the trial judge. Locke J was the only one in the majority who emphasized that the shares in the underlying companies representing the trust unit were kept separate from all others by the trustee, and when dividends were received they were immediately placed in a special trust account and all distributions made out of that account.[79] To him, it appeared that the fixity of the underlying investment played an important part in determining the application of *Baker*. On the other hand, Estey J, in the minority, emphasized that net income under the trust deed could include profits from realization of underlying shares, that transferable shares were issued, and that control of dividends received was not in the hand of certificate holders. He held that these factors and the deed as a whole did not support 'a construction that either a legal or an equitable right is created in favour of the certificate holders in respect to the dividends received by the trustee from the underlying companies'.[80]

In *Costa and Duppe Properties Pty. Ltd.* v. *Duppe*,[81] a trust deed provided that units were to be issued and each unit was defined as an undivided part or share in the trust fund having the characteristics provided in the deed. Clauses 7(a) and 8(a) of the trust deed provided as follows. '7.(a) The beneficial interest in the Trust Fund as originally constituted and as existing from time to time shall be vested in the Unit Holders for the time being.' '8.(a) Each Unit shall entitle the registered holder thereof together with the registered holders of all other Units to the beneficial interest in the Trust Fund as an entirety but subject thereto shall not entitle a Unit Holder to any particular security or investment comprised in the

---

[79] [1955] 5 DLR 576 at 587.          [80] Ibid., at 586.          [81] [1986] VR 90.

Trust Fund or any part thereof and no Unit Holder shall be entitled to the transfer to him of any property comprised in the Trust Fund other [*sic*] than in accordance with the provisions hereinafter contained.' The trustee was given wide investment powers, including the power to carry on a trade or business. There was no manager. The units issued were held equally by two trustees of two discretionary private trusts. The trust fund comprised three parcels of land under the Transfer of Land Act 1958. A unitholder registered a caveat in respect of each parcel. On an application by the trustee of the unit trust to vacate the caveats, the question posed to the court was whether the unitholder had an estate or interest in land within the meaning of section 89(1) of the Act. Brooking J of the Supreme Court of Victoria held that the unitholder had such an estate and interest to support the caveats.

Thus, *Baker* was applied in a situation which hitherto had not been encountered; it was a situation of a conflict of claims of parties to the trust. To Brooking J, it is an inescapable conclusion of *New Zealand Insurance*[82] and *Charles*[83] that the unitholders have proprietary interests in all properties, which clause 7(a) recognizes. His logic was that '[i]f there is a proprietary interest in the entirety, there must be a proprietary interest in each of the assets of which the entirety is composed'.[84] Clause 8(a) was confined to its narrowest limit to mean that 'no unitholder can claim to have any particular asset appropriated to his share or transferred to him otherwise than in accordance with the deed'. In effect, the position would be the same even without these two clauses.[85]

In *Softcorp Holdings Pty. Ltd.* v. *Commissioner of Stamps*,[86] a unit trust was formed by a deed between a settlor and a trustee under which the settlor had paid the trustee a nominal sum and the trustee was to hold the trust fund for the benefit of those who later were to hold units. A unit was defined to be an undivided part or share in the trust fund. Nine units were issued and held by three unitholders equally. By a subsequent amending deed, a new B class unit was created conferring the right to receive *in specie* one-quarter shares in a company upon those shares forming part of the trust fund. This amending deed also conferred a discretion to the trustee to transfer assets *in specie* to other unitholders. After the execution of the amending deed, the trustee did acquire those company shares and distribution *in specie* was made accordingly. The Commissioner of Stamps assessed *ad valorem* duty on the transfers of shares to each of the unitholders. On appeal to the Supreme Court of South Australia, the question was whether each transfer fell within the exemption as 'a transfer of property to a person who has the beneficial interest in the property by

---

[82] [1973] VR 659.  [83] (1954) 90 CLR 598.  [84] [1986] VR 90 at 96.
[85] Id.  [86] (1987) 18 ATR 813.

virtue of an instrument that is duly stamped'. Bollen J held that on
construction, the combined effect of the trust deed and the amending deed,
which provided for transfer of shares *in specie*, was that each unitholder
was to have one-quarter of the company shares.[87] For the exemption to
apply, it is not necessary for the transferee to have 'the' beneficial interest
in precisely 'the' actual shares transferred, as argued for the Commissioner.
Having one-quarter of the whole of the shares was having the beneficial
interest in the property.

Bollen J regarded his decision as one of 'interpretation of the relevant
provisions of the Stamp Duties Act and the application thereof to the
facts'[88] rather than an application of precedents.

## C. An Analysis

### (1) What Does *Baker* Decide

Despite the number of post-*Baker* cases, there is still no consensus on the
*ratio decidendi* of *Baker*. To those dissatisfied with *Baker*'s doctrinal
position, it is best to be considered as a case explicable of no more than a
tax law principle,[89] or to be applicable only when there is only one
beneficiary.[90] A broader interpretation is to see the life tenant in *Baker* as
having a proprietary interest in the trust assets that generated the income
paid into her account by the trustee. In subsequent litigation in *Archer-
Shee* v. *Garland*,[91] Viscount Dunedin said:

My Lords, the first and indeed crucial point of this case is to make up one's mind as
to what was the true *ratio decidendi* in the former case [*Baker* v. *Archer-Shee*], for
by that decision we are bound. I think the *ratio decidendi* very clearly appears by
comparing the judgment of Viscount Sumner, who was in the minority, with the
majority judgment which prevailed. . . . [Viscount Sumner's] view was rejected by
the majority on the view that *there was in the beneficiary a specific equitable interest
in each and every one of the stocks, shares, etc., which formed the trust fund* . . .[92]

---

[87] (1987) 18 ATR 813 at 818.
[88] Ibid., at 822; Bollen J did not consider himself as following precedents. He regarded
*Costa and Duppe Properties Pty. Ltd.* v. *Duppe* [1986] VR 90 and cases cited therein as
'helpful in a generally educative way' (at 821).
[89] As Lord Morison in *Reid's Trustees* v. *CIR*: text accompanying fn. 38, *ante*. Similarly,
although Callan J in *Stannus* did not regard *Baker* as confined to tax situations, he
distinguished *Nelson* v. *Adamson* on this basis: see fn. 58, *supra*.
[90] 'After careful consideration of their speeches, it appears inescapable that in *Baker* v.
*Archer-Shee* the majority of their Lordships have enunciated that under English law the sole
life tenant of a residuary estate, which has been finally ascertained and settled, is entitled in
equity specifically during her life to the dividends upon the stocks in which such residuary
estate is for the time being invested.' Per Callan, J in *Stannus* [1947] NZLR 1 at 24.
[91] [1930] AC 212.
[92] Ibid., at 221; emphasis supplied.

*Baker* thus stands for the proposition that a beneficiary has a proprietary interest in 'each and every one' of the specific underlying assets of the trust. In this sense, *Baker* has imputed transparency to the trust; the interposition of the trust between the persons enjoying the property and its legal owner of that property is functionally useless, at least where the trust is fully constituted and there is only one beneficiary.

An impelling undercurrent of this proposition is its treatment of the trustee as a mere conduit and its potential equation of a trustee with an agent.[93] That would cut deep into the root of the trust institution. Perhaps, here is the real menace facing theorists. This could not be the intention of the majority in *Baker*. Indeed, *CSD (Qld.) v. Livingston*[94] must have subtly set the limit to which *Baker* can expand, given the similarity between an unadministered estate and a trust with complex administrative duties or a discretionary trust. Even for the most pragmatic, there is a need to locate a point of reconciliation so that *Baker* can fit into the rest of trusts law. Latham suggests that *Baker* applies, or rather the courts will attach a beneficiary's interest to specific trust assets, where 'problems of social and economic importance are involved'.[95] Latham's test is criticized by Waters as 'haphazard and unpredictable'.[96] In its place, Waters draws on the judgment of Kitto J in *CSD (Qld.) v. Livingston*[97] and suggests a test of 'sufficiently direct and exclusive'. Although these two tests are based on extensive research into cases before and after *Baker*, if they are applied *post facto* to all cases just surveyed, it is still a matter of guesswork of what the result would be. For example, there is still no answer to the question why the beneficiary in *Schalit* v. *Nadler*[98] (or, indeed, the beneficiaries in *Reid's Trustees*[99] and *Stannus*[100]) could not have been regarded as having a sufficiently direct and exclusive interest in the rent to be collected.

As *Baker* is so influential in the law of both private trusts and unit trusts, it is worth looking again at the facts and decision of *Baker*. The court was required to decide whether the life tenant was the owner of the net income from investments that had actually been paid into her account by the trustee. Of course, she was—the money was in her account already! The

---

[93] *Reid's Trustees.*   [94] [1965] AC 694.

[95] This is the conclusion reached by Latham in 'The Right of the Beneficiary to Specific Items of the Trust Fund' (1954) 32 *Can BR* 520. His analysis also suggests that the applicability may also depend on how specific the interest of a beneficiary is in relation to the trust assets. This may be compared with the test of 'sufficiently direct and exclusive' of Waters in the article referred to in the succeeding footnote.

[96] Waters, 'The Nature of the Trust Beneficiary's Interest' (1967) *Can BR* 219 at 228. Note that Latham is incorrectly referred to as Dr Korah in the article.

[97] [1965] AC 694.   [98] [1933] 2 KB 79; 49 *LQR* 480; 50 *LQR* 158.

[99] (1929) 14 TC 512.   [100] [1947] NZLR 1.

majority was simply realistic, without concern for any juristic lumber.[101] None of their Lordships were asking the question whether the beneficiary had any interest in specific properties of the trust, namely, the shares and stocks. They were concerned purely with the dividends. Lord Wrenbury said:

My Lords, *the question is* not what the trustees have thought proper to hand over and have handed over (which is question of fact) but *what under the will Lady Archer-Shee is entitled to* (which is a question of law). . . . Under Mr Pell's will Lady Archer-Shee (if American law is the same as English law) is, in my opinion, as matter of construction of the will, entitled in equity specifically during her life to the dividends upon the stocks.[102]

He also said:

I have to read the will and see what is Lady Archer-Shee's right of property in certain ascertained securities, stocks and shares now held by the Trust Company 'to the use of my said daughter.' It is, I think, if the law of America is the same as our law, an equitable right in possession to receive during her life the proceeds of the shares and stocks of which she is tenant for life. Her right is not to a balance sum, but to the dividends subject to deductions as above mentioned. Her right under the will is 'property' from which income is derived.[103]

Lord Carson said:

In my opinion upon the construction of the will of Alfred Pell once the residue had become specifically ascertained, the respondent's wife was sole beneficial owner of the interest and dividends of all the securities, stocks and shares forming part of the trust fund therein settled and was entitled to receive and did receive such interest and dividends.[104]

If a trust is conceived as an institution that divides ownership into title and right of enjoyment between the trustee and the beneficiary, the court in *Baker* was ascertaining that right of enjoyment in order to determine if such right was taxable under the relevant statute. In all the passages quoted, their Lordships confined themselves to the question 'what under the will Lady Archer-Shee is entitled to' and they were careful to confine their conclusion to interest and dividends, rather than the shares and securities.

In almost all cases subsequent to *Baker*, the courts were asking themselves if the beneficiary in question had an interest in specific

---

[101] To borrow the phrase of Waters, *supra*, at 228. It is interesting to note the paucity of cases quoted in the judgments of the majority. Does this suggest they did not have any doctrinal concern?

[102] [1927] AC 844 at 865–6; emphasis supplied.

[103] Ibid., at 866; emphasis supplied. Lord Atkinson, after criticizing judgments of the courts below, said he concurred with the view of Lord Wrenbury (at 863).

[104] Ibid., at 870.

properties or if he had merely a right to compel the trustee to due administration. In posing the question in such manner, they were in effect compartmentalizing equitable rights as either rights *in rem* or rights *in personam* under different phraseologies; they were still labouring under the shadow of the great debate. The truth is that a beneficiary must have some interest under the trust. The court in *Baker* was asking what was the beneficiary's interest in question.

It is therefore submitted that (within the context of those cases) the correct approach is a two-step one. The first question is to determine what is a particular beneficiary's right of enjoyment as conferred by the instrument constituting the trust, or the nature of that right. Secondly, the language of the relevant statute or the relevant principle of law has to be considered to see if that right falls within its reach.[105] This will avoid any oversimplification of all legal issues concerning beneficiaries as being one and the same thing, namely, his rights in specific properties. It admits of the reality of a variety of trusts with diverse purposes and constitutions.

It is, thus, not difficult to visualize that the beneficiary under a bare trust, where he can call on the trustee to transfer the legal title to him at any time, can be regarded as an equitable owner of the underlying property having a title good against the whole world except a bona fide purchaser for value without notice. He may have a right of termination of the trust under the principle of *Saunders* v. *Vautier*.[106] But, until he exercises his right to call for the legal title, the trust does not give him a right of administration, which remains vested in the trustee.[107] If the trust consists of land, he cannot sue for the rent directly but can compel the trustee to account.[108] A beneficiary under a discretionary trust has the right to be considered as a recipient of the trust benefit; he does not have any right to any property because the trust does not confer such right on him. This does not preclude him from exercising his tracing remedy which is a remedial right given by equity. Under this analysis, it is not necessary to know if the right was a right *in rem* or *in personam*. Of course, it has to be admitted that the task for the court will not be an easy one but this approach, it is

---

[105] Questions of whether income is 'profits from business or profits arising from carrying on or carrying out of a profit-making scheme' (as in *Charles*) and of whether a person has 'the beneficial interest in the property' (as in *Softcorp*) are different by nature. Moreover, the context may require an altogether different approach. Thus, although a beneficiary may have no interest in specific assets of unadministered estate, if that beneficiary makes a will of a specific item in that unadministered estate, the court sitting in the armchair of a testator will no doubt give effect to his wishes when that item ultimately passes to him (*Smith* v. *Layth* (1953) 90 CLR 102). See also *Horton* v. *Jones* (1935) 53 CLR 475.

[106] (1841) 4 Beav. 115.

[107] *Re Brockbank* [1948] Ch. 206; cf. *Butt* v. *Kelsen* [1952] 1 All ER 167.

[108] *Schalit* v. *Nadler* [1933] 2 KB 79.

submitted, brings into focus the relevant without being tied down by Latinisms. This was exactly what the majority in *Baker* did.

## (2) A Question of Construction

What then are the rights of a unitholder in the trust fund?[109] The first proposition begins with the qualifier 'unless the trust instruments provide specific interests in the underlying assets'. This serves to emphasize that it is always a question of construction of each trust deed as to the right of a particular unitholder. The passages quoted from the majority of their Lordships support this point. Lord Wrenbury, for instance, considered himself to be construing the will of Lady Archer-Shee's father to ascertain her right.[110] The determination of the income of the beneficiary in *Macfarlane*[111] also depended on the construction of the trust instrument. Bollen J in *Softcorp* was most explicit to consider the issue as one of construction of the deed before him and the relevant statute. He considered authorities as of general educative value only.[112] Implicitly, *Charles* is also to the same effect.[113]

This approach is also supported by cases on the nature of shares in companies constituted by deeds of settlement.[114] In the mid-nineteenth century, courts were called upon to decide the nature of shares in deed of settlement companies as well as in companies constituted by Acts of Parliament. All cases turned upon the question whether shares were

---

[109] In the preliminary analysis, s. 1B, *ante*, it has been pointed out that a unit is a bundle of rights of which interest in the trust fund is only one of them. What that bundle consists of is also a question of construction of the trust deed and all other documents constituting the trust fund.

[110] Text accompanying fn. 102.

[111] (1929) 14 TC 532. The court has to decide if the entitlement of a beneficiary from the trust is net amount after expenses or the gross amount.

[112] Fn. 88, *supra*.

[123] *Re Whitehead's Will Trusts* [1959] 2 All ER 497 was a case on fixed investment trusts decided at about the same time as *Charles*. An estate of a testator consisted of sub-units in three fixed investment trusts. The trustees of the will sought directions on the allocation of distributions from the investment trusts between beneficiaries interested in income and those interested in capital. Although *Baker* was not considered, since Harman J considered the question as one of apportionment between capital and income beneficiaries, he also approached it by way of construing the trust deeds to find out if they directed the trust to alter the nature of the money received. He held that they did not and that the will trustees therefore had to enquire in any case of doubt into the source of each distribution as if they were the direct shareholders (at 501 and 503).

[114] The use of deed of settlement companies as historical antecedents is supported by *Elders Trustee and Executor Co. Ltd.* v. *EG Reeves Pty. Ltd.* (1987) 78 ALR 193 (promoter of unit trusts); *Gra-ham Australia Pty. Ltd.* v. *Perpetual Trustees WA Ltd.* (1989) 1 WAR 65 (majority's duty as to amendment of deeds); *Smith* v. *Permanent Trustee Australia Ltd.* (1992) 10 ACLC 906 (unitholders' requisition of a meeting). See ch. 1, s. 5E, *ante*, for their historical connections.

interests in land within the Mortmain Acts[115] or section 4 of the Statute of Frauds.[116] The leading authorities of *Bligh* v. *Brent*,[117] *Myers* v. *Perigal*[118] and *Watson* v. *Spratley*[119] considered it to be a question of construction whether the shares conferred on the shareholders individually an interest in land as land, or whether the shareholders' interest was represented by mere money.[120]

There are three possible alternative ways of construing the terms of a unit trust deed. The first is that each unit represents a proportional share of underlying assets. The second is that the unit trust is a trust for conversion and each unitholder is also entitled to an interest in the underlying assets. The third alternative is that each unit represents a proportion of the net value of the trust fund. Their interests are from the beginning to the end in money.

## (3) Specific Interest in the Underlying Assets

The early company cases regarded the company as a trustee for its shareholders.[121] It followed naturally that the equitable title to real estate was vested in the shareholders. Cases on the New River Company established this.[122] However, in *Bligh* v. *Brent*,[123] Alderson B regarded the issue as one of construction. His Lordship held that the shares before him were personalty. For him, shares would confer proprietary interests in

---

[115] Prohibiting interests in land being devised by will for charitable uses.

[116] Requiring disposition of interests in land to be in writing.

[117] (1837) 2 Y & C Ex. 268. This is a case where the court had to decide the nature of shares in the Chelsea Waterworks Company for the purpose of the Statute of Frauds. The company was incorporated by an Act of Parliament. Martin B, in *Watson* v. *Spratley*, considered that there was no reason why the principle established in statutory companies should not be applied to companies constituted by deeds of settlement (1854)10 Ex. 222 at 238. *Bligh* v. *Brent* was relied on expressly by Martin B, Alderson B, and Parke B in *Watson* v. *Spratley*.

[118] (1852) 2 De GM & G 599.  [119] (1854) 10 Ex. 222.

[120] It is not surprising that the result of this approach was that in the majority of cases the shares were held to be personal property. But, until the statutory provision (Companies Act 1862, s. 22) declaring shares to be personalty (now Companies Act 1985, s. 182(1)(a) ), the correct principle should be that it was a question of construction: see Lindley, *A Treatise of the Law of Companies, Considered as a Branch of the Law of Partnership*, 5th edn., Sweet and Maxwell, 1889, p. 451, and Page Wood VC in *Hayter* v. *Tucker* (1858) 4 K & J 243 and *Entwistle* v. *Davis* (1867) LR 4 Eq. 272 also regarded *Myers* v. *Perigal* and *Watson* v. *Spratley* as establishing that the question is one of construction.

[121] *Child* v. *Hudson's Bay Co.* (1723) 2 P Wms. 207 at 208–9, per Lord Macclesfield, discussed in Cooke, *Corporation, Trust and Company: An Essay in Legal History*, Manchester UP, 1950, pp. 69–71.

[122] *Drybutter* v. *Bartholomew* (1723) 2 P Wms. 127, *Townsend* v. *Ash* (1745) 3 Atk. 336, *Stafford* v. *Buckley* (1750) 2 Ves. Sen. 171, *Swayne* v. *Fawkener* (1696) Show. PC 207, *Sandys* v. *Sibthorpe* (1778) Dick. 545, quoted in Cooke, ibid., at p. 70 fn. 3. Other early cases on the same point were referred to in the judgment and counsels' arguments in *Bligh* v. *Brent* (1837) 2Y & C Ex. 268.  [123] (1837) 2Y & C Ex. 268.

underlying assets if, as in the New River case: 'the individual corporators have the property. The corporation have only the management of it . . . [T]he property given to the corporation was real property, which they are to manage for the good of all. They have no powers of converting it into any other sort of property, but must keep it and make a profit from it as it is, viz. as real property.'[124]

In the unit trust context, the most likely candidate to fall within this construction was the early version of the fixed investment trust which had the composition of each unit predetermined, and each sub-unit was an undivided share of the unit. These fell within the *Bligh* v. *Brent* interpretation that the underlying assets were to be held by the unitholders as such and the trustee was to have only the management, with no power to convert into any other properties. The intention, therefore, was to confer interest in underlying assets. *Trans-Canada Investment*[125] is a clear example of this type of trust. Although the administration of the trust was complex, the majority must have been influenced by the fact that each unit's investments were kept separate.[126] In *Charles*,[127] although it was not structured as units and sub-units, the trust was a fixed investment trust. The trustee's expenses were to be paid not out of the trust fund, but from the initial charge of the manager. All investments were therefore kept completely intact as no payment could be made out of them. The trustee's obligation to hold the investments for the unitholders was even clearer when the trust deed provided the right to exchange units for underlying investments.

The modern example is the single property trust constituted under section 76(4)–(6) of the Financial Services Act 1986 and the Financial Services Act 1986 (Single Property Schemes) (Exemption) Regulations 1989.[128] Under the Act, a single property scheme can obtain exemption only if the property of the scheme consists of '(a) a single building (or a single building with ancillary buildings) managed by or on behalf of the operator of the scheme' or '(b) a group of adjacent or contiguous buildings managed by him or on his behalf as a single enterprise'.[129] The Regulations require the trust deed to provide 'for the trustee to hold the land and the building or group of adjacent or contiguous buildings forming part of the property subject to the scheme on trust for sale . . . for participants in

---

[124] (1837) 2Y & C Ex. 268 at 295–6.                [125] [1955] 5 DLR 576.
[126] Text accompanying fn. 79, *ante*.              [127] (1954) 90 CLR 598.
[128] These regulations are made by the Secretary of state. The power to make regulations for the marketing and operation of single property schemes has been delegated to the Securities and Investments Board (the Financial Services Act 1986 (Delegation) (No. 2) Order 1988) which made the Financial Services (Single Property Schemes) (Supplementary) Regulations 1989 for these purposes.
[129] See the discussion in ch. 1, s. 5D, *ante*.

proportion to their respective entitlements as determined by the number of units in respect of which they are registered'.[130] Thus there is a trust for sale of the real property in favour of unitholders as tenants in common in the proportion of their respective unitholdings. This is likely to be construed as creating in favour of each unitholder an interest in the buildings as it is not contemplated by such a scheme that there will be a constant change of underlying assets.

## (4) Trust for Conversion

This is the second type of possible construction of the terms of a unit trust deed.

A unit trust is a fixed trust. A fixed trust can be a fixed investment trust, a flexible trust or of any character that the draftsman wants. *Charles*[131] has virtually been regarded as the authority as to the nature of unit trusts generally. In truth, it was concerned only with a fixed investment trust, a fixed trust which has its investments almost fixed. It was never the intention of the court to decide beyond the trust deed before them.[132] The position of flexible trusts operating under the cash fund principle has therefore to be examined separately.

One possible construction of the cash fund trust is that when the cash subscriptions are paid by unitholders, there is a trust for conversion into the permitted assets of the unit trust and the unitholders are beneficial owners of underlying assets, as in the fixed investment trust in *Charles*. If the trustee has, at the direction of the manager, exercised borrowing powers or incurred liability, they are owners of the assets subject to liabilities.

There are three objections. First, in order to effect a conversion, there must be an imperative direction in the trust deed. In a cash fund trust, the trustee is not under any 'imperative' obligation to convert cash into investment as the manager instructs since the trustee has to consider all investment policies and restrictions have been observed.[133] The powers of investment are powers, not directions.[134] Moreover, the trust deed will give the manager the power to vary investments. Underlying investments may therefore fluctuate. Secondly, the doctrine of conversion operates only to convert realty to personalty and vice versa. It will not apply to

---

[130] Reg. 6(b)(vi).    [131] Ibid.    [132] See text accompanying fn. 76, *supra*.

[133] Thus, the monitoring role of the trustee prevents the exercise of the manager's power from being considered as a direction to the trustee. Even if the court considers the manager as directing the trustee in investment matters, there is no conversion until the direction is given: *In re Goswell's Trusts* [1915] 2 Ch. 106.

[134] Powers to sell, unlike directions to sell, will not cause conversion: *In re Dyson* [1910] 1 Ch. 750.

convert cash into securities or other types of personal properties. Thirdly, when a unitholder redeems his units, under this analysis, a second conversion is necessary. This is a double conversion,[135] the artificiality of which is apparent. It is difficult to find any imperative direction in the second conversion. As the redemption money could have been paid by the trustee out of the cash of the trust, the provision enabling the sale of assets to meet redemption invariably is a discretion. Such a provision is also difficult to be construed as a direction, on account of the lack of identification of assets.

### (5) A Proportion of the Net Value Calculated and Realizable in Manner Provided by the Trust Deed

The third construction is that a unit confers a proportion of the net value, rather than any specific interest. Under this, the nature of underlying assets is irrelevant; the unitholders' interest is money, the investment capital. This construction, it is submitted, best represents the position of modern unit trusts operating on a cash fund principle and an authorized unit trust is a typical example.

Five points can be made to support this construction of the cash fund trust.

1. In a cash fund trust, the property entrusted is money. The trust fund as a whole is in the nature of capital, fluctuating from time to time.[136] Each unitholder is interested only in the return of this capital plus the accrued surplus value of the money he invested. Whilst the trust is a going concern, unitholders expect the return to be by way of redemption, or in some cases, realization on the Stock Exchange. If the trust is terminated, again, the expectation is the return of the capital together with its surplus value after realization of all assets by the trustee. Thus, this description of a unit does not have much difference from that of a share found in company law textbooks.

It was the capital character and profit motive that led Alderson B in *Bligh* v. *Brent*[137] to come to the conclusion that a share of the deed of

---

[135] This is not reconversion. Reconversion is the election by a beneficiary to take the original property. The election discharges the direction to convert. Reconversion may also take place by operation of law. (See *Snell*, pp. 499–502.) Double conversion is where the settlor gives direction to convert from one type of property into the other and then back to the original type. E.g., the trustee is directed to sell one house and use the proceeds to buy two houses for two beneficiaries.

[136] S. 1A of this ch., *ante*.

[137] (1837) 2Y & C Ex. 268. *Bligh* v. *Brent* was applicable to deed of settlement companies: see fn. 138 and 147, *infra*.

settlement company before him was personalty unconnected to the nature of the company's assets:

> It is of the greatest importance to look carefully at the nature of the property originally entrusted, and that of the body to whose management it is entrusted: the powers that body has over it, and the purposes for which these powers are given. The property is money—the subscriptions of individual corporators. In order to make that profitable, it is entrusted to a corporation who have an unlimited power of converting part of it into land, part into goods; and of changing and disposing of each from time to time; and the purpose of all this is the obtaining a clear surplus profit from the use and disposal of this capital for the individual contributors.[138]

2. The second point is a corollary of the first: all assets are not to be enjoyed as assets *per se*. They are instruments to achieve the objective of gain. This differs from private trust assets, which are for the enjoyment of beneficiaries according to the wishes of the settlors. Gearing, hedging techniques, and management of all assets as a single portfolio implicitly reflect the intention that no parties shall have any interest in individual assets. The two leading cases on deed of settlement companies, *Myers* v. *Perigal*[139] and *Watson* v. *Spratley*,[140] suggest that it is a question of the intention with regard to underlying assets.

In *Myers* v. *Perigal*[141] the issue was whether a bequest of shares in a banking company constituted by a deed of settlement and with assets in land was within the Mortmain Act. It was held that the shares were not interests in land. Lord St Leonards considered this to be a question of intention. He said:

> The true way to test it would be to assume that there is real estate of the company vested in the proper persons under the provisions of the partnership deed. Could any of the partners enter upon the lands, or claim any portion of the real estate for his private purposes? Or if there was a house upon the land, could any two or more of the members enter into the occupation of such house? *I apprehend they clearly could not; they would have no right to step upon the land; their whole interest in the property of the company is with reference to the shares bought, which represent their proportions of the profits.*[142]

*Myers* v. *Perigal* was consistently applied in subsequent cases[143] and it can be said that: '[s]ince the decision in *Myers* v. *Perigal*, the test is not whether

---

[138] Ibid., at 295. *Bligh* v. *Brent* was followed in *Humble* v. *Mitchell* (1839) 11 AD & E 205, *Duncuft* v. *Albrecht* (1841) 12 Sim. 189; *Sparling* v. *Parker* (1846) 9 Beav. 450, *Walker* v. *Milne* (1849) 11 Beav. 507 and *Ashton* v. *Lord Langdale* (1851) 4 De G & Sm. 402 (following *Sparling* v. *Parker* and *Walker* v. *Milne*). In *Watson* v. *Spratley*, *infra*, it was finally established that its principle is equally applicable to companies constituted by deeds of settlement, rather than Acts of Parliament.      [139] (1852) 2 De GM & G 599.
[140] (1854) 10 Ex. 222.      [141] (1852) 2 De GM & G 599.
[142] Ibid., at 620–1; emphasis supplied.
· [143] *Linley* v. *Taylor* (1850) 1 Giff. 67; *Edwards* v. *Hall* (1855) 6 De GM & G 74; *Walker* v. *Bartlett* (1856) 18 CB 844; *Powell* v. *Jessop* (1856) 18 CB 337; *Hayter* v. *Tucker* (1858) 4 K & J 243; *Entwistle* v. *Davis* (1867) LR 4 Eq. 272.

the holder of the shares can in some sense be said to be interested in land, but whether the share is such a share as, under any ordinary state of circumstances, can result to him in the shape of land. In other words, is the right of the shareholder merely a right to call for his share of the profits, and not for a specific part of the land itself?'[144]

*Watson* v. *Spratley*[145] was interesting; the unincorporated company considered in it had features similar to modern unit trusts. It was a mining company conducted on cost book principles. The legal rights in mines were acquired by a purser. The interest in the company was divided into a fixed number of shares, which were taken up by different members who contracted to supply the necessary capital in proportion to their respective shares. Shares were transferred freely by a certificate of sale, addressed by the vendor to the purser and countersigned with an acceptance by the purchaser; on receipt of the certificate the purser would substitute the purchaser for the vendor in the cost book. Sometimes, the shareholder could sign off his name in the cost book and the purser would pay him the value of shares. The purser was the trustee of the grant of mining rights. The plaintiff was a purchaser of shares suing the vendor for failing to complete the sale upon a parol contract.[146] One of the issues was whether the contract was a sale of interests in land within section 4 of the Statute of Frauds. It was held that it was not.

Parke B looked at the intention with regard to the assets. He said:

. . . If the purser of the mine, who had himself the let or grant of the mine, had the mine and the machines and plant vested in him, in trust to employ the machinery in working the mine and making the most profit of it for the benefit of the co-adventurers, who were to share the profit only, such interest was transferable by parol, and might be bargained for by parol.

If he held the mine in trust for himself and the co-adventurers present and future in proportion to their number of shares, then there was a direct trust in the realty, for the right to get the minerals was a real right, and could not be granted without deed, nor a trust in it transferred without note in writing, nor a bargain be made for a share of that direct trust without note in writing. This is clearly a question of fact, and depends on the evidence as to what was the mutual agreement of the parties.[147]

---

[144] Per Page Wood VC, *Entwistle* v. *Davis* (1867) LR 4 Eq. 272 at 275.

[145] (1854) 10 Ex. 222.

[146] Martin B regarded the question as an important one because the practice of the mining share market was not to make any written contract but for each party to make a memorandum on its own book, in manner very similar to the then Stock Exchange. (Ibid, at 234–5.)

[147] Ibid., at 245–6. Alderson B took a similar approach to the issue but he was relying on cases of companies incorporated by statutes. In his view, the principles were the same. The other two judges, Martin B and Platt B, came to the conclusion that the entitlement of the share was in profits, not interest in land. It was not clear if they considered this to be a question of construction. Also, unlike Parke B, both Martin B and Platt B did not regard this to be a question of fact for the jury.

Both *Myers* v. *Perigal* and *Watson* v. *Spratley* were applied in subsequent cases.[148] Applying these two cases to unit trusts, it can be said that there is no intention that the unitholders of a unit trust should enjoy underlying assets both when the trust is a going concern and when it is terminated. At all times it is intended that the unitholders have interests only in the capital and its increase in value. Indeed, a somewhat cynical approach[149] is to say that if the unitholder were to have rights in specific assets, he would have a right to obstruct[150] the well-being of the portfolio as a whole, which is never intended by any of the parties to the transaction, neither the manager, the trustee, nor the unitholders.

3. Moreover, some deeds of offshore unit trusts frequently provide that a unitholder has no interest in specific assets. The following is an example:

Each unit shall entitle the unitholder together with other unitholders of all other units to the beneficial interest in the trust fund as an entirety but subject thereto shall not entitle a unitholder to any particular asset comprised in the trust fund and no unitholder shall be entitled to the transfer to him of any property comprised in the trust fund other than in accordance with the trust deed.

It is submitted that this type of provision is merely declaratory in nature. In any event, it supplies the express intention that judges in *Myers* v. *Perigal* and *Watson* v. *Spratley* looked for—the intention that each unit only confers the net value. Unfortunately, when this clause was considered in *Costa and Duppe Properties Pty. Ltd.* v. *Duppe*,[151] Brooking J took the view that the meaning of this clause was that no unitholder can claim the

---

[148] *Linley* v. *Taylor* (1850) 1 Giff. 67; *Edwards* v. *Hall* (1855) 6 De GM & G 74; *Walker* v. *Bartlett* (1856) 18 CB 844; *Powell* v. *Jessop* (1856) 18 CB 337; *Hayter* v. *Tucker* (1858) 4 K & J 243; *Entwistle* v. *Davis* (1867) LR 4 Eq. 272. The same kind of reasoning was not limited to deed of settlement companies. In an earlier case, *March* v. *The Attorney General* (1842) 5 Beav. 433, it was held that policies of assurances by which the directors or trustees of insurance companies engage 'to pay out of the funds' or 'that the funds shall be liable' or 'that a share of the funds shall be paid' did not entitle policyholders to underlying assets and accordingly the Statute of Mortmain did not apply. This is a strong case as in one of the policies the policyholder was expressly admitted to be a member of the insurance society and another policy consisted of covenants by two trustees that they, upon the payments becoming due, would pay out of the stock or fund of the society unto the executors of the assured the full sum assured.

[149] According to Stoljar, *Groups and Entities: An Inquiry into Corporate Theory*, Australian National University Press, Canberra, 1973, pp. 84–5, the rule that a partnership share is personalty is to obviate the opportunity of heirs of a deceased partner to obstruct the business which other partners may wish to carry on. *A fortiori*, in groups such as joint stock companies and unit trusts where there is no question of mutual confidence, the right of obstruction should not exist. However, the learned author's rationale does not appear to be based on judicial precedents. The two cases quoted, *Thornton* v. *Dixon* (1791) 3 Bro. CC 199 and *Balmain* v. *Shore* (1808) 9 Ves. 500, do not seem to go as far.

[150] e.g., by registering a caveat, as in *Costa and Duppe Properties Pty. Ltd.* v. *Duppe*, *supra*.        [151] [1986] VR 90; discussed in s. 2B, *ante*.

appropriation of any particular asset[152] and the position to be the same even when this clause was not in the deed.

It is submitted that *Costa and Duppe* was wrongly decided in this regard. The interpretation offered only gives effect to the provision that '. . . no unitholder shall be entitled to the transfer to him of any property . . .'. It renders the part '. . . shall not entitle a unitholder to any particular asset comprised in the trust fund . . .' meaningless. There seems no question that the literal meaning of this part is that a unitholder has no right whatever in any specific part of the trust fund. The underlying intention is, as in *Watson* v. *Spratley* type of cases, to give a unitholder a right to call for his share of the gain and the return of his capital in accordance with the trust deed.[153] Brooking J did not explain why an express part of a clause should be denied of its effect. His Honour was under the misapprehension that the situation before him fell squarely within the matrix of *Charles*,[154] a decision which was binding upon him. Indeed, his Honour did not analyse the reach of the cases of *Baker* and *Charles* at all and also did not explain why they should be extended to a conflict of claims between beneficiaries to the trust. For him, '[i]f there is a proprietary interest in the entirety, there must be a proprietary interest in each of the assets of which the entirety is composed'.[155] Perhaps, his Honour was concerned to find the equitable owners of individual unit trust assets. As explained later,[156] this is an untenable doctrinal position.

4. A unit is an object of ownership. It is a *res*, a thing to be owned, mortgaged, disposed of by sale, gift or will. The trust deed intends a unit to be dealt with as an item of property and only to be transferred in the manner laid down in the deed. In general, a transfer in a unit trust contemplates a novation whereby the transferee is substituted for the transferor. The stipulated transfer excludes other means of disposal and is operative irrespective of the nature of the underlying assets.[157]

5. For units sold on the Stock Exchange, it is self-evident that it is the unit as an object of ownership which is being realized. Unit trusts not listed on the Stock Exchange invariably provide for the manner in which the net value of the unit can be ascertained and realized. The process may not involve the realization of underlying assets. Again, it is the unit, as an object of ownership, which is realized. As a going concern, an open-ended trust, such as an authorized unit trust, invariably provides a mechanism for

---

[152] See s. 2B, *ante*.
[153] Cf. the test of Page Wood VC in *Entwistle* v. *Davis* (1867) LR 4 Eq. 272 at 275, text accompanying fn. 144, *supra*.
[154] (1954) 90 CLR 598, discussed in s. 2B, *ante*.
[155] [1986] VR 90 at 96.                                    [156] S. 2C(6), *post*.
[157] This is discussed in s. 4B of this ch., *post*.

redemption.[158] This involves the contractual consent[159] of all parties to methods of valuation for different assets, timing of valuation, and calculation of the price of redemption. It also involves the agreement of the manager to buy units and, in the case when the manager requests the trustee to cancel the relevant units, the agreement of the trustee to pay out of the trust fund or to sell underlying assets. Beneficiaries have impliedly agreed to use the redemption methods in the unit trust deed or the regulations as means of realization to the exclusion of the method prescribed by ordinary trust principles.

Two aspects serve to demonstrate the point that it is the value of units as distinct items of properties that is being realized in the redemption process. For an authorized unit trust, it is the manager's obligation to redeem units. If the manager does not proceed to instruct the trustee to cancel the units 'redeemed' from a unitholder, those units may continue to exist; the trust fund remains intact. Ordinarily, unitholders are paid the value of the units according to the formula which includes the manager's charges for redemption; no assets will be transferred.

This forms a clear contrast with the position of a beneficiary who is *sui juris* and who has an absolutely vested interest in a share of a trust fund. His position is one of realization of underlying assets, whether in terms of value, timing or right. Such a beneficiary is entitled to have transferred to him an aliquot share of each and every asset of the trust fund. This presents no difficulty so far as division is concerned with assets such as cash, money at bank or stock exchange securities. As regards land and other assets not readily realizable[160] the beneficiary cannot insist on an aliquot share and must wait until the assets are sold before he can call on the trustee as of right to account to him for his share of the assets.[161]

Regulation 4.28 of the Financial Services (Regulated Schemes) Regulations 1991 provides for *in specie* redemption of units in an authorized unit trust in certain circumstances. However, it does not alter the basic position that it is the value of units that is being realized in redemption. By paragraph 1 of this regulation, it applies where:

---

[158] Redemption is discussed in s. 4A, *post*.

[159] For the analysis that all unitholders are in contractual relationships, see ch. 2, s. 2B(5), *ante*.

[160] *Re Weiner's Will Trusts* [1956] 2 All ER 482; *Lloyds Bank plc* v. *Duker* [1987] 3 All ER 193 (private company shares); *Re Marshall* [1914] 1 Ch. 192 at 199 (mortgage debt).

[161] *Stephenson (Inspector of Taxes)* v. *Barclays Bank Trust Co. Ltd.* [1975] 1 All ER 625 at 637–8, per Walton J where he regarded these as 'elementary propositions'. In *Lloyds Bank plc* v. *Duker*, ibid., the court ordered majority shareholding of a private company to be sold rather than allocating a proportionate fraction to a beneficiary as such shareholding would be worth more when it is sold.

(a) a participant requests redemption of a number of units representing in value not less than 5% (or any lower percentage stated in the trust deed) of the value of the scheme as a whole, and
(b) transfer to that participant of property of the scheme, instead of the proceeds of redemption, is either
 (i) chosen by the manager by his serving a notice of election on the participant, or
(ii) requested by the participant (in a case where he is permitted to do so by the terms of the trust deed) at the same time as his request at a.

Paragraph 4 provides that where there is to be a transfer of property,[162] whether by election or request, the trustee must cancel the units and transfer to the participant his proportionate share of the property of the scheme. The term 'proportionate share' is defined in paragraph 5 to mean:

(a) such part of each description of asset in the property of the scheme as is proportionate to or as nearly as practicable proportionate to the participant's share, or
(b) such selection from the property of the scheme as the trustee shall, after consultation with the manager, decide is reasonable
having regard to the need to be fair both to the participant and to continuing participants.

The contractual nature of this provision needs no elaboration. The intention is for this provision to apply to large deals (5 per cent or any lower rate as provided by the trust deed) primarily to save the trouble of the manager having to redeem from unitholders and to instruct the trustee to cancel those units who most likely may have to sell some assets. It does not apply to every unitholder. It is a mutual agreement giving an option to the unitholder[163] of substantial unitholding and also to the manager receiving a redemption request from this unitholder. This provision does not preclude redemption being effected as in ordinary cases.

The formula for 'proportionate share' of assets to be transferred is different from the aliquot share that would be transferred to a beneficiary of a private trust. As a private trust is a means of disposition used by a settlor, usually, the trust portfolio does not comprise liability. In the case of a unit trust, a unitholder's interest is a pro rata interest in the difference in value between assets and liabilities.[164] Since distribution of the portfolio assets is not the aim of the trust and since the portfolio is a pool of capital to generate gain, proportionate distribution of assets may not be in the best interest of continuing unitholders.[165] This is particularly true of property

---

[162] If it is the manager's election to invoke the provision of this regulation, the participant is given the right to require the manager to sell the assets that would be transferred by the trustee and to pay the proceeds to the participant: reg. 4.28.3.
[163] If the unit trust deed so provides: see para. 1 cited.
[164] S. 1A of this ch., *ante*.                    [165] Cf. *Lloyds Bank plc* v. *Duker, supra*.

funds, futures and options funds, geared futures and options funds that may be authorized. The implementation of either limb of paragraph 5 by the trustee is most likely to result in the redeeming unitholder being allocated something very different than if the trust were a private trust.

It can therefore be said that a unit in a cash fund trust confers only an interest in the net value of the trust fund calculated and realizable in a stipulated manner.

## (6) Assets without Equitable Owners?

If the trust fund is not to be looked at as assets held for beneficiaries, each item of property in the unit trust will have no equitable owner. Is this possible? Dicta in the Full Court of Victoria in *New Zealand Insurance Co. Ltd.*[166] are against this possibility. Winneke CJ and Menhennitt J said in their joint judgment:

The principles applicable to a fully administered estate are, in our opinion, those enunciated in *Baker* v. *Archer-Shee*[167] . . . as reaffirmed in *Archer-Shee* v. *Garland*.[168] It is established by those cases, we think, that, once an estate is fully administered so that a trust fund consisting of the assets of the estate comes into existence, a beneficial interest or interests in each and all of the assets constituting the trust fund must be in some beneficiary or beneficiaries, whether it be absolutely or in remainder or liable to be divested or contingently.[169]

The sentiment of Brooking J in *Costa and Duppe* was also the same.[170] An answer to this is that it is a fallacy that at every moment of time the law requires the separate existence of two different kinds of estate or interest in property, the legal and the equitable. The common law and equity are not two separate systems of law, one recognizing a legal owner and the other recognizing an equitable owner. Equity is not a 'complete' system; it only complements the common law. It does not say that the beneficiary is the owner of trust properties; it says that the trustee is the owner of those properties, but adds that he is bound to hold them for the benefit of the beneficiary.[171] An absolute owner does not hold two estates, a legal estate and an equitable estate.[172] When a trust beneficiary, who is fully entitled to

---

[166] [1973] VR 659.      [167] [1927] AC 844.      [168] [1931] AC 212.

[169] [1973] VR 659 at 664. They approved of Sir William Grant's view that '[t]he equitable interest in that estate must have resided somewhere: the trustees themselves could not be the beneficial owners; and if they were mere trustees, there must have been some cestui que trust'. *Pearson* v. *Lane* (1809) 17 Ves. 101 at 104. Smith J's dictum was to the same effect (at 669–70).

[170] According to Brooking J, all unitholders own the whole of the trust fund and the logic must be that they own each and every asset: see text accompanying fn. 84.

[171] Maitland, *Equity: a Course of Lectures*, 2nd edn. by Brunyate, Cambridge UP, 1936, p. 17.

[172] Thus, a man cannot be a trustee for himself: *Goodright* v. *Wells* (1781) 2 Doug. KB 771.

a trust property, acquires the legal estate of the property, his equitable interest merges into the legal estate.[173] He is a legal owner with all legal rights; there are no equitable rights vested in him. The truth is that equity in fact calls into existence and protects equitable rights and interests only where their recognition has been found to be required in order to give effect to its doctrines.[174] Thus, the objects of discretionary trusts have no interest in the trust funds[175] but this fact does not preclude them from seeking equitable remedies when trustees refuse to properly exercise their discretion to consider all objects of the trusts.

## (7) Units as Personal Property

The conclusion of this analysis is that units of trusts operating under cash fund principle are interests in money and therefore are personal property. The end result is arrived at not by participating in the *in rem-in personam* debate and classifying the unitholder's interest as a right *in personam* but by looking at the reality of rights conferred on units. Those rights comprise not only interests in the trust fund but also a bundle of other rights as a result of the interaction of trust and contract. So far as that part of the rights relating to the trust fund is concerned, the right is represented by money.

### 3. A UNIT AS A BUNDLE OF RIGHTS (THE SECOND PROPOSITION)

The second proposition describes the composition of rights comprised in a unit. In broad terms, rights of a unit can be analysed in terms of interests in the trust fund (which have already been discussed), rights of parties *inter se*, rights against third parties, and statutory rights.

## A. Rights of Parties *Inter Se*

The essence of the unit trust deed is the provision of a trust of assets and a deed of covenants amongst the parties.[176] As suggested in the foregoing chapters, three consequences follow:

---

[173] *Fung Ping Shan* v. *Tong Shun* [1918] AC 403. In a similar vein, when an assignment or transfer has been executed in favour of a purchaser, the purchaser's equitable interest under the contract merges with the assignment or transfer.

[174] Per Viscount Radcliffe, *CSD (Qld.)* v. *Livingston* [1965] AC 694 at 712. See also *DKLR Holding Co. (No. 2) Pty. Ltd.* v. *CSD* [1980] 1 NSWLR 510 at 519–20 per Hope JA and *Re Transphere Pty. Ltd.* (1986) 10 ACLR 776.

[175] *Gartside* v. *IRC* [1968] AC 553.

[176] Which may incorporate legislative provisions as part of the terms of the deed: see ch. 2, s. 2A(2), *ante*.

(1) The combination of the trust and the contract gives rise to rights conferred by the body of law derived from the use of the trust in family dispositions as well as contractual rights. These two distinct sources give rise to distinct rights.[177]

(2) Principles developed around private trusts may not be appropriate to commercial circumstances. The contract is the tool to alter trust principles in their application to a particular unit trust.[178] Some alterations are results of necessity from the structural split of trusteeship[179] between the trustee and the manager. Thus, the right to due administration of the trust has assumed a new character by reason of the fact that investment decisions are now in the hand of the manager, rather than the trustee. Some alterations cater for the commercial objectives of particular unit trusts. For example, income which is to be distributed may be added to the principal.[180] They are in the nature of contractual rights.

(3) Unit trusts are ongoing vehicles of collective investment. Their ongoing character necessitates provisions for adjustment of rights according to new circumstances. Thus, through contractual provisions for amendment of trust deeds, rights of particular unitholders are alterable and defeasible by other unitholders acting in unitholders' meetings held in accordance with the trust deed.[181]

## B. Benefits of Third Party Contractual Promises

Third party contractual promises occupy an important position in an investor's assessment of whether to buy units of a particular unit trust. For example, banks or leading financial institutions may provide guarantees of the return of capital for futures and options funds. In some offshore unit trusts, insurance companies may provide insurance benefits. Such rights given by third parties not only distinguish the units from other competing

---

[177] For example, the trust gives unitholders standing to ask the court to exercise its equitable jurisdiction to make a general administration order (*McLean* v. *Burns Philp Trustee Co. Pty. Ltd.* [1985] 2 NSWLR 623 at 633). Contract law enables unitholders to require the manager to redeem units according to valuation provisions. See ch. 2, *ante* and s. 4A of this ch.

[178] For example, when the trust is a going concern, a unitholder cannot require the trustee to sell unit trust assets for equal division. He must redeem his units in accordance with the provision for redemption.                    [179] Ch. 4, s. 1B(2), *ante*.

[180] This is the term of accumulation units.

[181] Ch. 2, s. 2B(5), *ante*. In *Gra-ham Australia Pty. Ltd.* v. *Perpetual Trustees WA Ltd.* (1989) 1 WAR 65 unitholders who submitted requests for redemption before amendments of trust deed but remained unpaid were held by the Full Court of the Supreme Court of Western Australia to be subject to the amendments that defeated accrued rights. Modification of the trust deed of an authorized unit trust is subject to Part 11 of the Financial Services (Regulated Schemes) Regulations 1991.

unit trusts, they also affect the degree of risk which a unitholder is taking.

Other types of third party contracts include those made in the course of execution of investment decisions such as contracts for the services of investment advisers, registrars of units, brokers, custodians, bankers, estate agents, property management agents or auditors, and contracts for the sale or purchase of investment assets. Such contracts may be entered into by the trustee or the manager.

From an analytical viewpoint, third party contractual rights can be classified into four categories:

(a) contractual promises made under a contract between a third party and the trustee (or manager) for the benefit of unitholders. The contract is a contract conferring benefits on non-parties.

(b) contractual promises, made under a contract between a third party and the trustee (or manager), to be held by the trustee (or manager) on trusts for the unitholders severally. These are trusts of contractual promises.

(c) contractual promises made under a contract between a third party and the trustee (or the manager) acting as the trustee (or the manager) of the unit trust.

(d) promises by a third party under a deed poll.

## (1) Category (a): Promises for the Benefit of Non-Contracting Parties

It is a fundamental principle of common law that only parties to a contract are bound by and entitled to enforce its terms. When a contract confers benefit on a third party, the cause of action against the promisor is vested solely in the promisee. The third party cannot sue. He can only sue if he can establish that he is a beneficiary under a trust of that promise or the promisee is merely his agent or the promisor is estopped. Whether the third party can fall within one of the exceptions, the trust exception in particular, is always very blurred. In practice, all alternatives should be pleaded by the third party suing.

A likely example of the category (a) type of contract is a guarantee of the return of capital for participants in a futures and options trust given by a bank or financial institution. Such guarantee is often incorporated in an agreement under which the manager gives an indemnity to the guarantor.[182]

---

[182] The simple reliance on an indemnity is possible where both the manager and the bank are within the same financial conglomerate. There are overseas examples whereby the trustee is joined in to provide security out of the trust fund. For an authorized unit trust, this is prohibited: reg. 5.67 of the Financial Services (Regulated Schemes) Regulations 1991. For the major problems associated with guaranteed unit trusts in the UK, see Securities and Investments Board, *Regulated Collective Investment Schemes: Key Policy Issues* (Discussion Paper) 1993, paras. 5.1–5.12.

In some jurisdictions, there are also examples of master insurance policies being taken out by the manager with an insurer under which unitholders will be automatically insured.[183] Where the relevant banking legislation permits, some trusts that invest in deposits and financial instruments with no risk of loss of capital, contracts may be entered into with banks to provide cheque books and automatic teller machine cards to enable redemption by drawing cheques and withdrawing from automatic teller machines. Possibilities of other contractual arrangements are infinite. All depends on the ingenuity of the person designing the financial products.

As will be seen shortly, it is always open to the court to construe these examples to be cases of the manager holding promises of the third parties on trust for individual unitholders. But the classic position is that a unitholder in such circumstances acquires no right against the third party. Nor can he compel the manager to sue. It is a different question whether the manager may be liable to him for misrepresentation contained in the scheme particulars relating to the issue, a question which is more complicated for a unitholder acquiring by transfer, or transmission on death, from another unitholder.

The manager can sue. As a general principle, the manager can only recover damages to the extent that he suffers damage. This is likely to be nominal for it is the unitholder who has suffered substantial damage. Recent cases have indicated that there is an exception to the general rule and the measure of damages should be based on the full amount suffered by the unitholder.[184] However, the width of this exception is still debatable.[185] What is appropriate is for the manager to ask for an order of

---

[183] e.g., an accidental death insurance and life insurance may be taken out for the benefit of unitholders making certain level of investments.

[184] Lord Pearce in *Beswick* v. *Beswick* [1968] AC 58 at 88 took the view that the damages assessed would be substantial damages of the person for whose benefit the promise was made. Lord Diplock in *Albacruz* v. *Albazero (The Albazero)* [1977] AC 774 at 847 recognized that in a commercial contract concerning goods where it is in the contemplation of the parties that the proprietary interests in the goods may be transferred, an original party, if such be the intention, is treated as having entered into the contract for the benefit of the transferee of goods and is entitled to recover loss suffered by the transferee. Lord Wilberforce in *Woodar Investment Development Ltd.* v. *Wimpey Construction UK Ltd.* [1980] 1 WLR 277 at 283 also recognized the possibility of a contracting party recovering for a member of a group in contracts such as ordering meals in restaurants or family holidays. *The Albazero* was applied in *Linden Garden Trust Ltd.* v. *Lenesta Sludge Disposals Ltd.* [1994] 1 AC 85 and *Darlington BC* v. *Wiltshier Northern Ltd.* [1995] 1 WLR 68. See also *Ruxley Electronics and Construction Ltd.* v. *Forsyth* [1996] 1 AC 344; Wallace, 'Assignment of Rights to Sue: Half a Loaf' (1994) 110 *LQR* 42; Tettenborn, 'Loss, Damage and the Meaning of Assignment' [1994] *CLJ* 53; Berg 'Assignment, Prohibitions and the Right to Recover Damages for Another's Loss' (1994) *JBL* 129; Law Commission, *Privity of Contract: Contracts for the Benefit of Third Parties*, HMSO, 1996.

[185] Law Commission, *Privity of Contract: Contracts for the Benefit of Third Parties*, HMSO, 1996, para. 2.37–2.46.

specific performance on the basis that award of damages is inadequate in the circumstances.[186]

There are a number of statutory exceptions and of some possible relevance is section 11 of the Married Women's Property Act 1882 which provides that a life insurance policy taken out by someone on his or her own life, and expressed to be for the benefit of his or her spouse or children, creates a trust in favour of the objects named in the policy. This section does not apply if the third party beneficiary is someone other than a spouse or child, such as a cohabitee or parent. It applies only to a contract of life insurance taken out by someone on his own life. Consequently, a master policy effected by the manager upon the lives of unitholders will not fall within this description.

Also relevant to the unitholder's right to enforce against the third party is the Australian High Court decision in *Trident General Insurance Co. Ltd.* v. *McNiece Bros. Pty. Ltd.*[187] It is not certain if there is any single principle which English courts may follow.[188] In this case, the insurance company agreed under the policy to indemnify 'the Assured against all sums which the Assured shall become legally liable to pay in respect of . . . bodily injury to . . . any person'. The 'Assured' was defined to include 'all its subsidiary associated and related companies, all contractors and subcontractors and/or suppliers'. The question before the High Court of Australia was whether a contractor, engaged after the policy was effected, can claim as a matter of contract law. The issue of the insured as a trustee of a promise did not arise as leave to amend the pleadings was refused when the appeal was first heard in the New South Wales Court of Appeal. It was held by a majority of 4–3 that the contractor could claim. The joint judgment of Mason CJ and Wilson J upheld the Court of Appeal decision that a person who was not a party to the insurance policy but fell within the class of persons expressed to be insured by the policy was entitled to be indemnified in accordance with the policy. This principle was an exception to the doctrine of privity and the rule that consideration must move from the promisee.[189] Toohey J took the same line of approach but proposed a narrower proposition.[190] In effect, their decisions were a common law

---

[186] *Beswick* v. *Beswick* [1968] AC 58, *Coulls* v. *Bagot's Executor and Trustee Co. Ltd.* (1967) 119 CLR 460; Law Commission, ibid., para. 2.47.

[187] (1988) 80 ALR 574.

[188] There is a hint of its possible acceptance in Lord Goff's judgment in *The Mahkutai* [1996] 3 WLR 1 at 11–12.                                    [189] Ibid., at 575 and 585.

[190] His Honour said: 'When an insurer issues a liability insurance policy, identifying the assured in terms that evidence an intention on the part of both insurer and assured that the policy will indemnify as well those with whom the assured contracts for the purpose of the venture covered by the policy, and it is reasonable to expect that such a contractor may order its affairs by reference to the existence of the policy, the contractor may sue the insurer on the

abrogation of the third party rule in insurance contracts. Gaudron J's decision was a principle of unjust enrichment. To her, as a matter of law and not contract, 'a promisor who has accepted an agreed consideration for a promise to benefit a third party owes an obligation to the third party to fulfil that promise and the third party has a corresponding right to bring action to secure the benefit of the promise'.[191] In effect, the principle of unjust enrichment was extended to protect expectations rather than used to reverse benefits acquired at the expense of the plaintiff.[192] Given the different reasons of the majority decision, it is uncertain as to the future direction of the law in this respect.

Is it possible for the manager to be regarded as the agent of each unitholder? For an agent to make a contract on behalf of a principal, the principal must be ascertainable even though his identity is undisclosed. Mason CJ and Wilson J in *Trident*[193] took a restrictive approach and thought that the insured could not be the agent of the contractor who was not yet engaged at the time of the issue of the insurance policy. However, Lord Reid in *Midland Silicones Ltd.* v. *Scruttons Ltd.*[194] considered that there could exist a contract (in terms of an exemption clause in a bill of lading) between the shipper and the stevedore made through the agency of a carrier if (i) the carrier had authority from the stevedore or the stevedore ratifies and (ii) consideration moving from the stevedore was proved.[195] Lord Reid's statement was subsequently applied in a number of cases beginning with the Privy Council decision of *New Zealand Shipping Co. Ltd.* v. *AM Satterthwaite and Co. Ltd., The Eurymedon.*[196] The analysis of this type of situation is that the bill of lading brings into existence a bargain, initially unilateral but capable of becoming mutual, between the goods owner and the stevedore made through the carrier as its agent. This becomes a full contract when the stevedore has performed services by discharging the goods. The performance of those services was the relevant consideration.[197] The stevedore may not necessarily be known at the time

---

policy, notwithstanding that consideration may not have moved from the contractor to the insurer and notwithstanding that the contractor is not a party to the contract between the insurer and assured.' (Ibid., at 621.)

[191] Ibid., at 624.

[192] Law Commission, *Privity of Contract: Contracts for the Benefit of Third Parties*, HMSO, 1996, p. 38, fn. 186; Soh, 'Privity of Contract and Restitution' (1989) 105 *LQR* 4.

[193] (1988) 80 ALR 574 at 577.                                    [194] [1962] AC 446 at 474.

[195] The other two conditions laid down by his Lordship were that the bill of lading made it clear that the stevedore was intended to be protected by the exemption clause and that the bill of lading made it clear that the carrier intended to contract for itself as well as for the stevedore.

[196] [1975] AC 154; *Port Jackson Stevedoring Pty. Ltd.* v. *Salmond and Spraggon Pty. Ltd.* (1980) 144 CLR 300; *Celthene Pty. Ltd.* v. *WKJ Hauliers Pty. Ltd.* [1981] 1 NSWLR 606; *Life Savers (A'asia) Ltd.* v. *Frigmobie Pty. Ltd.* [1983] 1 NSWLR 431. See Cheshire and Fifoot, pp. 594–6.                                    [197] [1975] AC 154 at 167–8.

of the bill of lading and this does not appear to be relevant.[198] It is not clear if the *Eurymedon* line of cases is to be confined to exemption clauses,[199] though the focuses of the judgments are on privity and consideration. As the editor of the sixteenth edition of *Bowstead and Reynolds on Agency* observes:[200] '. . . since an agent need not always name his principal but may and often does act for a completely unnamed principal (e.g. "bought for our principals"), ratification should be possible in such a case also. If the third party is willing to deal on this basis, he should arguably be bound under the doctrine of ratification just as under the normal principles of authority.' Indeed, the editor is able to point to marine insurance cases that the agent who procures the insurance need not at that moment have in mind any person as an intended principal.[201] Therefore, courts should not be deterred from holding that the master policies and other contracts made by the manager are ratified by individual unitholders at the time when they enter into the contracts for purchase of units with the manager and the performance of those contracts by payment of subscription moneys provides the requisite consideration.[202] A finding of an agency means that individual unitholders are in direct contractual relationships with the relevant parties and can sue without joining the manager.

## (2) Category (b): Contractual Promises Held on Trust for Unitholders

Falling within category (b) are rights of a beneficiary under an ordinary trust, except that the subject matter is the benefit of the promise by the person contracting with the manager or the trustee. If a trust of a promise is established, the trustee (or the manager) can sue as a party to the contract; or if the trustee (or the manager) refuses to sue, unitholders can sue by joining the trustee (or the manager) as a defendant as well.[203] The damages recovered would be the losses suffered by the unitholder, rather

---

[198] This is clear since the New South Wales Court of Appeal decision in *Life Savers (A'asia) Ltd.* v. *Frigmobie Pty. Ltd.* [1983] 1 NSWLR 431.

[199] In these cases, the third party is relying on the exemption clause as a defence and not enforcing a promise made in a contract.

[200] *Bowstead and Reynolds on Agency*, 16th edn., Sweet and Maxwell, 1996, para. 2–063.

[201] *Boston Fruit Co.* v. *British & Foreign Marine Insurance Co.* [1906] AC 336 at 389; *P Samuel & Co. Ltd.* v. *Dumas* [1924] AC 431; *Routh* v. *Thompson* (1811) 13 East 274; *Robinson* v. *Gleadow* (1835) 2 Bing. NC. They are cited at p. 75 fn. 90.

[202] In *The Eurymedon* [1975] AC 154, the stevedore was under a contractual obligation with the carrier to unload the goods and this fact was held not to be a bar for providing the requisite consideration for the promise of the exemption by the goods owner. Thus, the fact that the unitholder is already under an obligation to pay for the units is not relevant.

[203] Joinder of parties is necessary to prevent a double claim against the promisor but since this is for the benefit of the promisor, the promisor can waive (*Les Affreteurs Reunis, SA* v. *Leopold Walford (London) Ltd.* [1919] AC 801).

than the loss of the trustee (or the manager).[204] This is the position even though only the trustee (or the manager) sues and the unitholder, as the beneficiary of the promise, does not sue. In other words, the court will award substantial damages based on the loss of the beneficiary of the promise rather than nominal damages suffered by the trustee of the promise. Common law recognized this manner of assessment long before the fusion of courts of common law and equity.[205] In effect, a common law wrong was enlarged by the presence of an equitable obligation.

In order to establish a trust, an intention to create it must be established. The cases on intention to create a trust of a promise are voluminous and often contradictory.[206] As Treitel has said: 'There is no point in trying to reconcile all these cases. They represent different stages of development and show that the courts became at one stage reluctant to apply the trust device, because, once a trust was held to have been created, the parties to the contract lost their right to rescind or vary that contract by mutual consent.'[207] That stage was reached in the House of Lords decision of *Vanderpitte* v. *Preferred Accident Insurance Corp. of New York*[208] where Lord Wright said the intention to create a trust must be 'affirmatively proved' and 'cannot necessarily be inferred from . . . mere general words' used in the contract.[209] In this case, it was held that a daughter driving with consent of her father cannot sue the insurance company under her father's policy, which was stated to be 'available . . . to any person . . . while . . . legally operating' his car. He was not a trustee for her benefit. The cases show that the court is concerned to maintain a dividing line between the case of a trust and the simple case of a contract made between two persons

---

[204] In *Lloyd's* v. *Harper* (1880) 16 Ch. D 290 at 321, Lush LJ said: 'I considered it to be an established rule of law that where a contract is made with A for the benefit of B, A can sue on the contract for the benefit of B, and recover all that B could have recovered if the contract had been made with B himself.' This was approved by Lord Upjohn in *Beswick* v. *Beswick* [1968] AC 58 at 101. Lush LJ was referring to a contract where A was trustee of the promise: per Windeyer J, *Coulls* v. *Bagot's Executor and Trustee Co. Ltd.* (1967) 119 CLR 460 at 501 and per Mason CJ & Wilson J, *Trident* v. *McNiece Bros. Pty. Ltd.* (1988) 80 ALR 574 at 581. Cf. Lord Denning MR in *Jackson* v. *Horizon Holidays Ltd.* [1975] 3 All ER 92 where this statement was applied to a situation where A was not a trustee of the promise for B. Lord Denning's reasoning in *Jackson* was disapproved in *Woodar Investment Development Ltd.* v. *Wimpey Construction UK Ltd.* [1980] 1 WLR 577. See also *Linden Gardens Trusts* v. *Lenesta Sludge Disposals Ltd.* [1994] AC 85.
[205] The common law cases of *Lamb* v. *Vice* (1840) 6 M & W 467, *Robertson* v. *Wait* (1853) 8 Ex. 299, *Pugh* v. *Stringfield* (1858) 4 CB (NS) 364, and *Stansfeld* v. *Hellawell* (1852) 7 Ex. 373 awarded substantial damages based on the loss of the beneficiaries of the promise rather than nominal damages suffered by the trustee: Greig and Davis, p. 1026.
[206] Cheshire and Fifoot, pp. 607–8, have attempted to illustrate 'the melancholy unpredictability of the recourse to the trust principle in third party benefit contracts' by a tabulation of seven categories of situations where both decisions importing and negativing the trust can be found.
[207] Treitel, *The Law of Contract*, 9th edn., Sweet and Maxwell/Stevens, 1991, p. 579.
[208] [1933] AC 70.                                                        [209] Ibid., at 80.

for the benefit of a third party.[210] Unless an intention to create a trust is clearly to be collected from the language used and the circumstances of the case the court will not be astute to discover indications of such an intention.[211]

In Australia, a swing in the pendulum of judicial thinking back to the relaxed view of equity[212] before *Vanderpitte* began with the judgments of Rogers J in the *Ipec* litigation.[213] It is not certain whether the same type of swing will occur in English decisions.[214] In *Home Insurance Co.* v. *Ipec Holdings Ltd.*,[215] a parent company guaranteed the liability of its subsidiary in the London reinsurance market under a guarantee executed in favour of another broker in the market. The question was whether the principal of the broker could sue under the guarantee. Rogers J held that commercial necessity demanded that a trust be imputed.[216]

In *Eslea Holdings Ltd. (formerly Ipec Holdings Ltd.)* v. *Butts*,[217] the additional issue was whether the principals of companies of the same group as the broker could enforce the guarantee. There was evidence that all parties acted as if the guarantee covered the whole group. Rogers J decided in favour of the principals of the group on the basis of estoppel but not on the ground of trust. The Court of Appeal upheld the estoppel ground. Samuels JA, with whom Kirby P agreed, held in addition that a trust also existed in favour of all principals of the whole group. He was

---

[210] *Re Schebsman* [1944] Ch. 83 at 84, per Lord Greene MR.

[211] Ibid., at 104, per du Parcq LJ.

[212] This statement was borrowed from the extrajudicial comments of Rogers J in 'Contracts and Third Parties' in Finn, *Essays on Contract*, Law Book Co., 1987, ch. 3 at p. 86, where he was referring to an appeal against his Honour's own decision, *Eslea Holdings Ltd.* v. *Butts* (1986) 6 NSWLR 175. The credit of this judicial swing should be attributed to him rather than the Court of Appeal.

[213] *Home Insurance Co.* v. *Ipec Holdings Ltd.*, Rogers J, Supreme Court of NSW, 25 Nov. 1983, unreported, extensively discussed in Greig and Davis, *The Law of Contract*, Law Book Co., 1987, pp. 1027, 1029–30; *Oakeley Vaughan and Co. Ltd.* v. *Ipec Holdings Ltd.*, Rogers J, 22 Mar. 1984, unreported; *Eslea Holdings Ltd. (formerly Ipec Holdings Ltd.)* v. *Butts* (1986) 6 NSWLR 175, an appeal from Rogers J to the Court of Appeal.

[214] See *Darlington BC* v. *Wiltshier (Northern) Ltd.* [1995] 1 WLR 68 at 75.

[215] Unreported, ibid.

[216] He said: 'The guarantee was not required by the brokers for their own protection. . . . The only entity intended to be secured and therefore benefited by the [parent's] guarantee was [the broker's principal]. The only way that it was commercially sound to proceed, in order to ensure the security of the various principals for whom the brokers might from time to time be agents, was to obtain a guarantee in the form actually given. The one instrument of guarantee enured for the benefit, and to the extent required, of those who, from time to time, became the principals of the broker and entered into contractual relations with [the subsidiary] on the security of this guarantee. The only unarguably sound legal basis on which they could give effect to all the foregoing commercial needs and pressures, as well as the common intention of the parties, was for the brokers to hold the guarantee on trust . . .'— quoted in Greig and Davis, *supra*, at 1029.

[217] (1986) 6 NSWLR 175.

extending Rogers J's 'commercial necessity' a step further. He reasoned as follows:

Commercial necessity is relevant because it goes to support the existence of the intention requisite for the constitution of the trust: see *Re Schebsman*.[218] In the present case it is clear that both . . . were aware that [the group companies of the broker] were introducing business to [the subsidiary] and all involved did so only on the footing that [the subsidiary] was good for its engagements solely by reason of the [parent] guarantees. It is, of course, the intention of the promisee . . . which is critical: *Re Webb*,[219] although the rule may well depend upon the nature of the transaction from which the trust is said to arise. . . . In my view the necessary intention—and bearing in mind the warning of du Parcq LJ in *Re Schebsman*[220]— was made out . . .'[221]

This approach has the support of Mason CJ and Wilson J in their joint judgment in *Trident* v. *McNiece Bros. Pty. Ltd.*[222] They suggested that:

the courts will recognise the existence of a trust when it appears from the language of the parties, construed in its context, including the matrix of circumstances, that the parties so intended. We are speaking of express trusts, the existence of which depends on intention. In divining intention from the language which the parties have employed the courts may look to the nature of the transaction and the circumstances, including commercial necessity, in order to infer or impute intention. See *Eslea Holdings Ltd.* v. *Butts*.

Moreover, Deane J, though dissenting on the point of the privity exception, was prepared to decide on the basis of a trust of a promise and to stand down the case pending amendment of the pleadings.

Given this state of the law, it is possible to argue that the master policies and contracts entered into by the manager as part of the unit trust arrangement can be analysed in terms of trust after *Eslea Holdings Ltd.* and *Trident*. But an argument is not enough to satisfy the demands of commercial reality. There is no reason why a draftsman should not make express the intention of trust in the relevant document.[223] There are good grounds for joining the trustee of the unit trust in the contract, to be a promisee holding the promises in trust for all unitholders.

What then is the subject matter of this trust of promises? All depends on the nature of rights underlying the promises. If the promise is the grant of a right to use a bank's facilities such as automatic teller machines and current

---

[218] [1944] Ch. 83 at 104.
[219] [1941] Ch. 225 at 234.
[220] See text accompanying fn. 211, *supra*.
[221] (1986) 6 NSWLR 175 at 189.
[222] (1988) 80 ALR 574 at 583.
[223] The use of the word 'trust' or 'trustee' suffices: see *Fletcher* v. *Fletcher* (1844) 4 Hare 67 and *Bowskill* v. *Dawson* [1955] 1 QB 13.

accounts, it is a benefit of a contract, which is a chose in action. There is no doubt that a chose in action can be the subject matter of a trust.[224]

Doubt, however, can arise in relation to guarantees and insurance policies. Yeldham J, for example, has questioned whether the benefit of a guarantee, at a time when no money is owing and when it is uncertain whether any would become owing in the future, is a future chose in action.[225] The so-called income guarantee or capital return guarantee is in fact not a guarantee in the legal sense. A guarantee is by definition an accessory contract to cover any default of a principal debtor. Nothing of this nature is intended in the guarantees used in unit trusts. The guarantor is promising to pay, in the case of an income guarantee, a sum being the difference between the actual and expected income return and the loss suffered in the case of a capital return guarantee. There is, in the normal course of events, no breach on the part of the manager or the trustee in investing the money under the guarantees. These guarantees are indemnities in the nature of insurance. However, the point raised by Yeldham J is still relevant as the obligation to pay is to happen at a future date specified in the guarantee but that obligation may never arise. The answer perhaps is that the promise to pay a sum to be ascertained upon future eventuality is a present promise.[226] As it is a term of the contract, it is a chose in action in respect of which consideration has been given. It is property of value, which is represented by the premium or guarantee fee charged by the insurance company or the guarantor. Moreover, courts have long accepted guarantees and insurance policies[227] as choses in action capable of being subject matters of trusts.

---

[224] 'The scope of the trusts recognised in equity is unlimited. There can be a trust of a chattel or of a chose in action or of a right or obligation under an ordinary legal contract; just as much as a trust of land.' *Lord Strathcona SS Co. Ltd.* v. *Dominion Coal Co. Ltd.* [1926] AC 108 at 124, per Lord Shaw; *Underhill and Hayton*, p. 160.

[225] *Sacher Investments Pty. Ltd.* v. *Forma Stereo Consultants Pty. Ltd.* [1976] 1 NSWLR 5 at 10 where he invited the parties to argue on this point in relation to the question of enforceability by an assignee of the reversion from the landlord of a guarantee of rental payment by the tenant. His invitation was not accepted. See also *Re Cook's Settlement Trusts* [1965] Ch. 902 and Lee, 'The Public Policy of Re Cook's Settlement Trusts' (1969) 85 *LQR* 213.

[226] *Hanbury and Martin*, p. 127. According to this view, the trust *res* is the promise, not the property which will be obtained by its performance. This is clearly supportable by cases quoted in the next footnote. The real doctrinal issue, perhaps, lies in the nature of the 'property which will be obtained by its performance' through enforcement, which is the heart of any right of action. As Rickett has argued, the right is a right or liberty to go to court and remedies, whether damages or an order for specific performance, are given because of a rule of law, not because of the contractual promise which has come to end upon breach. Consequently, if damages awarded are held on trust, that trust will be one imposed by the court, a constructive trust: 'The Constitution of Trusts: Contracts to Create Trusts' (1979) *Current Legal Problems* 1 at 8–9; 'Two Propositions in the Constitution of Trusts' (1981) *Current Legal Problems* 189 at 192–4.

[227] *Lloyd's* v. *Harper* (1880) 16 Ch. D 290 (insurance policy); *Metcalf* v. *Bruin* (810) 12 East 400 (guarantee).

### (3) Category (c): Contractual Promises Made to the Trustee (or the Manager) as a Trustee (or a Manager)

A distinction has to be made between the above type of promise and promises in contracts made by the trustee or the manager in the execution of the terms of the unit trust deeds—i.e., category (c) above mentioned. The trustee may execute the manager's investment decision and enter into leases with tenants. It may enter into contracts for acquisition and disposal of trust properties. Promises made in these types of contracts by other parties are choses in action. Of course, such choses in action form part of the trust corpus. A unitholder has no right of administration of the trust assets of the unit trust.[228] The trustee as the owner of such choses is a proper person to sue without joining the unitholders.[229] Whether these promises should be enforced is a question of the discretions and powers of the trustee. Except where breaches of trusts or fiduciary duties are involved, an individual unitholder cannot enforce the promises. The point here is that the trust in the unit trust is a single trust and the rights that a unitholder has are as one of the beneficiaries. In the case of promises in insurance policies or guarantees, the promises are made to individual unitholders severally. Thus, if a unitholder's estate is entitled to claim under a master life insurance policy, the benefits belong to the estate and not the unit trust. Similarly, if a bank guarantees the return of capital of a unitholder, it guarantees that his capital will be returned, not that the money will be paid into the trust corpus of the unit trust. The importance of this point is particularly clear where the trust is an open-ended trust where unitholders may join at different levels of unit prices. Thus, the benefits of these types of contracts are held on trusts for unitholders severally.

It follows that insofar as benefits of third party contracts are conferred on units severally, a unit confers rights beyond the trust corpus.

### (4) Category (d): Deed Poll

The position that rights of unitholders under guarantees are separate is even clearer if the guarantee is in the form of a deed poll. There are instances where guarantees for return of capital in the form of deed polls have been used. If the deed is an *inter partes* deed, the privity rule

---

[228] Ch. 3, s. 1D(2)(b), *ante*.

[229] In *Murphy* v. *Lew* (1994) 13 ACSR 10 it was held (*inter alia*) that actions by trustees against third parties for breach of contract or in tort would form the trust property available to successors in office of the trustee. See also *Harrison* v. *Tew*, *The Times*, 30 Nov. 1988.

applies.[230] The position is different with a deed poll.[231] It is well established that a person for whose benefit a covenant in a deed poll is expressed to be made, at any rate if sufficiently named by reference, can sue on it.[232] However, it has been suggested that the right of persons who are not existent at the date of the deed to sue is not entirely clear.[233] It is submitted that the very nature of a deed poll is that a person uses it to express his intention addressed to the public at large and the court gives effect to what is expressed in it. The real question always is whether the person suing falls within the class to be benefited by the express intention.[234]

It is a question of construction whether a deed of guarantee is a bilateral deed or a deed poll.[235] Factors which will indicate that the deed is not *inter partes* are the absence of a clause at the beginning of the deed referring to the parties to the deed and the fact that the deed is expressed in the first person.[236]

## C. Statutory Rights of Unitholders

In the case of a non-authorized unit trust and an offshore trust, rights of unitholders are determined by the unit trust deed. The Financial Services

---

[230] *Norton on Deeds*, 2nd edn. by Morrison and Goolden, Sweet and Maxwell, 1928, (1981 reprint by Gaunt & Sons, Florida), p. 28.

[231] See generally, *Norton, supra*, pp. 28 *et seq*; Bullen, 'The Rights of Strangers to Contracts under Seal' (1977–1978) 6 *Adelaide LR* 119 and *Halsbury's Laws of England*, 4th edn., Vol. 12, 1975, para. 1303.

[232] *Sunderland Marine Insurance Co.* v. *Kearney* (1851) 16 QB 923 at 938; *Moss* v. *Legal and General Life Assurance Society of Australia* (1851) 1 VLR 315; *Re A and K Holdings Pty. Ltd.* [1964] VR 257 at 261; *Norton, supra*, pp. 28–9.

[233] *Re A and K Holdings Pty. Ltd.* [1964] VR 257 at 262, per Sholl J. In the instant case before him, the guarantee by way of deed poll was 'a continuing guarantee, and shall be enforceable by every unsecured creditor . . .'. He did not find it necessary to rule whether the deed covers unsecured creditors existent after the guarantee has been made because no demand in the form required has been made. There is a problem whether transferees of existing unitholders can have the benefit of the guarantee. In *Consolidated Trust Co. Ltd.* v. *Naylor* (1936) 55 CLR 423, the High Court of Australia held that the benefit of a guarantee incorporated in a mortgage did not pass with an assignment of a mortgage. An express assignment of the benefit of the guarantee is necessary. (Note that the view expressed in *Consolidated Trust* on whether a guarantee touches and concerns the land must be read subject to *P and A Swift Investment* v. *Combined English Stores Group plc* [1988] 2 All ER 885 and *Lang* v. *Asemo* Pty. Ltd. [1989] VR 773. These cases should not affect a guarantee in respect of choses in action such as shares and units.)

[234] It is clear from the cases such as *Sunderland Marine Insurance Co.* v. *Kearney, supra*, *Moss* v. *Legal and General Life Assurance Society of Australia, supra*, and *Chelsea & Walham Green Building Society* v. *Armstrong* [1951] Ch. D 853 that the court regards entitlement to sue as a question of construction.

[235] *Chelsea & Walham Green Building Society* v. *Armstrong*, ibid.; *Re A and K Holdings Pty. Ltd.*, ibid.

[236] *Chelsea & Walham Green Building Society* v. *Armstrong* [1951] Ch. D 853 at 857.

(Regulated Schemes) Regulations 1991 do not regulate the content of such a trust deed, though it may regulate the provision of scheme particulars.

For an authorized unit trust, the position is more complicated. As noted in chapter 2, the rights and obligations of the parties are governed by a hierarchy of statute, regulations, trust deed, and scheme particulars. The provisions of the Financial Services (Regulated Schemes) Regulations 1991, which are primarily made under section 81, are particularly important as they cover almost every aspect of the operation of a unit trust.

Section 81 of the Financial Services Act 1986 provides that regulations made under this section are 'binding on the manager, trustee and participants independently of the contents of the deed and, in the case of the participants, shall have effect as if contained in it.'[237] As between unitholders, the regulations are to be considered as part of the terms of the trust deed and are enforceable as such.

As between a unitholder and the manager or the trustee, if the terms of the Regulations have been incorporated into the trust deed, which often is the case, again, the terms of the Regulations are enforceable just like any other terms of the deed. But it is not mandatory for a trust deed to incorporate the Regulations expressly. If they are not so incorporated, there is a question of how a unitholder can enforce the terms that are 'binding . . . independently of the contents of the deed'. Logically, one would expect the legislation to provide for the right of enforcement by the unitholders. Otherwise, unitholders cannot enforce the terms of the provisions against the manager or the trustee and this scenario would be worse than that under the 1958 Act.[238] Unfortunately, the Act does not provide a straightforward answer.

The Financial Services Act provision that gives rights to investors to sue for contravention of the Act and the regulations is section 62. This is the section which a unitholder of an authorized unit trust has to invoke if the terms of the Regulations are to be enforced against the manager or the trustee. This section does not have a happy history. Because of the potential floodgate of civil liability for market players that this section could generate, it was met with resistance.[239] The response of the Government and the regulator was one of sympathy and it was diluted subsequently through amendments in the main Act and subsidiary

---

[237] S. 81(3) of the Financial Services Act 1986.

[238] Prevention of Fraud (Investments) Act 1958: see ch. 1, s. 4C, *ante*.

[239] It was said that s. 62 would be 'a lawyer's paradise': *Financial Times*, 29 Sept. 1987, cited in Posner, *International Securities Regulation: London's 'Big Bang' and the European Securities Markets*, Little Brown & Co., 1991, p. 294.

legislation.[240] One incidental and perhaps unintended result is that in order to determine the right to sue for breach of the Financial Services (Regulated Schemes) Regulations 1991—which were intended to be the statutory substitute of the trust deed—it is necessary to meander through a maze of legislative provisions. For this purpose a distinction has to be drawn between private investors and non-private investors.

## (1) Application of Section 62 to Unit Trusts

Section 62(1) provides that:

. . . a contravention of—
(a) any rules or regulations made under this Chapter [V];[241]
(b) any conditions imposed under section 50[242] above;
(c) any requirements imposed by an order under section 58(3)[243] above;
(d) the duty imposed by section 59(6)[244] above;
shall be actionable at the suit of a person who suffers loss as a result of the contravention subject to the defences and other incidents applying to actions for breach of statutory duty.

By subsection (2), section 62(1) is extended to:

a contravention by a member of a recognised self-regulating organisation . . . of any rules of the organisation . . . relating to a matter in respect of which rules or regulations have been or could be made under this Chapter in relation to an authorised person who is not such a member . . .

On the face of it, section 62 cannot apply to any breach of the Financial Services (Regulated Schemes) Regulations 1991 because these regulations are not made under Chapter V. The principal provisions of these Regulations govern authorized unit trusts. The source of authority is derived from section 81 of Chapter VIII. A small portion of provisions

---

[240] Initially, the Government suspended the operation of s. 62. This was followed by the Securities and Investments Board proposing to amend the business conduct rules to provide a defence against a professional, business or experienced investor if a firm can show it has taken all reasonable steps to comply with the rules. Finally, the Government enacted s. 132(1) of the Companies Act 1989 which introduced the new s. 62A, discussed below: Posner, ibid., pp. 293 *et seq.*

[241] This Chapter empowers the Securities and Investments Board to regulate the conduct of business, market making, investment advertisement, appointed representatives, financial resources, reporting requirements, indemnification, compensation fund, and clients' money.

[242] This section deals with the modification of business and financial resources rules for particular cases.

[243] This subsection gives the power to the Treasury to give exemption from restrictions on advertising.

[244] The duty imposed by this subsection is on an authorized person and an appointed representative to take reasonable care not to employ or continue to employ a person in contravention of a disqualification direction.

relate to recognized collective investment schemes and they are also derived from Chapter VIII of the principal Act. The regulations are made by the Securities and Investments Board by virtue of the power delegated to it by the Treasury—which in turn had its powers transferred from the Secretary of State. Accordingly, subsection (1) does not apply. As the Regulations are not rules of a self-regulating organization, they are not covered by subsection (2) either.

The application of section 62 to unit trusts is by virtue of section 95 which provides:

A person who contravenes any provision of this Chapter [VIII], a manager or trustee of an authorised unit trust scheme who contravenes any regulations made under section 81 above and a person who contravenes any other regulations made under this Chapter shall be treated as having contravened rules made under Chapter V . . . or, in the case of a person who is an authorised person by virtue of his membership of a recognised self-regulating organisation . . . the rules of that organisation . . .

It is a requirement for authorization of a unit trust that a manager or a trustee must be an authorized person.[245] If the manager or the trustee is in breach of the Financial Services (Regulated Schemes) Regulations 1991, then under this section 95, it shall be treated as having contravened the rules of the self-regulating organization to which the manager or the trustee belongs. By virtue of this deeming provision, section 62(2) applies. Consequently, a unitholder may bring an action against the manager or the trustee under section 62(1). The manager or the trustee may suffer the additional sanction given by the relevant self-regulating organization, including expulsion which may cause it to lose the status of an authorized person.

Offshore unit trusts recognized under the Financial Services Act 1986,[246] are governed by two parts of the Financial Services (Regulated Schemes) Regulations 1991 that are not derived from section 81.[247] If the manager or the trustee of such unit trust scheme is in breach of these Regulations, it is caught by section 95 as 'a person who contravenes any other regulations made under this Chapter' and 'shall be treated as having contravened rules made under Chapter V'. This deeming provision will bring the contravening manager or trustee under section 62(1)(a).

Thus, section 62(1) applies to both authorized unit trusts and offshore unit trusts recognized under the Act, though through different routes.

---

[245] S. 78(4).       [246] Ss. 86–8; see ch. 1, s. 5C, *ante*.
[247] Part 3 of the Regulations, relating to scheme particulars, is made under ss. 85, 87(5), and 88(10) of the Act and Part 14, containing provisions specific to recognized schemes, is made under ss. 86(3), 87(4), 90, and 52 of the Act: see reg. 1.05.

## (2) *Locus Standi* of Unitholders

In response to market criticism of the extensive reach of section 62, the Government introduced a new section 62A[248] which provides that:

(1) No action in respect of a contravention to which section 62 above applies shall lie at the suit of a person other than a private investor, except in such circumstances as may be specified by the regulations made by the Secretary of State.
(2) The meaning of the expression 'private investor' for the purposes of subsection (1) shall be defined by regulations made by the Secretary of State.

The intention to draw a line between private investors and non-private investors is clear. As contemplated by this section, it is for the relevant regulations to determine who is a private investor and to define the circumstances under which a non-private investor may sue.

For the purpose of section 62A, the Financial Services Act 1986 (Restriction of Right of Action) Regulations 1991 define a private investor as 'an investor whose cause of action arises . . . in the case of an individual, otherwise than in the course of carrying on investment business; and in the case of any other person, otherwise than in the course of carrying on business of any kind'.[249] If a unitholder can fall within this definition of a private investor, he or she can bring an action under section 62 of the Financial Services Act 1986.

If a particular unitholder is not a private investor, regulation 3 of the Financial Services Act 1986 (Restriction of Right of Action) Regulations 1991 has to be considered. This regulation provides:

The following circumstances are specified for the purposes of section 62A(1) as being circumstances in which action may be brought at the suit of a person other than a private investor—
(a) circumstances in which the contravention in question is not a contravention of a kind mentioned in section 62(1) or (2) of the Act;
(b) circumstances in which the contravention in question is a contravention of any rule . . . prohibiting a person from seeking to make provision excluding or restricting any duty or liability;
(c) circumstances in which the contravention in question is a contravention of any rule . . . directed at ensuring that transactions in an investment are not effected with the benefit of unpublished information which, if made public, would be likely to affect the price of the investment; and
(d) circumstances in which the action would be brought at the suit of a person in a fiduciary or representative capacity ('the representative') and the following conditions are fulfilled—

---

[248] This was added by Companies Act 1989, s. 193.
[249] Reg. 2. A government, local authority or public authority is also excluded from the definition of a private investor.

(i) the cause of action arises as a result of anything done or suffered at a time when the person to whom the representative owed a duty or for whom he was acting was [a private investor as defined]; and

(ii) any recovery would be exclusively for the benefit of such a person and could not be effected through action brought otherwise than at the suit of the representative.

Paragraph (b) covers a contravention of a prohibition against exemption clauses such as section 84 of the Financial Services Act which renders void any provision of the trust deed exempting the manager or the trustee from liability for any failure to exercise due care and diligence.[250] Paragraph (c) covers insider trading and may not be applicable to unit trusts.[251] Paragraph (d) enables a trustee or other representative to sue on behalf of its beneficiary or principal who is a private investor. A non-private investor may rely on these provisions if the prescribed circumstances are applicable.

The main question is whether paragraph (a) gives non-private investors in unit trusts a 'blanket' right to enforce the Financial Services (Regulated Schemes) Regulations 1991. A breach of these Regulations by a manager or a trustee of an authorized unit trust is deemed to be a breach of the rules of the relevant self-regulating organization, a contravention 'mentioned' in section 62(2). A breach of these Regulations by a manager or a trustee of an offshore unit trust recognized under the Act is deemed to be a breach of the rules or regulations made under Chapter V, a contravention 'mentioned' in section 61(1). Paragraph (a) enables non-private investors to sue in respect of a contravention not of a kind mentioned in section 62(1) or (2) of the Act. The question is whether this paragraph extends to cover deeming contraventions. It is submitted that the word 'mentioned' should be interpreted literally. A contravention of the Financial Services (Regulated Schemes) Regulations 1991 is not a contravention mentioned in section 62(1) and section 62(2). If a literal interpretation is not adopted, there would be the anomaly that a unitholder of an offshore trust recognized under the Act could sue the manager or the trustee for breach of the terms of the scheme's constitution, since the content of the constitution is not regulated by the Financial Services (Regulated Schemes) Regulations 1991, whereas a unitholder of an authorized unit trust could not do so because the trust's main constitutional provision is found in the Regulations.

To conclude, section 62 enables both private and non-private investors to enforce the Financial Services (Regulated Schemes) Regulations 1991.

---

[250] Ch. 4, s. 2C(2)(b), *ante.*

[251] Part V of the Criminal Justice Act 1993 applies only to securities specified in Sch. 2 of that Act, which do not include unit trusts (s. 54).

(3) Nature of a Section 62 Action

Section 62(1) of the Financial Services Act provides that 'a contravention
. . . shall be actionable . . . subject to the defences and other incidents
applying to actions for breach of statutory duty'. Any cause of action under
section 62 therefore must establish the 'incidents' of an action for breach of
statutory duty. In other words, the tort of breach of statutory duty is
'imported' into the Financial Services Act regime. Arguably, this section is
merely declaratory because a person who suffers any loss as a result of a
breach of a statute may always bring an action for breach of statutory duty
where on the true construction of an Act it is apparent that the obligation
or prohibition is imposed for the benefit or protection of a particular class
of individuals or where the statute creates a public right and a particular
member of the public suffers particular direct and substantial damage
different from that which is common to all the rest of the public.[252] In this
sense, the objections of the financial services industry might have been an
over-reaction. However, its application to breaches of the rules of self-
regulating organizations[253] is an extension of liability of statutory duty
since such rules are not delegated legislation but rules of professional
organizations, which are contractual in nature.

After establishing that section 62 is applicable to a particular provision,
like any action for breach of statutory duty, the plaintiff must prove the
'incidents' of this tort, namely, (a) the injury he has suffered is within the
ambit of the statute; (b) the statutory duty was not fulfilled; and (c) the
breach of duty has caused his injury.[254]

A statutory duty is imposed to prevent some particular form of injury.
The plaintiff has to prove that the damage he suffered was within the scope
of the contemplated injury. There are old cases in industrial safety
legislation which applied the 'ambit' rule so vigorously that the result might
appear to be absurd.[255] It is a matter of speculation whether a more liberal
attitude may be taken in the context of the Financial Services Act 1986.
Presumably, the court may take into account the objective of investor
protection contemplated by the legislation.

---

[252] *Lonrho Ltd.* v. *Shell Petroleum Co. Ltd. (No. 2)* [1982] AC 173 at 186; *Clerk and
Lindsell on Torts*, 17th edn. by Brazier, Sweet and Maxwell, 1995, para. 11–01.
[253] A breach of the Financial Services (Regulated Schemes) Regulations 1991 by a manager
or a trustee of an authorized unit trust is deemed to be a breach of the rules of the relevant
self-regulating organization.
[254] *Clerk and Lindsell, supra*, paras. 11-06–11-33.
[255] In *Close* v. *Steel Company of Wales Ltd.* [1962] AC 367, the statutory duty to fence
every dangerous part of any machinery was held to be a duty to prevent the operator himself
from coming into contact with the machinery, and thus did not give rise to liability for
materials flying out of the machine.

There are also the questions of what type of 'loss' is recoverable under section 62 for a breach of the Financial Services (Regulated Schemes) Regulations 1991 and what sort of remoteness rule is applicable. In relation to an authorized unit trust, this set of regulations is meant to be the mandatory terms of the equivalent of a unit trust deed. The logical outcome is that contractual principle as to foreseeability should apply. However, an action for breach of statutory duty is a tort. It will be a matter which the court has to decide.

The tort of breach of statutory duty is one of strict liability because once a breach is proved, questions as to whether the breach is unavoidable and whether the defendant is negligent are not relevant. But a particular regulation may not impose absolute duty and may have elements of reasonable care and skill so that a manager or a trustee acting with such care and skill may not be in breach of that regulation.

There is also the requirement of causation which a plaintiff must prove. It must be shown that on balance of probabilities the damage was caused, both in fact and as a matter of law, by the defendant's breach of duty.[256] This is no different from the test applicable to negligence.

Under section 62, 'a contravention . . . shall be actionable . . . subject to the defences . . . applying to actions for breach of statutory duty'. It was established in a House of Lords decision[257] that *volenti non fit injuria* is not a defence to an action for breach of statutory duty imposed by industrial safety legislation. The rationale is that as a matter of public policy if Parliament has required certain precautions to be taken by an employer to protect his employees, the former should not be entitled to neglect those precautions and then to rely on an express or implied agreement that the employee should bear the loss of injury. It is uncertain whether the court will distinguish the case in an action under section 62 of the Financial Services Act 1986. Arguably, the court should not because the rationale for the very detailed provisions of the Act is an underlying concern that investors cannot protect themselves and disclosure alone was regarded as inadequate.

Contributory negligence is a defence to a breach of statutory duty. It was a complete defence at common law but the Law Reform (Contributory Negligence) Act 1945 empowers the court to apportion the responsibility and award the plaintiff reduced damages. The availability of this defence again raises the tension between contractual principle and section 62. For an authorized unit trust, the Financial Services (Regulated Schemes)

---

[256] *Clerk and Lindsell, supra,* para. 11-28.
[257] *Imperial Chemical Industries Ltd.* v. *Shatwell* [1965] AC 656, approving *Wheeler* v. *New Merton Board Mills Ltd.* [1933] 2 KB 669; see also *Burnett* v. *British Waterways Board* [1973] 1 WLR 700.

Regulations 1991 are a contractual substitute. If the consequence of a breach of these Regulations by a manager or a trustee is compared with a breach of the terms of a trust deed of an offshore unit trust, it appears that the defence of contributory negligence is available to a breach which would otherwise be in the nature of contract.

In general, it is not open to the defendant in an action for breach of statutory duty to say that it has delegated the responsibility to a third party.[258] However, under regulation 7.15 of the Financial Services (Regulated Schemes) Regulations 1991, apart from delegation of the manager's management functions and delegation to associates, a manager or a trustee may avoid liability by showing that the matter was delegated, that it was reasonable for a delegate to be employed, that the agent was and remained competent to undertake the function delegated, and that the manager or the trustee had taken reasonable care to ensure that the function delegated was undertaken in a competent manner.[259]

In an action for breach of the Financial Services (Regulated Schemes) Regulations 1991, it is not a defence to show that liability for such a breach is exempted or excluded by the terms of the trust deed.[260]

In conclusion, a unitholder of an authorized unit trust is given the right to enforce the terms of the Financial Services (Regulated Schemes) Regulations 1991, the major constitutional provisions of an authorized unit trust. While there is no objection to such a conclusion, much can be said about the manner of arriving at this conclusion. Even when a unitholder's right to sue is established, there is the anomaly that tort principles, rather than contractual principles, are applicable in the assessment of the loss payable.

### 4. A UNIT AS A CHOSE IN ACTION OF A SPECIAL KIND (THE THIRD PROPOSITION)

The nature of rights of each component of a unit has been examined. The third proposition states that a unit is an indivisible chose in action redeemable and transferable in manner provided by the trust deed. It looks at the unit as a single item of property. Redemption distinguishes units from shares and transferability distinguishes them from beneficiaries' interests in private trusts.

---

[258] Unless on construction of the relevant statute, delegation is a discharge of that duty.

[259] This regulation is discussed in ch. 4, s. 5, *ante*.

[260] Financial Services Act 1986, s. 82; Financial Services Act 1986 (Restriction of Right of Action) Regulation 1991, reg. 3(b).

## A. Redemption

Units of an authorized unit trust are created by the trustee on the instruction of the manager[261] which will issue such units to investors subscribing units. Issue is the sale of units by the manager as principal.[262] Redemption is the converse of the issue of units. It is the purchase of units from a participant by the manager as a principal.[263] This may be followed by the manager surrendering those units to the trustee for cancellation.[264] The manager is entitled to retain the units if it so wishes.

The process for creation, issue, redemption, and cancellation and even terminology may be different for a non-authorized unit trust or an offshore unit trust. However, redemption has been a feature of the unit trust since its first emergence.[265] The right of the manager to repurchase units at the option of the manager appeared in unit trusts in the 1930s.[266] In effect, the manager provides a market for its investors by buying back and reselling units at a price based on the value of the trust's investments.[267]

Regulation 4.18.1 of the Financial Services (Regulated Schemes) Regulations 1991 provides that:

> The manager must at all times during the dealing day be willing to redeem units in the scheme; and, accordingly, must at the request in writing of any participant agree to redeem units owned by that participant at a price arrived at under these regulations.

There are a very limited number of exceptions to this obligation to redeem. The manager may refuse to redeem if the number of units redeemed is less than the minimum stated in the trust deed or if the redemption will result in

---

[261] The Financial Services (Regulated Schemes) Regulations 1991, reg. 4.08.

[262] Ibid., Sch. 4; reg. 4.15.

[263] Ibid., Sch. 4; reg. 4.18. The use of the expression 'redemption' has been criticized as conveying 'the incorrect impression that units are charges or incumbrances on the trust fund' and '[i]t is therefore preferable to speak of the repurchase of units by the manager'. (Pennington, *The Law of the Investment Markets*, Blackwell Law, 1990, p. 546 endnote 136.) The term 'buy-back' is used in the Australian Corporations Law.

[264] Ibid., reg. 4.10.

[265] The Foreign and Colonial Government Trust formed in 1868 contained provisions for redemption out of surplus moneys after payment of expenses and interest: Walker, 'Unincorporated Investment Trusts in the Nineteenth Century' (1940) 15 *Economic History* 341. It is important to bear in mind that the manager did not exist in the type of unit trust of the nineteenth century. Consequently, redemption was a payment out of the trust fund, and not a purchase by the manager.

[266] In the First British Fixed Trust, which was the first unit trust based on the American model, the manager undertook to reacquire units issued: see ch. 1, s. 4B, *ante*.

[267] Per Brooking J, *Gra-ham Australia Pty. Ltd.* v. *Corporate West Management Pty. Ltd.* (1990) ACSR 682 at 683.

the unitholder holding below the minimum holding requirement.[268] The manager may also refuse to redeem in the case of an initial offer or unitization[269] and during the period of suspension.[270] The manager may suspend dealing of units only with the prior agreement of the trustee but the trustee may require the manager to suspend dealing. Suspension cannot be longer than twenty-eight days and there must be good and sufficient reason to suspend dealing having regard to interests of participants.[271]

Redemption or repurchase provisions can also be found in non-authorized unit trusts or offshore unit trusts. The obligation on the part of the manager to redeem, however, may be subject to more stringent restrictions where the unit trust invests in assets that are not readily realizable.

It will be observed that redemption is a transfer of an existing interest to the manager for a consideration; the manager takes over ownership of the units redeemed. The trust fund is intact until there is a request for cancellation by the manager. This differs from a trustee paying a beneficiary his interest and discharging its trustee's obligation.

The obligation to redeem on the part of the manager is an option granted to each unitholder. It is an option to sell to the manager the units at a price calculated at an agreed formula that relates to the value of underlying assets. It is exercisable by the unitholder subject to the conditions and restrictions contained in the regulations or the trust deed. A request made to the manager under this regulation is the exercise of an option. The sale to the manager effected in this manner is not a separate contract outside the trust deed.

This interpretation is supported by the Australian case *Gra-ham Australia Pty. Ltd.* v. *Corporate West Management Pty. Ltd.*[272] This case was a result of the collapse of stock markets worldwide in 1987, an event of 'melancholy notoriety'.[273] A unitholder, in the morning of the day of the stock market crash, 20 October 1987, made enquiries about selling back to the manager and received its assurances. It then delivered to the manager a request for repurchase in the form required by the trust deed. According to the deed's provision, the price for repurchases requested between 8 October and 7 November should be based on the net value of the fund as at 30 September, which apparently would be substantially higher than that on 20 October. No payment was made to the unitholder. Instead, the manager called a meeting of all unitholders which resolved to amend the deed to provide that from 7 October the value of units repurchased should be

---

[268] The Financial Services (Regulated Schemes) Regulations 1991, reg. 4.18.2.
[269] Ibid., reg. 4.18.2.          [270] Ibid., reg. 4.18.5.          [271] Ibid., reg. 13.02.
[272] (1990) ACSR 682 at 683.          [273] Per Brooking J, ibid., at 683.

determined as at the date of repayment and a supplemental deed was executed. The Full Court of the Supreme Court of Western Australia decided that the supplemental deed was valid and binding on all unitholders, including those who made requests before the passing of the resolutions, saving only any rights arising under any contract made between a unitholder and the manager and not arising under the trust deed.

The question before Brooking J was whether there was a separate contract between the unitholder and the manager in the morning of 20 October. His Honour held that there was not.[274] He said:

> . . . I have of course considered with care his Honour's reasons for decision. It seems to me that the different results reached by Beach J and by me are difficult to account for satisfactorily by differences in the facts . . . I have been influenced in a way which his Honour was not by the pre-existing contractual relation between the unitholder and manager—the existence of a contract whereby, among other things, the unitholder had what a man of business would nowadays call a put option. Once that option was exercised, the units had to be bought, and I have explained the events of 20 October in terms of the exercise of that option . . . Beach J said: 'That the defendant would enter into agreements of that nature with unitholders was always within the contemplation of the parties. That much is clear from the provisions of the trust deed to which I have referred.' Those provisions are the parts of the deed which provide for requests to repurchase units. His Honour treats these provisions as making it more probable that a contract of sale outside the deed would be made. My own view is that the existence of a so-called 'put option' as part of the contract between the plaintiff as a unitholder and the manager tends against the suggestion that a contract of sale outside the deed was made on 20 October and in favour of the view that there was an exercise of the option coupled with discussion of its effect. In other words, the provisions relied on by his Honour were contemplating, not a contract outside the deed, but the exercise of the option conferred by it.[275]

As redemption is an exercise of an option pursuant to the terms of the trust deed or the regulations, the manager cannot negotiate a new price according to the supply and demand condition in the market. In this respect, the manager is not the same as an ordinary purchaser from the unitholder.

Although redemption is an obligation, it also provides the opportunity for the manager to make a profit out of the operation. A manager may make a charge for redemption if the trust deed so provides.[276] In addition,

---

[274] *Fay* v. *Corporate West Management Ltd.*; *Tauman* v. *Corporate West Management Ltd.* (17 Mar. 1988, Beach J, SC (Vic.), both unreported) were not followed.

[275] Ibid., at 689.

[276] Reg. 4.21 of Financial Services (Regulated Schemes) Regulations 1991 provides that the trust deed may permit the manager to impose redemption charges calculated as a fixed sum or a percentage of the proceeds of redemption.

trusts invariably provide two prices[277] for redemption and issue of units. The former is calculated by dividing the value of the trust fund on a cancellation basis by the total number of units which are issued;[278] the latter is calculated on a creation basis.[279] In normal circumstances, if the manager purchases from the redeeming unitholder and sells to an incoming unitholder, it will earn a profit represented by the difference between the issue and redemption prices. It seems that the manager is not a fiduciary when it is dealing in units. It should be entitled to retain this profit.[280] In the case of an authorized unit trust, the manager may only do so if this is disclosed in the scheme particulars.[281]

A unit therefore differs substantially from a trust beneficiary's interest which generally does not have a ready market. In effect, the obligation of the manager to redeem or repurchase units has assumed a central position in unit trust. It is the 'essence' and 'machinery' forming the framework of a unit trust.[282] In the absence of any other right conferred by the deed, this right to require the manager to redeem or repurchase precludes any right to require the trustee to sell underlying assets for the purpose of distribution, at least while the unit trust is a going concern. This right of realization is also subject to such conditions and restrictions which the trust deed or the regulations may provide, including amendment powers given in the trust deed, which may divest or diminish such rights. As between a unitholder and a manager, units are dealt with as items of property.

## B. Transferability

A beneficiary's interest in a private trust is an equitable chose in action[283] and as an equitable chose, it can only be alienated by an equitable

---

[277] It is common practice of funds in the European Community to operate systems of single pricing. There has been a suggestion that the UK should adopt single pricing: Securities and Investments Board, *Regulated Collective Investment Schemes: Key Policy Issues* (Discussion Paper) 1993, pp. 8–15.

[278] Reg. 4.11.

[279] Reg. 4.09.

[280] Ch. 3, s. 4B and ch. 4, s. 2A(3), *ante*.

[281] Reg. 8.05.3.

[282] In *Eagle Star Trustees Ltd.* v. *Heine Management Ltd.* (1990) 3 ACSR 232 at 237, Phillips J took the view that the provisions for buy-back and the buy-back period are the 'essence' and 'machinery' forming the framework of a unit trust.

[283] *Pigott* v. *Stewart* [1875] WN 69. It is a right to sue the trustee for due administration of the trust. Whether a beneficiary has an interest beyond the equitable chose depends on the construction of the trust instrument and whether the trust is a discretionary, fixed or bare trust.

assignment[284] or a statutory assignment,[285] and where desirable or necessary by giving notice to the trustee.[286]

Modern unit trusts provide for the transfer of units by way of instruments of transfer to be executed by the transferors and the transferees and to be delivered to the trustee.[287] The Financial Services (Regulated Schemes) Regulations 1991 or trust deeds invariably provide that the transferee is not a unitholder until his name is entered in the register.[288] The trustee of an authorized unit trust is required to keep a register of unitholders.[289] Disposal of units therefore takes the form of a transfer, rather than an assignment, and is effective only by an entry in the register book. This resembles the transfer of shares in a registered company and was a method adopted by unincorporated associations and deed of settlement companies using the trustee device at least as early as the late seventeenth century.[290] In relation to deed of settlement

---

[284] The basic requirement of an assignment of choses in action in equity is a manifestation by the assignor of an intention to assign. It may be couched in the language of command, request or mere permission. The language is immaterial if the meaning is plain. (*William Brandt's Sons & Co.* v. *Dunlop Rubber Co.* [1905] AC 454 at 462, per Lord Macnaghten; *Norman* v. *FCT* (1963) 109 CLR 9; *Shepherd* v. *FCT* (1965) 113 CLR 385.) As the assignment of a beneficiary's interest is a disposition of a subsisting equitable interest within the Law of Property Act 1925, s. 53(1)(c), it has to be in writing and signed. Joinder of the assignor is necessary in any action by the equitable assignee. Giving of notice to the trustee, however, is not mandatory but obviously desirable to preserve the priority of the assignee's interest. See Marshall, *The Assignment of Choses in Action*, Pitman, 1950, ch. III; Starke, *Assignment of Choses in Action in Australia*, Butterworths, 1972, ch. 3; Meagher, Gummow and Lehane, *Equity: Doctrines and Remedies*, 3rd edn., Butterworths, 1992, ch. 6.

[285] Under the Law of Property Act 1925, s 136(1) (re-enacting s. 25 of the Judicature Act 1873). Basically, any absolute assignment in writing signed by the assignor of any chose in action, of which notice in writing is given to the trustee or debtor, is effective: see Marshall, *supra*, ch. V; Starke, *supra*, ch. 4.

[286] Notice is desirable for an equitable assignment and necessary for a statutory assignment: see preceding two footnotes.

[287] Reg. 6.12 of the Financial Services (Regulated Schemes) Regulations 1991 requires the transfer of units in an authorized unit trust to be left with the trustee. For other unit trusts, trust deeds may provide the manager to be the registrar and the transfer will be delivered to it.

[288] Ibid., reg. 6.12.3.

[289] Ibid., reg. 6.02. In the register, the name and address of each unitholder, his unitholding, and the date of becoming a unitholder have to be entered.

[290] The practice of transfer on books could be traced to the East India Company which received its first charter in 1600 granting it monopoly of trade with the Indies. (The transfer on books of the company was apparent from the case *Johnson* v. *East India Company* (1679) Rep. Temp. Finch 430, where the transferee with notice of fraud was ordered to transfer back the shares to the rightful owner and this was done by joining the company as a defendant. According to Scott, *The Constitution and Finance of English, Scottish and Irish Joint-Stock Companies to 1720*, Cambridge UP, 1912 (Peter Smith reprint, 1951), Vol. 1, p. 161, the company's shares were widely traded in the company's early years and in many cases by way of auction as the East India commodities.) It was also used by other statutory companies of the early period: Greenland Company, 1692, Bank of England, 1694, and National Land Bank, 1695 (Cooke, *Corporation, Trust and Company*, Manchester UP, 1950, p. 73). It is clear from DuBois, *The English Business Company after the Bubble Act 1720–1800*, 1938

companies, it can be said that interests in trusts had long been transferred before the modern development of the law relating to assignments of choses in action.[291] What happened was that courts were pragmatic in their approach and gave their recognition to practices in the market-place. Thus, characterization of the share in a deed of settlement company was not a prerequisite to determine the method of alienation or disposition, but, illogical as it may appear, the mode of transfer laid down in the constitution was regarded as one of the attributes that the court would consider to determine the nature of the share.[292]

The juridical nature of transfer as a mode of disposition does not appear to have been judicially considered. The transfer has its origin in a deed of bargain and sale which derived its terminology from the law of real property.[293] The transfer method was a result of a process of simplification of the deed of bargain and sale to meet the commercial need of a more efficient capital market. In the end, as observed by DuBois,[294] the entry in

(Octagon Books reprint, 1971), that transfer on books was the method used by deed of settlement companies such as Sun Fire Office, the Temple Brass Mills, and the West New Jersey Society (pp. 360 and 405 n. 106). These companies were established in 1707, 1695, and 1692 respectively (pp. 218, 493, and 494). (The description of the use of the trust to hold property by these companies is at pp. 217–19.) During the Bubble period, there were many modes of transfer of shares, including transfer by deeds and by endorsement on share certificates, but transfer on books remained the most common (pp. 358–62). It was highly probable that this method predated the passing of the Bubble Act 1720 (6 Geo. 1, c. 18) as the Act was a reaction to share speculation and according to Scott, ibid., Vol. 1, pp. 442–3, the stock market in London then was highly organized with put and call options and bear and bull accounts.

[291] Share transfer was quite common in the late 17th century (the preceding footnote). It is difficult to trace legal decisions as to their efficacy. Various opinions extracted in DuBois, ibid., did not suggest its invalidity. Its validity possibly was based on the view that the transfer was part of the contractual agreement as to holding of shares and their disposal found in the deed of settlement: *Ashby* v. *Blackwell and the Million Bank Co.* (1765) Amb. 503 at 506, per Lord Northington. By contrast, legal choses in action, with certain exceptions, notably the King's assignment and negotiable instruments, were not assignable since the expulsion of the Jews in the 13th century: *Lampet's Case* (1612) 10 Co. Rep. 46b (the objection of maintenance); *Winchester's Case* (1853) 3 Co. Rep. 1a, 3b (the 'too personal' objection). They were assignable only after 1873. Although the Chancellor began to give effect to assignments of debts as early as the 15th century, the principles on equitable assignment were not settled until the 19th century, notably with *Kekewich* v. *Manning* (1851) 1 De GM & G 176. For a historical account on this aspect, see Bailey's three-part article, 'Assignments of Debts in England from the Twelfth to the Twentieth Century', especially Part III (Part I: (1931) 47 *LQR* 516; Part II: (1932) 48 *LQR* 248; Part III: (1932) 48 *LQR* 547). In any event, there is no doubt that shares had been transferred for almost two centuries before they were settled by the House of Lords to be choses in action in *The Colonial Bank* v. *Whinney* (1886) LR 11 AC 426. (It was so decided in an earlier case of *Humble* v. *Mitchell* (1839) 11 Ad. & E 205.)

[292] This was the approach of Alderson B and Parke B in *Watson* v. *Spratley* (1854) 10 Ex. 222 at 243–4 and 246 respectively. Martin B did not regard the mode of transfer as determinative (at 241). Platt B did not consider the issue.

[293] Probably because of the decisions that shares of the New River Company were realty: see cases quoted at fn. 122, *supra*.                            [294] *Supra*, at 361.

the register book became crucial; it was not a record of the assignment between the transferor and the transferee but the process of assignment itself. If judicial authority for this proposition is wanting, there is nothing better than the decision of *Milroy* v. *Lord*.[295] As an integral part of the process of transfer and before an entry was made in the register book, invariably the acceptance of the transferee was required. The consequence was that the transferor would cease to be liable as a member of the deed of settlement company and the transferee would be liable to contribute thereafter.[296] Thus, the transfer method is a novation[297] whereby all parties concerned agree that the transferee shall be substituted for the transferor as a member, with the same rights as the transferor possessed and subject to the same obligations as those to which the transferor was subject.

A typical modern unit trust transfer form provides that:

I/We, . . . in consideration of the sum of $ ... paid to me/us by . . . (hereinafter called 'the transferee') do hereby transfer to the transferee . . . units in . . . Trust to hold the same unto the transferee upon and subject to the deed dated . . . and I/ We the transferee hereby agree to take the same units subject to the said conditions.[298]

In substance, this is indistinguishable from the form of transfer used by deed of settlement companies.[299] Transfer of units in modern unit trusts is

---

[295] (1862) 4 De GF & J 264, the facts of which appear below (text relating to fn. 305).

[296] *Re Monmouthshire and Glamorganshire Banking Co., Cape's Executor's Case* (1852) 2 De GM & G 562; *Re Pennant and Craigwen Consolidated Lead Mining Co., Mayhew's Case* (1854) 5 De GM & G 837; *Re Mexican and South American Co., Grisewood and Smith's Case* (1859) 4 De G & J 544.

[297] Pennington, *Company Law*, 6th edn., Butterworths, 1990, p. 339. The learned author's view may also be supported by the fact that at the time when shares in deed of settlement companies were widely traded, the law did not recognize assignment. Novation was a widely used avoidance device (Marshall, *supra*, pp. 67–71). Practitioners of the day had no choice other than novation.

[298] *Australian Ency. F & P*, Vol. 3, p. 1069.

[299] The form used in *Watson* v. *Spratley* was: 'To [the purser of the Boscean mine]. I, [transferor] do herby certify, that I have this day sold unto [transferee] four hundred and fortieth parts or shares of and in a certain mine or adventure called Boscean, situate &c., together with the like shares or proportions of and in all the engines and tools, tackle, materials, ores, halvans, monies, and all other appurtenances thereunto belonging, together with all dividends and advantages to be derived therefrom. And this is your authority for transferring the said parts or shares into his name in the usual way. . . .' 'I, the above-named [transferee] do hereby accept the said parts and shares, subject to the same terms and conditions, rules, and regulations, as the said [transferor] held the same.' ( (1854) 10 Ex. 222 at 225–6.) According to DuBois, *supra*, a simpler formula was used by many deed of settlement companies. For example, at p. 405 n. 107, the example of West New Jersey Society was similar to modern unit trusts: 'I . . . do sell, assign, and transfer unto . . . 20 Shares of my Interest and Credit in the Land and Stock of the West New Jersey Society together with all present and future Proceeds thereof.' 'I accept of the above-mentioned Share according to the Conditions expressed in the Preamble of this book dated April 4, 1692, and oblige myself to the True Performance thereof.'

also in the nature of novation. An existing unitholder's right of transfer is a
right to insist on substituting a new unitholder who agrees to be bound by
the same terms as the existing unitholder.

One of the implications of *Costa and Duppe*[300] would be that, as the
unitholder has an interest in the underlying real property, any contract of
disposition must be evidenced by a memorandum in writing signed by the
defendant.[301] However, conventional sale and purchase of property trust
units in the stock market will not satisfy the requirement; nor will
computerized trading.[302] More importantly, *Costa and Duppe* would also
require that alienation of units has to be by way of assignment.[303] This will
render ineffective any alienation by way of transfer; the trust deed
provisions for transfer are also rendered void. There is a further problem.
A transfer has the effect of novation so that the transferee will be bound by
the terms of the trust deed, but under an assignment the burden may not
pass and there is the question of enforceability of the terms of the trust
deed against assignees from existing unitholders.

There is no reason why a court in this situation should deny the right of
parties to contract themselves. The approach of *Watson* v. *Spratley*[304] was
to give precedence to the transfer method and indeed to use it as evidence
of the intention of the parties as to rights in the underlying assets.

Implicit in any trust deed provision prescribing transfer as a mode of
alienation of a unitholder's interest is its exclusion of any assignment as a
mode of disposition. In *Milroy* v. *Lord*,[305] shares in the Louisiana Bank
were transferable by the execution of a transfer and its registration in the
books of the bank. It was held that the purported transfer by the settlor of
the shares by deed in favour of the trustee was ineffective. If the transfer of
company shares can be traced back to deed of settlement companies there
is good reason to regard *Milroy* v. *Lord* as an authority on unit trusts.

---

[300] [1986] VR 90, discussed in ss. 2B and 2C(5) of this ch., *ante*.
[301] Law of Property Act 1925, s. 40(1) re-enacting in part s. 4 of the Statute of Frauds 1677.
This was the type of problem raised in cases such as *Watson* v. *Spratley* (1854) 10 Ex. 222,
discussed in s. 2C of this ch.
[302] Under the old out-cry system, there would be no signed memorandum that satisfied the
Statute of Frauds. This was what happened in *Watson* v. *Spratley*, ibid.
[303] As an assignment of interests in land: Law of Property Act 1925, s. 53(1)(a).
[304] (1854) 10 Ex. 222.
[305] (1862) 4 De GF & J 264. The *ratio decidendi* of this case, as stated in various texts, is
that for a gift to be effective, the donor must have done everything which according to the
nature of the property is necessary to be done in order to transfer the property. This *ratio*
must be premised on the statement herein that alternative transfer methods are ineffective for
otherwise the donor in that case would have done all that was necessary. For the difficulties in
applying this ratio, see *Anning* v. *Anning* (1907) 4 CLR 1049 at 1057 (per Griffith CJ), 1069
(per Issacs J), and 1081–2 (per Higgins J) and compare *Re Fry* [1946] Ch. 312 and *Re Rose*
[1952] Ch. 499 (followed in *Tett* v. *Phoenix Property and Investment Co. Ltd.* [1984] BCLC
599).

Thus, units are transferred solely by means of a change in the register of unitholders. This distinguishes unit trusts from private trusts and brings them closer to companies. This closeness is also reflected in the common provision in trust deeds that no notice of any trust shall be entered on the register[306] or that the manager and the trustee are not bound to take notice of any trust or equitable interest.[307] Their proximity, however, stops here, as some unit trusts make detailed provisions for notification of mortgagees' interests, payment of income to the mortgagees, and the requirement of the mortgagees' consent on transfer.[308] This practice is intended to encourage borrowing by investors and to protect lenders within the same financial conglomerate as the manager.

The resulting position for a transferee in the event of successive dealings by his transferor is very complicated. No doubt, in priority questions, courts will have to rely on first principles and also pay due regard to the attributes of units. Several observations can be made.

1. The starting-point of consideration may be the two basic principles of property law. The first is where equities are equal, the first in time prevails.[309] The second is where equities are equal, the law prevails; and for this purpose a bona fide purchaser for value of a legal interest without notice of a prior equitable interest has a better equity.
2. The first principle, the 'first in time' rule, is a principle that determines priority according to the time of creation of competing interests. This principle, however, has no application where property is held by a trustee. Dispositions by a beneficial owner will rank in the order in which notices of the disposition are given to the trustee. This is the rule in *Dearle* v. *Hall*.[310] It has been extended to debts, many kinds of choses in

---

[306] This common provision is an illustration of the danger of a direct transplant of company provisions in drafting unit trust deeds. This provision only precludes the notice of trust from being entered on the register. In some non-authorized unit trusts, the registers may be kept by the manager; what will be the position if a notice of trust is given to the unit trustee in accordance with *Dearle* v. *Hall*? The unit trust is not a separate legal entity which is significant in this context. A better drafting approach is to provide that the manager and the trustee are not bound to take notice of any trust or equitable interest. It may also be desirable to insert both provisions.

[307] Cf. reg. 6.03.2 of the Financial Services (Regulated Schemes) Regulations 1991 which provides that '[n]o notice of any trust, express, implied, or constructive, which may be entered in the register in respect of any unit shall be binding on the manager or the trustee.'

[308] Although this is not common for an authorized unit trust, it seems that such a provision in the trust deed will not contradict the terms of Financial Services (Regulated Schemes) Regulations 1991.

[309] The maxim is *qui prior est tempore potior est jure*: he who is earlier in time is stronger in law. This principle applies both in law and in equity. See *Snell*, pp. 46–7; Megarry and Wade, p. 987.

[310] (1828) 3 Russ. 1 where a beneficiary of an annuity under a will trust made three successive assignments for consideration and the last assignee who gave notice to the trustee was held to have priority over the others.

action, and properties that can only reach the beneficiary in the form of money.[311]

3. In the two House of Lords decisions of *Shropshire Union Railways and Canal Company* v. *R*[312] and *Société Générale de Paris* v. *Walker*,[313] it was established that priority principles established in property law apply to questions of competing equitable interests in shares. *Société Générale de Paris* v. *Walker* was also applied to shares in a deed of settlement company in *Roots* v. *Williamson*.[314]

4. On questions of priority affecting equitable interests of units of unit trusts, the court will have to choose between *Dearle* v. *Hall* and *Société Générale de Paris* v. *Walker*. In almost every case that priority questions arise, the court has to decide which of the innocent parties has to suffer. The tendency is to regard *Dearle* v. *Hall* as an exception[315] not to be extended. Lord Macnaghten in *Ward* v. *Duncombe*[316] said:

I am inclined to think that the rule in *Dearle* v. *Hall* has on the whole produced at least as much injustice as it has prevented. . . . [I]t seems to me that when your Lordships are asked to extend the rule to a case not already covered by authority, it is proper to inquire into the principles upon which the rule is said to be found. For the reasons which I have already given, I do not think that those principles are so clear or so convincing that the rule ought to be extended to a new case.

In the light of this dictum, any application of *Dearle* v. *Hall* would probably necessitate a search for its justifications, of which many have been advanced. To sum up, in some authorities, the giving of notice in respect of a chose in action has been likened to delivery of a chose in possession. In some cases, courts have emphasized the necessity of preventing frauds by beneficiaries who create successive encumbrances without disclosing the earlier ones. In some, emphasis was on the duty of the assignee to do all that he could to obtain possession of the subject matter of the assignment.[317]

5. These justifications may not be wholly convincing because they are

---

[311] See Fisher and Lightwood, *Law of Mortgage*, 10th edn. by Tyler, Butterworths, 1988, pp. 493 *et seq.*, where a succinct account of the origin of the rule is given.
[312] (1875) LR 7 HL 496.                                            [313] (1885) 11 App. Cas. 20.
[314] (1888) 38 Ch. D 485. This case was relied upon in *Moore* v. *North Western Bank* [1891] 2 Ch. 599 and *Ireland* v. *Hart* [1902] 1 Ch. 522. See also *Colonial Bank* v. *Cady* (1890) 15 App. Cas. 267; *Peat* v. *Clayton* [1906] 1 Ch. 659; *Hawks* v. *McArthur* [1951] 1 All ER 22; *Perrier-Jouet* v. *Finch Co.* [1982] 1 WLR 1359.
[315] In *Shropshire Union Railways and Canal Co.*, *supra*, the House of Lords did not consider *Dearle* v. *Hall* at all. Earl Selborne in *The Société Générale de Paris* v. *Walker* (1885) 11 App. Cas. 20, at 30–1 approached *Dearle* v. *Hall* on the basis that it did not apply to shares in the absence of authority or good reason. Other Law Lords did not consider *Dearle* v. *Hall*.
[316] [1893] AC 369 at 393–4.
[317] *Re Wyatt, White* v. *Ellis* [1892] 1 Ch. 188 at 209, per Lindley LJ, reading the judgment of the Court of Appeal which was drawn up by Fry LJ.

based on the conduct of the parties. It is now established that conduct of the parties is no longer a relevant consideration for the rule.[318] At the end, the reality may simply be that it is not a principle of justice but a rule applied by analogy to the order and disposition provision in bankruptcy law.[319] If this is the only rationale, there is clear reason to reject *Dearle* v. *Hall* in the unit trust context. In *Société Générale de Paris* v. *Walker*,[320] the question was one of priority between an equitable mortgagee by deposit of the share certificate and a blank transfer and a subsequent equitable mortgagee which was given a blank transfer by the mortgagor who stated that the share certificate was lost or mislaid. The subsequent mortgagee purported to register the transfer before the first equitable mortgagee by deposit gave notice to the company. The company refused registration as the transfer was not accompanied by the share certificate. The company's articles provided for transfer by deed and on the face of the share certificate 'there was an engagement under the company's common seal that no transfer of any portion of the shares thereby represented should be registered without delivery of the certificate'.[321] In an action by the subsequent equitable mortgagee for a declaration of priority, the House of Lords held that nothing had happened to displace the original priority in order of time. Earl Selborne rejected *Dearle* v. *Hall* by reference to its 'bankruptcy origin'. After stating that it was irrelevant for the first mortgagee to give notice to the company, as the company was not under any obligation to accept notice, he said:

No authority was cited to shew that the doctrine of *Dearle* v. *Hall* had been applied to such shares; and *the reasons for that doctrine are, in my judgment, not applicable.* The case is not like those under the bankruptcy laws, in which the fact, or presumption, of a continuance (after a change in the equitable title) of the prior state of 'order and disposition,' or reputed ownership, 'with the consent of the true owner,' has to be in some way disproved. But in the case before your Lordships, that was actually done by the company's engagement under the deed[322] in the respondents' possession, which could not have been done by any mere notice.[323]

---

[318] *Re Dallas* [1904] is illustrative. A beneficiary charged his legacy under a will of a living testator to two chargees in succession. Upon the death of the testator, both chargees gave notice to the administrator immediately after they knew of his appointment. The first chargee lost priority to the second chargee as the second chargee's notice was received first and although there was no fault on his part. Further, failure to make enquiry by the subsequent encumbrancer was irrelevant (*Meux* v. *Bell* (1841) 1 Hare 73; *Re Brown's Trusts* (1867) LR 5 Eq. 88).

[319] The judgment of Plumer MR in *Dearle* v. *Hall* was said to be based on *Ryall* v. *Rowles* (1750) 1 Ves. Sen. 348, which held that pawnees of goods permitting bankrupts to continue in possession or to have the goods in their order or disposition had no specific liens against their assignees: see Fisher and Lightwood, *supra*, p. 493, fn. (o).

[320] (1885) 11 App. Cas. 20.     [321] Ibid., at 29.

[322] i.e. the engagement stated on the face of the certificate: see the text accompanying the preceding footnote.     [323] Ibid., at 31; emphasis supplied.

6. As shown in this chapter, a unit is more than just an interest in a trust fund; it is a bundle of contractual, trust, and statutory rights with its own modes of redemption and alienation; it is a product of a combined operation of the contract and the trust. On balance, therefore, it bears closer resemblance to a share in a deed of settlement company than to a beneficiary's interest in a private trust. If an issue of priority is to be decided by way of analogy, cases of deed of settlement companies offer better precedents. It is submitted that priority principles of property law should apply to decide priority questions in units in unit trusts.

7. In applying such priority principles, regard has to be had to trust deed provisions. It is common that the trust deed will provide that no notice of any trust shall be entered in the register. However, the absence of this provision should not preclude the court from applying the principle of *Société Général de Paris* v. *Walker* because none of their Lordships in this case considered this to be a factor relevant to the priority question before them. Exclusion of trusts from the register was only discussed by Earl Selborne and only in the context whether the prior mortgagee by deposit of the share certificate had better equity. In *Shropshire Union Railways and Canal Company* v. *R.*,[324] the other House of Lords case applying property law priority principles, a trust interest was in fact entered at one time on the register of the company concerned. Express provisions for notation of mortgagees' interests on the unit trust register are by no means uncommon. Ironically, this creates novel points for the court even if the court applies *Société Générale de Paris* by analogy. It is difficult to speculate whether the court will regard equities as equal between a holder of an equitable interest in the unit and a competing mortgagee who does not register in accordance with the mortgage notification provision of the trust deed. It is also an indeterminate question whether failure to register the mortgage affects its validity. This is a question of construction of the relevant provisions and of the nature of the notation or register of mortgagees' interests that is intended.

8. If the court decides that the issue falls within the realm of *Dearle* v. *Hall*,[325] the court will have to decide upon whom the notice is to be served, the trustee or the manager, the former being a fundholder and the latter having control of the fund, though subject to the monitoring function of the trustee.[326]

---

[324] (1875) LR 7 HL 496.          [325] (1828) 3 Russ. 1.

[326] In an offshore unit trust or a non-authorized unit trust, the court may also have to consider the fact that the manager is the person to maintain the register of unitholders. If the court is to draw on existing case-law on the application of *Dearle* v. *Hall* to multiple trustees, the difference in juridical nature of the office of the trustee and the manager must be examined. For the rules relating to giving of notice to several trustees, see *Phipps* v.

9. *Dearle* v. *Hall*,[327] *Shropshire Union Railways and Canal Company* v. *R*,[328] *Société Générale de Paris* v. *Walker*,[329] and *Roots* v. *Williamson*[330] are concerned with the question of priority in competing equitable interests. A separate principle is that acquisition of the legal title to property by a bona fide purchaser for value without notice of any prior equitable interests will have absolute title. In the case of company shares, the entering on the register of the name of the purchaser is the only means of acquisition of legal title.[331] In relation to unit trusts, however, it may be questioned that a unit is an equitable interest only and, as such, no question of competition between legal and equitable interests can arise. It is submitted that even in such a position the unit registered should have priority as if it is a legal interest. The reason is that equity does not appear to have difficulty in ranking equitable interests of different qualities. An equitable interest has long been regarded as having better quality than a 'mere equity'.[332] An equitable interest with a superior right to the legal estate can also defeat a prior equitable interest.[333] The general rule is that the 'first in time' rule applies where equities are equal. The person on the register complies with the constitution of the unit trust and therefore has better equity. He should be given priority.

## C. Characterization as an Indivisible Chose

What is a chose in action is a jurisprudential question[334] in itself which is beyond the present investigation. For the present purpose, it suffices to start with Fry LJ's much cited dictum that: 'all personal things are either in possession or in action. The law knows no *tertium quid* between the

---

*Lovegrove* (1873) LR 16 Eq. 80; *Hallows* v. *Lloyd* (1888) 39 Ch. D 686; *Re Wyatt, White* v. *Ellis* [1892] 1 Ch. 188; *Ward* v. *Duncombe* [1899] AC 369; *Re Phillips' Trusts* [1903] 1 Ch. 183; *Re Wasdale* [1899] 1 Ch. 163; *Snell*, pp. 68–9.

[327] *Supra.*   [328] (1875) LR 7 HL 496.   [329] (1885) 11 App. Cas. 20.
[330] (1888) 38 Ch. D 485.

[331] In *Ireland* v. *Hart* [1902] 1 Ch. 521, where the directors had no power to refuse transfer of shares, it was held that the lodging of the transfer for registration did not pass the legal title. This differs from Earl Selborne's view in *Société Générale de Paris*, *supra* at 28, that 'a present absolute right to have the transfer registered' may pass the legal interest in the share.

[332] Such as the right of rectification and the right to set aside a transaction for fraud or mistake.

[333] *Taylor* v. *London and County Banking Co.* [1901] 2 Ch. 231; Megarry and Wade, pp. 145–6; *Snell*, pp. 49–50.

[334] Marshall, *supra*, pp. 1–71, where the learned author suggests this question can only be answered by taking a combined analytical and historical approach. For various meanings of the term, see *Halsbury's Laws of England*, 4th edn. (Reissue), Vol. 6, Butterworths, 1991, para. 1, and *Crossley Vaines on Personal Property*, 5th edn., by Tyler and Palmer, Butterworths, 1973, pp. 262 *et seq.*

two.'[335] Thus, a chose in action is to be understood in negative terms, viz., something of which it is impossible to take physical possession. It is not confined to things that can only be enjoyed by taking actions. Used in this wider sense, it has been held that both partnership shares[336] and company shares[337] are choses in action.

The analysis relating to the first and second propositions[338] of this chapter has demonstrated that a unitholder has a bundle of rights comprising contractual, trust, and statutory rights and, in exceptional cases, interests in underlying assets. However, a unit is more than a mere bundle of rights. It is an item of property in itself, one that comprises various choses and rights. It is indivisible in nature and is dealt with in the market-place as such. It is an object of ownership that can be sold, bought, mortgaged or disposed of in other manner. It can be said that the trust deed provisions regarding redemption, transfer, and unit register implicitly preclude any possibility of transferring component rights independent of the unit itself. Moreover, rights to vote and to request the trustee to call meetings of unitholders can only be meaningful if they are conferred on each unit representing the totality of choses. They cannot stand in a vacuum or be detached from other rights for they are inchoate in nature and are to be used for the furtherance of other objectives that will affect proprietary rights or their value.

Thus understood, a unit is an item of property indivisible in nature. The grant of fractional units by some trust deeds does not affect this conclusion for, in the first place, the so-called 'fraction' is by nature nothing but a unit of account for the purposes of the trust deed and in respect of which the trust deed will define its rights. For example, the deed may allow a fractional unit to enjoy income on a pro rata basis but may say that it is not counted for the purpose of voting. The attribute of indivisibility is that a unitholder cannot detach different component choses otherwise than in accordance with the terms of the trust deed. He cannot, for example, assign all beneficial rights other than the right to attend unitholders' meetings and to vote at them. Nor can he assign the income of the units

---

[335] *Colonial Bank* v. *Whinney* (1885) 30 Ch. D 261 at 285 when his Lordship was giving a dissenting judgment, which was subsequently approved on appeal by the House of Lords: (1886) 11 App. Cas. 426. This dictum is said to have acquired 'the sanctity of a truism' (Marshall, *supra*, p. 2).

[336] *Re Bainbridge, ex p. Fletcher* (1878) 8 Ch. D 218; *Anning* v. *Anning* (1907) 4 CLR 1049; *FCT* v. *Everett* (1980) 143 CLR 440; *United Builders Pty. Ltd.* v. *Mutual Acceptance Ltd.* (1980) 144 CLR 673. Cf. *Canny Gabriel Castle Jackson Advertising Pty. Ltd.* v. *Volume Sales (Finance) Pty. Ltd.* (1974) 131 CLR 32.

[337] *Colonial Bank* v. *Whinney* (1886) 11 App. Cas. 426.

[338] Ss. 2 and 3, *ante*.

while retaining the capital; the register does not cater for such type of transfer.[339]

What then is the character of this indivisible unit? Is it in the nature of a chose in possession, or a chose in action? With the wider interpretation of the term chose in action by Fry LJ, it is not difficult to conclude that a unit is a chose in action. His reasoning in the following passage dealing with the nature of a share can *mutatis mutandis* apply to units of unit trusts:

Such a share is, in my opinion, the right to receive certain benefits from a corporation, and to do certain acts as a member of that corporation; and if those benefits be withheld or those acts be obstructed, the only remedy of the owner of the share is by action. Of the share itself, in my view, there can be no occupation or enjoyment; though of the fruits arising from it there may be occupation, enjoyment, and manual possession. Such a share appears to me to be closely akin to a debt, which is one of the most familiar of choses in acton; no action is required to obtain the right to the money in the case of the debt, or the right to the dividends or other accruing benefits in the case of the share; but an action is the only means of obtaining the money itself or the other benefits *in specie*, the right to which is called in one case a debt and in the other case a share. In the case alike of the debt and of the share, the owner of it has, to use the language of Blackstone, 'a bare right without any occupation or enjoyment.' A debt, no doubt, differs from a share in one respect, that it confers generally a more limited right than a share, and that when once paid it is at an end; but this distinction appears to me immaterial for the purpose now in hand.[340]

The similarity between shares and units as choses in action cannot extend further. Units of unit trusts stand as a class of their own, although the deed of settlement company provides the historical commonality of the unit trust and the company. But there is no doubt that there is now a distinct body of company law, even though trust and equity may have asserted their influence in different contexts. This body of law will form the analytical base of the chose of the share. Rights and liabilities may have attached to shares by reason of the fact that a company is a legal person and the fact that a shareholder is contracting with this legal person.[341] A unitholder will not have any contractual relationship with the unit trust for the trust is not

---

[339] If he does so and receives consideration from the assignee, he will be a constructive trustee of such income. Of course, there is nothing improper for him to declare himself a trustee holding the units on trust for himself as to capital and for the purported assignee as to income. Cf. *FCT* v. *Everett* (1980) 143 CLR 440 where a partner assigned a fraction of his partnership income to an assignee and it was held by the High Court of Australia that the assignment was an equitable assignment constituting the assignor trustee of the assignee's interest, which was a fraction of an equitable chose.

[340] *Colonial Bank* v. *Whinney* (1885) 30 Ch. D 261 at 286–7. His Lordship also approved the decision of *Ex parte Agra Bank* (1868) LR 3 Ch. App. 555 where shares in a mining company were held to be choses in action.

[341] Under the statutory contract constituted by the memorandum and articles: Companies Act 1985 s. 14.

an entity. Units in the unit trust will continue to have the trust and the contract as their sources of rights and obligations.[342] The contractual source will provide attributes of the unit that will distinguish it from a beneficiary's interest in a private trust.[343] In a sense, the unit trust's provision of investment services through the use of the trust device and the deed of covenants is new wine in an old bottle.[344]

The dynamic character of the unit trust means that it is possible, though nowadays it is less common, to give unitholders rights in the underlying real property held by the trustee.[345] Thus, a unit may comprise real property interest and choses in action in the form of benefits of contract; it may comprise both equitable as well as legal interests. This phenomenon may not be as alarming as it first appears. A natural person can own all types of proprietary interest, be they equitable or legal interests, at any one time. A unit is simply a medium which gives him different types of proprietary interests at a single time, and for a single consideration. If these component rights have to be enforced, their respective nature will determine the courses of action and the remedies available.

In short, the unit is a chose in action founded on principles of the trust and the contract and is redeemable and transferable in manner provided by its constituting instrument rather than by way of equitable or statutory assignment.

## D. Implications

Units are items of property in their own right. As such, they can be acquired by trustees of private trusts,[346] agents or other fiduciaries having investment responsibilities. In the course of so doing, they are acquiring assets and it cannot be asserted that they are delegating their investment duties to the manager of the unit trust. Instead, the primary question should be whether investment in unit trusts falls within the relevant investment power. If this is answered in the positive, the risk-nature of the

---

[342] S. 3A of this ch., *ante*.

[343] Noticeably in the nature of realisation and manner of alienation.

[344] i.e., the bottle being the form of deed of settlement company.

[345] See s. 2C(3) of this ch.

[346] The Trustee Investment Act 1961 considers unit trust units as items of properties. Units of an authorized unit trust will be 'wider-range' investments (Sch. 1, Part III, para. 3) and units of a gilt unit trust are 'narrow-range' investments within Part II of Sch. 1 (Trustee Investments (Additional Powers) (No. 2) Order 1994). If, which is not uncommon, the Trustee Investment Act provisions are excluded, the investment powers of a particular trust will have to be construed whether units are permitted.

relevant unit trust may have to be considered in the context of negligence or in the construction of investment restrictions in relevant instruments.

In the construction of any document or statute, units of unit trusts will fall within the term 'securities' if this term is used in the wide sense of investment property.[347] They should not have any stigma of speculation or risk. The unit trust structure is neutral in terms of risk. The risk comes from the investment objectives, the manner of exercise of the trust's investment power, and whether the parties have fulfilled their contractual and fiduciary obligations. It also follows that the Unfair Contract Terms Act 1977 does not apply to unit trust deeds.[348]

---

[347] In *Re Douglas's Will Trusts* [1959] 2 All ER 620 Vaisey J held the word 'securities' in the context of the will before him meant investments and not secured investments. This approach may be contrasted with the classic statement by Viscount Cave in *Singer* v. *Williams* [1921] 1 AC 41 at 49: '. . . the normal meaning of the word "securities" is not open to doubt. The word denotes a debt or claim the payment of which is in some way secured. The security would generally consist of a right to resort to some fund or property for payment; but I am not prepared to say that other forms of security (such as personal guarantee) are excluded. In each case, however, where the word is used in its normal sense, some form of secured liability is postulated. No doubt the meaning of the word may be enlarged by an interpretation clause contained in a statute . . . or the context may show . . . that the word is used to denote, in addition to securities in the ordinary sense, other investments such as stocks or shares. But, in the absence of any such aid to interpretation, I think it clear that the word "securities" must be construed in the sense above defined . . .' Viscount Cave's dictum was applied in various contexts: *In Re Smithers* [1939] 1 Ch. 1015 (legacy proceeds of 'my securities' in a home-made will); *In Re United Law Clerks Society* [1947] 1 Ch. 150 (investment power of a friendly society); *Boyd* v. *Cowell* [1952] VLR 288 (will trustee's investment power); *Westminster Bank Executor and Trustee Co. (Channel Islands) Ltd.* v. *National Bank of Greece SA* [1969] 3 WLR 468 (statutory interpretation). These cases take a restrictive interpretation of Lord Cave's statement in that the narrow sense of the word is presumed unless some express intention to use it in the wide sense of investment is found. This approach leads to an extraordinary result in *Maddaford* v. *de Vantee* [1951] SASR 159. In this case, the defendant went from house to house offering units in a scheme under which the company contract with each unitholder to plant olive trees and to pay the profit to a trustee under a trust deed which will be distributed eventually. The land was held in the joint names of the company and the trustee. The question was whether the defendant contravened the Companies Act in going from house to house offering to the public shares for subscription or purchase. The term 'shares' was defined in the Act to mean 'the shares of a company . . . and includes stock, bonds, debentures, debenture stock, and other securities and units, whether having the benefit of security over the assets of the company or not'. All three members of the Supreme Court of South Australia unanimously held that the defendant was not offering securities. Abott J went as far as saying: 'As far as I can see, the scheme, considered as a whole, offers to the public a mere speculation by which the "unit holder" may make a profit at the expiration of ten years, or may lose all, or nearly all, the money he has invested. To say that he has any "security" seems to me a contradiction in terms.' (At 277.) The legislative intent to regulate investments (through the wide definition of shares) was clearly ignored. It is clearly absurd that the legislature intended to regulate secure investments but not insecure investments. It is submitted that the correct approach is that this term carries two meanings and it is for the court to ascertain which meaning should be ascribed to in a particular context; there is no reason why a particular meaning should take precedence. This is particularly so where the term 'securities' has been widely used as a synonym of 'investments'.

[348] This is because the Act does not apply to any contract so far as it relates to the creation or transfer of securities: ch. 4, s. 2C(1), *ante*.

At least in the majority of cases of unit trusts operating on a cash fund basis considered in this work, the unit is a property of monetary value. Such a unit invariably does not carry rights to underlying assets. Any asset-based tax issues should be examined on this basis. Similarly, where a unit trust invests in shares, its unitholders should not be regarded as having interests in those shares for the purpose of applying the Companies Act. Thus, for example, where a unit trust invests in the shares of one of its corporate unitholders, that corporate unitholder should not be regarded as having a beneficial interest in its own shares in determining whether there is a breach of the prohibition against self-acquisition contained in the Companies Act 1985.[349] This approach should also apply to questions of exercise of rights and of attachment of liability with respect to ownership of underlying assets.[350]

It follows from the above that the location of the underlying assets does not have any bearing on the *situs* of the unit. The unit is a kind of property and hence its *situs* is to be determined separately. The unit is a unique chose in that it comprises other choses. Thus, on questions of its *situs*, the court should draw a distinction between issues of location of the unit *per se* and issues of location of underlying choses. On the former, the place where the transfer is to take place may be held by the court to be the location of the *situs*.[351] This is based on the analogy with company shares.[352] In the

[349] Companies Act 1985 ss. 143–9 and Sch. 2. Arguably, this is also relevant to the directors' obligation of disclosure of shareholdings under ss. 324–8. If the analysis in this chapter is accepted, para. 11 of Sch. 13 of the Act is merely declaratory. But it should be noted that the provision in para. 11 only disregards interests in authorized unit trusts and not other types of unit trusts. In all these circumstances the unitholder may not even be aware of the portfolio of the unit trust.

[350] Liability of unitholders, theoretically, may also arise if unitholders are partners of the trustee or the manager or if they are principals of the trustee or the manager. In such circumstances, liability is the result of the act of the unitholders, rather than from having an interest in underlying assets. Whether the relationships of partnership can exist amongst the unitholders, the manager, and the trustee, see ch. 3 generally.

[351] Thus, if under the trust deed, the unit is transferable by a change in the register, it is transferred at the place where the register is located. If it is a bearer unit, it is located at where the document is. (Cf. company share cases of *Re Clark* [1904] 1 Ch. 294; *Re Aschrott* [1927] 1 Ch. 313; *R v. Williams* [1942] AC 541; *Treasurer of Ontario* v. *Aberdein* [1947] AC 24; *Standard Chartered Bank Ltd.* v *IRC* [1978] 1 WLR 1160; *Winans* v. *AG (No. 2)* [1910] AC 27.)

[352] There is a particular danger in relying on company shares cases in the private international law context where this position, arguably, is subject to the supremacy of the law of the place of incorporation of the company. As explained by the editor of Dicey and Morris, *The Conflict of Laws*, 12th edn. by Collins, Sweet and Maxwell, 1993, Vol. 2, pp. 931–2, a share, as an interest in the company, is subject to the law of the place of incorporation of the company, which governs all matters concerning the constitution of the company. The transfer at the place of the register is effective because the law of the place of incorporation gives effect to such transfer. This explains the Canadian authorities of *Braun* v. *The Custodian* [1944] 4 DLR 209 and *Brown, Gow, Wilson* v. *Beleggings-Societeit NV* (1961) 29 DLR (2d)

majority of cases, it is where the register is located.[353] But, for some cases where the register is nominally located to achieve different domicile for political or tax purposes, the *situs* may be at the branch register where the units are most effectively dealt with.[354] If the right in question is one of enforcement of trust duties against the unit trustee, it may be located at the place where the trustee is domiciled.[355] Likewise, any right of the underlying choses given to a unitholder will be located in the place where the underlying chose can be enforced.

At a conceptual level, the recognition of the unit as a chose in action, rather than as an aggregate of choses and rights, means that the unit trust is a device capable of creating proprietary interest. Equity has a long history of property creation.[356] There should be no misgiving that the unit trust, as a trust built upon contractual covenants, is capable of continuing equity's capability in this regard. Its product, the unit, has distinct attributes which also form part of the attributes of the unit trust as a legal institution. The trust, with its elasticity, will continue to serve a variety of purposes, be they altruistic or commercial ones; and the unit trust by enlisting the contract to its service will prove to be more flexible and more responsive to the tax, political, and commercial environment at any particular time.

---

673 which could have been interpreted as establishing that the *situs* of shares is located at the place of incorporation (see Nygh, *Conflict of Laws in Australia* 5th edn., Butterworths, 1991, pp. 445–6). The unit trust position is far more complicated. As a unit trust is not a legal person, there is no law of the place of incorporation to decide the validity of the transfer of units. If the mode of transfer is characterized as a matter of administration of the trust, it is uncertain if the proper law or the law of the place of administration should apply. Sykes and Pryles *Australian Private International Law*, 3rd edn., Law Book Co., 1991, pp. 715–19 and Graveson, *Private International Law*, 7th edn., 1974, p. 538, support the view that the proper law governs matters of administration and the editor of the 10th edn. of Dicey and Morris, *The Conflict of Laws*, 10th edn. by Morris, 1980, p. 683 and Nygh, *Conflict of Laws in Australia*, 5th edn., 1991, pp. 477–9 regard that the law of the place of administration governs. However, the editor of the 12th edn. of Dicey and Morris (12th edn. by Collins, *supra*) says, 'it seems advisable to discard a rigid distinction, advocated in earlier editions of this work . . . between the validity, interpretation and effect of a trust on the one hand and questions of "administration" on the other . . .' (pp. 1092–3). See also Wallace 'Choice of Law for Trusts in Australia and the United Kingdom' (1987) 36 *ICLQ* 454 at 473 *et seq*. If the mode of transfer is regarded as part of the disposition of interest in a unit trust, the nature of units, the subject of this chapter, will be called into question; in which event, the issue is the choice between the proper law and the *lex situs*.

[353] Cf. *New York Breweries Co.* v *AG* [1899] AC 62; *CIR* v. *Maple & Co. Ltd.* [1908] AC 22; *Brassard* v. *Smith* [1925] AC 371; *London and South American Investment Trust* v. *British Tobacco Co. (Australia)* [1927] 107; *Erie Beach Co. Ltd.* v. *AG for Ontario* [1930] AC 161.

[354] *Re Clark* [1904] 1 Ch. 294; *Re Aschrott* [1927] 1 Ch. 313; *R* v. *Williams* [1942] AC 541; *Treasurer of Ontario* v. *Aberdein* [1947] AC 24; *Standard Chartered Bank Ltd.* v. *IRC* [1978] 1 WLR 1160.

[355] *Archer-Shee* v. *Garland* [1931] AC 212.

[356] To quote a few examples, estate contracts, restrictive covenants, equity of redemption, proprietary estoppel, and the short-lived deserted wife's equity.

# Bibliography

American Law Institute, *American Restatement of the Law: Trusts 2d*, American Law Institute Publishers, 1959.

Ames, *Lectures on Legal History and Miscellaneous Legal Essay*, Harvard UP, 1913.

Arnaud, *Investment Trusts Explained*, Woodhead Faulkner Ltd., 1977.

Ashburner, *Principles of Equity*, 2nd edn. by Browne, Butterworths, 1933.

Athena Guaranteed Financials Ltd. (Prospectus dated 10 January 1992).

Atiyah, *The Rise and Fall of Freedom of Contract*, Clarendon Press, 1979.

Atiyah, *Essays on Contract*, Clarendon Press, 1986.

Austin, 'The Income Tax Assessment Act, Section 102(1)(B): Trusts for Unmarried Infant Children' (1974) 4 *U Tas. LR* 137.

*Australian Encyclopaedia of Forms and Precedents*, Vol. 3, 2nd edn. (rev.), Butterworths Australia, 1985.

Australian Law Reform Commission and Companies and Securities Advisory Committee, *Collective Investment Schemes* (Discussion Paper 53), 1992.

Australian Law Reform Commission and Companies and Securities Commission, *Collective Investments: Other People's Money*, Report No. 65, 1993.

Baker, 'The Future of Equity' (1977) 93 *LQR* 529.

Bean, *Fiduciary Obligations and Joint Ventures: the Collaborative Fiduciary Relationship*, Clarendon Press, 1995.

*Bowstead and Reynolds on Agency*, 16th edn., Sweet and Maxwell, 1996.

Bullen, 'The Rights of Strangers to Contracts under Seal' (1977–1978) 6 *Adelaide LR* 119.

Burns, 'The "Fusion Fallacy" Revisited' (1993) 5 *Bond LR* 152.

Butler, 'Modern Portfolio Theory and Invesment Powers of Trustees: the New Zealand Experience' (1995) 16 *NZULR* 349.

Carson, 'Unit Investment Trusts' (1960) 30 *The Australian Accountant* 88.

Cheshire and Fifoot, *Law of Contract*, 6th Australian edition by Starke, Seddon and Ellinghaus, Butterworths, 1992.

Chesterman, 'Family Settlements on Trust: Landowners and the Rising Bourgeoisie' in Rubin and Sugarman (eds.), *Law, Economy and Society, 1750–1914: Essays in the History of English Law*, Professional Books, 1984.

*Chitty on Contracts*, 27th edn. by Guest, Sweet and Maxwell, 1994.

*Clerk and Lindsell on Torts*, 17th edn. by Brazier, Sweet and Maxwell, 1995.

Cockburn, 'Trustee Exculpation Clauses Furnished by the Settler' [1993] *ABR* 163.

Collyer, *A Practical Treatise on the Law of Partnership*, Sweet, Stevens and Maxwell, 1832 (American edition by Phillips and Pickering, Merriam, 1839).

Companies and Securities Law Review Committee, *Prescribed Interests*, Discussion Paper No. 6, 1987.

Company Law Committee, *Report* (the Jenkin's Committee) (Cmnd. 1749), HMSO, 1962.

Cook, 'The Mysterious Massachusetts Trusts' (1923) 9 *American Bar Association Journal* 763.

Cooke, *Corporation, Trust and Company, An Essay in Legal History*, Manchester UP, 1950.

*Crossley Vaines on Personal Property*, 5th edn. by Tyler and Palmer, Butterworths, 1973.

Davidson, 'The Equitable Remedy of Compensation' (1982) 13 *Melb. ULR* 349.

Davies, 'The Variety of Express Trusts' (1986) 8 *U Tas. LR* 209.

Day and Harris, *Unit Trusts*, Oyez, 1974.

Dicey and Morris, *The Conflict of Laws*, 12th edn. by Collins, Sweet and Maxwell, 1993.

Downe, 'Investing for Income' (1987) 25 *Law Society Journal* 54.

DuBois, *The English Business Company after the Bubble Act 1720–1800*, 1938 (Octagon Books reprint, 1971).

Emery, 'The Most Hallowed Principles—Certainty of Beneficiaries of Trusts and Powers of Appointment' (1982) 98 *LQR* 551.

Emery, 'Do We Need a Rule Against Perpetuities?' (1994) 57 *MLR* 602.

Evershed, 'Reflections on the Fusion of Law and Equity after 75 years' (1954) 70 *LQR* 326.

*Financial Services in the United Kingdom: A New Framework for Investor Protection* (Cmnd. 9432), HMSO, 1985.

Finn, *Fiduciary Obligations*, Law Book Co., 1977.

Finn, 'The Fiduciary Principle' in Youdan (ed.), *Equity, Fiduciaries and Trusts*, Carswell, Toronto, 1989.

Finn, 'Contract and Fiduciary Principle' (1989) 12 *UNSWLJ* 76.

Finn, 'Fiduciary Law and the Modern Commercial World' in McKendrick (ed.), *Commercial Aspects of Trusts and Fiduciary Obligations*, Clarendon Press, 1992.

Fisher, *The Collected Papers of F. W. Maitland*, Vol. III, Cambridge UP, 1911 (William S. Hein reprint, Buffalo, 1981).

Fisher and Lightwood, *Law of Mortgage*, 10th edn. by Tyler, Butterworths, 1988.

*Fixed Trusts: Report of the Departmental Committee Appointed by the Board of Trade*, 1936 (Cmd. 5259).

Flannigan, 'The Fiduciary Obligations', (1989) 9 *OJLS* 285.

Fletcher, *The Law Relating to Non-profit Associations in Australia and New Zealand*, Law Book Co., 1986.

Ford, 'Unit Trusts' (1960) 23 *MLR* 129.

Ford, 'The Unit Trust as a Production Joint Venturer' [1985] *AMPLA Yearbook* 1.

Ford, 'Public Unit Trusts' in Austin and Vann (eds.), *The Law of Public Company Finance*, Law Book Co., 1986.

Ford and Austin, *Principles of Corporations Law*, 7th edn., Butterworths Australia, 1995.

Ford and Hardingham, 'Trading Trusts: Rights and Liabilities of Beneficiaries' in Finn (ed.), *Equity and Commercial Relationships*, Law Book Co., 1987.

Ford and Lee, *Principles of the Law of Trusts*, 3rd (looseleaf) edn., LBC Information Services, 1996.

Formoy, *The Historical Foundation of Modern Company Law*, Sweet and Maxwell, 1923.

Frankel, *The Regulation of Money Managers*, Little, Brown & Co., 1978.

Free, 'Can Parties in Contractual Relations be Liable to Each other in Tort?' (1978) 3 *Auckland ULR* 243.

French, 'The Contract/Tort Dilemma' (1983) 5 *Otago LR* 236.

Gautreau, 'Demystifying the Fiduciary Mystique' (1989) 68 *Can. BR* 1.

Goff and Jones, *The Law of Restitution*, 4th edn. by Jones, Sweet and Maxwell, 1993.

Gonski, 'The Unit Trust as a Production Joint Venturer' [1985] *AMPLA Yearbook* 17.

Goodhart and Jones, 'The Infiltration of Equitable Doctrine into English Commercial Law' (1980) 43 *MLR* 489.

Gower, 'Rayfield v Hands—A Postscript and a Drop of Scotch' (1958) 21 *MLR* 657.

Gower, 'The Contractual Effect of Articles of Association' (1958) 21 *MLR* 401.

Gower, *Review of Investor Protection: A Discussion Document*, HMSO, 1982.

Gower, *The Principles of Modern Company Law*, 5th edn., Sweet and Maxwell, 1992.

Graveson, *Private International Law*, 7th edn., 1974.

Gray J. C., *The Rule against Perpetuities*, 4th edn. by R. Gray, Little, Brown & Co., 1942.

Greig and Davis, *The Law of Contract*, Law Book Co., 1987.

Gummow, 'Compensation for Breach of Fiduciary Duty' in Youdan (ed.), *Equity, Fiduciaries and Trusts*, Carswell, Toronto, 1989.

Halbach Jun., 'Trust Investment Law in the Third Restatement' (1992) 77 *Iowa LR* 1151.

*Halsbury's Laws of England*, 4th edn. (Reissue), Vol. 6, Butterworths, 1991.

*Halsbury's Laws of England*, 4th edn., Vol. 12, Butterworths, 1975.

Hanbury, 'A Periodical Menace to Equitable Principles' (1928) 44 *LQR* 468.

Hanbury, *Modern Equity, Being the Principles of Equity*, Stevens, 1935.

*Hanbury and Martin's Modern Equity*, 14th edn. by Martin, Sweet and Maxwell, 1993.

Harman, 'Emerging Alternatives to Mutual Funds: Unit Investment Trusts and Other Fixed Portfolio Investment Vehicles' [1987] *Duke Law Journal* 1045.

Harris, 'Trust, Power and Duty' (1971) 87 *LQR* 31.

Harris, *Variation of Trusts*, Sweet and Maxwell, 1975.

Hart, 'The Place of Trust in Jurisprudence' (1912) 28 *LQR* 290.

Haskell, 'The Prudent Person Rule for Trustee Investment and Modern Portfolio Theory' (1990) 69 *NCLR* 87.

Hayton, 'Trustees and the New Financial Services Regime', 10 *The Company Lawyer* 191.

Hayton, 'Trading Trusts' in Glasson, *International Trust Law*, (looseleaf), Chancery Law Publishing, 1992.

Hayton and Marshall, *Cases and Commentary on the Law of Trusts*, 9th edn., Sweet and Maxwell, 1991.

Heydon, Gummow and Austin, *Cases and Materials on Equity and Trusts*, 4th edn., Butterworths Australia, 1993.

Holdsworth, 'Equity' (1935) 51 *LQR* 142.

Holdsworth, *A History of English Law*, 2nd edn., Methuen and Sweet and Maxwell, 1937.

Hughes, *The Law of Public Unit Trusts*, Longman Professional, 1992.

Hunt, *The Development of the Business Corporation in England 1800–1867*, Harvard UP, 1936 (Russell & Russell edition, 1969).

International Organisation of Securities Commissions, *Principles for the Regulation of Collective Investment Schemes*, 1994.

*Jackson & Powell on Professional Negligence*, 3rd edn., Sweet and Maxwell, 1992.

Jacobs, *Law of Trusts in Australia*, 5th edn. by Meagher and Gummow, Butterworths Australia, 1986.

*Jarman on Wills*, 8th edn., by Jennings, Sweet and Maxwell, 1951.

Johnson, 'Speculating on the Efficacy of "Speculation": An Analysis of the Prudent Person's Slipperiest Term of Art in Light of Modern Portfolio Theory' (1996) 48 *Stanford LR* 419.

Jones, 'The Massachusetts Business Trust and Registered Investment Companies' in Youdan (ed.), *Equity, Fiduciaries and Trusts*, Carswell, Toronto, 1989.

Keeton, 'The Director as Trustee' (1952) 5 *Current Legal Problems* 11.

Keeton, 'The Thellusson Case and Trusts for Accumulations' (1970) 2 *NILQ* 131.

Keeton, *Modern Developments in the Law of Trusts*, Northern Ireland Legal Quarterly, 1971.

Keeton and Sheridan, *Law of Trusts*, 12th edn. (by Sheridan), Barry Rose, 1993.

Knight, 'Capital Maintenance' in Patfield (ed.), *Perspectives on Company Law: I*, Kluwer Law International, 1995, 52.

Langbein, 'The Contractarian Basis of the Law of Trusts' (1995) 105 *Yale LJ* 625.

Latham, 'The Right of the Beneficiary to Specific Items of the Trust Fund' (1954) 32 *Can. BR* 520.

Law Commission, *Fiduciary Duties and Regulatory Rules: a Consultation Paper* (Consultation Paper No. 124), HMSO, 1992.

Law Commission, *Fiduciary Duties and Regulatory Rules* (Report No. 236), HMSO, 1995.

Law Commission, *Privity of Contract: Contracts for the Benefit of Third Parties* (Report No. 242), HMSO, 1996.

Lawson, *Introduction to the Law of Property*, Clarendon Press, 1958.

Lee, 'The Public Policy of Re Cook's Settlement Trusts' (1969) 85 *LQR* 213.

Lee, 'Trust and Trust-like Obligations with Respect to Unincorporated Associations' in Finn (ed.), *Essays in Equity*, Law Book Co., 1985.

*Lewin on Trusts*, 16th edn. by Mowbray, Sweet and Maxwell, 1964.

Lewis and Boyd, *Savings: Australia in Crisis?*, The Financial Review Library, 1993.

Lindley, *A Treatise of the Law of Companies, Considered as a Branch of the Law of Partnership*, 5th, edn., Sweet and Maxwell, 1889.

*Lindley & Banks on Partnership*, 17th edn. by l'Anson Banks, Sweet and Maxwell, 1995.

McCamus, 'Remedies for Breach of Fiduciary Duty' in *Special Lectures of the Law Society of Upper Canada 1900: Fiduciary Duties*, De Boo, Ontario, 1991.

McDermot, 'Jurisdiction of the Court of Chancery to Award Damages' (1992) 108 *LQR* 652.

MacDougall, 'Mutual Funds and Unit Trusts' (1960) 33 *ALJ* 331.

Maitland, 'Trust and Corporation' in Fisher, *The Collected Papers of F. W. Maitland*, Vol. III, Cambridge UP, 1911 (William S. Hein reprint, Buffalo, 1981).

Maitland, *Equity: a Course of Lectures*, 2nd edn. by Brunyate, 1936.

Maitland, 'The Unincorporate Body' in Fisher, *The Collected Papers of F. W. Maitland*, Vol. III, Cambridge UP, 1911 (William S. Hein reprint, Buffalo, 1981).

Manitoba Law Reform Commission, *Report on the Rule in Saunders v Vautier*, Report No. 18, Winnipeg, 1975.

Marsh, *Corporate Trustees*, Europa Publications, 1952.

Marshall, *The Assignment of Choses in Action*, Pitman, 1950.

Martin, 'Fusion, Fallacy and Confusion: a Comparative Study' [1994] *Conv.* 13.

Mason, 'Themes and Prospects' in Finn (ed.), *Essays in Equity*, Law Book Co., 1985.

Mason, 'Contract & Tort: Looking Across the Boundary from the Side of Contracts' (1987) 61 *ALJ* 228.

Mason, 'The Place of Equity and Equitable Doctrines in the Contemporary Common Law World: an Australian Perspective' in Waters (ed.), *Equity, Fiduciaries and Trusts*, Carswell, Toronto, 1993.

Matthews, 'The Efficacy of Trustee Exemption Clauses in English Law [1989] Conv. 42.

Maudsley, *The Modern Law of Perpetuities*, Butterworths, 1979.

Maurice, 'The Office of Custodian Trustee' (1960) 24 *Conv.* 196.

Meagher, Gummow and Lehane, *Equity: Doctrines and Remedies*, 3rd edn., Butterworths Australia, 1992.

Megarry and Wade, *The Law of Real Property*, 5th edn., Stevens, 1984.

Merriman, *Unit Trusts and How They Work*, 2nd edn., Pitman, 1959.

MGA Pacific Fund B Ltd. (Prospectus dated 27 March 1992).

Millet, 'The Quistclose Trust: Who Can Enforce It?' (1985) 101 *LQR* 269.

Moffat, 'Trusts Law: A Song Without End?' (Review Article) (1992) 55 *MLR* 123.

Moffat, *Trusts Law: Text and Materials*, 2nd edn., Butterworths, 1994.

Moret and Storey, 'The Massachusetts Business Trust and Registered Investment Companies' (1988) 13 *Delaware Journal of Corporate Law* 421.

Morgan, 'The Negligent Contract-Breaker' (1980) 58 *Can BR* 299.

Morris and Leach, *The Rule Against Perpetuities*, 2nd edn., Stevens, 1962.

*Norton on Deeds*, 2nd edn. by Morrison and Goolden, Sweet and Maxwell, 1928, (1981 reprint by Gaunt & Sons, Florida).

Notes (1933) 49 *LQR* 480.

Notes (1934) 50 *LQR* 158.

Nygh, *Conflict of Laws in Australia*, 5th edn., Butterworths, 1991.

Odgers, *Construction of Deeds and Statutes*, 5th edn. by Dworkin, Sweet and Maxwell, 1967.

Paling, 'The Trustee's Duty of Skill and Care' (1973) 37 *Conv.* 48.

Palmer, *Company Law*, 7th edn., 1909.

*Palmer's Company Law*, 25th (looseleaf) edn. by Morse, Sweet and Maxwell, 1992.

Parker and Mellows, *The Modern Law of Trusts*, 6th edn. by Oakley, Sweet and Maxwell, 1994.

Partlett, *Professional Negligence*, Law Book Co., 1985, chapter 6.

Pash, 'Property Trusts', a Paper Presented at the Taxation Convention on the Taxation of Investments, arranged by the South Australia Division of the Taxation Institute of Australia, April 1984.

Pearce, 'Directing the Trustee' (1972) 36 *Conv. (NS)* 260.

Pennington, *Company Law*, 2nd edn., Butterworths, 1967.

Pennington, *The Investor and the Law*, MacGibbon & Kee, 1968.

Pennington, *Company Law*, 6th edn., Butterworths, 1990.

Pennington, *The Law of the Investment Market*, Blackwell Law, 1990.

Pettit, *Equity and the Law of Trusts*, 7th edn., Butterworths, 1993.

Pollock, *Law of Partnership*, 6th edn., Stevens & Sons, 1895.

Posner, *International Securities Regulation: London's 'Big Bang' and the European Securities Markets*, Little, Brown & Co., 1991.

Pritchard, 'An Innovation in Unit Trusts' (1985) 23 *Law Society Journal* 134.

Redmond, *Companies and Securities Law: Commentary and Materials*, 2nd edn., Law Book Co., 1992.

Reynolds, 'Torts Actions in Contractual Situations' (1985) 11 *NZULR* 215.

Rickett, 'The Constitution of Trusts: Contracts to Create Trusts' (1979) *Current Legal Problems* 1.

Rickett, 'Two Propositions in the Constitution of Trusts' (1981) *Current Legal Problems* 189.

Rickett, 'Different views on the Scope of the Quistclose Analysis: English and Antipodean Insights' (1991) 107 *LQR* 608.

Robinson, 'Unit Trusts: an Accountant's View of Practical Tax Problems', a Paper Presented at the State Convention of the New South Wales Division of the Taxation Institute of Australia, Leura, New South Wales, 1983.

Rogers, 'Contracts and Third Parties' in Finn, *Essays on Contract*, Law Book Co., 1987.

Rosenbalm, 'The Massachusetts Trust' (1964) 31 *Tennessee LR* 471.

*Salmond and Heuston on the Law of Torts*, 19th edn., by Heuston and Chamber, Sweet and Maxwell, 1987.

Salmond and Williams, *Principles of the Law of Contract*, 2nd edn., Sweet and Maxwell, 1945.

Sappideen and Butt, *The Perpetuities Act 1984*, Law Book Co., 1986.

Scott, A. W., 'The Nature of the Rights of the Cestui Que Trust' (1917) *Columbia LR* 467.

Scott, A. W., 'The Fiduciary Principle' (1949) 37 *Cal LR* 539.

Scott, A. W., *Scott on The Law of Trusts*, 4th edn. by Fratcher, Little, Brown & Co., 1987.

Scott, W. R., *The Constitution and Finance of English, Scottish and Irish Joint-Stock Companies to 1720*, Cambridge, 1912 (Peter Smith reprint, 1951).

Sealy, 'Fiduciary Relationships' [1962] *CLJ* 69.

Sealy, 'The Director as Trustee' [1967] *CLJ* 83.

Sealy, 'The Enforcement of Partnership Agreements, Articles of Association and Shareholder Agreements' in Finn, *Equity and Commercial Relationships*, Law Book Co., 1987.

Sealy, 'Fiduciary Obligations, Forty Years On' (1995) 9 *JCL* 37.

Securities and Investments Board, *Unit Trust Only Personal Equity Plan* (Consultative Paper 22), 1989.

Securities and Investments Board, *Regulated Collective Investment Schemes: Key Policy Issues* (Discussion Paper), 1993.

Securities and Investments Board, *Open Ended Investment Companies* (Consultative Paper 93), 1995.

Shepherd, *The Law of Fiduciaries*, Carswell, Toronto, 1981.

Shindler, 'Note of Recent Cases' (1980) 44 *Conv.* 155.

Sin, 'Enforcing the Unit Trust Deed Amongst Unitholders' (1997) 15 *C&SLJ* 108.

Sinclair, 'Property Income Certificates (PINCs) Explained' (1987) 6 (Issue 4) *IFLR* 6.

Smille, 'Negligence & Economic Loss' (1982) 32 *U of Toronto LJ* 231.

Smith, *A Compendium of Mercantile Law*, 6th edn. by Dowdeswell, Stevens, Norton and Sweet, 1859.

Smith, *Cases and Materials on Development of Legal Institutions*, West Publishing, 1965.

*Snell's Equity*, 29th edn. by Baker and Langan, Sweet and Maxwell, 1990.

Sparkes, 'How to Simplify Perpetuities' [1995] *Conv.* 212.

Spavold, 'The Unit Trust: A Comparison with the Corporation' (1991) 3 *Bond LR* 249.

*Special Lectures of the Law Society of Upper Canada 1990: Fiduciary Duties*, Dee Boo, 1991.

Spence, *The Equitable Jurisdiction of the Court of Chancery*, Lea and Blanchard, 1846 (William S. Hein reprint, 1981), Vol. 1.

Spry, *Equitable Remedies*, 4th edn., Law Book Co., 1992.

Starke, *Assignment of Choses in Action in Australia*, Butterworths, 1972.

Stephenson, 'Co-trustees or Several Trustees?' (1942) 16 *Temple ULQ* 249.

Stewart, 'Unit Trusts—Legal Relationships of Trustee, Manager and Unitholders' (1988) 5 *C&SLJ* 269.

Stoljar, *Groups and Entities: An Inquiry into Corporate Theory*, Australian National University Press, Canberra, 1973.

*Story's Commentaries on Equity Jurisprudence*, 13th edn. by Bigelow, Little, Brown & Co., 1886 (1988 reprint by Rothman & Co.).

Swanton, 'The Convergence of Tort and Contract' (1989) 12 *Syd. LR* 40.

Sykes and Pryles, *Australian Private International Law*, 3rd edn., Law Book Co., 1991.

*Theobald on Wills*, 15th edn., by Clark, Sweet and Maxwell, 1993.

Treitel, *The Law of Contract*, 8th edn., Sweet and Maxwell/Stevens, 1991.

Trotman, 'Articles of Association and Contracts' in Farrar, *Contemporary Issues in Company Law*, CCH (NZ), 1987.

Trotman, 'The Enforcement of Partnership Agreements, Articles of Association and Shareholder Agreements' in Finn, *Equity and Commercial Relationships*, Law Book Co., 1987.

*Underhill and Hayton's Law Relating to Trusts and Trustees*, 15th edn. by Hayton, Butterworths, 1995.

Vaughan, *The Regulation of Unit Trusts*, Lloyd's of London Press, 1990.

Walker, 'Unit Trust', an unpublished thesis submitted for the degree of Ph.D. in Economics in the University of London in 1938.

Walker, 'Unincorporated Investment Trusts in the Nineteenth Century' (1940) 15 *Economic History* 341.

Wallace, 'Choice of Law for Trusts in Australia and the United Kingdom' (1987) 36 *ICLQ* 454.

Walsh, 'Unit Trust' [1978] *Taxation in Australia* 446.

Walsh, 'Unit Trust' in Grbich, Munn and Reicher, *Modern Trusts and Taxation*, Butterworths Australia 1978.

Waters, 'The Nature of the Trust Beneficiary's Interest' (1967) 45 *Can BR* 219.

Waters, *Law of Trusts in Canada*, 2nd edn., Carswell, Toronto, 1984.

Waters (ed.), *Equity, Fiduciaries and Trusts*, Carswell, Toronto, 1993.

Wedderburn, 'Company Law—Effect of Articles as Contract—Remedy against Directors' (1958) *CLJ* 148.

Whelan, 'Automation within the Australian Securities and Future Markets' (1990) 8 *C&SLJ* 37.

Williams, 'The Three Certainties' (1940) 4 *MLR* 20.

Williams, 'The Origins and Logical Implications of the *Ejusdem Generis* Rule' (1943) 7 *Conv. (NS)* 119.

*Williams's Law Relating to Wills*, 6th edn., by Sherrin, Barlow and Wallington, Butterworths, London, 1987.

Winfield, *Province of the Law of Tort*, Cambridge UP, 1931.

Wordsworth, *The Law of Joint Stock Companies*, 3rd edn., John Littell, 1843.

Wordsworth, *The Law of Railway, Banking, Mining and Other Joint Stock Companies*, 5th edn., William Benning & Co, 1845.

Wrightington, 'Voluntary Associations in Massachusetts' (1911–1912) 21 *Yale LJ* 311.

# Index